Romanticism and Subversive Suicide

Edinburgh Critical Studies in Romanticism
Series Editors: Ian Duncan and Penny Fielding

Available Titles

A Feminine Enlightenment: British Women Writers and the Philosophy of Progress, 1759–1820
JoEllen DeLucia

Reinventing Liberty: Nation, Commerce and the Historical Novel from Walpole to Scott
Fiona Price

The Politics of Romanticism: The Social Contract and Literature
Zoe Beenstock

Radical Romantics: Prophets, Pirates, and the Space beyond Nation
Talissa J. Ford

Literature and Medicine in the Nineteenth-century Periodical Press: Blackwood's Edinburgh Magazine, *1817–1858*
Megan Coyer

Discovering the Footsteps of Time: Geological Travel Writing in Scotland, 1700–1820
Tom Furniss

The Dissolution of Character in Late Romanticism
Jonas Cope

Commemorating Peterloo: Violence, Resilience and Claim-making during the Romantic Era
Edited by Michael Demson and Regina Hewitt

Dialectics of Improvement: Scottish Romanticism, 1786–1831
Gerard Lee McKeever

Literary Manuscript Culture in Romantic Britain
Michelle Levy

Scottish Romanticism and Collective Memory in the British Atlantic
Kenneth McNeil

Romantic Periodicals in the Twenty-first Century: Eleven Case Studies from Blackwood's Edinburgh Magazine
Edited by Nicholas Mason and Tom Mole

Godwin and the Book: Imagining Media, 1783–1836
J. Louise McCray

Thomas De Quincey: Romanticism in Translation
Brecht de Groote

Romantic Environmental Sensibility: Nature, Class and Empire
Edited by Ve-Yin Tee

Romantic Pasts: History, Fiction and Feeling in Britain, 1790–1850
Porscha Fermanis

British Romanticism and Denmark
Cian Duffy

The Lady's Magazine (1770–1832) and the Making of Literary History
Jennie Batchelor

Mary Wollstonecraft: Cosmopolitan
Laura Kirkley

Romanticism and Consciousness, Revisited
Edited by Richard Sha and Joel Faflak

Remediating the 1820s
Edited by Jon Mee and Matthew Sangster

Romanticism and the Poetics of Orientation
Joey S. Kim

Romantic Women's Writing and Sexual Transgression
Edited by Kathryn Ready and David Sigler

Law, Equity and Romantic Writing: Seeking Justice in the Age of Revolutions
Edited by Michael Demson and Regina Hewitt

Kirkyard Romanticism: Death, Modernity and Scottish Literature in the Nineteenth Century
Sarah Sharp

Walter Scott on Monarchy: Royal Bodies and the Body Politic
Tara Ghoshal Wallace

Romanticism and Subversive Suicide: Human Rights, Existential Freedom and Biopower
Michelle Faubert

Contesting Cosmopolitan Moments in the Long Eighteenth Century
Enit Karafili Steiner

Visit our website at: www.edinburghuniversitypress.com/series/ECSR

Romanticism and Subversive Suicide

Human Rights, Existential Freedom and Biopower

Michelle Faubert

EDINBURGH
University Press

Edinburgh University Press is one of the leading university presses in the UK. We publish academic books and journals in our selected subject areas across the humanities and social sciences, combining cutting-edge scholarship with high editorial and production values to produce academic works of lasting importance. For more information visit our website: edinburghuniversitypress.com

Edinburgh University Press Ltd
13 Infirmary Street
Edinburgh EH1 1LT

First published in hardback by Edinburgh University Press 2025

Typeset in 10.5/13pt Sabon LT Pro
by Cheshire Typesetting Ltd, Cuddington, Cheshire, and
printed and bound in Great Britain

A CIP record for this book is available from the British Library

ISBN 978 1 3995 2753 8 (hardback)
ISBN 978 1 3995 2754 5 (paperback)
ISBN 978 1 3995 2755 2 (webready PDF)
ISBN 978 1 3995 2756 9 (epub)

Contents

Figures

Acknowledgements

This book is the culmination of a project I've been developing for over a decade. My output for it began as articles, chapters, conference presentations and campus talks, and later grew into an edition of a novel and two journal issues, but I always envisioned a book as the crowning glory of my efforts. I may not have accomplished anything glorious here, but I can say that I'm glad I did not write the book I had in mind when I first began my research into Romanticism and suicide, as the present study provides deeper insights into the historical and cultural roots of the period's fascination with suicide than I anything I could have written in those early days. I'm referring to my examination of the role of transatlantic slavery in shaping British cultural ideas about suicide and its relationship to biopower as the predominant political mode in the period. During my research on suicidal contagion for an article in *Literature & Medicine*, I discovered in the British Library a manuscript by Granville Sharp on the *Zong* slave-ship massacre; the letter's presence there was hitherto unknown to anyone, the British Library included. I describe this discovery in my book *Granville Sharp's Uncovered Letter and the* Zong *Massacre* (Palgrave, 2018), the writing of which forced to my attention the importance of slavery for ideas about suicide in British culture at the time. This research, which seemed at first to be an interruption and almost a distraction from my research into suicide and Romanticism, was crucial to the formation of *Romanticism and Subversive Suicide: Human Rights, Existential Freedom and Biopower*.

I could not have completed this book without generous funding from the Social Sciences and Humanities Research Council of Canada (through a multi-year, major grant, 'Romanticism and Revolutionary Suicide', the proposal for which Elyssa Warkentin offered advice), as well as from the University of Manitoba, the Faculty of Arts and the Department of English, Theatre, Film & Media at the University of Manitoba, the Gerda Henkel Stiftung program, and Northumbria

University in England; a special thanks goes to Allan Ingram and Clark Lawlor, who were instrumental to arranging my Visiting Fellowship at Northumbria.

I am also grateful to the many people and who have aided me in thinking through the complexities of this sensitive topic. Michelle Fu, Emma Winram, Tiffany Humble, Shoshannah Bryn Jones Square, Katie Leitch and Lauren Chochinov were wonderful research assistants, who helped gather excellent secondary and primary sources for various stages of the project, while the students in the various iterations of my graduate seminars 'Romantic Suicide' and 'Romantic Radicalism' offered unique insights into Romantic-era suicide, as did students in other courses, such as Sean Hetherington. Joel Faflak was an early supporter of this project, partly by inviting Nicole Reynolds and me to edit a volume of *Literature Compass* on Romanticism and suicide in response to our conference panel on the topic. Similarly, Alan Vardy invited me to submit an article to *Essays in Romanticism* in response to a conference paper I presented on Mary Shelley's *Mathilda*. I am also thankful to those who edited my chapters on Romantic literature and suicide in various volumes: Michael Demson and Regina Hewitt; Gerold Sedlmayr; and Diane Piccitto, Angela Esterhammer and Patrick Vincent. The same goes for those who accepted my invitations to contribute to journal volumes on the topic: Eric Parisot, Shoshannah Bryn Jones Square, Kirsty Cameron, Deanna Koretsky, Kate Singer, Margaret Higonnet, Kelly McGuire, Andrew Bennett and Leigh Wetherall Dickson. I would like to address particular thanks to Nicole Reynolds, with whom I edited the *Literature Compass* volume and wrote the introductory essay.

I can't thank Allan Ingram enough for his unwavering support of and interest in my work. Allan read and offered invaluable commentary on multiple drafts of this book, not to mention the proposal. (Clark Lawlor also read and offered advice on the book proposal; thanks, Clark!) Allan, you've been instrumental to the successful completion of this book. Thank you!

I'm also immensely grateful to the editors at Edinburgh University Press – Elizabeth Fraser and Emily Sharp, and, especially, the Series Editors, Ian Duncan and Penny Fielding – for believing in this project and helping me to deliver the finished product. Ian Duncan and Penny Fielding offered thorough, creative, inspiring feedback on drafts of this book that improved it immensely. Their attention to detail is unmatched; any remaining errors are mine alone. I also want to thank the anonymous readers of this book, who provided me with advice and queries that helped me to improve it. Closer to home, Ben Dueck, Librarian at the University of Manitoba, aided me in sourcing the images included here, while my brother-in-law Ken Juneau helped with French translation.

Throughout it all, my husband, Javier Uribe, has been a constant source of support and encouragement. Thanks for listening to my ramblings about suicide and slavery all these years, Javi. I'll try to choose a more cheerful topic for the next project!

Finally, for her love, I'd like to thank my mom, Yvonne Faubert, who passed away during the last year of writing this book.

Part I

Introduction and Context

Introduction: Romantic Subversive Suicide and Biopower

> Send this man to the mine this to the battle
> Famish a naked beggar at your gates
> And let him die by inches – but for worlds
> Lift not your hand against him – Live Live on
> As if this earth owned neither steel nor arsenic
> A rope a river or a standing pool
> Live as if you dread the pains of hell, or think
> Your corpse would quarrel with a stake – alas
> Has misery then no friend? – if you would die
> By licence, call the dropsy and the stone
> And let them end you – strange it is
> And most fantastic are the magic circles
> Drawn round the thing called life – till we have learned
> To prize it less we ne'er shall learn to prize
> The things worth living for. – (William Wordsworth, 'Argument for Suicide')

Although the only poem that William Wordsworth devoted entirely to the topic of suicide is not famous, it is important for what it demonstrates about influential Romantic writers' interest in the topic of suicide and their approach to it. Entitled 'Argument for Suicide' (1797) and provided above in full, the poem points out the hypocrisy of the prohibition against suicide. Even while power allows deaths through war, work or starvation, it still denies the right to choose death. Suicide prohibition appears thus motivated by a desire to manage the subject's body as an expression of control and authority – key components of biopower, the episteme of political power Michel Foucault describes as establishing itself on a society-wide scale in this period and characterised by the supervision, management and maintenance of human life. When Wordsworth's speaker directs the would-be suicide to 'call the dropsy and the stone/ And let them end you' (10–11), then he counsels the aid of the enemy of medicine, illness, as the only hope for those who would 'die/ By licence' (9–10), recognising that medicine is ranged on the side of biopower in the effort to control the subject's body. So, too, is religion: the speaker's ironic instruction that the addressee 'live *as if* you dread the pains of hell' (7; my emphasis) confirms the increase in atheism in the period and suggests the more frequent irrelevancy of the religious proscription against suicide, which pervaded even legal discussions of its impermissibility. Wordsworth refers to this proscription with his mention of the 'stake' (8) threatening the corpse, a common punishment for (particularly low-class) suicides then. Meanwhile, the mention of the 'magic circles/ Drawn around this thing called life' (12–13) frames as mere superstition religion's prohibition of suicide on the grounds that life is sacred. By undermining the legitimacy of Christianity's opposition to suicide, Wordsworth presents the religious prohibition of it as an aspect of biopower's denial of individual autonomy, as I do in this study. While it may appear that religion is devoted to the spiritual life of the subject, its excessive attention to the continuation of the body in the explosion of anti-suicide texts in the Romantic period reveals it as a functionary of biopower. Wordsworth suggests in 'Argument for Suicide' that the denial of one's right to choose death is an illogical and baseless superstition designed to curb individual freedom, and he expresses elsewhere that such unfreedom undermines the very nature of what it means to be a Briton in his time. In 'It is not to be Thought of', a sonnet from 1803, the poet echoes the spirit of the French and American revolutions: 'We must be free or die, who speak the tongue/ That Shakespeare spake' (11–12). According to Wordsworth, individual liberty to the point of death defines what it is to be English, and many of his contemporaries agreed.[1] Insofar as English – or, more broadly, British – state power was concerned, though, the subject's existential autonomy was not total. The prohibition against suicide demonstrates this limit to the Western liberal subject's claim to individual freedom.

Romantic-era awareness of the workings of biopower, comprising the realisation that British subjects are not totally free, despite the Enlightenment definition of the human as an autonomous being, demonstrates the broad cultural influence of the British slave trade, which shaped national awareness of what it meant to be a subject and evolving notions about what constituted human being. In *Slavery and the Romantic Imagination* (2002), Debbie Lee argues that by turning 'people into chattels', transatlantic slavery 'led to the interpretation in Western culture of slavery as the polar opposite of freedom. Transatlantic slavery gave European culture its definition of freedom because in a very real sense, enslaved blacks created freedom for whites in Europe and America' (18). The trade's importance to Britain, in particular, cannot be underestimated, since

> Britain was one of the most successful slave-trading countries. Together with Portugal, the two countries accounted for about 70% of all Africans transported to the Americas. Britain was the most dominant between 1640 and 1807 and it is estimated that Britain transported 3.1 million Africans (of whom 2.7 million arrived) to the British colonies in the Caribbean, North and South America and to other countries. (Anon., 'Slavery' n.p.)

Seymore Drescher confirms that the Romantic period was particularly lively when it came to the slave trade: 'The British share of the trade rose sharply at the end of the eighteenth century and was maintained through 1805, reaching a peak or near peak just before abolition. Britain remained the premier carrier of slaves to the end, accounting for over half the world total between 1791 and 1806' (30). The transatlantic slave trade's vastness and its importance to the British economy and culture are undeniable, even if direct references to it in canonical Romantic-era literature are often indirect, as Lee recognises (28). British colonial slavery represented more than a major source of Britain's wealth in the period: it shaped the national imagination and made Britons aware of the workings of biopower.

The establishment of biopower in the eighteenth century was inspired by the massive, lucrative and influential British transatlantic slave trade, the quintessential and original biopolitical state. The teleological purpose of the slave trade was to manage the bodies of the Africans kidnapped into it through feeding, exercising and giving medical attention to the enslaved on the ships in the Middle Passage so that they could be sold at a profit in the New World. Once there, it was incumbent upon slave-owners to keep their expensive purchases alive and healthy so that they could be productive plantation workers. Such biopolitical management of bodies became especially important after the abolition of the slave trade in Britain in 1813, when the production of additional enslaved people through births became central to the continuing success of colonial society. While, for good reason, history has focused mostly on the pervasive violence and murders associated with slavery, this emphasis has, nevertheless, detracted from an awareness of slavery as one of the earliest and most potent forms of biopower. Understanding slavery's role in British politics and the national imagination in the Romantic period reveals not only biopower's importance, but also the significance of the pervasive theme of suicide in texts from the time. The plethora of literary works about slave suicide in abolitionist literature of the eighteenth century present it as a refusal to surrender agency or submit meekly to the requirements of biopolitical rule, a rejection of life as managed, maintained, forced into productivity in biopolitical society. I contend that, accordingly, certain key works of British Romanticism show an increased interest in biopower, often using the language of slavery to gesture to it, and the theme of suicide as the ultimate means of subverting it.

The issue of suicide pervaded texts from the eighteenth century into the early nineteenth century, to the extent that one may speak of a distinctly Romantic-era suicide debate. I argue that the topic became so heated at this time because of the concurrent rise of biopower, to which suicide was the ultimate threat, coupled with recent and developing Enlightenment ideas proclaiming the Western liberal subject as existentially free, which the prohibition against suicide denied. By far, most texts about suicide agitated against it, urging readers to recognise that they were not the sole owners of their bodies: an apt expression of biopower. In this context, the many positive depictions of suicide in Romantic-era literature – such as a desirable escape from life or the final choice of a sympathetic protagonist, as I will detail in Chapter 2 – are all subversive, as they illustrate the individual's claim to ownership of the body, despite power's denial of this right. Such references to suicide usually occur in passing and in texts that do not have clear political resonances, but a few key, substantial texts from the period on which I focus – by Mary Wollstonecraft, Mary Shelley and Lord Byron – make subversive suicide their main focus while adumbrating how it undermines the expression of biopower. Since this literary expression of suicide as rebellion has roots in eighteenth-century abolitionist literature, and the cultural awareness of power's desire to control the subject's body to the point of enforcing life can be traced in part to the transatlantic slave trade, many of these key works use the trope of slave suicide to underscore the destabilising threat to biopower of the suicidality depicted in them. When biopower began to establish itself over the course of the eighteenth century, suicide became recognised as the ultimate form of resistance to it, one of its first 'astonishments', as Foucault comments (*Sexuality* 138–9), since it enacts a refusal to allow the body to be subjected to biopower's management, administration and supervision – to be a contributing, productive member of biopolitical society. This book considers how some major works of British Romanticism understood suicide as an expression of personal autonomy in defiance of power's management of the body and its demand that the subject live. More broadly, this study argues for the centrality of the slave trade to Romanticism through the pervasive trope of subversive suicide.

Theoretical, Methodological and Organisational Approaches

The facets of the literary trope of rebellious suicide on which I focus in this study – slave suicide, female suicide and anti-religious suicide[2] – exemplify the defiant response to what I term 'enforced life', a concept related to Foucault's notion of biopower, as outlined in 'Right of Death and Power over Life', Part V of the first volume of *The History of Sexuality*. As opposed to what Foucault calls the 'characteristic privilege ... of sovereign power' – 'the right to decide life and death', or, rather, 'the right to *take* life or *let* live' (135, 136; emphasis in original) – biopower concerns the management of life. During biopower's formation in the second half of the eighteenth century (Cisney and Morar 5), when the Romantic period began, biopower was increasingly associated with increasing, ordering, controlling and maintaining life in the interest of the health of the overall population (*Sexuality* 136, 137), such that individuals' significance became subordinated to their function within the larger whole of society. The lives of the individual members of society ruled by biopower are thus managed, maximised and, of greatest interest for this study, maintained; such enforced life is less a privilege than a duty to society, ruled by a master – slaver, patriarch or God – who enforces its robustness. If one disagrees with one's treatment by this master – if one wishes to withdraw from the system of biopower and rebel against it as an assertion of one's individuality and autonomous human worth – then suicide is the most poignant and perhaps only practical means of expressing this refusal. To quote Ian Marsh, 'Suicide therefore represents a failure of power to preserve life, and further, it is a waste of life – the loss of an asset to power' (99). Viewed thus, under the system of biopower, every suicide is rebellious, regardless of motivation.

Subversive suicide is an expression of radical autonomy that opposes enforced life. Foucault comments on the significance of suicide for understanding biopower:

> It is not surprising that suicide – once a crime, since it was a way to usurp the power of death which the sovereign alone, whether the one here below or the Lord above, had the right to exercise – became, in the course of the nineteenth century, one of the first conducts to enter into the sphere of sociological analysis [i.e. in Émile Durkheim's *On Suicide* (1897)]; it testified to the individual and private right to die, at the borders and in the interstices of power that was exercised over life. This determination to die, strange and yet so persistent and constant in its manifestations, and consequently so difficult to explain as being due to particular circumstances or individual accidents,

> was one of the first astonishments of a society in which political power had assigned itself the task of administering life. (138–9)

What was a crime was transformed into a social problem, a challenge to the maintenance of a robust society. Foucault identifies the preceding form of power – 'the sovereign' power represented by earthly and divine power ('whether the one here below or the Lord above') – as less erased than changed into biopower, the injunction to live, which explains why Romantic-era discussions of suicide often revolve around whether it was a crime or sin to be punished via threats to the body of the would-be suicide and the corpse of accomplished suicides, or whether it was a problem requiring medical and psychological treatment: for a time and to varying degrees, both modes of power existed as biopolitical rule developed. Biopower originally 'centered on the body as a machine: its disciplining, the optimization of its capabilities, the extortion of its forces,' all of which 'was ensured by the procedures of power that characterized the *disciplines*: an *anatamo-politics of the human body*' (*Sexuality* 139; emphasis in original). By the end of the Romantic period, the newly medicalised view of suicide was an expression of the broad biopolitical effort to deter, rather than punish, suicide and therefore maintain citizens' bodies as assets to power.

Biopower developed over a broad period: during the course of the 'classical age', writes Foucault, 'a power [developed] whose highest function was ... to invest life through and through' (139). He continues: '[S]tarting in the seventeenth century, this power over life evolved', the first phase of it focusing on the individual body – 'the optimization of its capabilities, the extortion of its forces, the parallel increase of its usefulness and docility, its integration into systems of efficient and economic controls' – while the second phase 'formed somewhat later' and focused on 'the species body': 'propagation, births and mortality, the level of health, life expectancy and longevity' (139). The formation of the first stage of biopower, attending to the individual body as a machine, was concurrent with the establishment of the British colonies in the seventeenth century (Zeuske 381) and the formation of the second stage of biopower – when it expanded into its society-wide form and became, thus, more evident – occurred in the second half of the eighteenth century (Cisney and Morar 5). What Foucault calls 'this power over life' is key to understanding the political and social underpinnings of the literature about suicide, autonomy and slavery I examine in *Romanticism and Subversive Suicide* (*Sexuality* 139).

Suicide in this framework is the ultimate test case for what Achille Mbembe, in 'Necropolitics', calls the 'romance of sovereignty': that which 'rests on the belief that the subject is the master and the controlling author of his or her own meaning. Sovereignty is therefore defined as a twofold process of *self-institution* and *self-limitation* (fixing one's own limits for oneself)' (13; emphasis in original). The often illogical, counter-intuitive prohibition of suicide in the period demonstrates that the subject has no sovereignty and is far from being in control. Slave, female and anti-religious suicides, in particular – the topics of the following chapters – rebel against the expectation that they must live, that their lives are not theirs and that their bodies are the property of a master – that they are mere cogs in the machine of biopower. Chloë Taylor notes that 'biopower works primarily through the state' ('Biopower' 238), and so it is with respect to these forms of subversive suicide, which oppose the colonial project, patriarchy and religious-based laws and institutions in Britain in the period.

While Foucault's examination of biopower forms a large part of the theoretical basis for this study, I offer something of a corrective to it in my focus on the theme of slave and female suicide. I am not the first to interrogate the foundations of Foucault's work. Giorgio Agamben's *Homo Sacer*: *Sovereign Power and Bare Life* (1998) takes as its starting point a rejection of Foucault's thesis that the historical rise of biopower marked the threshold of modernity by claiming that biopower and sovereignty are linked. Of greater moment to this study, though, is another lacuna in Foucault's discussion of biopower: he does not consider women and the enslaved. With regard to the latter group, citing Alexander G. Weheliye and Zakiyyah Iman Jackson, Gwen Bergner recognises this problem: 'Michel Foucault's biopolitics and Giorgio Agamben's state of exception and bare life – arguably the predominant critical frameworks for analyzing state violence and inequality as constituent aspects of democratic formation – neglect the history and legacy of racialization, colonialism, and slavery' ('Introduction' 447–8). I wish to expand this consideration to the treatment of women in the system of biopower, but not because I believe the trials of the enslaved and women were the same, either in kind or, usually, severity. I argue that the bodies of individuals in these groups were managed similarly in the system of biopower in its drive to maintain the population by controlling the subject's body, sometimes forcing it to reproduce, and denying the right to suicide. While Foucault does not mention the enslaved and women specifically, he seems to gesture to these groups in relating biopower to sexuality when he invokes

> the background that enables us to understand the importance assumed by sex as a political issue. It was at the pivot of the two axes along which developed

> the entire political technology of life. On the one hand it was tied to the disciplines of the body: the harnessing, intensification, and distribution of forces, and adjustment and economy of energies. ('Sexuality' 145)

The enslaved and women, in particular, were managed sexually, their fecundity made the focus, however implicit, of their roles in relation to British society, colonial and familial, as I will demonstrate in Chapters 3 and 4. Given their sexualised identities in the system of biopower, the cultural treatment of their suicidality takes on an intensified and paradigmatic aspect.

As one of Agamben and Foucault's most astute interrogators, Mbembe focuses on biopower's willingness to assign death to certain populations. My focus is, rather, on the enforcement of life – in the case of the enslaved, as a result of the very racism that Mbembe describes in terms of colonised societies:

> In Foucault's formulation of it, biopower appears to function through dividing people into those who must live and those who must die. Operating on the basis of a split between the living and the dead, such a power defines itself in relation to a biological field – which it takes control of and vests itself in. This control presupposes the distribution of human species into groups, the subdivision of the population into subgroups, and the establishment of a biological caesura between the ones and the others. This is what Foucault labels with the (at first sight familiar) term *racism*. (16–17; emphasis in original)

While Mbembe focuses on British colonialism in Africa, my focus is on the eighteenth-century British imperial project that involved kidnapping Africans to work in the West Indian colonies. Needless to say, racism was central to that project: only by identifying Africans as essentially different from white populations could slavers justify enslavement as not anti-British – that is, inhumanly predatory and contemptuous of mankind's natural rights, an affront to British law, cultural norms and Christian belief. In biopower's devotion to enforcing life ('those who must live'), the 'subdivision of the population into subgroups' moves to the foreground; the enslaved are in many ways defined as a subgroup by their very lack of bodily autonomy, a criterion that Mbembe recognises (21). He adds, 'In the economy of biopower, the function of racism is to regulate the distribution of death and to make possible the murderous functions of the state' (17). My topic is, to an extent, the reverse of Mbembe's, for I examine the dehumanising intervention of the state into the continued bodily existence of such subjects. The lives of the enslaved and women, I argue, were enforced, strictly maintained and compelled to multiply. They are, thus, the ultimate subjects of biopower.

The establishment of British biopower in transatlantic slavery made the British public aware of this new kind of power and thus able to recognise it in other areas of society. Women writers, such as Mary Shelley (hereafter 'Shelley') and Wollstonecraft, observed the subtle workings of the patriarchy's control over the female body in these terms, which they expressed by using the language of slavery in their works of feminist protest and by developing plots that revolved around suicide as subversive of such power. Byron, meanwhile, uses the theme of suicide to express the individual's autonomy in the face of religious control. We are not free from biopower today. The biopolitical treatment of the enslaved and women in the (proto-) Romantic period is a stark and early example of a situation that haunts broader Western society. Enforced life is an existential problem with which Jean Améry claims we all contend if we are not at liberty to choose death (43). In *Romanticism and Subversive Suicide*, I detail specific, political situations that exemplify the problem of such unfreedom, as expressed in Romantic literature. These works ultimately express the common human concerns to which Améry points: the demands for individual dignity, autonomy and independence – and biopower's challenge to them.

Chapter Breakdown

I have chosen to focus on a few major literary texts in this study – Wollstonecraft's *Mary, A Fiction* (1788) and *The Wrongs of Woman, or Maria* (1798), Shelley's *Mathilda* (written in 1819; published in 1959), and Byron's *Manfred* (1817) – for three main reasons. First, they are all British, which is why I do not examine Johann Wolfgang von Goethe's *The Sorrows of Young Werther* (1774; published in English in 1779) or Jean-Jacques Rousseau's *Julie, ou La Nouvelle Héloïse* (1761) in great detail, although both are reference points for my examination of literary suicide as expressive of personal freedom and receive attention in Chapter 2. Secondly, the texts on which I concentrate are substantive (novellas and a drama) and, uniquely, address suicidality from beginning to end or present the resolution of the protagonist's story as ending in suicidality, as distinct from those that simply mention suicide in passing, such as John Keats's 'Ode to a Nightingale' (1820) or Shelley's *The Last Man* (1826), in which the character Perdita kills herself. Thirdly, the major texts I examine present suicide as an answer to the biopolitical control of the body, such as under slavery, patriarchy and religious rule. For this latter reason, I do not examine in detail Percy Bysshe Shelley's 'Alastor' (1816); even though much of the poem is devoted to following the poet-character as he makes his way to chosen death, he does so through a desire to merge with the ideal world, not explicitly in rebellious response to biopower. I show how other references to suicide in period literature contribute to broad cultural notions about it, but the texts that receive the most detailed close readings in this book answer to the above strictures.[3]

In the following chapters, I examine key Romantic literary works that embody aspects of subversive suicide. By demonstrating how slavery increased British cultural awareness of the workings of biopower as it became established in the eighteenth century and tracing the ubiquity of the theme of slave suicide in abolitionist works, I provide the framework necessary to recognise the biopolitical resonances of suicide in these works by Wollstonecraft, Shelley and Byron, which enables new readings of them. Via literary form and the theme of suicide, the main texts I explore suggest the removal of the body from the sphere of biopower, making them subversive rather than constitutive of biopower – the contrary of how works of sentiment in the American context seek to regulate the body as a force of biopower, according to Kyla Schuller in *The Biopolitics of Feeling: Race, Sex, and Science in the Nineteenth Century* (2018) (*passim*). The slave memoirs I examine seek to replace the excessive attention to the Black body under slavery with a text, an intellectual object; as memoirs, they are ideal representations of the authors' selves, or, at least, their experiences, that bypass the physical body. Similarly, Shelley's *Mathilda* seeks to replace a woman's body – the source of her woe – with text, specifically the suicide note. Literary form is important for Wollstonecraft's works, too: seeking to reach a female audience with her message of women's rebellious suicide as a form of feminist protest, the author not only uses the novel genre – as opposed to the genre of a polemical tract, as in her famous *Vindications* – but she also chooses novelistic forms that were especially popular with women readers: the novel of sensibility in *Mary* and the Gothic novel in *The Wrongs of Woman*. In this way, Wollstonecraft addresses her message of suicidal protest to readers who are most concerned with it. Finally, the form of Byron's *Manfred*, mental drama, denies the actor's body its usual role as the conveyor of the dramatic work, echoing the aim of subversive suicide: to remove the body from the field of action as a form of resistance to the status quo. Thus, in all these works that use the theme of suicide to undermine biopower, expressed as slavery, misogyny or religious oppression, the genres in which they are written convey the message of subverting biopower as surely as do their direct references to subversive suicide.

In addition to this attention to form, my theoretical approach in each chapter is encapsulated in Foucault's theory of biopower, particularly the idea that – viewed from the perspective of biopower – suicide is essentially rebellious, despite its other meanings in the culture or its significance to the individual who chooses it, because it always undermines biopower's aim to maintain itself through the bodies it manages and seeks to maximise. My methodology is New Historical beyond my response to Foucault's philosophy of biopower. In this interdisciplinary study, I examine extra-literary primary sources to provide historical and cultural contexts for the literary works. Such often-ignored or under-studied sources demonstrate that the forces of biopower were not created and distributed conceptually through a top-down organisation of tyrants in the government, law and religious institutions of the time – although all these systems of power were certainly powerful purveyors of the ideology of enforced life, against which subversive suicide opposed itself. I study a web of period texts from across British culture that illustrate the development of, and build ideas about, enforced life, as well as suggest suicide's role in undermining it. In addition to investigating a range of literature across genres, such as poetry, plays, novels, short stories and memoirs, my sources, many of which have not been republished since their first appearance, include the following: legal texts; media reports; coroners' inquest reports; court documents, such as trial reports; tracts; essays; personal letters; medical texts; sermons; protest works; and visual art. Together, these sources exemplify Foucault's dictum that power is everywhere, and show the interconnectedness of the literature I interpret with the broad culture of the time. By submitting texts not usually considered to be literary to the methods of close reading, I demonstrate how literary criticism can help us to trace the formation of the concept of subversive suicide across the culture.

In Chapter 1, 'Period Approaches to Suicide', I provide the historical context of subversive suicide in Romantic-era literature by outlining the dominant views on the topic from non-literary fields, such as the religious, philosophical, political, legal and medical. I also discuss how suicide appeared in the media and popular culture, with particular attention to the different treatments of suicides by important political figures versus low-class subjects of lesser biopolitical value. Chapter 2, '"Give me Liberty or give me Death": The Literary Context of Romantic Subversive Suicide', offers an overview of the literature on suicide in the eighteenth century and Romantic period that influenced the formation of, or provided a foil for, the major texts I examine in this study. Following a discussion of Thomas Gray's 'The Bard' (1757) as a well-known example of rebellious suicide committed in opposition to sovereign power, and Aphra Behn's *Oroonoko* (1688) as one of the first major British texts depicting the suicidal rebellion of the enslaved, I show that

Joseph Addison's celebrated play *Cato* (1713) reveals an early recognition of the eighteenth-century understanding of biopower as linked to slavery. I then consider several of the most famous literary references to suicide in the Romantic era, both British and the most influential ones from elsewhere in Europe. Recognising that some eighteenth-century poets' biographies were also influential for the Romantics' conceptualisation of suicide, I discuss Thomas Chatterton and William Cowper's suicidality as crucial to the Romantic-era discussion about the significance of suicide.

Chapter 3, 'The Dying Negroes: Enforced Life and Slave Suicide as the Spectacle of Sentiment,' inaugurates Part II of this book ('Slavery, Biopower and Literary Subversive Suicide') and demonstrates how abolitionist works of the period were essential to the formation of the literary trope of suicide as subversive of biopower. The major texts I examine – Olaudah Equiano's *The Interesting Narrative of the Life of Olaudah Equiano, Or Gustavus Vassa, The African* (1789), Mary Prince's *The History of Mary Prince, a West Indian Slave* (1831) and Thomas Day and John Bicknell's *The Dying Negro* (1773, 1775) – describe in painful detail how the tortures of transatlantic slavery can lead to the wish to escape the system by choosing death; Day and Bicknell's poem recovers the figure of the honourable suicidal hero from the classical period and recasts him for the contemporary political climate. These works and others are formative expressions of rebellion against the system of slavery as enforced life, the quintessential expression of biopower. I also show how the use of the trope of slave suicide to engage the reader's sympathy in abolitionist texts by white writers could undermine their message of protest: the techniques of sensibility make pain and suffering available for aesthetic enjoyment, in a kind of ideological enslavement. (Given this issue, it was with some trepidation that I chose the cover image for this monograph, James Neagle's etching of an enslaved Black man apparently about to commit suicide on the deck of a ship, particularly since Neagle was a white man, and I am a white woman.[4] The image, however, is not a sentimental one: the figure's pride and defiance evoke respect, rather than pity, despite the implied desperation of his suicidal state. That this etching was the frontispiece of the 1793 edition of Day and Bicknell's *The Dying Negro*, one of the most famous abolitionist poems of the period and one which Equiano honours by mentioning in his *Interesting Narrative*, confirms the image as fitting for the cover.) Although slave memoirs similarly convey the torments of the Black body as a feature of their abolitionist appeal to the reader, their more immediate effect is to subvert the biopolitical regime that would treat Black authors as bodies alone: not only do they deny their former subjugation and exert control over their life-narratives by organising them into stories, but they also replace their former existences as enslaved bodies with an intellectual expression of their lives. The authors thereby remove themselves, particularly their bodies, from the sphere of biopower via the form of the memoir itself. To understand the revolutionary significance of slave suicide in these texts, I provide a historical overview of the topic that includes writings by pro-slavery writers, with a focus on what I call the 'inverted world' of transatlantic slavery, wherein the common meanings and values of British eighteenth-century society were perverted into a horrific other that saw people as property, and growth – such as on the plantations – as the source of death. Here, in this biopolitical world of enforced life, suicide is a form of freedom.

In Chapter 4, 'Refusing the Burden of the Body: Mary Wollstonecraft, Mary Shelley and the Suicide Note as Literary Form', I show how some early feminist fiction depicts female oppression as an aspect of the system of enforced life by tracing its presence chiefly in Wollstonecraft's *Mary, A Fiction* and *The Wrongs of Woman, or Maria*, and Shelley's *Mathilda*. In these novellas, patriarchy appears in the form of fictional husbands and fathers, the deputy agents of biopower, who burden women with the tasks of creating and maintaining maximum life, oppressing them as dependents and sex objects. The female protagonists of these novellas protest their subordination through suicidality – and, in the case of Shelley's protagonist Mathilda, by replacing her body, the site of her subjugation, with a suicide note, which, I argue, becomes Shelley's method of developing a literary form distinct from the masculine canon. This chapter also delineates how the literary theme of female subversive suicide borrows the terms of slave suicide as rebellion, demonstrating the strong influence of abolitionist literature on early feminist writing as such writers began to recognise female oppression as akin to the biopolitical management of bodies practised in the British slave trade. This framing is problematic, though, in that these texts sometimes predatorily and insensitively co-opt the terms of abolitionism for their own ends. Another concern with the theme of female suicide is that it may be seen as promoting misogynist ideals about women as weak, passive and so dependent upon men that they cannot live without masculine support, an idea that, in historical and media representations of female suicide, was often offered as the most common reason for female suicide. This explanation for female suicide not coincidentally frames it as the opposite of rebellious, as it positions the suicidal woman as an asset to biopower, rather than an autonomous being. I will demonstrate that this popular understanding of female suicide is connected to the ambiguously represented suicides of Wollstonecraft's and Shelley's protagonists.

Chapter 5, '"Earth! take these atoms!": The Religious Tract War and Suicidal Rebellion in Byron's *Manfred*', builds upon the visceral reality of the enforcement of life as described in the foregoing chapters to demonstrate how it also functioned more generally – and was ideologically established – throughout society in religious doctrine. The seemingly more abstract divine injunction that humans must maintain their grip on life becomes lived oppression through its basic denial of individual autonomy, and some of the texts in this chapter – chief of which is Byron's *Manfred* – protest this situation through the theme of rebellious suicide. Although Christianity may seem devoted solely to the spiritual life of the subject, its excessive concern with the enforcement of life shows that it is an arm of biopower. Practically every period text that agitates against choosing death does so from a religious perspective, such that the biopolitical enforcement of life gained legitimacy and strength from the almost totally consistent Christian demand that every person must live. In short, the influence between these fields of biopower – slavery, patriarchy and religion – was mutually enforcing. Simon Critchley maintains, 'as long as we keep this power [of suicide] in our hands, then we are, in some minimal but real sense, free ... Religions like Christianity prohibit suicide because of the real threat of insubordination that it poses' (72). Thus, in this case, too, the agents of biopower – here the representatives and supporters of religion, or what Foucault would call 'pastoral power' – oppose self-killing as defiance, an affront to its very existence: for what is a religion without adherents? This chapter also describes the development of the religious enforcement of life through historical and literary texts in and beyond the Romantic period by elucidating six major arguments they present for and against suicide. Byron, influenced by the discussion of suicide as a human right, tackles this radical topic in *Manfred*, which centres on the eponymous protagonist's wish to die from the play's beginning to the end, and in defiance of religious authorities of all kinds. Byron echoes this theme of suicide as the subversion of biopower through literary form in *Manfred*, for mental drama removes the actor's body from the conveyance of the dramatic work. To draw attention to the significance of the physical silence wrought by mental drama, Byron moreover makes constant references to silence in the dialogue of the play. In short, the mental-drama form functions as more than an expression of defiance against the Licensing Act of 1737, which greatly limited playwrights' artistic freedom of expression, another type of state oppression. Using the literary form of the mental drama and multiple references to silence in the dialogue of his play about suicide, Byron rails against any oppressive attempt to deny the freedom of the individual.

A notable feature of the main texts about suicide I study here is that they do not all feature accomplished suicide, but, rather, suicidality, which can include a death wish. (I often use the simple and direct term 'suicide', though, to gesture to the general topic.) In this way, they differ from their eighteenth-century forebears in the tradition I am outlining; one that stems from depictions of rebellious suicide in, especially, Gray's 'The Bard' and Addison's *Cato*, both of which feature the accomplishment of the heroes' chosen deaths. Ambiguously represented rebellious suicide may be viewed as showing Romantic writers' recognition of the problem with these figures from classical and neoclassical literature: their victory over tyranny is undermined by their mode of protesting it, their own death. As I will ask regarding slave suicide and philosophical treatments of suicide in general, how can the subject be free if he is no longer? I argue that the equivocal nature of these treatments of suicide does not divest it of protesting power, however. Slave memoirists' depictions of their suicidality can only be unaccomplished, else the memoir – a powerful form of abolitionist protest – could never have been written. When Wollstonecraft's and Shelley's female protagonists wish to die to protest the patriarchal control of their bodies, but do not accomplish the act, then the authors implicitly acknowledge and refuse to contribute to the long history of misogynistic fantasy about lovely female corpses. Byron's Manfred yearns for death for the entirety of the play, although his death at the end can only marginally be classified as a suicide. In this instance, the vagueness of the representation of suicide functions as a refusal of the narrative demand in readerly texts to present a neat, closed dénouement, in which the protagonist accomplishes the wish to die. That refusal is a gesture of subversion, as the theme of suicide itself is in *Manfred*. Just as suicidality destabilises biopolitical society, so does it destabilise plot.

Finally, the Conclusion of *Romanticism and Subversive Suicide* – 'The Afterlife of Romantic Subversive Suicide' – considers objections to the very idea of suicide as a victory through the lens of philosophers from the long eighteenth century to the present. Such philosophers as Immanuel Kant and Albert Camus query how choosing death can establish the successful rebellion of the suicide if the victorious subject ceases to exist. I address this concern with reference to the eternising nature of textuality in the literary trope of rebellious suicide and suicide as a means of defining subjecthood, as Mbembe, Martin Heidegger and Maurice Blanchot discuss. Améry asserts that suicide is motivated by such highly personal concerns that the victorious nature of the accomplished act can scarcely be communicated, and that suicide must therefore be understood as, simply, the establishment of one's human rights on the point of death as the 'privilege of the human' (97, 28, 43). *Romanticism and Subversive Suicide* ends with a consideration of how current changes in attitudes towards suicide in Western culture suggest that we might finally be moving beyond the long-standing reticence to discuss suicide and the one-dimensional view of it as significant only of insanity, both of which have plagued the issue from the Romantic period until recently. Changes in laws concerning euthanasia in Canada and expanded public debates about the topic in Britain suggest that the Romantic-era emphasis on suicide as a human right is, again, entering the cultural conversation.

The Critical Context for *Romanticism and Subversive Suicide*

While the present study is the first to offer a thorough historical background of subversive suicide in this period, it is not the first to study suicidality in the literature of the time. Two notable book-length works on the topic are *Dying to be English: Suicide Narratives and National Identity, 1721–1814* (2012) by Kelly McGuire, and Deanna Koretsky's *Death Rights: Romantic Suicide, Race, and the Bounds of Liberalism* (2021). In the former, McGuire studies the literary trope of suicide not as an individual act, but as a national one, with a focus on how suicidal women are depicted as sacrificial exemplars for England in literature from 1721 to 1814, a framing that understands suicide as conservative – constitutive of state power. Although this approach differs sharply from my focus on Romanticism, with its associations of rebellion and understanding of suicide as subversive of state power, McGuire's exploration nevertheless shares with mine the idea of suicide as heroic. Also similar is our attention to the universalising element in literature about suicide. I argue that the repeated expression of literary subversive suicide establishes it as a recognisable trope, rendering the individual characters who commit rebellious suicide representatives of a type. Crucially, though, in my study, the characters themselves choose suicide out of a desire for autonomy – to opt out of the system of biopower that would crush its members into 'close conformity', to borrow a phrase from Marianne Moore's 'To a Steam Roller' (4), and deny them the freedom of individual choice. In that sense, they oppose nationhood and community, rather than exemplify it, as do the suicidal female literary figures in McGuire's study.

Koretsky's recent monograph, meanwhile, focuses on racial politics and interrogates the very basis of my approach by arguing that the trope of Romantic suicide is based on a chimera, a baseless cultural belief in individual autonomy that both undergirds and belies liberalism itself through a racist ideology of white male supremacy. As Koretsky puts it, 'liberalism most clearly reveals itself as a system that enables freedom for some people at the expense of others' precisely in the trope of Romantic suicide, which (she claims, as I do) was chiefly established via British abolitionist literature about suicides of the enslaved (*Rights* 4). While our studies both approach Romantic suicide as a bid to establish the autonomy of the individual, they differ in breadth and methodology. Koretsky's emphasis is on Romantic suicide as 'the literary and critical commonplace that extols the singularity of white male genius, even in death' (*Rights* 5), as opposed to the specifically subversive suicide which is my focus. Koretsky also maintains a narrower focus on Romantic suicide as a key expression of the racist and misogynist foundations of 'modern liberalism'. She specifies 'how eighteenth- and nineteenth-century authors in Britain and the Atlantic world engaged the trope of suicide in ways that buttress antiblackness' and idealise 'white male supremacy' as the foundation of modern liberalism itself (*Rights* 2, 4), adding that, in abolitionist literature, 'The trope of suicide ... was often (albeit not always) aimed toward emancipatory ends, [whereas] this book will argue that these well-meaning efforts more often reflected, and functionally served to maintain, liberalism's foundational inequities' (*Rights* 4). While recognising this latter point, I argue that literary suicidality from the period can undermine racist and misogynist ideology and expresses a burgeoning recognition of and opposition to the emerging system of biopower, including its violent enforcement of life and denial of human autonomy. Most of all, *Romanticism and Subversive Suicide* differs from *Death Rights* in establishing the broad historical and cultural context of Romantic suicide through a more comprehensive view of the topic. I approach the primary texts as representations of and contributions to a far-reaching cultural understanding of subversive suicide and the limits of personal freedom, rather than deconstruct them as essentially oppositional to their stated import and confirming a system of white male supremacy. Our studies of literary suicide in the period may be read in tandem: they investigate similar topics, although from different theoretical perspectives.

Other works about suicide that form the critical context for my work investigate the theme in literature from other periods. Barbara T. Gates's *Victorian Suicide: Mad Crimes and Sad Histories* (1988) stands as an early study of the topic of suicide in literature from the Victorian period and beyond; Andrew Bennett's *Suicide Century: Literature and Suicide from James Joyce to David Foster Wallace* (2017) investigates the topic in the modern to contemporary periods; and Eric Langley's *Narcissism and Suicide in Shakespeare and his Contemporaries* (2009) examines the early history of literary suicide. About the broad period under investigation, important articles have appeared over the years; some of the most essential are by Margaret Higonnet, whose groundbreaking work on the topic of female suicide in nineteenth-century literature is foundational to my own approach. Another important literary treatment of suicide that is not a work of literary criticism is Al Alvarez's much-cited *The Savage God: A Study of Suicide* (1971), which examines suicide and literature over the span of several periods, focusing most closely on the life, work and death of Sylvia Plath, to whom Alvarez was a personal friend. The breadth and age of these studies of the literary treatment of suicide raise the question: why is the exploration of the theme in Romantic literature so scant and recent?

No examination of suicide can overlook the influence of French sociologist Émile Durkheim's foundational text *On Suicide*, which was the first book-length sociological study devoted entirely to the topic. Claims Richard Sennett, 'Durkheim taught the modern world how to think about suicide' (xi). For good reason, Jeffrey Watt calls Durkheim 'the giant who still towers above all others in the sociological study of suicide' ('Gender' 139). Durkheim's commentary has been formational to other disciplinary approaches, as well, such as that of psychology. I also recognise Durkheim's influence on the present literary-critical study, with its interdisciplinary aims. Durkheim approached the topic of suicide free of judgement, not sentimentally, or as sin, crime or rebellion, as was common before him; nor did he explicitly frame his study as an instrument to reduce the number of suicides. Rather, he presented self-chosen death as a serious sociological phenomenon that could reveal something important about the workings of the society from which the suicidal person originates. I take a similar approach to suicide in the Romantic period, as the present study is not an attempt to point out the error in our historical conceptualisation of suicide or an effort to address the problem of suicide in the present day. Like Durkheim, I interpret the phenomenon of suicide in the period as a powerful expression of a range of cultural concerns, and I agree that suicide should be understood in the wider context of social pressures and ideals.

Some concepts from Durkheim's book have leapt from the realm of sociology into public conversation, so commonly accepted are they. Many trace the origins of the phrase 'suicidal contagion' to *On Suicide*. Durkheim was not the first to recognise the related concept of imitative suicide, as the concern over 'Werther-mania', which I will discuss hereafter, shows a culture-wide acceptance of the basic idea in Europe in the late eighteenth century. However, Durkheim appears to have been the first to have coined the phrase 'suicidal contagion' and articulate it in detail – and, importantly, he disambiguates it from the kind of culture-wide suicidal phenomena that 'Werther-mania' denotes, maintaining that suicidal contagion only works on an individual level and does not have the power to affect broad sociological rates of suicide (140). He also establishes that contagion only occurs if the social groundwork exists to inspire the consideration of suicide, since a person will not commit suicide through contagion if they were not predisposed to do it in the first place (140). Also well known are Durkheim's three categories of suicide – anomic, egotistical and altruistic:

> Egotistical suicide derives from the fact that men no longer see any sense in living; altruistic suicide from the fact that this sense appears to them to be situated beyond life itself; and the third kind of suicide, ... from their activity being disrupted and from their suffering as a result. Because of its origin, we shall call this last kind *anomic suicide*. (283; emphasis in original)

In these familiar terms, we can view subversive suicide as a combination of egotistical suicide, for the subversive suicide sees no point in living to satisfy a tyrannical other, and anomic suicide since the subversive suicide rejects the disruption to his individual desires imposed from without. Durkheim himself recognised that these types of suicide are closely related: 'Both come from the fact that society is not sufficiently present for individuals' (284). Such is precisely the case with the subversive suicide, insofar as the suicide refuses to function as a cog in the machine of biopower. In several recognisable ways, Durkheim provides important, basic approaches to suicide that I use in this book.

A less familiar passage from Durkheim's *On Suicide* is even more pertinent to the present study, standing as the first to theorise about and define the significance of rebellious suicide. Durkheim treats suicide by enslaved people as the exemplar of this virtually unrecognised, fourth category:

> We can see by the preceding that there is a type of suicide ... that results from an excess of regulation, the one committed by those whose future is pitilessly confined and whose passions are violently constrained by oppressive discipline ... For the sake of completeness, we must therefore establish a fourth type of suicide ... [I]t could be that it has some historical interest. Is this not the kind of suicide of slaves that is said to be common in certain circumstances ... ? In short, all those suicides which could be attributed to an excess of physical or moral despotism? To indicate the inescapable and inflexible character of the rule over which one has no power, and in contrast to the term 'anomie' ... we might call it 'fatalistic suicide'. (305n)

Here, Durkheim describes precisely the kind of suicide that is the focus of the present study: that which is in response to 'physical ... despotism', the attempt to control the subject's body. For the literary figures I study, 'fatalistic suicide' is a powerful statement of liberty in the face of such oppression.

By tracing the roots and expression of the literary theme of subversive suicide in the British Romantic era through key texts from different genres, from novels to letters, and poems to plays, this book aims to demonstrate the significance of the concept for the period. A range of commentaries on suicide – including newspaper reports, coroners' inquests, religious tracts, sermons, medical studies and legal texts – reveals the existence of a distinctly Romantic-era suicide debate, the fervour of which reflects the rise of biopower, to which suicide was the ultimate threat. This debate also shows the spirited defence of Enlightenment ideas proclaiming the Western liberal subject as existentially free, which the prohibition against suicide denied. These concerns demonstrate the broad cultural influence of the British slave trade, which shaped national awareness of what it meant to be a subject and evolving notions about what constituted human being at the time.

Notes

1. Andrew Bennett considers several other Wordsworth poems, all from *Lyrical Ballads* (1798, 1802), as concerned with the topic of suicide: 'The Female Vagrant', 'Ruth', 'Ellen Irwin', 'The Idiot Boy', 'The Brothers' and ''Tis said, some have died for love' (44); I do not study any of these poems in detail, as they do not feature subversive suicidality in response to biopower.
2. I use the term 'anti-religious suicide' to refer to suicide committed to protest religious, mostly Christian, power.
3. It cannot be coincidental that these writers have biographical connections, given that Wollstonecraft was Shelley's mother, and Shelley, with P. B. Shelley, lived near Byron while he resided at the Villa Diodati in 1816, a few years before he published *Manfred* and she penned *Mathilda* in Florence. However, I do not focus on these texts as an illumination of these relationships.
4. The British Museum has a sketch of Neagle depicting him clearly as a white man in their collections (Anon. 'Portrait of the engraver James Neagle').

Chapter 1

Period Approaches to Suicide

What is most notable about the period under discussion is that so many literary works broke with the most common views of suicide at the time – as either a sin, a crime or an unintentional act of insanity – by posing it as subversive, even heroic, a throwback to the understanding of suicide that is most associated with the classical period in the West. Romantic literary suicide often signifies personal autonomy, existential freedom in the face of oppression and the rebellious assertion of the sole self to 'live free or die', to recall a phrase associated with the American Revolutionary War, borrowed by the French Revolution (Schama 557). In more general terms, too, suicide likely regained this significance in the period because rebellions were common at the time and imbued the public imagination. The American Revolution (1775–83) saw the American colonies break away from British rule (and taxation); the French Revolution (1789–99) was motivated by a desire to establish the governing power of the citizens of France over and against the corrupt French monarchy and Catholic Church; and slave revolts in the colonies were a constant source of interest or concern, depending on one's political leanings and financial investments. Tacky's Rebellion of 1760–1 in Jamaica and the Haitian Revolution (1791–1804) and its aftermath were the most significant to touch British interests. Howard French comments:

> Determined to control the richest of the sugar islands following its seizure of Guadeloupe, in 1793 Britain sent the largest naval expedition it had ever assembled to capture Saint-Domingue, which under the leadership of Toussaint Louverture had risen up against the French. The former slaves of what would soon become Haiti, however, defeated the British; more of their soldiers died there in battle and from disease than had died in the American Revolutionary War two decades earlier. (n.p.)

Non-violent ideological and political movements also contributed to the period's association with rebellion. Carol Blum recognises that several of the major political battles of the long eighteenth century sought to establish the principle of ownership over another person as an affront to basic human rights, and to enshrine in law the prohibition against the human body ever being classed as property, be it Black, female, or low class (161). The 'woman question' concerning women's equality with men, most commonly associated with Wollstonecraft's influential tract *A Vindication of the Rights of Woman* (1792; hereafter *Rights of Woman*), was sometimes figured as betokening a female revolution against the patriarchy, while the Great Reform Act of 1832 enacted a sea change in the British electoral system, one that provided previously unrepresented (often low-class) voters with political representation for their interests by relaxing the stranglehold the British aristocracy had over the political system until that time. Christianity itself experienced a revolutionary moment in this period, during which a variety of different forms of Protestantism flourished, as Saree Makdisi, Daniel White and Mark Canuel have discussed.[1] These new types of Christianity challenged the hegemony of the official Protestant churches in Britain. To call the period from 1770 to 1830 revolutionary, therefore, is unexceptionable. What has been less commonplace is to note that this spirit is encapsulated in literary depictions of suicide.

Concerns over the number of people in the British population – and how to best maximise bodies for the good of the nation – were also related to the rebellious spirit of the time. Gunnar Thorvaldsen notes, 'The social unrest following the French Revolution alerted many British to the need to know the basis for raising an army and extra taxes in case of war', as did concerns over how to account for the number of poor people in need of government assistance after a catastrophic harvest in 1795 (52). Together, such social issues meant that the time was ripe for works such as Thomas Malthus's *Essay on the Principle of Population* (1798) and Sir John Sinclair's *Statistical Account of Scotland* (1791–9). The first efforts towards a national census also occurred at this time and were memorialised in print by John Rickman's 'Thoughts on the Utility and Facility of a General Enumeration of the People of the British Empire' (1796), after which censuses were performed every decade from 1801 (Thorvaldsen 52).[2] Such efforts constituted the move towards establishing biopolitical control over citizen's bodies through the management of them, especially in Britain, where utilitarianism was taking hold as a major organising ideology.

Jeremy Bentham, English jurist, philosopher and social reformer, is best known as the founder and main exponent of the principles of utilitarianism, a system of normative ethics that famously sought to establish how to foster '"the greatest amount of good for the greatest number"' of people (Driver n.p.). Proclaiming this goal, admirable in its attention to the equality of every individual's right to the good, utilitiarianism yet gave rise to the statistical analysis of the population and set the stage for 'big government' to quantify and assess its citizens as necessary tools for the achievement of 'the greatest good'. Julia Driver states: 'Bentham … sought to use utilitarianism to inform law and social policy' (n.p.). It is not that Bentham was opposed to individual independence or championed tyranny, as he 'view[ed] liberty and autonomy as good'; however, he saw them as such 'instrumentally, not intrinsically' (Driver n.p.), meaning that, if the statistical quantification of the population – so important to the establishment of biopower – could help garner the 'greatest good' for the largest number of people, then such assessment of individuals in society should, from a Benthamite perspective, win out over concerns about people's privacy and individual needs.

The very principle of the 'greatest good for the greatest number' is itself an expression of biopower's goal to foster, maintain and maximise life. Thomas Sowell points out that 'Malthusian population theory became one of the keystones of the set of doctrines known as "classical economics," developed and set forth uncompromisingly by the Benthamite Utilitarians' (268), and such study of populations, always aimed at increasing it, necessitates the classification and quantification of individuals as part of the social whole. Given that such utilitarian thinking was established in the nineteenth century – first by Bentham, later by Malthus and developed further in the Victorian period by John Stuart Mill – we should not be surprised to witness opposition to this new way of understanding the individual: not as inherently important as a person, but as a part of a whole that must continue to grow in this system of biopower, thereby effectively erasing the individual's autonomy and unique desires.[3]

This period is also associated with the rise of academic disciplines. The nineteenth-century establishment of the discipline of psychology as a professional field, with increasingly stringent rules for membership and codified means of assessing patients, is related to the utilitarian urge: along with it came greater methods for the classification and means of understanding individuals. This point is important for the present study because psychology sought to enlist itself as the chief means of understanding suicide – and it achieved this goal, retaining its hold to the present day, as commentators such as Thomas Szasz have protested. The Benthamite focus on 'the greatest good for the greatest number' would also eventually give rise to another discipline closely connected with the understanding of suicide through Durkheim's work: sociology. In the Victorian period, this new field relied on statistical records of population, health, births, deaths and other biological details about the population in order to maximise life. Quoting philosopher Ian Hacking, McGuire comments, 'The notion that … "one can improve – control – a deviant subpopulation by enumeration and classification," accounts for the fact that suicide has historically been the subject of sociological statistical analysis' (*Dying* 5), particularly after Durkheim's study in the late Victorian period. However, the seeds of this sociological drive to measure and study such populations to control them began much earlier in the nineteenth century. Together, the disciplines of psychology and sociology effectively provided new discourses for the deployment and expression of biopower. Améry takes aim at both disciplines for ignoring and suppressing the highly individualised reasons that motivate people to choose suicide, as well as for purporting to define what cannot be communicated systematically (8, 16). Foucault would say that these fields aimed not at understanding suicide, but at preventing it through the management of live bodies – that they are aspects of the biopolitical regime that 'focuses on the species body …: propagation, births and mortality, the level of health, life expectancy and longevity … Their supervision was effected through an entire series of interventions and *regulatory controls: a biopolitics of the population*' (*Sexuality* 139; emphasis in original). Such processes began around the turn of the nineteenth century.

This period was also defined by the Enlightenment focus on individual liberty and the 'rights of man', which increased interest in questions about individual autonomy – and suicide is the consummate example of how far personal liberty might go. Most notably, the *Encyclopédie ou Dictionnaire Raisonné des Sciences, des Arts et des Métiers* (1762–72) – or, simply, the Enlightenment *Encyclopedia* – offers a definition of what a person's natural rights are. This influential reference work, directed by Denis Diderot, includes many articles by such famous *philosophes* as Voltaire, Montesquieu and Rousseau that outline key Enlightenment concepts. Although the contributors to the *Encyclopedia* were by no means in agreement about all matters political and, especially, religious, the work does provide a coherent overview of the Enlightenment approach to issues that concerned the movement greatly, such as human rights. Importantly, the definition of 'slave trade' strongly denies its legitimacy on these very grounds:

> *Men and their freedom are not objects of commerce*; they can be neither sold, nor purchased, nor bought at any price …
>
> … [E]ach of those unfortunates who are merely considered slaves, has the right to be declared free since *he never lost his freedom and never could.* Furthermore, neither his prince, nor his father, nor anybody else in the world

> has the ability to own this freedom. Accordingly, the purchase of it is worthless: this Negro does not, nor could he ever, deprive himself of his *natural right*. He carries it everywhere, and can demand that he be allowed to enjoy it wherever he goes. It is thus an obvious inhumanity that, in the free country to which the Negro is transported, judges do not immediately decide to liberate him by declaring that he is free, as he is the judges' fellow man and has a soul like theirs. ('Slave trade' n.p.; my emphasis)

This powerful statement on the slave trade, which also functions as a definition of humankind, directs that humans cannot be owned, lose their freedom or be unequal to other humans since their 'natural right[s]' preclude such a fate. The description attests in no uncertain terms that humans are essentially, inherently autonomous beings with free agency. Appropriately, the Enlightenment *Encyclopedia* uses the most extreme example of the loss of human liberty – enslavement – to demonstrate its main point: that, by their very nature, human beings cannot be owned by others, even by their own choice. As I will detail in Chapter 3, the *Encyclopedia*, one of the major sources for Enlightenment thinking about human rights, was sometimes contradictory in approaching the topic of slavery.

Such thinking powerfully affected such events as the French Revolution, the American Revolution, abolitionism and the Reform Act of 1832, the last of which signals the final chapter of the British Romantic period, underscoring its strong identification with democratic principles. Most importantly for *Romanticism and Subversive Suicide*, these movements encourage the ultimate question about personal liberty: if humans are, by definition, autonomous, free agents, then may we not choose to end our own lives? This question is the core of the suicide debate in the period, when writers from many segments of the political spectrum declared their views on this important matter. The issue of suicide concerned beliefs about human equality; democracy versus monarchy and other forms of 'big government'; faith versus atheism; and human rights and freedoms versus social duty and the requirements of citizenship in a healthy society – all contentious issues at the heart of Romanticism.

In this context of the Enlightenment focus on human rights, increasing forces of control in British society and its fomenting revolutionary spirit, ideas about suicide took shape. These notions were also profoundly affected by centuries of thinking about the topic.[4] Attitudes towards suicide changed considerably over the centuries in the West. In Ancient Rome and Greece suicide was often linked with ideas about honour and status, but, after Augustine of Hippo declared in *The City of God* (c. 412–16) that the act was a direct violation of the Sixth Commandment ('Thou shalt not kill'), self-accomplished death become identified 'as a form of murder [that] repositioned the deceased as the perpetrator of a mortal sin. Later, a series of Canon Laws sought to criminalise self-killing' in 452 and 563, and the Church influenced legal entities, such as juries, to find suicides criminally culpable (Marsh 86, 88). In the Renaissance period suicide was linked with notions about melancholy, which might seem to mitigate beliefs about its culpability, yet church punishments for this crime continued into the seventeenth century. Suicide retained its status as an unmitigated sin until well into the nineteenth century. Romantic-era doctors almost invariably fell back on the Renaissance understanding of suicide as motivated by melancholy, with legal judgements on the motivations for suicide arguing in favour of *non compos mentis* (Latin for 'not of sound mind') in almost all cases by the turn of the nineteenth century: Michael MacDonald asserts that 'Less than 7 per cent of the suicides reported to King's Bench were declared to have been insane in the early 1660s, but the proportion more than doubled in the next two decades ... By the 1720s 90 per cent of all suicides were judged insane' ('Secularization' 60).[5] However, texts on suicide by religious writers at the time almost always condemned the act as a sinful rebellion against the authority of God. Concurrent with this broadly religious and social prohibition of suicide was the increasing view of it as cowardly, an attempt to escape the pressures of life through death. James Fordyce opines in *A Letter on Suicide, to a Friend who Meditated that Dreadful Crime* (1797) that the very tenor of Christianity is self-sacrifice and 'self-surrender': the devout Christian should therefore be willing to accept any sort of pain, rendering suicide a demonstration of extreme cowardice (22). The view of suicide as cowardly, so contradictory to the view of it as rebellious in many literary depictions of the act, was alive and well in the Romantic period, an indication of how energetic the debate about it was at the time.

What gave special urgency to the debate was the widely accepted view that the British believed themselves particularly prone to committing suicide. The first full-length discussion of suicide in English, according to Margaret Pabst Battin, was by a 'zealous Calvinist minister born in Scotland' named John Sym; his treatise *Lifes* [*sic*] *Preservative Against Self-Killing* (1637) frames suicide as an English epidemic (296). This belief only became more widespread in subsequent years, partly due to the highly influential discourse surrounding nerve theory that was popularised in the eighteenth century, especially by George Cheyne in *The English Malady* (1733), which posited melancholy (what we call 'depression' today) as endemic to the English. This disease often ended in suicide, a point to which Robert Burton attests in *The Anatomy of Melancholy* (1621), the most famous account of the disease for centuries: 'Seldom this malady procures death, except ... they make away themselves; which is a frequent thing, and familiar amongst them' (317–18). A few eighteenth-century literary writers almost succumbed to this condition, including James Boswell, who suffered from 'hypochondria' and, as Allan Ingram shows, felt suicidal several times in his life (19, 22). Accordingly, well-known literary statements on English suicidality also express alarm about it: the poet Edward Young bemoans, 'O Britain, infamous for suicide', in *Night-Thoughts* (1742–5) (442) and Robert Blair describes 'Self-murder' as 'our island's shame' (403) in *The Grave*, a poem first published in 1743. So many fretted about the British proclivity for suicide that it became part of the British identity.

The appropriate response to (supposed) British suicidality was a matter of dispute. Some eighteenth-century writers seemed nearly to revel in this national character. Roy Porter remarks, 'In the *Spectator*, [Joseph] Addison and [Richard] Steele had been making considerable play of the notoriety the nation had acquired on the Continent for its spleen, vapours, lowness of spirits, and, indeed, its propensity for suicide' (xxix). Writers from Europe were intrigued by it, too. Montesquieu took a long view of the matter:

> We do not find in history that the Romans ever killed themselves without a cause; but the English are apt to commit suicide most unaccountably; they destroy themselves even in the bosom of happiness. This action among the Romans was the effect of education, being connected with their principles and customs; among the English it is the consequence of a distemper, being connected with the physical state of the machine, and independent of every other cause. In all probability it is a defect of the filtration of the nervous juice: the machine, whose motive faculties are often unexerted, is weary of itself; the soul feels no pain, but a certain uneasiness in existing. (395)

Speaking in the language of nerve theory, Montesquieu surmises that the cause for British suicide was mechanical: ineffective plumbing of the 'nervous juice'. Why the English should be particularly susceptible to such faulty 'filtration' remains a mystery, but what Montesquieu's comment does reveal is that other European nationals accepted the existence of an English malady that led to suicide to the extent that they even searched for a physical cause for it, thereby investing the notion with objective substantiation that answered to the demands of empirical science in this age of Enlightenment. The story of suicide was written on the body and, by the Romantic period, the idea that the English killed themselves in alarming numbers had become accepted as a fact. McGuire states that the 'English nation [saw itself] as the bastion of an inordinately suicidal culture. Suicide and the English become synonymous over the course of the century' covered in her study (*Dying* xiii).

Accordingly, Mary Dawes Blackett laments in 1789, 'That the people of this country [i.e. England] are notoriously eminent for the commission of this crime [of suicide], is a truth that has long been admitted' (iii). Suicide had become as English as John Arbuthnot's John Bull, and this belief came to stand in for the British character as a whole – one whose independence of spirit and devotion to individual freedom extended to the point of choosing death for oneself.

The Suicide Debate: Religious and Philosophical Views

While I discuss the religious opprobrium against suicide in greater detail in Chapter 5, here it suffices to say that no one was more voluble about the transgressive nature of suicide than religious writers, who invariably associated it with sin. Despite plenty of protestations to the contrary in Enlightenment texts – such as in John Locke's *Two Treatises of Government* (1689), in which the empiricist philosopher memorably states that 'man [is] … master of himself, and *proprietor of his own person*' (225; emphasis in original) – these writers proclaim that suicide is forbidden because we are not our own masters. Many religious writers argue that God created us and therefore owns us (e.g. Croft 6), and we have no right to destroy his property. Despite writers of all stamps proclaiming the impermissibility of suicide on the basis of God's mastery over us, even those who subscribed to this belief might still commit suicide, as was the case with John William Polidori, Byron's physician, who wrote in his 'Essay on the Punishment of Death', '"All must agree that our being here originating from God it is not allowable to take into our own hands our own dismissal"' (quoted in Franklin 228n). Polidori, burdened by gambling debts, killed himself in 1821 at age 25, despite his pious animadversions.

Many religious writers feared that the very discussion of suicide as a matter of debate in the period indicated waning belief in God's mastery and an increase in atheism in Britain. The title of an anonymously authored tract from 1785 expresses their alarm: *A Dissertation or, Discourse on Suicide; Grounded on the Immovable Foundation of Scriptural, Rather than of Philosophical Principles*. This author's assertion that biblical sources are implicitly incontrovertible in their permanence, in contradistinction to philosophical ideas – which, the author suggests, are merely fashionable whims – communicates the common concern that debate itself, the soul of philosophy, could undermine faith. Taking aim at writers exploring the issue from a secular perspective, the author of *A Dissertation* declares that 'Whatever an ingenious, but *depraved* Reason may be able to alledge [*sic*] in Vindication of the sin' of suicide, it, nevertheless, is a sin 'against *God* [and] ... A Species ... of Murder, horribly unnatural; ... *all* MURDER, without Discrimination, has been declared by our Saviour himself, to *come out*' of evil (3; emphasis in original). Similarly, John Corry tells a long story about philosophy's pernicious effect on British piety in *The Suicide; or, The Progress of Error. A Moral Tale, for the Instruction of Young Persons* (1805?), in which one 'Mr R***', influenced by Wollstonecraft's 'Rights of Woman, [William Godwin's] Political Justice, ... and similar vehicles of sophistry and impiety [that had] excited the attention of the public', decides to kill himself after a row with his mistress because she denied Godwin was a greater philosopher than Sir Isaac Newton (7). He is rescued from a drowning attempt by one 'Mr Trueman' (14), whose 'vision' turns Mr R from the path of vice and 'infidelity', having himself been reclaimed from the temptations of 'modern philosophy' (15). Even though this story ends with an avoidance of suicide, the narrator nevertheless laments, 'But how few, alas, of those who wander along the flowery path of fashionable levity, sensuality, and irreligion, are thus reclaimed! how many sink into an imfamous [*sic*] course of the most grovelling sensuality? and how many perish even *in the blossom of their sin* by their own hand!' (28; emphasis in original). The message of these and many other authors of the time is that philosophical debate, especially about suicide, is the enemy of religion.

In such confident devotion to the axiomatic, though, these writers conveniently ignore that one of Britain's most admired religious writers, John Donne, had written a posthumously published treatise entitled *Biathanatos* (written in 1608; published in 1647), much of which is devoted to exploring whether suicide really is disallowed in Christian scripture, and which I will investigate closely in Chapter 5. It is important to recognise that Donne wrote the text before he took holy orders, and that he forbade his son to publish it, a command the latter disobeyed after his father's death (Seaver, 'Vicar' 40; Pabst Battin, Introductions 288). However, the fact remains that, at least in 1608 when Donne penned the work, he was confident enough in the propriety of examining the validity of the Christian injunction against suicide to produce a lengthy and well-researched text, the full title of which demonstrates his liberal approach to the topic: *A Declaration of that Paradoxe, or Thesis, That Self-homicide is Not So Naturally Sin, That It May Never be Otherwise. Wherein the Nature, and the Extent of All those Lawes, Which Seeme to be Violated by this Act, are Diligently Surveyed.* The laws against suicide to which Donne gestures in the title are scriptural, and his analysis of them undermines the notion that they are beyond debate or untouchable as ideology.

Given the existence of this major text on the possible permissibility of suicide by a well-respected religious writer, it would make sense if a study with a similar aim by a reputable philosopher from the subsequent century would be met with relative equanimity: but such was not the case. David Hume's *Essays on Suicide* was initially published and withdrawn in 1756 (Klibansky and Mossner 38–9n) and, when it was finally published again in 1783 with Hume's name, the editor practically disavowed the publication in the very subtitle: *With Remarks, Intended as an Antidote to the Poison Contained in These Performances*. Hume's text on suicide is doubtlessly the target of Anonymous's complaint about 'ingenious' writers of degenerate reason (*Immovable* 3) who debate the validity of strictures against suicide. To be sure, some of Hume's statements seem eminently reasonable:

> Were the disposal of human life so much reserved as the peculiar province of the Almighty, that it were an encroachment on his right, for men to dispose of their own lives; it would be equally criminal to act for the preservation of life as for its destruction. If I turn aside a stone which is falling upon my head, I disturb the course of nature, and I invade the peculiar province of the Almighty, by lengthening out my life beyond the period which, by the general laws of matter and motion he had assigned to it. (11)

While it is easy to see why religious writers would have felt threatened by Hume's essay, since this conclusion is difficult to assail, some, such as William Cowper, were perfectly capable of offering their own logical rejoinders. Hume's next statement, 'It would be no crime in me to divert the *Nile* or *Danube* from its course, were I able to effect such purposes. Where then is the crime of turning a few ounces of blood from their natural channel?' (12), inspired Cowper to offer the sound counterargument: 'His [Hume's] silly assertion, that, because it would be no sin to divert the course of the Danube, therefore it is none to let out a few ounces of blood from an artery, would justify not suicide only, but homicide also' (*Works* 174). Cowper then falls into an ad hominem attack that weakens his rational position: 'But the life of a man and the water of a river can never come into competition with each other in point of value, unless in the estimation of an unprincipled philosopher' (*Works* 174). Many other religious writers, such as Solomon Piggott (216), challenge Hume's text on suicide in similarly unconvincing ways. Perhaps most memorable is George Clayton's claim in a footnote from *The Dreadful Sin of Suicide* (1812):

> Mr Hume's Essay on Suicide has been a source of incalculable evil. How affecting is the thought, that he should have spent his last hours in 'forming a project for destroying the souls, and abridging the lives of his fellow-creatures!'

> It is said, that having presented this piece to an intimate friend, such was its effect on his mind, that he first returned his thanks to the author, and immediately afterwards put an end to his existence. (48n)

Such dramatic stories, so ripe for repetition regardless of how questionable their claims to truth are, suggest to the reader the immediate danger of the suicide debate from a religious perspective and the desire to shut it down completely.

The troubled publication history of Hume's discussion of suicide exemplifies the fearful reaction to it. At least one of Hume's fellow philosophers recognised the injustice of its reception. In the nineteenth century, Arthur Schopenhauer writes in 'On Suicide':

> It is a great disgrace to the English nation that a purely philosophical treatise, which, proceeding from one of the first thinkers and writers in England, aimed at refuting the current arguments against suicide by the light of cold reason, should be forced to sneak about in that country, as though it were some rascally production. (25)

Despite being treated unfairly, Hume's writings on suicide would reshape the debate for the British Romantic movement, and not only with respect to fellow philosophers, such as Godwin, who appears to respond to Hume's *Essays on Suicide* in his appendix on the topic in *Political Justice*.

Politics and Legal Approaches to Suicide

The discussion of suicide was attended by fear in the period, as it often is today in the West, and for some of the same reasons, such as the provocation of religious and moral disapprobation or the dread of conveying suicidal contagion. After all, Goethe's *The Sorrows of Young Werther* was reputed to have caused a rash of suicides amongst young Europeans, who sought to replicate the beloved protagonist in dress, in attitude and in choosing death, as I will detail further in Chapter 2. One major difference between then and now regarding the fear of discussing suicide is the political baggage that attended the issue in Romantic-era Britain, when the most profound source of that fear was, doubtlessly, the French Revolution. In the 1790s, the legalisation and acceptance of suicide were associated with French Revolutionary sympathies. Dominique Godineau asserts, 'the [French] revolutionaries decriminalised suicide: the Penal Code of 1791 did not put it in the list of crimes prosecuted by the law, and the Code of Crimes and Punishments of 1795 states that death annuls any prosecution' (127; my translation).[6] Moreover, as Jeffrey Merrick points out in 'Suicide and Politics in Pre-Revolutionary France,' suicide was used as 'a deliberate political statement [by] ... political figures who killed themselves, in heroic Roman style, during the Revolution' (43).[7] In the wake of the Revolution, writes William Stewart, 'criminal penalties for attempting to commit suicide were abolished in European countries, the United Kingdom being the last to follow suit in 1961' (479).[8] This point underscores the extent to which English authorities resisted the revolutionary decriminalisation of suicide. Unsurprisingly, then, the mere discussion of suicide was suppressed in England, where fears of revolution were codified into the Habeas Corpus Suspension Act of 1794, which was instituted to 'empower his Majesty [George III] to secure and detain such persons as his Majesty shall suspect are conspiring against his person and government', as the long title of the Act asserts.[9] Any kind of rebellion was strictly policed at the time. A royal subject's assertion of her sole right over and ownership of her body through the act of suicide could easily be construed as rebellion.

It is difficult to divide a consideration of the political from the religious significance of suicide in a period that framed it as a crime against God, who invested the British monarchy with the right to rule. Suicide was therefore seen as a crime against the sovereign, the highest political figure in Britain. When religious authorities discuss the sin of suicide in militaristic terms, they are not only using a metaphor to make a theological point; they are also confirming religious power's support of the political order and drawing attention to suicide's rebellious significance as much as its blasphemous nature. Nor were religious writers the only ones to insist on this point. In *Historia Placitorum Coronæ: The History of the Pleas of the Crown* (1778), Matthew Hale associates God and the sovereign in their right to our lives: 'No man hath the absolute interest of himself, but 1. God almighty hath an interest and propriety in him, and therefore self-murder is a sin against God. 2. The king hath an interest in him, and therefore the inquisition in case of self-murder is' a felony (412). My examination of religious suicide, for which I take Byron's *Manfred* as the literary exemplar, is as much about worldly biopower as are the two chapters that precede it.

The religious injunction against suicide in the period is observable in the legal treatment of suicides' corpses, as well as suicides' families, since British common law strongly reflected Christian principles. The religious flavour of William Blackstone's statements about the crime of suicide in his authoritative *Commentaries on the Laws of England* (1765–70) demonstrates the point:

> the law of England wisely and religiously considers, that no man hath a power to destroy life, but by commission from God, the author of it: and, as

> the suicide is guilty of a double offence; one spiritual, in invading the prerogative of the Almighty, and rushing into his immediate presence uncalled for; the other temporal, against the king, who hath an interest in the preservation of all his subjects; the law has therefore ranked this among the highest crimes, making it a peculiar species of felony, a felony committed on one's self [or *felo de se*, criminal suicide]. (*Commentaries* (1773) 189)

A common legal punishment for suicides was also very much a religious one: the denial of a church burial to the suicide's corpse. The posthumous punishment of suicide did not end there, as the anonymous author of *Thoughts on Suicide* comments:

> The wretched victim is to be buried in a four-cross-road, and a stake is to be driven through his body, without any of those decent ceremonies, which attend a fellow-creature to the recesses of the dead. And yet we deem it not sufficient to stop here ... We confiscate the property of the deceased, and deprive the disconsolate widow, the fatherless children, and the relatives, who may have depended upon him for support, of the common necessaries of life. We hold *them* up, probably no less estimable than ourselves, to indignation and scorn. (25; emphasis in original)

The anonymous author emphasises the absurdity as well as injustice of such penalties: 'But you cannot inflict a *punishment* on the man, who commits an act of Suicide. He is insensible to suffering, shame, and disgrace' (25; emphasis in original). Paul S. Seaver notes that punishments on suicides' corpses were meant 'not so much to punish the suicide – she was in any case beyond the reach of the authorities – as ... to dramatize the horror of the act of self-destruction and to deter similar acts by jeopardizing the survival of a suicide's family' ('Vicar' 27). Why punish the family members for what they did not do? Beyond the fantasy of deterrence, the illogicality of such penalties is revealing. It is intriguing to consider that, until the end of the Romantic period, suicides' corpses were treated in the same way as were the bodies of vampires, according to fictional treatments of the latter: as Edward Barry directs in *The Present Practice of a Justice of the Peace* (1790), the suicide 'shall be buried ignominiously in the highway, with a stake driven through his body' (413). Gates reasons that, 'Since they were considered the ultimate sinners, suicides had been staked to prevent their restless wanderings as lost souls' that could pose a threat to the living (6). Such socially sanctioned, legally required, brutally physical handling of the suicide's body appears to be a superstitious horror of suicide disguised as social protection.

As gory as the treatment of the suicide's corpse seems to us today, the financial repercussions of punishment for suicide were, perhaps, even more extreme. John Paris and John Fonblanque declare in *Medical Jurisprudence* (1823):

> as to what a *felo de se* shall forfeit, it seems clear that he shall forfeit all chattels, real or personal, which he hath in his own right; and also all chattels real, whereof he is possessed jointly with his wife, or in her right; and also all bonds and other personal things in action, belonging solely to himself; and also all personal things in action, and as some say, entire chattels in possession, to which he was entitled jointly with another. (106)

The authors recognise that coroners' juries rarely applied this punishment, suggesting that the motivation for avoiding it is a too-strict adherence to the definition of sanity:

> SELF-MURDER is ranked among the higher crimes being a peculiar species of felony, as implied in the technical term *felo de se*. To constitute this offence, the party must be in his senses, else it is no crime; but this excuse ought not to be strained to that length to which our coroner's juries are too apt to carry it, (a) *viz*. that the very act of suicide is an evidence of insanity; as if every man who acts contrary to reason, had no reason at all. (Paris and Fonblanque 104)

While they recognise that juries in the period often found the suicide *non compos mentis*, Paris and Fonblanque fail to acknowledge that the cruel and unjust nature of the attendant punishment for the suicide's family was part of what motivated juries to avoid finding culpability. Despite the infrequent application of this penalty, it remained in British law until the twentieth century, demonstrating that, on an official level, suicide was threatening enough to warrant the sternest of responses, long beyond the Romantic period.

All the same, punishments for suicide at this time were neither as harsh as they used to be, nor as Sir Thomas More, the author of *Utopia* (1516), would have them be for those who embrace death without official sanction: 'he that killeth himself before that the priests and the council have allowed the cause of his death, him as unworthy either to be buried or with fire to be consumed, they cast unburied into some stinking marsh' (239). Throughout the ages, the spirit of the penalties for suicide appears to be less about meting out appropriate punishment for a crime than demonstrating the culture's anger at and fear of the liberty taken by the suicide – alarm at his claim of autonomy over his own existence and disapprobation of his choice to opt out of the social contract.

Dramatic punishments for suicide waned over the years. Their nature changed to make them appear useful and less motivated by vengefulness or other emotions, as the following example suggests:

> the last recorded degradation of the corpse of a suicide in England took place in 1823, when a man called Griffiths was buried at the intersection of Grosvenor Place and the King's Road, Chelsea. But even then self-murderers were not left in peace: for the next fifty years the bodies of unclaimed and destitute suicides went to the schools of anatomy for dissection. (Alvarez 64)

Doubtlessly, the plan to use suicides' corpses for dissection seemed simply practical to many (why waste a good corpse?), as the progress of medicine depended on doctors' and medical students' access to dead bodies to complete their knowledge. In this way, suicides, so subversive of biopower, were transformed into its tools by making their corpses the means for training physicians to promote the health and longevity of the population. That the same treatment was meted out to murderers reveals the punitive impetus behind the choice of suicides' corpses for this practice. The author of *Thoughts on Suicide* calls the dissection of suicides' corpses a 'revolting ... measure' and apparently condemns both the coldly utilitarian reasons for dissecting them and its aim of deterrence. He quotes another anonymous writer's comment that

> 'by the more frequent dissection of such bodies, the cause of that most melancholy of all human maladies, insanity, might be more accurately investigated ... [W]hatever the number of bodies were given for dissection, by so many would be the necessity of body-stealing diminished, and a horrible race of ruffians, the resurrection-men, as they are called, eradicated.' (29)

Again, then, we arrive at punishments for suicides' corpses as a form of deterrent for the living, to threaten them so they may not opt out of the system of biopower.

By the Romantic period, 'In most cases of suicide – the jury ... [found] a verdict of lunacy' (29) or *non compos mentis*, according to the author of *Thoughts on Suicide*. The ruling recognises the unintentional nature of the death in order to obviate the application of the penalties meted out for criminal suicides, those deemed *felo de se*. Deterrents may only be effective in reducing acts made by choice, and are useless against unintentional ones. Michael MacDonald comments that the trend for such findings began long before:

> The increasing frequency of *non compos mentis* verdicts in the 1680s and 1690s signaled the beginning of a fundamental change in the cultural significance of suicide. As we have already seen, the rise of the *non compos mentis* verdict was prompted initially by its attractiveness as a way of escaping the fiscal penalties for self-murder, and for a long time this no doubt remained a major aspect of its appeal to coroners' juries. But, unlike the other methods of avoiding forfeiture, declaring that suicides were mad unavoidably challenged durable popular beliefs about the crime. A *non compos mentis* verdict was an implicit rejection of religious and folkloric interpretations of suicide that condemned it utterly, in favour of medical explanations that excused it. Used more and more commonly, it became the manifestation of the secularization of suicide. ('Secularization' 75–6)

What may have started as an attempt to ameliorate an injustice to suicides' families also had the effect of reflecting a broader cultural change in attitudes towards choosing death.[10] It was not the case that cruel punishments disappeared after the turn of the nineteenth century; they did, however, become rarer. Such attitudes were in keeping with the turn from sovereign power to biopower, with the former regime characterised by penalties to control the subject, and the latter by the imperative to foster and maintain the population – in this case via an understanding of the psychological underpinnings of suicide, implying that, with treatment, it could be avoided in future.

Suicide in the Media and Popular Culture

That the usefulness of the subject's body to the biopolitical regime was a key driver of attitudes towards suicide was apparent in the uneven application of penalties for suicide according to social class and status. Those who were deemed of high social value were sometimes labelled as ill, while suicides of less biopolitical worth were treated more punitively. This divergence is most notable in cases of political figures who killed themselves, a particular 'image problem' for the biopolitical regime since politicians represented power itself and the smooth running of society, and suicide signified the opposite. By framing such suicides as a tragic and unintended result of the politicians' excess of devotion to society, media reports avoided the appearance that power was dismantling itself.

When Whig leader and Member of Parliament Samuel Whitbread chose death in 1815, there was no talk of punishment. An article from *The Statesman*, 11 July 1815, calls him a 'lamented Patriot and Statesman' and notes his body will be 'interred to-day in the family vault at Cardington, a small village in Bedfordshire' in a private funeral (Anon., *Tributes* 16), rather than buried at a crossroads with a stake through his heart. Of note, too, is the narrative of Whitbread's death in the following tribute:

> his resolution never slackened, his zeal never cooled, and he was ever at his post ... but the mind of the most vigorous may exert itself too much. *Mr Whitbread* was sensible that this rigorous discharge of his duty must be fatal to his health, but he seems to have offered himself up as a sacrifice on the altar of public utility. The abrupt termination of *Mr Whitbread's* valuable life was, doubtless, justly attributable to a physical cause. (Anon., *Tributes* 17; emphasis in original)

This eulogy asserts that Whitbread's death was proof of the parliamentarian's devotion to his social duty. Far from his memory being shamed, Whitbread is cast as having generously sacrificed his health and, ultimately, his very life to public service. The anonymous journalist does not call for the degradation of the body of a man who had slit his own throat; rather, he plays the lay-physician, arguing that Whitbread inherited a 'plethoric habit' from his father that drove him mad and caused his death (Anon., *Tributes* 17). The writer thereby medicalises the suicide, implying a hope that the period's great strides in disciplines devoted to fostering the health of the population might prevent such deaths in the future. Sir Samuel Romilly summarises the posthumous judgement of Whitbread: '"the only faults he had proceeded from an excess of his virtues"' (quoted in Fisher n.p.).

Other ruling members of British society killed themselves, too, and interpretations of their suicides tended to be equally forgiving. Romilly's liberal assessment of Whitbread's suicide foreshadowed how others would respond to his own death by the same method in 1818, which was largely attributed to his grief over the death of his beloved wife only a few days prior (Melikan n.p.). The anonymous author of *Thoughts on Suicide* urges his reader to consider Romilly's suicide in a generous light:

> His solicitude for the declining health of a wife ... appears completely to have impaired the vigour of his intellectual frame; and he fell – *a martyr to sensibility* – respected by men of all ranks and parties, beloved by all who knew him, and admired by all who knew him not. – Who can call the circumstance of his death a crime? Who will dare to blame the deed? No! ... visit it not with the severity of censure. (44; emphasis in original)

As in the case of Whitbread, Romilly's suicide is treated as a sacrifice, here to 'sensibility', the honoured lawyer and parliamentarian's excessive feeling. According to the anonymous author of an editorial submitted to *The Examiner*, this characteristic made him a powerful advocate for the most beleaguered people (quoted in Anon., *Thoughts* 54), such as the enslaved, Catholics and those on death row (Andrew 175, 176). Such an assessment would have been almost unheard of before the Romantic period. Watt comments, 'Had he died a century earlier, public reactions almost certainly would have been overwhelmingly negative, condemning this self-inflicted death as a grievous sin and a cowardly act' ('Introduction' 8). By framing Romilly's suicide as a result of his immense sensibility, Anonymous suggests that the man was superlatively beneficent and caring, a victim to his devotion to others, such that he cannot be found culpable for taking his life even on religious grounds: 'Humanity drops a tear over her lifeless advocate, and Religion declares, that in her shrine he is entombed' (*Thoughts* 44).

Romanticism's devotion to the ideals of sensibility is another important feature of the period's extraordinary interest in suicide. While some influential works associated with the tradition contribute to the subversive significance of suicide in the period, others appear devoted to upholding the biopolitical regime, Schuller has argued. We usually associate sensibility with the literature of the period; the above news report demonstrates how far it went beyond novels and poems into the broader culture, to recall G. J. Barker-Benfield's contention in *The Culture of Sensibility: Sex and Society in Eighteenth-Century Britain* (1992). However, to point out the broad popularity of ideas about sensibility and its prevailing principles of sympathy for others, even those below one's own class, is not to say that the culture was entirely democratic; members of the higher ranks of society were thought to have finer nerves, which made them more sensitive to strong emotions, and, thus, more susceptible to the 'English malady'. Cheyne suggests that the upper classes were plagued by this disease because of their social status and the lifestyle that attended it (ii, 49). The too-frequent result of the illness – suicide – could then also be recast as laudable, rather than shameful. In this way, suicide could be associated with aristocracy and reinterpreted as constitutive of a carefully ranked biopolitical society, one that Foucault describes as using 'segregation and social hierarchization' to guarantee the 'relations of domination and effects of hegemony' needed to manage the explosion of life aimed at by biopower (*Sexuality* 141).

When Romilly's suicide was deemed a product of extreme sensibility, he was enshrined positively not only as a generous, beneficent man who cared for others and strove (too hard) to be a productive member of society, but also as a fashionable representative of the upper classes. Donna Andrew comments, 'Romilly's final act was described [in media reports] as springing "from an excess of feeling, or rather from a sentiment, which is the most binding one in our social system" and thus rather too much of a good thing than a crime or an evil' (182). She also recognises the hypocrisy in this positive judgement: when one Mr Green killed himself over the death of his wife thirty years previously, 'the *Times* rather facetiously noted that "to be inconsolable for one's wife, and to follow her to the grave – is *madness*"' (179).

Some period commentators noted the double standard. Byron mocks Romilly's suicide by mentioning it blithely in Canto I of *Don Juan* (1819) (115–20). He is even more scathing about the 1822 suicide of Viscount Castlereagh (Robert Stewart) – Conservative Leader of the House of Commons, defender of the government's attack at Peterloo and all-round enemy to liberals in Romantic-era England. Although Byron jeered at Castlereagh's suicide in a lengthy footnote to the Preface of Cantos VI to VIII of *Don Juan* (1823–4), many other Britons viewed it as they did Romilly's death: as a tragedy that showed his self-sacrifice for his country. Clara Tuite reports that Dr Bankhead, Castlereagh's physician, 'convened an inquest that found Castlereagh had suicided as a result of overwork' (122) – framing his suicide not as undermining of biopolitical society, but, like Romilly's and Whitbread's, as a tragic result of his laudable devotion to it. Accordingly, Castlereagh received a tearful, public farewell and dignified burial at the seat of honour, Westminster Abbey. Famously dubbing Castlereagh the 'Werther of Politics' in reference to the suicidal protagonist of Goethe's hit novel of sensibility, Byron suggests the classist reasons behind the outpouring of affection at Castlereagh's death: 'the Minister was an elegant Lunatic – a sentimental Suicide' (590, 589). Rankled by this hypocritical judgement, Byron writes, 'Of the manner of his death little need be said, except that if a poor radical ... had cut his throat, he would have been buried in a cross-road, with the usual appurtenances of the stake and mallet' (589).[11]

This injustice of British law was evident in popular publications about legal matters, too. *The Newgate Calendar*, a much-read publication detailing the crimes and punishments of those in Newgate prison and other malefactors, provides additional insight into the common view of suicidality.[12] Consider the narrative of 'the Reverend James Hackman', who was executed for the murder of the woman with whom he was obsessed, Martha Reay (sometimes spelled 'Ray'), Lord Sandwich's mistress of twenty years and the mother of nine children. She had decisively refused Hackman's proposals of marriage twice, to which commentators attributed Hackman's motive for the murder (Knapp and Baldwin 81). This event formed the basis of *Love and Madness* (1780), a novel by Herbert Croft (Knapp and Baldwin 81, 85). Having noted Hackman's attempted suicide after the murder – 'He then beat himself with the butt end [of the murder weapon] on his head, in order to destroy himself, so fully bent was he on the destruction of both' (Knapp and Baldwin 82) – the account in *The Newgate Calendar* concludes the story with a sentimental poem and the lament, 'Such was the end of a young gentleman who might have been an ornament to his country, the delight of his friends, and a comfort to his relations, had he not been led away by the influence of an unhappy passion' (Knapp and Baldwin 84). Love, it seems, was to blame for the innocent Reay's murder and Hackman's attempted suicide, rather than the latter's possessive violence and criminal sense of entitlement over a woman. The very next narrative bemoans that similar stories may be found amongst 'the lower orders', specifically in the case of one Thomas Giles, a barber: Giles murdered a 'servant girl' who rejected him, and he committed suicide immediately thereafter. 'Like all those who kill themselves', *The Newgate Calendar* warns, 'his body was buried in a cross road, and a stake driven through it with every mark of ignominy' (Knapp and Baldwin 85).[13] We may ask, why is Giles branded with 'ignominy' while Hackman's case is conveyed by purple prose and a sentimental poem in the same publication? Admittedly, Giles succeeded in committing suicide, instead of only attempting it, but surely being executed for murder, as Hackman was, could not explain the sympathetic response to his case. Again, the marked difference in these responses appears to reflect the perpetrators' class status and centrality to biopolitical society, for Reverend Hackman was a representative of a powerful arm of biopower.

Besides such sensational publications as *The Newgate Calendar*, other sources of narratives about suicide tied to the legal realm are records of the proceedings of the Old Bailey and, for texts that are slightly more narratively coherent, coroners' inquests. These are official legal documents and, as such, they cannot be praised for their gripping writing style; but they were a source of information about a topic of great interest to many readers. George Man Burrows complains in *Commentaries on … Insanity* (1828) that coroners' inquest reports had wide public appeal: 'the public taste has become more vitiated and debased; and hence, nothing is found so attractive as tales of horror and of wonder, and every coroner's inquest on an unhappy being who has destroyed himself is read with extraordinary avidity' (448; also quoted in Gates 42). About coroners' inquests, Andrew reports that, 'When someone died in unusual or unknown circumstances, English law required that a coroner's inquest be called, a jury sworn in, and a decision reached on the cause of death' (175), while *London Lives* details, 'Coroners' Inquests were held within forty-eight hours of a suspicious death, and were normally conducted at a local alehouse, parish workhouse or in the building in which the death occurred'; the source also mentions that 'A little over 1 per cent of all deaths were felt to be suspicious enough to warrant an inquest' (n.p.). While the comparative rarity of the occasions that could generate a coroner's inquest helps to explain their interest to the broader public, the literary merit of the subsequent formal legal report cannot, as they are tedious and ungrammatical. A typical example relating to a suicide from the period, dated 3 December 1762, demonstrates the point:

> the said Thomas Philpot not being of sound Mind Memory and Understanding, but lunatick and distracted on the Second day of December in the Year aforesaid, at the Parish aforesaid in the Liberty and County aforesaid, one End of a certain Piece of small bord unto a Brass Hook Fastened into the Wainscott, in a Room one pair of Stairs, in the dwelling House of Peter Swan situate[d] and being at Pimlico in the Parish Liberty and County aforesaid and the other End thereof about his own Neck did fix tye and fasten, and therewith did

> then and there hang, suffocate, and strangle himself, of which said Hanging Suffocation and Strangling[.] He the said Thomas Philpot then and there instantly Died: And so the Jurors aforesaid upon their Oath aforesaid. do say, that the said Thomas Philpot, not being of sound Mind Memory and Understand[ing], but Lunatick and distracted, in Manner and by the Means aforesaid, did Kill Himself. (Coroner's Inquest (hereafter 'C.I.'), Philpot n.p.; editorial oddities in original)

The dry and repetitive phrasing, not to mention the numerous technical errors, are typical of such legal documents. However, they were popular reading for a public hungry for works about suicide at a time when the topic was very much a matter of popular debate.

My review of dozens of coroners' inquest reports in the period supports several of the most common claims of other scholars on suicide, such as that most recorded suicides were by men (e.g. Watt, 'Gender' 141).[14] My research also confirms that the legal findings on suicide were commonly for insanity, or *non compos mentis*, although this Latin phrase was not used in the reports themselves; the preferred phrasing was that the victims were not of sound mind when they died or 'lunatic' (sometimes spelled 'lunatick'). The following report on the death of Peter Cope, dated 20 June 1789, is a typical example:

> Peter Cope not being aforesaid mind memory and understnding but lunatic and distracted on the twenty ninth day of June in the twenty ninth year aforesaid at the Parish and Ward aforesaid in London aforesaid one and of a certain Handkerchief of the value of one penny round the rail of a certain Bed stead in the dwelling house of him the said Peter Cope their situate and the other and of the said Handkerchief round and about his own Neck then and there did fix tye and Faston [i.e. fasten] and did thereby then and there hang strangle and suffocate himself Of which said hanging strangling and suffocation he the said Peter Cope did then and there die And so the jurors aforesaid upon their oath aforesaid do say that the said Peter Cope not ... of ... [sound] mind memory and understanding but lunatic and distracted in manner and by the means aforesaid did hang and kill himself. (C.I. Peter Cope, n.p.; editorial oddities in original)

Partly due to monotonous phrasing, such documents provide little information and, even when new information is introduced, the reader is often struck by its apparent extraneousness. Why, one wonders, is the cost of the handkerchief Cope used to hang himself pertinent? Despite such flaws, these texts were sources of popular reading, which indicates how robust the interest in suicide was at the time. The topic touched a nerve at a point in British history when ideas about one's right to one's own body to the point of death were a source of great public interest.

The Medical Understanding of Suicide

From a medical perspective, however, reading about suicide could be dangerous. Writing of the public's fascination with reading coroners' reports, Man Burrows claims: 'The increase of suicide, I am convinced, is mainly attributable to these causes. Were the offence to be less noticed, it would be less frequent' (448). He thus cautions that such texts could be a source of suicidal contagion, causing others to commit the act by affecting – or, rather, infecting – the mind of the reader with suicidality. Man Burrows voices the most common medical explanation for suicides in the period: that they were almost invariably caused by mental illness. (Presumably, a text could not expose the reader to a physical or diabolical cause of suicide.)[15] Some resisted the psychological interpretation of suicide, with its suggestion that the act is unintentional and therefore beyond social control and punishment. On the other hand, identifying the suicide as *non compos mentis* divests the act of its rebellious significance, which aligns the emerging discipline of psychology (not yet so called) as a tool of biopower. Practically, too, psychology can be viewed as constitutive of biopower, as it proposed to treat and prevent suicidality, the greatest threat to biopolitical society.

In the Romantic period, the discipline of psychology was as yet fluid and encompassed a range of concerns which we would identify as belonging to other fields today, such as literature, ethics, criminology and religion. It is therefore sometimes difficult to source primary texts on suicide that are inarguably psychological in approach; nor are there many texts by doctors of the mind devoted solely to suicide. This is not to say that there is a dearth of period writing on the psychological basis for suicide. Many lay writers comment on suicide from an apparently medico-psychological perspective. Even Granville Sharp – better known as the first British abolitionist and a writer on politics, linguistics, music and religious matters – attempts such a commentary in *A Tract on the Law of Nature and Principles of Action in Man* (1777). Following his warning against the temptations of Satan, Sharp writes,

> real *Madness*, or Lunacy, and other *natural* distempers and frenzies, are frequently the *Principles of Action* which occasion Suicide; but we have too many instances of *deliberate Self-Murder*, wherein no such *natural* causes can with Justice be alledged, though generally assigned by the coroner's juries, through a false notion of mercy, which inclines them to adopt the erroneous maxim, that '*all Men are mad who kill themselves*.' But nothing is more false! (174–5; emphasis in original)

Sharp's reference to '*natural* distempers and frenzies' constitutes his foray into theorising about the medico-psychological reasons for suicide, but he quickly transforms this consideration into a denial of the prevalence of such causes for suicide. Often, lay writers consider the psychological explanations for suicide as equivocating, a dishonest or misguided attempt to attribute suicide to involuntary reasons that exculpate the agents, instead of holding them accountable for what the writer sees as their great crime or, in this case, sin.

Other writers attempt to combine medical with religious language, essentially to undercut the exculpatory effects of arguing that suicide is the result of insanity and therefore involuntary. Although Piggott's very title, *Suicide and its Antidotes* (1824), suggests that he will recommend a medical 'antidote' to the problem of suicide, his major focus is to illuminate how 'Guilt paves the Way to the Crime' (xviii). He considers the bodily causes of suicide, but they lead, he argues, to sin and culpability. 'Sin [is] a Poison to the Soul', he claims, mixing the physical and spiritual, and 'Vicious Indulgence [is] a moral Suicide' he warns, showing his view that sinful decisions about how we treat our bodies can lead to suicide, thereby undermining the argument that suicide caused by insanity is devoid of guilt. Thus, even as he considers psychological aspects of suicide, such as 'Mental Maladies', 'Lunacy', as well as the 'Predisposing natural causes of suicide', including 'Excess in Animal Food', 'Spiritous Liquors', 'Strong Tea' and 'Luxury' – all very Cheynian concerns – Piggott refuses to regard these causes as exculpatory (xviii, xix).

This creative blending of the medical with the religious to discuss suicide did not begin in the period on which I focus. It was well established for more than a century earlier: Burton's influential masterpiece, *The Anatomy of Melancholy*, with its encyclopedic consideration of melancholy from a vast array of writers from the classical world on, is exemplary. Quoting Lucretius ('He voluntary dies, to ease his smart'), Burton considers the torments of the disease as a cause of suicide:

> In such sort doth the torture and extremity of his misery torment him, that he can take no pleasure in his life, but is in a manner inforced to offer violence unto himself, to be freed from his present insufferable pains. So some ... *in fury, but most in despair, sorrow, fear, and out of the anguish and vexation of their souls, offer violence to them selves; for their life is unhappy and miserable. They can take no rest in the night, nor sleep: or, if they do slumber, fearful dreams astonish them.* In the day time, they are affrighted still by some terrible object, and torn in pieces with suspicion, fear, sorrow, discontents, cares, shame, anguish, &c. as so many wild horses, that they cannot be quiet an hour, a minute of time, but, even against their wills, they are intent, and still thinking of it; they cannot forget it; it grinds their souls day and night; they are perpetually tormented, a burden to themselves, as Job was. (318; emphasis in original)

In this detailed and sensitive description of the cruel miseries of melancholy, Burton shows his familiarity with the illness, perhaps because Burton was himself 'diagnosed as suffering from melancholy', biographer J. B. Bamborough asserts (n.p.). Part of the above passage shows Burton's psychological perspicuity, particularly in the comment that, for the afflicted, such suffering and such an end happen involuntarily. However, Burton then moves into religious territory in the mention of Job from the Old Testament in the Christian Bible. Thereafter, even though he has recognised only a few pages previously that suicide can be considered as involuntary, Burton affirms that it is a crime against God and therefore destroys the suicide's very soul (325). Burton's influence on Romanticism cannot be understated. The *Anatomy* was a favourite of Keats (his annotated copy of it resides at the Keats House Museum in Rome), who studied medicine at Guy's Hospital in London. While Burton may not have been a physician himself, he influenced those who were.

Given such a precedent, it is not surprising to find a blend of medical and religious concerns in period texts on suicide. The anonymous author of *A Remedy for Self-Murder. Suggested in a Letter to a Friend* (1819) subordinates the medical approach to suicide to religious concerns through creative diction:

> It is at such times, when the soul is in gloom and heaviness, that the transforming power, and medicinal virtues of Religion are felt and understood; and the patient, who has been *early* accustomed to the use of that regimen which she prescribes, will best know *how*, *then*, and at *all times* to counteract and eradicate those diseases which the *passions of a disordered nature* engender, and which, like a moth fretting a garment, would destroy both body and mind, unless met and resisted in their daily march by her powerful applications and her triumphant remedies! (59–60; emphasis in original)

This passage is rich in the vocabulary of medical discourse: language such as 'medicinal', 'patient', 'regimen', 'prescribes', 'diseases', '*passions of a disordered nature*' and 'remedies' seems to orient the text scientifically, but it does so only to subordinate this discourse to the religious, for, here, the ultimate aim is to recommend the 'medicinal virtues of Religion' (59). Lay writers found creative ways to employ the new language of psychology for traditional – often religious – purposes.

Arguably, lay writers sometimes used the language of medicine to comment on what they saw as the sin of suicide because they feared that the common medical interpretation of suicide as indicative of insanity, exculpatory as it was, might encourage it. And, in fact, by locating the causes of suicide in the body and even the brain, medical writers on suicide did sometimes imply that suicide could be considered as a natural death, an involuntary end caused by illness. John Reid considers such causes of suicide in his *Essays on Insanity, Hypochondriasis, and Other Nervous Affections* (1816) (23, 96, 103, 139). Meanwhile, in *A Chemical Analysis and Medical Treatise ... on that Corporeal Derangement and Painful Mental Sympathy which Not Unfrequently Leads to The Commission of Suicide* (1828), Ralph Alderson boldly asserts, 'I cannot and do not believe that we in this age ever met with a case of what the law designates *felo de se*, that is to say, the commission of suicide in a state of sanity' (58). Alderson argues that there is always a psychosomatic reason for suicide. Considering the 'ossification of the valves of the cavities' that causes a

> general anarchy in the circulating system, ... we distinctly trace that mental gloom, that desponding melancholy, that agony of imagination that has tumbled into ruin the most stupendous intellect, soured every noble and delightful enjoyment, cast around the most resplendent objects of ambition a sickly ray of disgust, made the man of genius and of learning, in the very zenith of his fame weary of life, disgusted with its enjoyments, sick of its charms, and, finally, driven him to seek refuge, as a fugitive chased by despair, in the dreadful, dark, and unhallowed grave of the suicide. Thus it was, I have no doubt, that their country was deprived of the virtue, genius, and patriotism of a Whitbread and a Romilly. (56–7)

Alderson does not distinguish between body and mind. Rather, he attests that the mind is affected by corporeal afflictions. He continues,

> mental agitation, gloom, despondency, and finally that despair wich [*sic*] leads to suicide, may, and is, to be traced to a vitiated and deranged condition primarily of the digestive organs and ultimately of the nervous and vascular systems ... [T]his state of vitiation of the chylo-poetic functions we may by proper expedients in medicine and regimen invariably relieve, and consequently prevent the supervention of the immediate or proximate cause which has occasioned so many melancholy terminations of life. (61–2)

Alderson's point is that the mind and body cannot be teased apart, particularly in an investigation of the causes for suicide. He may focus on the parts of the body associated with nerve theory – such as the stomach and vascular systems – but he does so as a means of explaining mental afflictions traditionally linked to psychology.

Alderson was far from unique in taking a holistic medical approach to the problem of suicide. In like manner, physician and man-midwife William Rowley treats suicide as a psychosomatic concern in *A Treatise on Female, Nervous, Hysterical, Hypochondriacal, Bilious, Convulsive Diseases; Apoplexy and Palsy; with Thoughts on Madness, Suicide, &c.* (1788). Given the medical orientation of the title, a reader might expect

Rowley's discussion of suicide to begin with a consideration of the bodily and even mental aspects of the act. However, the first several pages of the section entitled 'Suicide' detail the moral, sinful and criminal aspects of choosing death, such as the debt we owe to others who have helped us live in society, and denounce literary writers like Rousseau (in *Julie*) for their mistaken arguments in favour of the individual's right to choose death (334–7). Everything Rowley writes on suicide in this section suggests he views it in the traditional way: as a crime against society and God and evidence of the perpetrator's blackest guilt. However, once the man-midwife begins to deliver on the text's implicit promise of approaching suicide from a psychological perspective, his conclusions change dramatically: 'Physicians have frequent opportunities of observing the diminution of human courage and wisdom from ... bodily infirmities ... The man is then changed; his blood is changed', he attests, adding, 'It is certainly clear, that when a man meditates how he shall destroy life ... he is no longer *compos mentis*; the commission, therefore, of suicide must necessarily be always considered an act of *insanity*' (341, 342; emphasis in original). By stating that the suicide's 'blood is changed' and asserting that he is (therefore) always insane, Rowley seems to argue against juries ever finding guilt in an achieved suicide – a surprising about-face from his opening salvo against it.

Some writers were so devoted to the notion that suicide is a corporal problem – a bodily-based disease, rather than a moral failing – that they even attributed suidicality to a particular area of the brain, making it a matter of neuroscientific interest. The anonymously authored *Essay on the Application of the Organology of the Brain to Education* (1816?) includes a poem entitled 'Verses Found Inscribed on a Skull in a Churchyard' that suggests people with too much of 'the organ of ideality' (16n) are likely to commit suicide:

> But here that fiend of fiends doth dwell,
> Wild Ideality unshaken
> By facts or theory, whose spell
> Maddens the soul and fires our beacon.
> Whom memory tortures, love deludes,
> Whom circumspection fills with dread,
> On every organ he obtrudes,
> Until Destruction o'er his head
> Impends; then mad with luckless strife,
> He volunteers the loss of life. (16; no line numbers given)

A footnote to the last line of this passage explains: 'The frequency of suicide in persons who have much of this organ [of ideality] is probably here alluded to. People with this organ kill themselves for very trifling reasons' (16n). The author at once excuses those with enlarged 'organ[s] of ideality' who commit suicide, for they struggle with a physical predisposition to the act, and undermines their final choice by calling the reasoning 'trifling'. What is clear is that, in the opinion of some from the Romantic period, suicidality is almost ineluctable, rather than a choice.

The multiplicity of views and strenuous debates about suicide in the Romantic period show that ideas about the act were changing, and Romantic-era writers contributed to the conversation with texts that explored hitherto unfamiliar resonances of suicide. Recognising that the official prohibition of suicide was an expression of power's control over the subject and its demand to manage his life – a scenario recognisable from the British slave trade – some writers penned works that highlight this connection, framing suicide as subversive of such power, as I show in the next chapter.

Notes

1. See Makdisi's *William Blake and the Impossible History of the 1790s* (2003), Canuel's *Religion, Toleration, and British Writing, 1790–1830* (2002) and White's *Early Romanticism and Religious Dissent* (2007) for accounts of the wide variety of religious sects in England during the Romantic period.
2. Thorvaldsen explains, 'MP Charles Abbot[,] who later came to chair the House of Commons as Speaker, introduced the census bill of 1800, and in passing made Rickman the offer of supervising the census operation' (52).
3. Importantly, though, Mill was a latter-day champion of bodily sovereignty, despite his devotion to utilitarianism. John Wiltshire notes that, in *On Liberty* (1859), Mill 'was famously to proclaim as an individual's sole "sovereignty" over their own body' (106).
4. What follows is an overview of topics that I explore in greater detail in the subsequent chapters. Some parts of the following section have appeared in my previous publications, such as: 'Political Suicide: Castlereagh, Rebellion, and Self-Directed Violence' (2019); 'Introduction' to the 'Suicidal Romanticism: Origins and Influences' issue of *Studies in the Literary Imagination* (2018); 'Introduction' to the Broadview edition of Mary Shelley's *Mathilda* (1819; 1959); '*Werther* Goes Viral: Suicidal Contagion, Anti-Vaccination, and Infectious Sympathy' (2016); a co-written introduction to the 'Romanticism and Suicide' issue of *Literature Compass* (2015); 'The Fictional Suicides of Mary Wollstonecraft' (2015); 'The Wollstonecraftian Plot: Female Suicide as Slave Protest' (2015); 'Romantic Suicide, Contagion, and Rousseau's *Julie*' (2015); and 'A Family Affair: Ennobling Suicide in Mary Shelley's *Matilda*' (2013).
5. Such court findings of *non compos mentis* for suicide may indicate a greater public understanding of the psychological problems that may lead to suicide, but Szasz claims that this 'insanitizing' of the act is only one instance

of 'the vastly influential institutions of social control', the discipline of psychology itself, that delimited the possibilities for motivations to choose death (*Prohibition* 11, 10).

6. Godineau's original passage is: '*les révolutionnaires dépénalisent le suicide: le Code pénal de 1791 ne le met pas dans la liste des crimes poursuivis par la loi, et le Code des délits et des peines de 1795 précise que la mort éteint toute poursuite*' (127).
7. McGuire provides a contrasting view of the significance of suicide in the French Revolution: 'French institutions of power rigorously legislated against suicide at all times and with particular severity during the Reign of Terror' because it 'perceived suicide as a threat to its power [, which] is suggested by the regular guillotining of political prisoners even after their suicides' (*Dying* 177).
8. Relatedly, Napoleon drank poison four days after abdicating on 6 April 1814. The poison had lost its potency through age, however, and he merely vomited and convulsed, rather than died (Gibson 146–7).
9. The Romantic period also saw the strengthening of the Licensing Act of 1737, instituted by Robert Walpole, to the extent that one of the greatest of all English plays, William Shakespeare's *King Lear* (1608), was banned from the stage out of fear that its depiction of a mad king would stimulate rebellion in the subjects of an insane King George III.
10. See Robert Houston's 'The Medicalization of Suicide: Medicine and the Law in Scotland and England, circa 1750–1850' for more information on the differences in punishments for suicide across Britain in the period.
11. See Chapter 5 for more on Byron's response to Castlereagh's and Romilly's suicides.
12. As *The Public Domain Review* reports of the publication, 'the first one titled *The Newgate Calendar* was published in 1773. There are many versions of *The Newgate Calendar* existing under slightly different names, and in 1824, a new edition was published by two lawyers, Andrew Knapp and William Baldwin', who later published other versions of the text (n.p.).
13. Houston reports that burial of the suicide's corpse at a crossroad was 'said to disorient or dissipate the suicide's spirit' (*Punishing* 323).
14. Nevertheless, suicide retained associations with femininity (e.g. McGuire, *Dying*, *passim*, Higonnet 'Frames' and 'Representations', *passim*).
15. The latter of these explanations was the most commonly given reason for suicide in coroners' inquest reports in the previous centuries. Michael MacDonald explains: 'Coroners' inquests on the bodies of self-murderers, like other felony indictments, alleged that the crime had been committed "at the instigation of Satan," and at least until the late seventeenth century the legal formula expressed the almost universal belief that suicide was literally diabolical' ('Secularization' 55).

Chapter 2

'Give me Liberty or give me Death': The Literary Context of Romantic Subversive Suicide

Major British Eighteenth-Century Literary Depictions of Rebellious Suicide

> ... 'with joy I see
> The different doom our Fates assign.
> Be thine Despair and scept'red Care:
> To triumph, and to die, are mine.'
> He spoke, and headlong from the mountain's height
> Deep in the roaring tide he plung'd to endless night. (139–44)

These lines, the final ones of Gray's Pindaric ode 'The Bard', express poignantly the spirit and aim of the literary theme of Romantic rebellious suicide in literature from 1770 to 1830. Although Gray wrote them in the middle of the eighteenth century, his words embody the defiance of authority and bid for autonomy that is common to Romantic literary articulations of rebellious suicide. Writing of Gray's interest in Celtic literature, William Powell Jones comments that 'The Bard' 'started a flame' and 'the fire swept into the Romantic movement itself' (99). I would add that the poem's theme of subversive suicide was at least as influential in carrying the spark well into the turn of the nineteenth century and beyond. Yet the poem was not as well loved in its time. While Samuel Johnson heaps praise on Gray's 'Elegy in a Country Churchyard' (1751) in *Lives of the Most Eminent English Poets* (1779) – quipping famously, 'Had Gray written often thus, it had been vain to blame, and useless to praise him' (502) – he was less than enamoured with 'The Bard', commenting: 'To select a singular event, and swell it to a giant's bulk by fabulous appendages of spectres and predictions, has little difficulty; for he that forsakes the probable may always find the marvellous' (501). However, by the Romantic period, 'The Bard' had found its audience. Even one of the Romantic period's most (in)famous literary critics,

John Wilson Croker, attests to the enduring popularity of Gray's verses, writing – in a fit of generosity apparently reserved for dead poets – that 'Gray's odes are still on every table and in every mouth' (210n). Such praise, a far cry from Croker's cruel review of Keats's *Endymion* in the *Quarterly Review* (1818), suggests that 'The Bard' was widely known, even amongst a general readership.[1] Myriad illustrators from the time rendered the scene of the Bard poised to hurl himself from a high cliff in Snowdonia into the River Conwy below, including, most famously, Benjamin West (1778) and John Martin (1817), but also Thomas Jones (1774) and Charles Fox (1821), whose model was a lost painting by none other than Henry Fuseli. William Blake (1798) illustrated Grey's suicidal bard, too, although in a (typically Blakean) extreme way: the Bard is represented during his fall into the river. The Bard's suicide is perhaps the most iconic image of the Romantic period, replicated endlessly in modern publications about Romanticism. The strong association between the Romantic era and this image of the rebel-poet, choosing death for his freedom, demonstrates the significance of this topic for the period (Figures 2.1, 2.2, 2.3, 2.4).

In 'The Bard', the theme of rebellious suicide is enacted in the final act of the eponymous Welsh Bard who speaks the above lines to King Edward I, the conqueror of the Welsh in 1284. As Gray himself comments in his notes on the brutal invasion, King Edward I '"hanged up all their Bards, because they encouraged the Nation to rebellion, but their works (we see), still remain, the Language (tho' decaying) still lives, and the art of their versification is known, and practised to this day among them"' (quoted in Ketton-Cremer 133). Gray asserts that established authority cannot crush the independent and rebellious spirit of literary genius, an assessment befitting the British Romantic era that would follow his own at least as well as it does the ancient Welsh.[2] Most of the ode consists of the Welsh Bard's curse upon Edward I and his progeny, along with his promise to kill himself rather than allow the monarch and his men to kill him. This end he duly accomplishes in the poem's final lines, quoted above, in a defiant gesture like that of the many enslaved Africans who chose a similar fate in defiance of British oppression, conditions that influenced the formation of the literary theme of subversive suicide in the period.

Before the eighteenth century, the most famous literary depiction of slave rebellion appears in *Oroonoko* (1688) by Aphra Behn. In this 'true history', as the author terms it, the enslaved hero Oroonoko does not attempt to flee his captors after they quell the rebellion he leads, for which he will certainly be executed; but his refusal to escape is not wholly suicidal. Having murdered his beloved Imoinda – pregnant with

Figure 2.1 Benjamin West, 'The Bard', 1778. Available in the public domain via Wikipedia

Figure 2.2 John Martin, 'The Bard', 1817. Available in the public domain via Wikipedia

their child and a willing victim – to protect them from a life of slavery, Oroonoko (renamed 'Caesar' by his master) considers suicide but desires vengeance more: 'A thousand times he turned the fatal knife that did the deed, toward his own heart, with a resolution to go immediately after her, but dire revenge, which now was a thousand times more fierce in his soul than before, prevents him' (912). He lingers, mourning, by Imoinda's body too long thereafter and becomes so weakened by grief

Figure 2.3 Thomas Jones, 'The Bard', 1774. Available in the public domain via Wikipedia

Figure 2.4 William Blake, 'The Bard', 1798. Available in the public domain via Yale Center for British Art

and starvation that he cannot achieve his revenge when his persecutors find him (912). Only then does Oroonoko enact his suicidal wishes, declaring to the colonists:

> ''tis not life I seek, nor am I afraid of dying', and, at that word, cut a piece of flesh from his own throat, and threw it at them, 'yet still I would live if I could, till I had perfected my revenge. But oh! it cannot be. I feel life gliding

> from my eyes and heart, and, if I make not haste, I shall yet fall a victim to the shameful whip.' At that, he ripped up his own belly, and took his bowels and pulled them out, with what strength he could. (913)

The whip being a symbol of colonial slavery, Oroonoko expresses succinctly the reasons for his suicidal actions. Behn's narrative became popular in the eighteenth century only after Thomas Southerne's adaption of it into the hugely successful drama *Oronooko: A Tragedy* (1695), which, however, focused on the love story between Oroonoko and Imoinda, whom Southerne transformed into a white woman (Black et al. 879–80). By the end of the century, the political resonances of Behn's narrative came to the fore with physician John Ferriar's adaptation *The Prince of Angola* (1788), which 'was presented as a reworking of the plot to accurately portray the injustices of slavery in South America' (Black et al. 880). The subtitle announces it as a 'Tragedy, altered from the Play of Oroonoko. And Adapted to the Circumstances of the Present Times' – a clear reference to the slavery debate of the period. In this context, Oroonoko's choice of death for Imoinda and himself in the face of biopolitical oppression would have resonated with an audience primed to recognise its message.

The idea of suicide as rebellion against tyranny developed through the classical model, long before either British colonial slavery or King Edward I's invasion of Wales. One classical source, often mentioned in the long eighteenth century, is the case of Cato the Younger, the Roman Republican who killed himself rather than submit to the dictatorship of Julius Caesar. As Marsh puts it, Joseph Addison's drama *Cato* 'reinterpreted the main protagonist's actions in the light of contemporary political concerns and attitudes, and here Cato is represented as a virtuous figure – a beacon of liberty' (85). The reverberations of Addison's play continued well into the Romantic period, partly through the rather circuitous route of the American Revolution: Barry Alan Shain comments that Patrick Henry's famous 'Give me liberty or give me death!' speech – recorded by William Wirt and adopted as the motto of the American Revolution – was inspired by Addison's play, in which Cato declares, '"it is not now a time to talk of aught/ But chains or conquest, liberty or death"' (quoted in Shain 304). In the 1790s, Godwin considers the fame of Cato in the appendix to *An Enquiry Concerning Political Justice, and Its Influence on General Virtue and Happiness* (1793; hereafter *Political Justice*) entitled 'Of Suicide', in which he comments on 'the much admired suicide of Cato':

> if he were instigated by reasons purely benevolent, it is impossible not to applaud his intention, even if he were mistaken in the application ... The

> death of Cato ... was dwelt on with admiration by all the lovers of virtue under the subsequent tyrants of Rome. It seemed to be the lamp from which they caught the sacred flame. Who can tell how much it has contributed to revive that flame in after ages, when it seemed to have been so long extinct? (87)

Voltaire also discusses the case of Cato in his entry 'Cato. On Suicide, And The Abbe St Cyran's Book Legitimating Suicide' from his *Philosophical Dictionary*. He presents Cato as the very embodiment of revolutionary suicide: 'It was, I believe, because Cato's soul was always equal, and retained to the last its love for his country and her laws that he chose rather to perish with her than to crouch to the tyrant. He died as he had lived. Incapable of surrendering!' (20). Addison's *Cato* was revived to great acclaim in 1816 at Covent Garden by the famous actor John Kemble (Macready 132), further demonstrating the influence of the Cato narrative – the epitome of heroic suicide – for the Romantic movement.

Some thought Addison's play dangerous. Piggott blamed it for the suicide of Eustace Budgell, Addison's cousin – and for good reason, since Budgell's much-quoted suicide note read, '"What Cato did and Addison approved, Cannot be wrong"' (quoted in Gates 83). Piggott insists, in *Suicide and Its Antidotes*, that

> Addison's play of *Cato* has doubtless contributed to the same pernicious purposes; and the tragic end of Eustace Budgell, the unfortunate author of the 'Bee', and the coadjutor of Steele and Addison, occasioned by that play, is one of the many proofs which might be adduced of its mischievous tendency. (133)

Undoubtedly, there was an extra-literary reason for Budgell's suicide – he likely drowned himself because of despair over the litigation in which he was involved and financial losses in the South Sea Bubble (Gates 82). At the same time, he seems to have wished to replace the cloud of dishonour that had settled over his reputation with the light of courage and heroism by comparing himself to Cato in choosing death.

However, there is an important difference between these key eighteenth-century representations of rebellious suicide: Gray's 'The Bard' targets sovereign power, the episteme that preceded biopower,[3] while Addison's *Cato* depicts suicide as subversive of biopower. In Gray's poem, King Edward I threatens the Bard with death, as is evident in his list of the many Welsh poets the king has killed already: 'Cold is Cadwallo's tongue,/ That hush'd the stormy main;/ Brave Urien sleeps upon his craggy bed:/ Mountains, ye mourn in vain/ Modred, ... / ... / Dear lost companions of my tuneful art' (29–32; 38). Facing that threat, the Bard chooses his own way out in suicide and thereby undermines sovereign power, with its exclusive claim over the life and death of the subject. Chloë Taylor comments, 'Sovereign power, Foucault explains, is grounded either in blood-right or blood-conquest' ('Familial' 203). The ode does not emphasise slavery or the threat that the Bard will be forced to live under excessively regulated conditions, features of biopower in its attempt to manage, maintain and increase the lives of its subjects. These are precisely the reasons why Addison's Cato chooses death, though. As much as Caesar is framed as exemplary of sovereign power in his murderous ascent at the start of Addison's play, his specific relationship to Cato reveals a biopolitical urge, demonstrating Addison's recognition of the first phase of biopower at this early point in the eighteenth century. At the outset of the play, Portius, one of Cato's two sons (along with Marcus), reports, 'Already *Caesar*/ Has ravaged more than half the Globe, and sees/ Mankind grown thin by his destructive Sword:/ Should he go further, Numbers would be wanting/ To form new Battels, and support his Crimes' (1. 1. 6–10).[4] Over and against the democratically elected, but much reduced, Roman senate headed by Cato, who is exiled in Utica (now Tunisia, then a province of Rome), Caesar establishes his tyranny via blood-conquest. Still, Caesar wishes to preserve Cato and, in fact, protect his life, according to Decius, Caesar's ambassador, who enters the Roman senate greeting his former friend with the significant words, '*Caesar* sends Health to *Cato*' (2. 1. 112). Sent by Caesar to win over Cato to Caesar's side, Decius goes on, '*Caesar* see's/ The Streights to which you're driv'n; and as he know's/ *Cato*'s high Worth, is anxious for his Life' (2. 1. 116–18). Caesar's concern for Cato's well-being positions the tyrant as trading his sovereign power for biopower.

Decius does not say that Caesar will kill Cato if he does not side with him (although this implicit threat becomes ever more likely when Caesar's army attacks Utica at the end of the play). Rather, he explicitly states that Caesar considers Cato's continued life as a valuable asset to his power: '*Caesar* is well acquainted with your Virtues,/ And therefore sets this Value on your Life:/ Let him but know the Price of *Cato*'s Friendship,/ And name your Terms' (2. 1. 138–41). Cato, however, refuses to live under such rule: 'My Life is grafted on the Fate of *Rome*:/ Would he save *Cato*? Bid him spare his Country./ Tell your Dictator this, and tell him *Cato*/ Disdain's a Life, which he has Pow'r to offer' (2. 1. 119–22). When Cato is good to his word, killing himself offstage with his sword late in the play, then the significance of his act becomes apparent: it is a rebellious suicide committed to undermine the tyranny of biopower. Addison gestures to life under Caesar's rule as enslavement several times over the course of the play, using the word 'slave' or 'slavery' eight times, as well as in words that express the idea less directly, such as in the famous line, 'A Day, an Hour, of virtuous Liberty,/ Is worth a whole Eternity in Bondage' (2. 1. 101–2). Seeing their fate under British rule in similar terms, the founding fathers of the United States of America, such as George Washington, prized Addison's *Cato* as their favourite play (Fleming 11). Its significance – and the example of Cato, the historical figure – in America is evident: Utica in New York state was named after the site of Cato's last stand, the last outpost of Roman republicanism, in 1798 (Grafton 620). For all who feared not so much the punishment of death for opposing tyrannical rule but enforced life under oppressive conditions – whether early Americans or British Romantics – Addison's Cato expressed their concerns.

Romantic Literary Suicide

Some of the most recognisable literary forms of the British Romantic period are bound up with ideas about suicide. Many major texts that feature suicide are also classics of the literature of sensibility: the protagonist of Samuel Richardson's *Clarissa* (1747–8) arguably chooses death through starvation; Frances Burney's *Evelina; or, The History of a Young Lady's Entrance into the World* (1778) includes a would-be suicide in the Scottish poet Mr Macartney; and, in Jane Austen's *Sense and Sensibility* (1811), Marianne Dashwood admits that her self-imposed, near-fatal illness was an act of suicidality (350). Suicidal characters are also typical in Gothic novels, such as Robert Wringhim in James Hogg's *The Private Memoirs and Confessions of a Justified Sinner* (1824) and the Monster in Shelley's *Frankenstein; or, The Modern Prometheus* (1818), to name only two. So, too, are suicidal wishes expressed in some of the period's best-known verse, as I will discuss further in Chapter 4; these include Wordsworth's 'The Complaint of a Forsaken Indian Woman' and 'The Mad Mother', both from the *Lyrical Ballads*, as well as several poems from Charlotte Smith's *Elegaic Sonnets* (1784) and Felicia Hemans's *Records of Woman* (1828), which present the main female characters as wishing for death. Other canonical Romantic poems that treat the theme of suicidality in a positive manner include Keats's 'Ode to a Nightingale', wherein the speaker memorably muses, 'Now more than ever seems it rich to die,/ To cease upon the midnight with no pain' (55–6), while the closing consolation of P. B. Shelley's elegy 'Adonais' (1821) expresses the speaker's wish for death:

Seek shelter in the shadow of the tomb.
What Adonais is, why fear we to become?
. . . .
Why linger, why turn back, why shrink, my Heart?
Thy hopes are gone before: from all things here
They have departed – thou shouldst now depart!
. . . .
No more let Life divide what Death can join together. (458–9; 469–71; 477)

Here, Shelley presents life as an encumbrance that divides the living from desirable death. Indeed, a death wish appears in many of the most celebrated British Romantic-era literary works, making it so familiar we have almost forgotten to examine its significance.

Since prevailing attitudes towards suicide at the time were strongly condemnatory of it, one might expect the topic to appear most often in a negative light in the period's literature. However, of the works listed above, only Hogg's novel frames suicide as horrifying and additional proof of Wringhim's evil nature. It is also worth noting, though, that Samuel Taylor Coleridge wrote a little-known poem condemnatory of suicide. Just as Wordsworth penned 'Argument for Suicide', the poem that introduces this book, Coleridge penned a short verse entitled 'The Suicide's Argument. With Nature's Answer' (1811), which Andrew Bennett considers to be a response to Wordsworth's offering (44). Coleridge's poem begins with a defiant announcement of the individual's right to choose suicide – a strong protest against biopower's efforts to force its subjects to live:

Ere the birth of my Life, if I wish'd it or no
No question was ask'd me – it could not be so!
If the Life itself be the Question – a thing sent to try,
And to live on be YES: what can NO be? To die. (1–4)

The second stanza, entitled 'NATURE'S ANSWER', mitigates this anti-authoritarian position considerably:

Is't return'd as 'twas sent? Is't no worse for the Wear?
Think first, what You *are*! Recollect what You *were*!
I gave you innocence, I gave you hope,
Gave health and genius and an ample scope!
Return you me Guilt, Lethargy, Despair?
Make out th' invent'ry! Inspect, Compare!
    Then die – if die you dare! (5–11; emphasis in original)

That 'Nature' answers the suicide's contention, rather than God, suggests Coleridge's wish to avoid engaging with theological considerations of suicide, but the last line – with its threat of punishment – highlights the religious tone of the poem, for a posthumously punitive 'Nature' could only be a divine one. The lines that Coleridge added to the poem in the 14 October 1815 publication of it in *Felix Farley's Bristol Journal* further underscore the essentially Christian nature of this poetic discussion: 'But none e'er rushed to death, whose Life dar'd send/ A courteous Invitation to Life's End./ And when Death came, could say: Welcome in *God's name*, FRIEND!' (12–14; quoted in Mays 895; capitalisation and emphasis in original). These lines recall the spirit of the opening of 'The Suicide's Argument', which describes life as a gift, confirmed here as one from God and not merely Nature. Although many of the major Romantic writers shunned the popular condemnatory attitude towards suicide in their works, Coleridge's poem shows that this attitude was not entirely universal.

Most often, suicide appears in British Romantic literature as a means of appealing to the reader's sympathy, aligning it with attitudes from the culture of sensibility. I will not argue that the culture of sensibility is subversive, given its misogynistic celebration of female weakness and, as Schuller has convincingly argued, its use as a mechanism of biopolitical control. However, some expressions of sentimental suicidality align it with the subversive suicides I study when they function as a kind of Marcusian 'great refusal', an opposition to the Industrial Revolution's demand that the subject be a productive, useful and, most of all, future-oriented member of society – an asset to biopolitical society.

Two major works of criticism on literature and sexuality help to illustrate how suicide destabilises biopower by refusing futurity. Lee Edelman's *No Future* (2004) and Richard Sha's *Perverse Romanticism* (2009) both demonstrate, in different ways, how the denial of futurity through biological reproduction undermines conservative politics and the status quo. Edelman's *No Future* focuses on the 'impossible politics' of queerness, which refuses the heteronormative demand to contribute to society through reproduction, a political state that he calls 'reproductive futurism'. These terms, Edelman asserts, 'impose an ideological limit on political discourse as such, preserving in the process the absolute privilege of heteronormativity by rendering unthinkable, by casting outside the political domain, the possibility of a queer resistance to this organizing principle of communal relations' (2). By refusing to contribute to 'the Ponzi scheme of reproductive futurism' (4), Edelman claims, queerness subverts all political regimes, and becomes 'the negativity opposed to every form of social viability' (9). I argue that suicide functions analogously relative to biopower: it refuses 'social viability', rejects the social contract and removes the subject from the trap of biopolitical management. With more specific attention to the Romantic period, Sha argues that the Romantics sought to rescue sexual desire from purposiveness – from its role in reproduction – and embrace its ability to give pleasure, instead; this 'distrust of function' in Romantic literature Sha sees as the writers' attempt 'to engage readers otherwise stupefied by the "savage torpor" of industrialism' (1, 2). Likewise, I contend that the figures of subversive suicide in the texts I study protest against a biopolitical reality that treats them as cogs in the machine, bodies without individual agency, faceless contributions to the smooth, healthy running of society. In short, what both Sha and Edelman claim about this divorce from futurity – this refusal to see human bodies as achieving their highest teleological function in creating children, the symbol of the future – I argue the Romantics also represented through suicide. Framed thus, suicide is the most extreme expression of Romantic idealism: an active, even violent turning away from productivity. While individual writers opted out of the trap of British industrialism by running away to the Lake District or Italy, the literary protagonists I study in these works attempt to achieve the same goal in a more permanent way – through death. Keats's and Shelley's lines quoted above, with their dreamy embrace of death as a refusal of life's fret and worry, also exemplify how Romantic suicidality was sometimes a rejection of the engaged productiveness of the bourgeois Romantic subject in the biopolitical regime.

Arguably, too, the significance of suicide as the refusal to be a productive, well-disciplined member of society was introduced to British Romanticism from European works that are widely recognised as formative influences on the movement. Rousseau's *Julie, ou La Nouvelle Héloïse* and Goethe's *The Sorrows of Young Werther* not only helped to shape British sentimental expressions of suicide, but they also contributed to British Romantic writers' view of it as a matter of individual autonomy. In Rousseau's novel, Saint-Preux and his friend Lord Bomston discuss the topic of suicide 'peaceably, tranquilly' (311), as the former character directs that they should, helping to usher in the Romantic-era suicide debate to a British audience that read the book with great avidity.[5] Even Lord Bomston, the voice of conservativism in his effort to talk his young friend out of choosing death, acknowledges that suicide may be allowable in some cases. While he asserts that Saint-Preux 'owe[s] ... [his] preservation' to 'society' and 'the fatherland to which [he] ... belongs', sounding very much like an agent of biopower, he adds that we may judge for ourselves whether we have paid our debt to society through good deeds and then choose death in good conscience if we have done so, rendering suicide a principled rejection of future social duty (321). Moreover, when Saint-Preux and Julie fall in love, even though their differing class positions and his professional relationship to her as her tutor dictate that they cannot be together, the highly sympathetic characters model an opposition to the biopolitical regime that would regulate its subjects' sexual expression. Donald R. Wehrs notes that Julie's life at Clarens as Madame de Wolmar presents a situation in which 'individual desires are subordinated to the interests of the community as a whole and tight control is maintained by all-powerful Legislator (Wolmar)' (79), a picture of biopolitical control. Saint-Preux and Julie continue to love each other despite these strictures. That they are both suicidal – Wehrs calls Julie's death 'half-willful' (79) – in defiance of the social rules that divide them shows that this novel presents suicidality as subversive of the regulatory strictures that decide who may have sex with whom to maintain the classifications of humans that undergird social order. As one of the most popular European works at the time, the novel's message was surely influential for ideas about the significance of suicide in British Romanticism.

Meanwhile, in Goethe's novel, the too-passionate and undisciplined Werther debates the permissibility of suicide with Albert, the upstanding bourgeois husband of Charlotte, Werther's beloved. Albert accuses Werther of being '"quite wrong in comparing suicide ... with great deeds. For really it can't be thought anything but a weakness. Of course it is easier to die than to bear a life of torment with fortitude"' (41). Werther responds, '"You call that weakness? I beg you, don't be misled by appearances. A people groaning under the unbearable oppression of a tyrant, can you call it weakness when they finally rise up and break their chains?"' (41). Here, then, is a model for the Romantic understanding of suicide as an assertion of autonomy and an act of rebellion against oppression, specifically slavery in the reference to chains. When Werther quits the government job and upper-class social role his mother wishes for him, preferring artistic creation and the company of children, his opposition to well-regulated, productive, bourgeois society, represented by Albert, becomes more evident and his suicidality appears to be an extension of his identity as a rebel. In his letter to Wilhelm, 20 July, Werther writes, '"I am no great friend of rank"', adding:

> 'You say my mother would be glad to see me occupied. That made me laugh. Am I not occupied now? And in fact is it not all one whether I count peas or lentils? It's all a nonsense, and a man who at the behest of other people and not for his own passion or need works himself into the ground, or money or status or whatever else, is always a fool.' (34, 35)

Werther thereby announces his disdain for the bourgeois ideals of status and money, and rejects the biopolitical demand that every subject must perform work that is recognised as useful by others. Moreover, by calling such work '"count[ing] peas or lentils"', Werther expresses his view that society values the act of work itself – the control of the subject's body through the performance of usefulness to others – even more than the product of such work, which he frames as trivial (35). He would rather satisfy the demands of '"his own passion or need"' (35) and remain an autonomous individual with his own unique desires. Although Werther's suicide has usually been depoliticised as the expression of his unrequited love for Charlotte, this most famous figure of sentimental suicide also represents the rejection of biopolitical society, with its insistence that its members be disciplined, productive contributors. The influence of *The Sorrows of Young Werther* on British ideas about suicide was great, and not only for its rebellious resonances. The novel was said to have provoked copycat suicides across Europe when young people, in imitation of the protagonist, killed themselves. Dubbed 'Werther-mania', the fear of contagious suicide blossomed from these reports and remains a touchstone for contemporary sociological and psychological studies of the phenomenon.[6]

Another influential European writer is also worth mentioning here for her well-known comments on suicide. The French-Swiss novelist Madame de Staël (the *nom de plume* of Anne Louise Germaine de Staël-Holstein) penned a notable foray into the topic of suicide entitled *On the Influence of the Passions* (1798), which went so far as to recommend committing suicide for love, earning the author great notoriety and contributing to the volatility of the topic at the time. De Staël writes, 'None but men capable of resolving to commit suicide, can with any shadow of wisdom, venture to explore this grand path of happiness' (464), and she later adds,

> the terrors that suicide inspires concentrate themselves into the space of an instant: and, in order to effect the act of self-murder, a man must take in the picture of his misfortunes, like the spectacle of his final end, aided by the intense energy of one sentiment and of one single idea. Nothing, however, inspires more horror than the possibility of existing purely and simply; and that, for want of sufficient resolution to die. (466)

The author goes so far as to recommend suicide here. Her audience was duly alarmed, thinking these sentments could encourage impressionable people to kill themselves. Responding to criticism, de Staël published an apologia in *Reflections on Suicide* (1812), in which she admits, in a footnote: 'In my work "On the Influence of the Passions" I have applauded suicide, and I have ever since repented of that inconsiderate expression. I was then in all the pride and vivacity of early youth; but of what use is life, without the hope of improvement?' (467n). Despite protestations that she had amended her views on suicide to support the traditional view of it, de Staël may also have contributed to British notions of suicide as rebellious with yet another literary work. Caroline Franklin comments that de Staël 'depicted her first novel's heroine Delphine (1802) ... [as] taking poison as a self-affirmative protest against an oppressive society' (212). Here is subversive suicide of the sort I examine in this book.

Eighteenth-Century Literary Biographical Influences

Certain writers' personal lives – and the legends that grew up around them – give the literature of this period some of its most enduring links with suicidality. Thomas Chatterton's significance to Romantic literary history is inextricable from popular ideas about his suicide at age 17 as an expression of frustrated poetic talent. Chatterton is best known for the Rowley poems, a series of forgeries that he wrote under the pseudonym of Thomas Rowley, who Chatterton claimed was a medieval monk.[7] Certainly, Chatterton was admired for his great talent; Boswell reports that in 1776 Johnson remarked of the poet, '"This is the most extraordinary young man that has encountered my knowledge. It is wonderful how the whelp has written such things"' (*Life* 68). Chatterton's true significance in literary history has less to do, however, with his own poetic output and more with that of others who were inspired by and contributed to the myths surrounding his suicide. Chatterton's death was an inspiration for canonical Romantic poets such as P. B. Shelley, who mentions him in *Adonais*, Keats, who wrote a sonnet in Chatterton's honour and dedicated *Endymion* (1818) to his memory, and Coleridge, who penned the 'Monody on the Death of Chatterton' (1794). Robinson's 'Monody to the Memory of Chatterton' (1791) is an early example in the long list of poems about him, but the most famous tribute appears in two lines of 'Resolution and Independence' (1807), in which Wordsworth dubs the poet 'the marvellous boy' (43–4). By praising Chatterton's genius and bemoaning his fate, the Romantic poets showed their allegiance with disenfranchised artists, writers too sensitive to be appreciated by the dull masses and greedy bourgeoisie – disciplined contributors to biopolitical society. Keats asserts in 'Oh Chatterton! how very sad thy fate' (1848, written in 1816) that the young poet was 'A half-blown flower, which cold blasts amate', and would rest forevermore 'Above the ingrate world and human fears' (8, 12). This literary ideal – another expression of the culture of sensibility – was more appealing than the truth behind Chatterton's death.

Although the boy died at his own hands, recent evidence suggests that he may have accidentally killed himself with an overdose, perhaps of medication intended to treat a venereal disease. Nick Groom recounts, 'In 1970, on the two-hundredth anniversary of his death, Richard Holmes first seriously argued that it was an accidental overdose that killed Chatterton. Since then the evidence has grown, despite being rejected (or perhaps just overlooked) by subsequent biographers and many critics. The persistence of the suicide myth is remarkable' (116). The popular rejection of the evidence that Chatterton was not a suicide is telling: it suggests that commentators on the poet prefer to perpetuate the myth of his suicide handed down since the Romantic period. Such myth-making indicates that Chatterton is widely considered to be important largely because of his suicide, rather than because of his poetry. If Chatterton isn't a suicide, then he ceases to be the face of the literary movement subsequent to his lifetime, in which the idea of sympathetic suicide, especially of the disenfranchised, became so firmly entrenched. The many Romantic-era poems that tell of Chatterton's sad death thus reflect and perpetuate the imagined history with which British culture has invested him. Arguably, the origin of the myth of Chatterton's suicide is largely literary, too: it was formed to create an English Werther, a sensitive, artistic type who is pitiable for being driven to death by an unjust and unappreciative society.[8] This situation Koretsky describes as the 'the relationship between romantic literature and the myth of the tortured artist ... who is tragically undone by his own brilliance' (*Rights* 2), a status reserved for white men, Koretsky argues, suggesting even Chatterton's centrality to power. However, it is equally notable that the Romantic literati found these suicidal figures sympathetic for the opposite reason: because they were outsiders who did not contribute to industrial society in a practical (read, non-literary) way. So popular was this myth that Chatterton became the poster boy for an identity essential to the Romantic movement in England: the disenfranchised, sensitive, pitiable and suicidal poet.

William Cowper, another strong influence on British Romanticism, was also famously suicidal, although the apparent cause of his mental distress was religious.[9] As Maurice Quinlan notes, it was 'frequently suggested that Cowper's peculiar form of religious mania was induced by his adherence to Evangelical and Calvinistic beliefs' in his lifetime (110), and this belief persists today. Boswell notes in his private papers:

> 'Mr Sharpe joined us after dinner. He was acquainted with Cowper, the Poet, his account of whom was frightful, for with a great deal of genius and even pleasantry, he has at bottom a deep religious melancholy, to divert the shocking thoughts of which he is now translating Homer. He has been woefully

deranged – in a strait waistcoat – and now is sometimes so ill that they take away his shoe buckles, that he may have nothing within his reach with which he can hurt himself. It seems he apprehends himself in a state of reprobation, being impressed with the most dismal doctrines of Calvinism.' (quoted in Quinlan 110)

Beliefs about Cowper's suicidal Calvinism were particularly strong after the unauthorised publication in 1816 of Cowper's *Adelphi*, which detailed his mental breakdown and religious conversion. Jane Darcy asserts that Cowper's enthusiasm was an essential aspect of his reputation as a poet: 'Cowper's enormous popularity in his lifetime rested on his image as a religious melancholic' (144) who was driven to suicidality because of his illness, although he never succumbed to it. Part of the attraction to these suffering Romantic poets was their suicidality, a mark of their fragility and heightened capacity for feeling, characteristics that divided them from the ideally strong, productive and engaged subjects of society.

Cowper seems to represent his own despair in 'The Castaway' (1803), one of his best-known poems. The poem depicts a sailor tossed overboard from his ship in a storm:

Not long beneath the whelming brine,
Expert to swim, he lay;
Nor soon he felt his strength decline,
Or courage die away;
But waged with death a lasting strife,
Supported by despair of life. (13–18)

When the speaker concludes the poem with reference to his struggles, Cowper appears to express his own suicidal anguish: 'We perished, each alone;/ But I beneath a rougher sea,/ And whelmed in deeper gulfs than he' (64–6). Happily for the poet, his despair over the thought that he was eternally damned found a receptive audience in Nathaniel Cotton, a physician specialising in mental illness who established an asylum dubbed the '*Collegium Insanorum*' ('college for the insane' in Latin). Here Cowper lodged during some of the most dangerous periods of his insanity. Cowper reflects upon this time in a letter dated 4 July 1765: 'I reckon it one instance of the Providence that has attended me throughout this whole event, that ... I was carried to Dr. Cotton', because

I had so much need of a religious friend to converse with ... The doctor was as ready to administer relief to me in this article likewise [i.e. religious anxiety], and as well qualified to do it as in that which was more immediately his province. How many physicians would have thought this an irregular

> appetite and a symptom of remaining madness! But if it were so, my friend was as mad as myself, and it is well for me that he was so. (quoted in Walsh 315–16)

If Cowper depicts his own suicidality in 'The Castaway', then this passage shows him considering Dr Cotton – and religion – as the wished-for life raft. Cowper is recognised as a considerable influence on the Romantic movement, particularly in the confessional nature of his verse, so dazzlingly on display in the monumental *The Task* (1785). His poetic musing on his religious suicidality doubtlessly also encouraged the greater sympathy for suicides that characterises so much of Romantic-era literature.

A critical number of works on suicide, literary and otherwise, were published in this period, a circumstance that inspired further responses in a kind of snowball effect and demonstrates the importance of suicide for the culture. In this hubbub of publications on suicide, what is most notable about the literary depiction of the topic is that it was mostly positive, or at least sympathetic. This compassionate attitude is essential to the establishment of the literary trope of subversive suicide, the focus of Part II of this book. In developing this theme, authors seek to inspire the reader's sympathy, support, admiration and even respect for the suicidal. The following chapters show how the positive framework for reading suicide as more than sin or a symptom of mental illness meant that it could also function more specifically as an assertion of bodily freedom against the coercions of biopower that were increasingly established – and recognised – as the eighteenth century turned into the nineteenth. Building on the classical associations of (male) suicide with heroism, and with a focus on the oppressed body, in particular, the literary works I interpret in detail in Part II demonstrate the building awareness of oppression as less about the fear of punishment and death, the way that sovereign power established itself in the previous episteme, and more about the control and management of the body, power's insistence that the individual live and multiply. This system, developed and perfected through the colonial slave trade, was often answered in the most effective and direct way through the threat of suicide amongst the enslaved, and these combined issues frequently appear in texts associated with the trade, especially in abolitionist works. Responding to this reality and literary trend, Romantic writers Wollstonecraft, Shelley and Byron reveal how biopower characterises other forces of British society, such as patriarchy and Christianity and, like the abolitionist works that come before theirs, they use the theme of subversive suicide to agitate against it.

Notes

1. Not all of Gray's verse was well appreciated in the Romantic period, though. Indeed, in the Preface to the *Lyrical Ballads* (1800, 1802), Wordsworth singles out Gray's 'poetic diction' as 'curiously elaborate' and therefore needlessly complicated and esoteric – the opposite of verse in 'language really spoken by men', which Wordsworth champions (412).
2. The association between ancient British bards and suicide appears also in Scottish poet James Macpherson's Ossian poems from the 1760s about the actions of the third-century warrior-poet. See Dafydd Moore's 'Heroic Incoherence in James Macpherson's "The Poems of Ossian"' for more on what he calls the 'suicidal antics of the Ossianic heroes' (52). Notably, Goethe includes his own translations of passages from the Ossian poems in *Werther*.
3. I acknowledge that Foucault describes the eighteenth century as being the era of disciplinary power, but, as Chloë Taylor recognises, biopower functions with the tools of disciplinary power ('Biopower' 238).
4. All emphases (here in italics) and technical oddities (especially the erroneous use of possessives and odd spelling) appear in the source text.
5. Interestingly, among other long sections of the original novel, Saint-Preux and Lord Bomston's long suicide debate is excised from one of the few scholarly modern translations of the novel, published by Pennsylvania State University Press in 1968.
6. Although some contemporary writers have questioned whether a Werthermania really did sweep Europe (e.g. Hulse 12, Thorsona and Öbergb, *passim*), others accept the reality of the phenomenon (Walling 106, Phillips *passim*).
7. Chatterton's forgery was likely inspired by the *Reliques of Ancient English Poetry* (1765), edited by Thomas Percy, perhaps the first of the great ballad collections that inspired Coleridge and Wordsworth's *Lyrical Ballads*.
8. Chatterton's literary and sentimental standing was further established by Henry Wallis's iconic, Victorian-era painting 'The Death of Chatterton' (1856), featuring a beautiful, young George Meredith.
9. Some of the above discussion of Cowper derives from my article, 'Calvinism, Enthusiasm, and Suicide: The Regulation of Subjectivity in the Romantic Period' (2018).

Part II

Slavery, Biopower and Literary Subversive Suicide

Chapter 3

The Dying Negroes: Enforced Life and Slave Suicide as the Spectacle of Sentiment

Slave Suicide as Subversive

> There was no end to my toils – no end to my blows. I lay down at night and rose up in the morning in fear and sorrow; and often wished that ... I could escape from this cruel bondage and be at rest in the grave. (Mary Prince 20)

The above passage from the memoir *The History of Mary Prince, a West Indian Slave* (1831) – orally related by Prince to Susanna Strickland (thereafter Moodie) and edited by Thomas Pringle – echoes a sentiment that is expressed in countless works by formerly enslaved people in Britain during the Romantic period: the wish to die to escape slavery. Although Prince's commentary is exceptional in that, as Lee comments, it is 'the first text authored by a black woman in Britain' (223), the content of her work – from descriptions of the extreme brutality she experienced as an enslaved person to her resulting suicidal despair – echoes throughout several similar works written by men.[1] Other notable slave memoirists who discuss the desire to die to escape slavery include Equiano and Ottobah Cugoano in the eighteenth century. With respect to biopower the slave memoir as a form is subversive: it replaces the author's body, subjugated in the biopolitical system of transatlantic slavery and treated as the enslaved person's only ontological reality, with a narrative of the author's life that may be viewed as the author's self rendered ideally, intellectually. In this sense, the memoir represents a kind of suicide, to reason from the basis of Blanchot's assertions in 'Literature and the Right to Death' (1948): 'For me to be able to say, "This woman," I must somehow take her flesh-and-blood reality away from her, cause her to be absent, annihilate her ... The word is the absence of that being, its nothingness, what is left of it when it has lost being – the very fact that it does not exist' (322). It follows that the memoir is a kind of suicide, in the sense that the memoirist annihilates his own physical presence in telling of himself.[2] Both suicide and the slave memoir subvert biopower by denying it a body, making their joint appearance particularly powerful expressions of the topic of this book. Prince's *History* engages with the issue of her absence in relation to the text about her in a more complex way than do most other memoirs, as she may also be absented by the appropriation of her voice by Strickland and Pringle, a topic I discuss in greater detail below.

The importance of studying texts by the formerly enslaved – rather than only texts by white Britons about slavery – cannot be overstated. Although Prince was born in Bermuda and did not endure the Middle Passage, her memoir, as well as those of Equiano and Cugoano, is essential to an understanding of the experience of enslavement from the perspective of the enslaved. As Saidiya Hartman asks in 'Venus in Two Acts',

> how does one rewrite the chronicle of a death foretold and anticipated, as a collective biography of dead subjects, as a counter-history of the human, as the practice of freedom? ... The scarcity of African narratives of captivity and enslavement exacerbates the pressure and gravity of such questions. There is not one extant autobiographical narrative of a female captive who survived the Middle Passage. This silence in the archive ... has for the most part focused the historiography of the slave trade on quantitative matters and on issues of markets and trade relations. (3–4)

In their discussions of suicidality as rebellion, these narratives function as announcements of the authors' freedom and break the silence to which Hartman gestures, imbuing it with a human passion for liberty, a necessary counterpoint to the study of transatlantic slavery as an economic matter. Equiano, Cugoano and Prince's texts are only a few of many historical slave memoirs; Laura Murphy reports, 'Scholars have identified approximately two hundred narratives authored by formerly enslaved people during the era of transatlantic slavery' (3–4). Because slave memoirs illustrate the agency and control of the Black writers of the period in a way otherwise unavailable to them, both in their enslavement and in depictions of Black enslavement by white abolitionists, studying these works honours their voices and acknowledges their power. Sidonie Smith points out that the formerly enslaved memoirist 'recreates himself as the protagonist of his life story', rather than as a subject of the institution of slavery, and asserts control over the 'pain of the past through the imposition of artistic form on the matter of experience, thus gaining control and mastery over it' (11). According to Barbara Baumgartner, pain itself can become a productive way for the slave memoirist to forge a new identity – an assertion that counters Elaine Scarry's claim that pain destroys the self, one's language and one's world (cited in Baumgartner 256). Baumgartner writes of Prince's

> ability to utilize her body and its pain to suit her own purposes [, which] is reflected in a ... narrative shift ... that demonstrates her newfound emotional investment in her debilitated body once she is finally able to reclaim it from the clutches of slavery. (257)

The study of slave memoirs is essential to avoid the reproduction of textual subjugation, a topic of this chapter.

Another reason why we must examine texts by the formerly enslaved is to redress the excessive critical attention to literature about slavery by members of the colonising group. By far, the most common literary works on slavery in the period are by white British abolitionists, and contemporary studies of abolitionist literature reflect this weighting. Eighteenth-century abolitionist writers use the theme of slave suicide often and for a multitude of discrete reasons that are meant to emphasise their anti-slavery message and, at best, to motivate their audience to take part in the abolitionist cause. As I will show by examining a range of abolitionist works by white Britons, including Day and Bicknell's popular long poem *The Dying Negro*, the trope of slave suicide is slippery and can even undermine the white abolitionist's apparent point, such as when it becomes part of a self-indulgent sentimental message and thereby seems to revel in the pain it depicts and the tears it draws from readers. These texts encourage the repeated depiction of the theme of slave suicide without necessarily inspiring the reader to oppose the slave trade actively. They can also reify beliefs about the powerlessness of the enslaved and satisfy the fantasy of white control over the Black body, undermining the subversive message behind depictions of slave suicide.

Of all the slave memoirs I discuss in this chapter, none have generated more discussion about the appropriation of the Black voice by white writers than has *The History of Mary Prince*, given that Prince's orally conveyed narrative was transcribed by a white woman, Strickland, a Methodist, and edited by Pringle, a white man. Both collaborators wished to present Prince's memoir as an anti-slavery tract; indeed, Pringle was the secretary of the British Anti-Slavery Society. Their agendas probably aligned with Prince's, who was introduced to Christianity at a Methodist meeting in Antigua (although she later became a member of the closely related Moravian Church) and was herself, unsurprisingly, an opponent of slavery (Prince 31). In his preface to the text, Pringle stresses this point and seeks to establish Prince as the true author of it: the 'idea of writing Mary Prince's history was first suggested by herself. She wished it to be done, she said, that good people in England might hear from a slave what a slave had felt and suffered' (i). Nevertheless, the process through which the text was created raises questions about whether Prince's narrative was appropriated, and maybe even co-opted and changed, by Strickland and Pringle, the latter of whom admits to having 'pruned' it (i). It is also notable, as Jessica Allen reports, that 'at the 1833 trial in which Pringle sued Thomas Cadell for libel, Prince revealed on the witness stand that Strickland did not write down everything she narrated' (509). Recent critics have questioned the extent to which Pringle and Strickland may have appropriated Prince's narrative: Allen asserts that Pringle 'violate[d] her [i.e. Prince's] subjectivity by overlooking her authorial decisions' through what she characterises as his heavy-handed editing of the memoir (510), and Rachel Banner characterises the paratextual material included by Pringle – such as the Preface and appendices – as an 'authoritative white verification of a black author's intellectual abilities and good moral character' (298) that thrusts the Black voice into a humiliating position of requiring white approval. Baumgartner, meanwhile, focuses on how Prince's text represents her body and argues that, even in contemporary versions of the *History*, 'Prince's body and text remained (and remain) subject to ongoing appropriation and interpretation' (254). To some contemporary readers, white people's involvement with Prince's text ineluctably intrudes on Prince's message.

Not every recent reader believes the integrity of Prince's text is destabilised in this way, though. Some critics, such as Alan Bewell, assert that the 'complex cross-cultural collaboration' between Prince, Strickland and Pringle was vital to the 'success' of Prince's text for the anti-slavery cause, given the demands of the largely white Christian British readership ('Stranger' 235), while Sandra Pouchet Paquet maintains that 'These heteroglot voices compete with but do not dominate Mary Prince's fully integrated sense of self' in the text (37), suggesting that concerns about the white appropriation of the Black voice are secondary to the noble purpose of the *History* as abolitionist, or, at least, that they can be allayed in consideration of Prince's intact and strong authorial identity. Still others take this issue a step further: Michelle Gadpaille goes so far as to argue that the *History* should be viewed as a collaboration between Prince and Strickland and, therefore, considered in the context of Strickland's wider *oeuvre* (63), an approach that threatens to reify Strickland's appropriation of Prince's narrative. For the present study, the fact of Strickland's and Pringle's involvement in Prince's text serves to highlight the prevalence and dangers of white interference in efforts by the formerly enslaved to agitate for themselves in the period, although it should be noted that Prince was not literate – as so many enslaved people were not, quite by design in the world of slavery – and thus could not have published her story on her own. Despite this problematic frame, I understand Prince's *History* as hers alone and her references to her suicidality under slavery as what she wished to include in her story, rather than as coerced by her transcriber or editor.

References to suicide in slave memoirs are important because the effect of suicide is always subversive of biopolitical society, especially slave society. It should be acknowledged, however, that the topic of slave suicide in works by formerly enslaved people can appear to be a desperate response to an impossible situation – a claim to victimhood, not heroism. Richard Bell summarises this conflict with reference to the 'Newly United States' – to echo the title of his book – when he asks, 'Was a slave's suicide an act of principled yet costly resistance to tyranny that challenged the hypocrisy of the revolutionary settlement? Or was it a measure of abject victimhood that begged for humanitarian intervention?' (*No More* 203). Reading slave suicide as only rebellious can ignore such demands for aid, and it must therefore be balanced with an appreciation of other reasons for suicide amongst the enslaved. Nevertheless, some period writers worried about the opposite problem: that heroism amongst the enslaved was not sufficiently recognised. The most famous British abolitionist, Thomas Clarkson, writes to the Comte de Mirabeau, one of the great orators during the early stages of the French Revolution:

> Scenes of the brightest Heroism ... happen repeatedly in the Holds or on the Decks of the Slave-Vessels ... Authors of them often eclipse by the Splendour of their Actions the celebrated Character both of Greece and Rome ... But how different is the Fate of the one and of the other. The Actions of the former are considered as so many Acts of Baseness, and are punished with Torture or with Death, while those of the latter have been honoured with publick Rewards. The Actions of the former again are industriously consigned to oblivion, that not a trace, if possible, may be found, while those of the latter have been industriously recorded as Examples for future Times. (quoted in Rediker 300–1)

The kind of heroism of which Clarkson writes must have been insurrectionary, which was often explicitly suicidal – and, even when it was not so, it amounted to suicidality, for rebellions often cost the lives of the oppressed. Huey P. Newton's comments in *Revolutionary Suicide* (1973), the manifesto of the Black Panther movement, are pertinent here: to 'assault ... the Establishment' 'lies at the heart of the concept of revolutionary suicide. Thus it is better to oppose the forces that would drive me to self-murder than to endure them. Although I risk the likelihood of death, there is at least the possibility, if not the probability, of changing intolerable conditions' (3). Broadly considered, violent rebellion is often suicidal, and all suicide is subversive of biopower, even if the individual motivation for it is otherwise. A balanced approach to the means through which the enslaved fought for their freedom, in whatever form, is necessary.

While real-life suicidal heroism may have been censored in some cases, the trope was vastly popular in the literary realm and may even be said to characterise the period. In *The Problem of Slavery in the Age of Revolution, 1770–1823* (1975), David Brion Davis follows M. H. Abrams in arguing that 'the concepts of mastery and servitude became ... central "metaphors of mind" which pervaded romantic literature' (559n). Robin Blackburn agrees, claiming that 'debates around abolitionism were indeed central to British culture in the Romantic period, being taken up in a great variety of ways by poets, dramatists and novelists as well as statesmen and subversives' (1). More recently, Lee has explored the theme of slavery in some of the major works of the British Romanticism, spurred to the task by the striking realisation that, despite the oversized presence of the topic in the culture, it 'seemed to be missing from the era's most powerful poetry'; she continues, 'Since slavery was the great moral question of the age and Romanticism the great aesthetic development, it seemed logical to set these two movements side by side' (1).[3] Finally, Koretsky recognises that slave 'suicide became ... one of the master tropes of political movements occurring on the fringes of society, such as abolitionist projects that sought to open Enlightenment categories of personhood to include a wider spectrum of people', in a persuasive comment on one of the most common interpretations of the meaning of slave suicide in abolitionist texts: that it communicates the humanity of the victim ('Habeas' 23). Revolution against servitude, including its most egregious form, slavery, and the most potent form of insurrection against it, namely suicide, express essential qualities of the Romantic movement.

Eighteenth-century abolitionist texts, including slave memoirs, influenced this literary trend. Cugoano presents slave suicidality as explicitly insurrectionist in *Thoughts and Sentiments on the Evil and Wicked Traffic of the Slavery and Commerce of the Human Species, Humbly Submitted to the Inhabitants of Great Britain* (1787):

> when we found ourselves at last taken away, death was more preferable than life, and a plan was concerted amongst us, that we might burn and blow up the ship, and to perish all together in the flames; but we were betrayed by one of our own countrywomen, who slept with some of the head men of the ship, for it was common for the dirty filthy sailors to take the African women and lie upon their bodies; but the men were chained and pent up in holes. It was

> the women and boys which were to burn the ship, with the approbation and groans of the rest; though that was prevented, the discovery was likewise a cruel bloody scene. (232–3)

Cugoano describes a plan for mass suicide as full-scale rebellion, although he tempers its victorious resonances by mentioning the betrayal of the plot amongst the enslaved and that many could only 'groan' their approval of it, making their sadness and pain at least as central to the story as their heroism. Nevertheless, the ambitious scale of the plan shows its revolutionary significance, for it did not concern only a few individual suicides; it was intended to be a mass-murder suicide that would consume the entire ship. Marcus Rediker reports a comparable circumstance: 'The least common but most spectacular mass suicides involved blowing up the entire ship', as in January 1773, when the enslaved men on the *New Britannia* killed almost everyone on board by setting the gun powder room on fire, killing around 300 people (290). Finally, Niel Douglas relates a similar story in *The African Slave Trade: Or a Short View of the Evidence, Relative to That Subject, Produced Before the House of Commons* (1792). In a passage that describes 'insurrections' amongst the enslaved, he writes of a French slave ship off the coast of Africa: 'Having got her complement of slaves, and waiting only a fair wind, a number of them broke loose, and some how found access to set fire to the powder-room, by which means every soul on board perished, seven excepted', after which Douglas opines:

> Thus would they [i.e. enslaved Africans] always, if in their power, prefer an immediate and violent death to the protraction of life on [*sic*] such wretched conditions. Being deprived of every thing for which it is worth while to live, life itself becomes a loathed burden. Hapless people, you can plead reasons for Suicide, to which European self-destroyers have no claim! (28)

These enslaved people sought to become suicide bombers together, demonstrating the revolutionary significance of the act.

Certainly, slavers often perceived slave suicide as revolutionary, since it always undermined their efforts to convey as many Africans as possible to the colonies. Marc Hertzman recognises the

> brutal fact, widely acknowledged by historians of slavery (though almost always in passing), that masters and traders understood suicide as a drag on production, and indeed much more: a direct assault on capital investment and future earnings. For any society that depended on forced labor, suicide was not only a moral, religious, or medico-legal matter, but also a racial and economic one. While laziness or indolence could draw a master's ire and affect plantation production, suicide – regardless of the intention behind it – was a dramatic attack against white wealth. (321)

Slave suicide was always subversive, for it had the power to undermine the entire system of slavery.[4] The view of slave suicidality as rebellious is the basis of Terri Snyder's important book *The Power to Die: Slavery and Suicide in British North America* (2015). She explains that, regardless of the intention of the enslaved person who chose death in British North America, slave-owners and other white people in colonial society perceived the act as insurrectionist:

> For many European settlers in the slave societies of colonial America, a suicidal slave was the worst of rebels, akin to those who engaged in armed revolt against their captors and masters. Self-inflicted death by enslaved people defied their very ownership and deprived their masters of property. Slave owners also reviled suicide because they feared that the act was contagious and attributed it to particular African ethnic groups who appeared to prefer self-inflicted death to slavery. Perhaps above all, suicide by enslaved people not only challenged European beliefs about good and bad deaths, it also shattered their pretentions of power over bondpeople. (9)

Slave suicide undermined the slave-owning system, both economically and ideologically – and it did so legally, as well. Snyder adds:

> acts of self-destruction by slaves mattered to emerging slave codes, local courts, and colonial and state legislatures ... The law may have simultaneously defined slaves as human beings and chattel properties, but in the very act of killing themselves, slaves became criminally culpable persons under the law. Criminal acts, including suicide, were the outcome of *mens rea* or intention, and suicide, ironically, erased the civil death that was slavery. (*Power* 13)

In gesturing to enslavement as a 'civil death', Snyder points to the special circumstances of slavery, which I will describe hereafter as an 'inverted world', in which individuals cease to exist – legally, as well as in any definition of a dignified human life – and are forced to continue living under pain of torture for even attempting to cut short what lives are left to them.

Slave suicide was strongly influential in challenging social attitudes about a topic that so often came under the scrutiny of the British legal and religious rules. The British slave ship and colonial plantation were lawless, godless places that skirted the norms of British society, although they were managed by British people and declared British colonies. Even British clerics such as George Whitfield (also spelled 'Whitefield'), one of the founders of Methodism, was bound to admit that Christian proclamations against the taking of one's own life were suspended in the extreme world of slavery. Snyder reports that, in '1740, George Whitefield protested the sinfulness and injuriousness of slavery ... [i]n a letter to the "Inhabitants of Maryland, Virginia, North and South Carolina"', in which he stated that, '"considering what usage" enslaved people commonly met with, he wondered "that there were not more instances of self-murder among the negroes, or that they have not more frequently rose up in arms against their owners"', and argued that 'suicide by slaves was part of a holy war, one in which suicide and revolt by enslaved people were justifiable responses to their unchristian treatment, to the sin of slavery' (*Power* 127). Whitfield's commentary comes close to defending suicidal revolution amongst the enslaved, which is surprising, not only because of Whitfield's strict Christian morals, but also because he had once been a slave-owner himself in America and, in fact, had preached 'a fulsome defence of the institution, claiming its full scriptural justification. "As for the lawfulness of keeping slaves, I have no doubt"', he wrote in 1750 (Schlenther n.p.). The world of slavery was a peripheral zone – British in name and often not in law – where the bounds of ethical conduct were often deferred. Despite its peculiarity and distance from mainland Britain, though, the realities of slavery were not unknown. They haunted British culture like a guilty dream or repressed memory. Slave suicide was therefore revolutionary with respect to its effect on the slave trade, as well as broad cultural notions regarding the significance of suicide.

Slavery created non-societies, groups that defied the usual structure and purpose of social organisation. Mbembe comments on the lawlessness of colonial society, such as in Africa itself:

> the colonies are the location par excellence where the controls and guarantees of judicial order can be suspended – the zone where the violence of the state of exception [i.e. Agamben's term for the circumstance in which a political leadership disavows the law in the interest of the public good] is deemed to operate in the service of 'civilization.' That colonies might be ruled over in absolute lawlessness stems from the racial denial of any common bond between the conqueror and the native. (24)

The same may be said of the British transatlantic colonies peopled largely by kidnapped Africans and their European oppressors. These were not replacement societies or new cultures, but a lack of civilisation, a state of permanent lawlessness. Snyder discusses plantation law helpfully, simultaneously recognising the precariousness and extraordinary nature of the legal system in British transatlantic colonies: 'Statutes authorized slaveholders to visit all manner of violence – commonly referred to as "plantation justice" – on their slaves', which also 'authorized non-slaveowning whites to police slaves, and endorsed extraordinary corporal and capital punishments exclusively for slaves' (*Power* 82–3). Plantation justice was no justice for the enslaved, and the societies they were supposed to support were relatively lawless.

The enslaved were denied freedom at every turn: the legal personhood to claim freedom under British law, as well as the freedom to kill themselves, which should be their choice as extra-legal people, regardless of what the law proscribes for legal persons in that society. Such discursive acrobatics on the part of slavers to lay blame and seek recompense for the suicides of the enslaved demonstrate how knotty the problem of slave suicide was for colonial society, the members of which understood very well that, despite their extreme efforts to maintain complete control over every aspect of the bodies of the enslaved, the latter could nevertheless take their own lives.[5]

While my focus is largely on the broad significance of slave suicide in British literary culture, rather than on individual lives, it is nevertheless necessary for an understanding of the topic to attend to the number of people who died. As Snyder recognises, 'the question of how many slaves killed themselves in the early modern Anglo-Atlantic and British North America is unanswerable' because several impediments existed to the honest reporting of these numbers, such as a 1785 ruling in the British courts that rendered 'any suicide that occurred aboard ship in the absence of an insurrection ... not considered ... a form of mutiny', which meant that 'such a death was therefore uninsured. The legal decision gave captains and surgeons incentives to conceal evidence of self-destruction' (*Power* 21, 20; see also Rediker 291). Snyder additionally reports that 'there was no legal requirement that inquests be held on [the suicides of] slaves, and usually this was done only if owners planned to sue for damages' (*Power* 20), which, again, means that the historical record tallying slave suicides is incomplete.[6] Another reason why slavers frequently suppressed information about slave suicide is that many antislavery Britons interpreted it as the direct consequence of the cruel treatment they endured on the slave ship and used it to advance the cause of abolition (Rediker 291). However, some accounts do provide an idea of how many enslaved people chose death over a life of slavery. Rediker sampled the journals of eighty-six slave-ship surgeons from 1788 to 1897 and found that slave suicide occurred on twenty-five of them, a figure he calls '"a serious understatement"' (Rediker 291); a similar study by David Eltis, covering ninety-two slave-ship surgeons' accounts from 1792 to 1796, concludes that 7.2 per cent of deaths amongst the enslaved – both during the loading of the ship on the African coast and during the Middle Passage – were suicides (quoted in Snyder, *Power* 20); and Stephen Shapiro claims that 'Isaac Wilson, an English surgeon, attributed two-thirds of all shipboard deaths' to slave suicide from melancholy over leaving Africa (124). Regardless of these discrepancies, the number of suicides amongst the enslaved was evidently enormous. The extent of the problem is also demonstrated by the costly measures slavers employed to prevent it, such as the complicated system of netting that was installed around slave ships to catch those who attempted to jump overboard to their deaths – one of the best-known technologies of what I term 'enforced life'.

Most scholars of the history of slavery and abolition focus on the loss of life linked to the transatlantic slave trade, which spanned roughly four centuries – from the late fifteenth century, when Portuguese ships began the slave trade (Rediker 41–2), to 1888, when Brazil finally passed the last Act of Emancipation (Sherwood 5). However, the height of the trade was in the years 1700–1808. The historical attention to the deaths in the slave trade makes sense, given the great number of them. Pabst Battin claims that at the height of the slave trade in the eighteenth century, about six million Africans were kidnapped onto slave ships, adding: 'Altogether, an estimated 12 million left the African continent as slaves in the European trade; an estimated 10–20% died during the Middle Passage' (Introductions 586–7). In his monumental book *The Slave Ship: A Human History* (2007), Rediker reports that, of the 12.4 million Africans who were kidnapped onto colonial ships in the almost 400 years of the transatlantic slave trade, 1.8 million died in the Middle Passage, while another 1.8 million Africans died between the point of captivity and before being loaded onto ships off the coast of Africa; yet another one and a half million died 'during the first year of labouring life in the New World' (5). While the specific number of fatalities from the various stages of slavery cannot be determined, it is fair to say that it is huge – 'roughly 5 million men, women and children' died (Rediker 5). It is important to recognise, moreover, that many deaths in the slave trade were not accidents in the enforcement of life, which I will discuss hereafter. They were often deliberate murders. Alexander Falconbridge confirms, 'the common practice of the officers in the Guinea trade, I am sorry to say it, will, with very few exceptions, justify the assertion, that to harden the feelings, and to inspire a *delight in giving torture* to a fellow creature, is the natural tendency of this unwarrantable traffick' (60; emphasis in original). But how and why did slavers forget the chief goal of their business – to kidnap and keep alive as many Africans as possible for work in the colonies – in this way? Another physician, the Scottish author John Moore, ventures an explanation for this perversity through the narrator of his novel *Zeluco* (1789):

> It is a common argument against the necessity of new laws for the protection of slaves, that they need no protection from a just and humane master, because he will never injure them; nor from a master of an opposite character, because his own interest will be their protection: but let it be remembered, that men who are not naturally compassionate, who are devoid of religious impressions, and in the habit of giving vent to every gust of ill-humour, are apt, in the violence of rage, to become deaf to the voice of common sense and interest, as well as of justice and mercy … [H]ow often do we see men in an absurd rage abuse their most serviceable cattle? But a thousand causes, which must occur to every one, expose *human creatures* to the vindictive rage of ill-tempered proprietors in a much greater degree than inanimate things or the brute creation ever can be. And we find in fact, that cruel and passionate masters, however interested in other respects, do gratify their ill humour against their most valuable slaves at the expence of their interest. (115–16; emphasis in original)

Put otherwise, the violence and death that characterised the slave trade in so many ways represent yet another of its perversities, rather than a planned feature of it.

Other scholars have puzzled over the significance of the shocking and self-defeating cruelty of slavers. In his classic study *The Black Jacobins: Toussaint L'Ouverture and the San Domingo Revolution* (1989), C. L. R. James comments that 'for the least fault the slaves received the harshest punishment' and the planters exercised the great 'ingenuity … [of] a depraved imagination … to break their [i.e. the enslaved's] spirit': 'hot ashes were poured on the bleeding wounds', 'Mutilations were common, limbs, ears, and sometimes the private parts, to deprive them of the pleasures which they could indulge without expense', and 'masters poured burning wax on their arms and hands and shoulders, emptied the boiling cane sugar over their heads, burned them alive, roasted them on slow fires, [and] filled them with gunpowder and blew them up with a match' (12), amongst other forms of torture, maiming and murder. James then asks if these were 'merely isolated incidents, the extravagances of a few half-crazed colonists?' before deciding that the sheer number of described incidents indicates that 'these bestial practices were normal features of slave life' (13). I will argue that sometimes the perverse cruelty of the slave trade was an outcome of its violent methods of enforcing life.

While I acknowledge the many deaths associated with transatlantic slavery, my focus in this chapter is on the many ways in which slavery was by definition and in many of its expressions a machine of enforced life for its victims. The unwavering goal of the slave trade was to maintain the lives of the enslaved. Rediker notes:

> Thomas Starke put it clearly when he wrote to Captain James Westmore in 1700, 'the whole benefitt of the Voyage lyes in your care in Preserving

> negroes lives.' Two American merchants, Joseph and Joshua Grafton, made the same point in 1785: 'on the health of the slaves, almost your whole voyage depends'. (198)

Once on the plantations in the British colonies, the lives of the enslaved were viewed as valuable assets to the British Crown, as were British subjects more generally. Scottish physician George Pinckard writes in *Notes on the West Indies: Including Observations Relative to the Creoles and Slaves of the Western Colonies and the Indian of South America: Interspersed with Remarks Upon the Seasoning Or Yellow Fever of Hot Climates* (2 vols, 1816) that many 'creole' doctors were barely literate, have almost no education, and end up killing their patients, which he frames as a lamentable waste:

> When we reflect that the riches and prosperity of a country are intimately connected with its population, and that the lives of men are of the greatest importance to the state, it becomes [a] matter of surprise and astonishment, that, even in the remotest colony, such uninstructed pretenders should be permitted to disgrace the healing art. (212, 214)

He thereafter denounces the 'miscalculating policy which ... tolerates a tremendous host of empirics' who 'commit depredations upon the health, the purses, and *the lives* of His Majesty's subjects' (214; emphasis in original). Pinckard's explicitly biopolitical perspective reveals the attitude of physicians involved in the slave trade during the Romantic period: medical treatment worked to uphold state power. I explore how the system of slavery attempted to force kidnapped Africans to live, even against their most strenuous efforts to die; how some of its most horrifying tools of torture – such as the *speculum oris*, a medical device pushed down the throat to force-feed those who refused to eat – were designed to sustain hated life amongst the enslaved; and how slavery compelled additional lives through 'breeding' more enslaved people, particularly after the British abolition of the slave trade in 1813.[7] Colonial slavery, then, must be viewed as a brutal, official and government-sanctioned regime of enforced life. It was a broad-ranging – perhaps foundational – effort of early biopower. Accordingly, suicide was, in both life and the literature I examine, a common means of rebellion, for suicide is always the soundest retort to biopower. For these reasons, the Romantic-era writers I discuss hereafter who focus on suicide as subversive of power use the theme of slavery as shorthand for the import of their texts, but, in the present chapter, I will show how slave suicide in abolitionist works by white and Black Britons – as well as those by pro-slavery writers from the long eighteenth century – reveals the significance of the theme for biopower, the abolitionist movement, and the period's literary trope of subversive suicide.

Slavery as an Inverted World and Death as Freedom

To demonstrate the ultimately subversive significance of slave suicide, it is necessary to provide a historical view of it that contextualises its appearance in literature and propagandist writing. In so many ways, colonial slavery was an inverted world in which the usual significations, values and meanings of British eighteenth-century society were not just suspended, but perverted and twisted into a horrific other: people became property, torture enforced life, growing (such as the sugar cane and tobacco of the plantation) created death, and suicide equalled freedom. In the world of transatlantic slavery, people became assets, products, chattels – in a complete denial of the definition of the human that emerged in such Enlightenment discussions as Locke's, which James Griffin describes as based on the principle of equal respect and the individual's right to life (214). Locke declares in *Two Treatises of Government*, 'every man has a property in his own person: this no body has any right to but himself. The labour of his body, and the work of his hands, we may say, are properly his' (209). Paul Youngquist comments, 'No matter how little else a person possesses, *he possesses his body* and with it the right to use it as he sees fit' (20; emphasis in original). This platitude was palpably untrue for the enslaved. While eighteenth-century British politics and philosophy wrangled over basic human rights and the culture defined itself in accordance with the principles that resulted from these debates, they were ignored with respect to colonial slavery.

The French context reveals a similar situation. Such basic tenets are reflected in the French Universal Declaration of Human Rights, the first and best-known article of which declares that humans are born and remain free and equal in rights. However, those who drafted the Declaration overlooked their enslaved African brethren. As Jessica Whyte asserts, only

> in abolishing slavery, the ideas of the Enlightenment met with the ideas and the resistance of the slaves of San Domingue [i.e. Saint-Domingue, who participated in the Haitian Revolution of the late eighteenth century], who saw in them more than had those who drafted the Universal Declaration without imagining that it would apply to those who were, after all, barely considered human. (247–8)

To be sure, the definition of 'Negroes' in that esteemed Enlightenment manifesto, the *Encyclopedia*, contradictorily discusses Africans' cultural habits and characteristics in terms of their suitability, or lack thereof, for the plantation, even while sounding the alarm that slavery is contrary to the principle of 'natural law' (n.p.). The definition starts out true to the Enlightenment spirit of impartiality:

> For several centuries, Europeans have carried out a trade in these negroes, whom they take from Guinea and the other coasts of Africa, to support the colonies that they have established in several places in America and in the Islands of the Antilles. People try to justify what is odious and contrary to natural law in this trade by saying that normally these slaves find the salvation of their souls in the loss of their liberty; that the instruction in Christianity given them, joined to *their indispensability for the cultivation of sugar*, tobacco, indigo, *etc.* mitigates that which seems inhuman in a trade in which men buy and sell others just like beasts for cultivating land. (n.p.; my emphasis)

Parts of this passage strike the appropriate tone of opposition to the slave trade, such as in the implication that it is wrongheaded to justify enslaving people on account of their ability to cultivate colonial crops, as though such work is the function of certain humans. However, other statements that follow fall into the racist essentialism that the passage condemns. It goes on, 'The best negroes come from Cape Verde, Angola, Senegal', without stating what, exactly, constitutes a good 'negro' (n.p.). A subsequent passage then hints at the standards by which these people are being judged: 'Their hard nature demands that they be treated neither with too much indulgence nor too much severity' on the plantation (n.p.). In short, the writer assesses these Africans in terms of how their supposedly native characteristics help them adapt, or not, to life in the colonies, as though they are unique types of humans. The definition is also notable for its account of slave suicide:

> As soon as trading is completed, it is necessary to set sail without losing time since experience has shown that as long as these unfortunates are in view of their country, sadness overwhelms them or despair seizes them. The first causes illnesses which make a great number of them die in the crossing, the other brings them to take their own lives, either in refusing food or in plugging up their breathing in a manner known to them of folding and turning the tongue, which suffocates them every time, or in breaking their heads against the ship, or in throwing themselves in the sea, if they can find the opportunity. (n.p.)

The strange comment that Africans have a way of suffocating themselves with their own tongues emphasises their otherness. The passage recognises that slavery leads to suicide – and it may well have influenced developing notions about the links between the two evils in the period, especially in consideration of the *Encyclopedia*'s impact. It sounds some of the expected Enlightenment notes on the topic of slavery, but lapses into rank racism at other points.[8] In such ways, enslaved Africans are denied an identity as equal claimants to human rights in the very texts that one might expect to champion the opposite view, since the very definition of the Western liberal subject stems from them.

Such passages destabilise the notion that the Enlightenment was characterised by a devotion to equality and freedom from prejudice. Travelling back to Britain, that sceptic and lion of the Enlightenment, Hume, appended what Brycchan Carey calls a 'notorious footnote to his essay "Of National Characters"':

> 'I am apt to suspect the Negroes to be naturally inferior to the whites [...] In JAMAICA, indeed, they talk of one negroe as a man of parts and learning; but it is likely he is admired for slender accomplishments, like a parrot, who speaks a few words plainly.' (quoted in Carey, *Rhetoric* 110; brackets and ellipsis in original)

Although Enlightenment philosophers presented an admirable fantasy of egalitarian society, free of prejudice and tyranny, they stumbled over their own racism. Here, yet again, is an ideological inversion born of the world of slavery.

Slavery as Enforced Life: The 'Breeding' of the Enslaved

In 'Necropolitics', Mbembe directs readerly attention to transatlantic slavery in his discussion of biopower in the modern epoch. First it is necessary to review Foucault's definition of biopower as essentially different from the sovereign's right to kill or let live in the previous episteme:

> Since the classical age the West has undergone a very profound transformation of these mechanisms of power ... 'Deduction' is no longer the main method of control, but only one element among others, working to incite, reinforce, control, monitor, optimize, and organize the forces under it: a power bent on generating forces, making them grow, and ordering them, rather than one dedicated to impeding them, making them submit, or destroying them. (*Sexuality* 136)

Although the influential concept of biopower is reconsidered by Agamben and Hannah Arendt with regard to the death camps of the Holocaust, they do not discuss the slave trade, rendering Mbembe's treatment of the topic essential. He proposes, 'Any historical account of the rise of modern terror needs to address slavery, which could be considered one of the first instances of biopolitical experimentation' (21). Mbembe focuses on the death toll of colonial slavery and the political regimes connected to it: 'My concern is those figures of sovereignty whose central project is not the struggle for autonomy but *the generalized instrumentalization of human existence and the material destruction of human bodies and populations*' (14; emphasis in original). I will build upon Mbembe's work to suggest that the deathly terror wielded by the slavers was often in the service of enforced life, the ultimate goal of the slave trade. In *The Afterlife of Reproductive Slavery: Biocapitalism and Black Feminism's Philosophy of History* (2019), Alys Eve Weinbaum also discusses biopower and modernity in terms that echo Mbembe's, but with a twist:

> Whereas sovereign power was exercised over individual lives through the ability to *make die*, biopower is exercised by dividing populations into those who are made to live and those who are left to die. For this reason, Foucault observes, biopower represents the entrance of life into the realm of politics. This entrance signals the emergence of the modern episteme with which, I have argued, the slave episteme ought to be regarded as concomitant and co-constitutive. (114–15; emphasis in original)

While Mbembe's focus is on the African populations who are 'left to die', Weinbaum and I focus on 'those who are made to live', especially enslaved populations, such that, she notes, 'slave women's wombs were routinely treated as valuable objects and as sources of financial speculation' (7). The murder of enslaved Africans and their descendants in the colonies was a common occurrence, but it was not the *raison d'être* of slavery; it was, rather, the opposite.

With this focus, I aim to help close a gap in thinking about Foucauldian biopower: its relation to slavery. Mbembe's 2003 call to address the issue of biopower in the transatlantic slave trade has not received much attention until the last couple of years, such as in Weinbaum's book and an issue of the journal *American Literature*, edited by Gwen Bergner and Zita Cristina Nunes. Bergner writes in the introductory essay,

> This reconsideration of the plantation heeds recent calls to challenge the omission of race in much current theory of biopolitics and bare life. As Alexander G. Weheliye ... and Zakiyyah Iman Jackson ... note, Michel Foucault's biopolitics and Giorgio Agamben's state of exception and bare life – arguably the predominant critical frameworks for analyzing state violence and inequality as constituent aspects of democratic formation – neglect the history and legacy of racialization, colonialism, and slavery. (447–8)

If biopower is distinguished from sovereign power in that it seeks to manage and increase life at the level of population, rather than to threaten death to those individuals who want to undermine sovereign power, then the transatlantic slave trade is the definitive example of its function as a foundation of modern society. Many enslaved people's lives were lost and a great number of those killings occurred in an effort to terrorise the rest of their brethren into living – into eating, 'breeding' and shunning suicide. Rather than a spasm of violence issuing forth unpremeditatedly, often such cruelty – what Rediker aptly terms 'studied terror' (303) – was calculated to instill a dread of disobedience in the enslaved. This system was the pre-eminent example of what Foucault calls 'a power that exerts a positive influence on life, that endeavors to administer, optimize, and multiply it, subjecting it to precise controls and comprehensive regulations' (*Sexuality* 137). The threat of a brutally violent death was just one method of controlling and maintaining the lives of the enslaved.

The inverted world of slavery made even life's pleasures abhorrent in the effort to maintain and increase life. That which sustains it, increases it – or simply makes it bearable and enjoyable, such as dancing and sex – became weaponised against the enslaved. As Hartman asks in *Scenes of Subjection: Terror, Slavery, and Self-Making in Nineteenth-Century America* (1997), 'How does one survive the common atrocities of slavery yet possess a ... confidence in the possibilities of freedom? It is hard to imagine possibility, let alone freedom, within the context of such fatal incommensurabilities: cruel whippings and courting, death and dance' (64). Indeed, for the enslaved on the slave ship, singing and dancing, normally great sources of pleasure, became forms of torture imposed on them to ensure their continued lives through exercise. Falconbridge, a surgeon on several slave-ship voyages and a strident abolitionist at the close of his sea-faring life, recounts the misery of such activities in *An Account of the Slave Trade on the Coast of Africa* (1788):

> Exercise being deemed necessary for the preservation of their health, they [i.e. the enslaved] are sometimes obliged to dance, when the weather will permit their coming on deck. If they go about it reluctantly, or do not move with agility, they are flogged; a person standing by them all the time with a cat-o'-nine-tails in his hand for that purpose.
>
> Their musick, upon these occasions, consists of a drum ... The poor wretches are frequently compelled to sing also; but when they do so, their songs are generally ... melancholy lamentations of their exile from their native country. (29–30)

This wretched activity is turned into poetry by Hannah More and Eaglesfield Smith in 'The Sorrows of Yamba', in lines spoken from the perspective of an enslaved woman:

> At the savage Captain's beck,
> Now like Brutes they make us prance;
> Smack the Cat about the Deck,
> And in scorn they bid us dance. (5; no line numbers given)

Activities that humans usually perform voluntarily and with delight, expressing life and extending it, are perverted into forms of torture intended to impose health upon unwilling participants in the world of slavery.

Similarly, sex was wielded by the slavers as a cruel tool to create more people born into the non-existence of slavery. Douglas (pseudonymously 'Britannicus') attested for the House of Commons inquiry into the slave trade in 1792, 'In some parts of America, the breeding of slaves was considered so *profitable*, that people *held them for this purpose alone*, independently of any prospect from the fruits of their labour; as we do cattle in this country' (83–4; emphasis in original). African women were chosen by slavers not only for work, but also – and perhaps especially – to ensure that they would bear children on the plantation. The truth of the claim is obvious when one considers how much stronger men generally are than women, and that the work of the enslaved in the British colonies was of the most physically demanding kind, including growing and harvesting sugar cane in the fierce heat of the West Indies; the slavers likely would not have chosen female Africans at all if it weren't for the slave-owners' wish to increase their number of workers by encouraging childbirth amongst the enslaved. Women, who generally numbered roughly a third to one-half of those 'stolen from Africa', to quote the great Jamaican singer Bob Marley (line 4), were chosen for their good health and strength, as were their male counterparts, with an added focus on the women's sexual attractiveness, presumably so that they would be desirable partners.[9] Some merchants gave specific instructions to their slave-ship captains regarding the type of African women they should buy: they insisted that the women be '"very black and handsome"', but they seem to have been more intent on avoiding certain physical characteristics, such as '"fallen-breasted Women"' or, as another merchant put it, '"Long Tripeish Breasts",' as well as '"Ugly faces"' and '"Navells sticking out"' (Rediker 193, 34). These physical characteristics are superfluous to the physical fitness of the enslaved women for work in the fields. They pertain to the women's sexual appeal, making them more likely to have many children – with or often without their consent.[10]

Nor were the slave-merchants only concerned about the African women's attractiveness to enslaved men, as it was common for British overseers and slave-owners to rape the enslaved women under their control, often for the express purpose of creating more enslaved people for the plantation or slave market. Robert Wedderburn's disgust at this practice is palpable in *The Horrors of Slavery; Exemplified in the Life and History of the Rev. Robert Wedderburn* (1824):

> My father ranged through the whole of his household for his own lewd purposes; for they being his personal property, cost nothing extra; and if any one proved with child – why, it was an acquisition which might one day fetch something in the market, like a horse or pig in Smithfield [, England] ... [H]is pleasure was the greater, because he at the same time increased his profits. (7)

Such slavers as Wedderburn's Scottish father, who was a sugar-cane plantation owner, would sell their own children into slavery. Although Wedderburn himself – whose mother was kidnapped from Africa and became enslaved on Wedderburn Sr's property – escaped this fate, the son's righteous anger at his father was not assuaged.

Other writers from the period are considerably more complacent about the practice of 'breeding' enslaved women. Before he decided slavery was against Christian principles, Whitfield – then a 'most energetic, and conspicuous, evangelical defender and practitioner of slavery' – wrote, '"Blessed be God for the increase of the negroes"' (Schlenther n.p.). The cold calculations of the pro-slavery writers on the 'breeding' of the enslaved is notable. Adopting the euphemistic cloak of the title 'West-India Planter', one slave-owner opines,

> two-thirds of males and one of females generally constitute the assortment of a Guinea-cargo. Now, as I conceive that women are at least as necessary to propagation as men, I would propose that this rule ... should be reversed; or at least that every Guinea-ship should bring as many females as males. (32)

Here is an explicit statement of the kind of calculations made in the system of biopower to ensure the generation of more bodies. Even those abolitionist writers who have historically been recognised as effective exponents of the anti-slavery cause, such as James Ramsay (Carey, *Rhetoric* 111, 130), advocate for the 'breeding' of enslaved women to ameliorate other evils of the slave trade. In *Objections to the Abolition of the Slave Trade, with Answers* (1788), Ramsay answers the pro-slavery objection that the enslaved 'are encouraged to rear children, and will not', by countering,

> How few are put in the state, have food, clothes, or necessaries, to encourage them, or are indulged when pregnant, or when nurses [i.e. nursing]? . . . Those acquainted with the usual treatment of slaves, may wonder how so many children are reared, rather than so few. Indeed, the ordinary causes of the increase of slaves on particular plantations, shew how easily population may be promoted. (72)

Elsewhere in the text, Ramsay refutes the statement that '*Free negroes and mulattoes do not increase from the births*' by arguing that the enslaved only need more abundant 'means of living' (77; emphasis in original), as well as that the abolition of the slave trade would '"make the breeding and preservation of slaves more an object of attention"' (16), without disparaging the notion of 'breeding' people as though they are livestock. Rather, he seems to recommend it as a desirable alternative to continuing the slave trade.

If one of the great eighteenth-century British abolitionists held such views, can we be surprised at the encomiums on 'breeding' the enslaved by such pro-slavery writers as one 'Mr Stewart', quoted by James MacQueen, regarding the situation in Jamaica? Speaking in 1824 of the changes that have occurred on colonial plantations since the end of the British slave trade in 1808, Stewart attests:

> 'Many or most of the old abuses are removed; punishments are more rare and far less severe; the Slaves are not worked at unreasonable hours ...; the Slaves are better fed, clothed, and lodged; ... and above all, the breeding women are carefully attended to, and receive every necessary indulgence and assistance: atrocious cases of cruelty are rarely heard of.' (305)

In short, because the enslaved were more difficult to obtain after the abolition of the slave trade, attention to increasing their number was intensified. Stewart and his ilk considered themselves caring managers of human lives and congratulated themselves on the wise husbandry of their property, revealing themselves to be devoted minor agents of bio-power. Guides to the topic abounded around the turn of the nineteenth century, notes Paula Dumas in *Proslavery Britain Fighting for Slavery in an Era of Abolition* (2016), such as the ever-popular *Instructions for the Treatment of Negroes* by Sir Phillip Gibbes, which went into three editions by 1797, and *Practical Rules for the Management and Medical Treatment of Negro Slaves, in the Sugar Colonies* (1803). Dumas comments that the anonymous author of the latter text 'covered numerous topics, including seasoning, diet, clothing, lodging, *reproduction*, labor, discipline, and religion, and provided specific advice on each' (83; my emphasis). Here, then, is slavery as enforced life. In this light, the massive loss of life that attended the slave trade may be considered as an all-too-common by-product of a cruel institution that aimed at its opposite.

Clarkson discusses the unique horror that was the 'breeding' of enslaved women with a tone of disgust in the text that made him famous, *An Essay on the Slavery and Commerce of the Human Species, Particularly the African; Translated from a Latin Dissertation, Which Was Honoured with the First Prize in the University of Cambridge, for the Year 1785* (1788). His concern over the practice is evident in the length at which he discusses it here, which I give in full in recognition of its aptness:

> There are some traders upon the coast, who have slaves in their possession, and who make a practice of breeding from these, as a grazier from his stock, for the purpose of selling them to others. They are brought up to a certain age, when they are reckoned saleable ...
>
> ... It frequently happens, that a woman is selected for sale, who has a child. The black trader never parts with the latter, but reserves it for a few years, till its age will insure him a certain price. This being an established rule, the unhappy mother is obliged to leave it behind. The parting is truly melancholy and affecting. No pen can pretend to describe it faithfully. Thus separated from her child, and sold into slavery, there are two calamities instantly to tear and afflict her mind; and if I may add a third, it must be in the thought that *she has been obliged to bring into the world, and give suck to a being, that lives only for the use of another*, and who in little time is to partake of her fate.
>
> As to the child, it has certainly a respite for some years. But for what is it reserved? Food is given to it, as to the young of an horse, to qualify it to become an instrument of labour. Melancholy consideration! To be obliged to eat and drink to support life, to be put only at last into *a situation in which it is pain to live* – to become the slave of an European. (114; my emphasis)

Clarkson emphasises the perversity of the 'breeding' of enslaved women like livestock as much as he considers the unique horror that such mothers endure through the practice. He also recognises that these children have been raised to endure a life of suffering, perfectly summarising my argument about slavery as enforced life and hinting at suicide as an obvious response to 'a situation in which it is pain to live' (114). In this way, the enforcement of life in the transatlantic slave trade was closely tied, even causally related, to suicide amongst the enslaved; ironically, biopower leads to suicide, its soundest retort. Later in the same volume, Clarkson states more directly that the state of slavery 'frequently drives them [the enslaved] to the horrid extremity of finishing their own existence' (202). Whereas death is usually viewed with horror, it became a welcome escape, a form of freedom, under colonial slavery – another of its perversities.

No white writer can comment on the 'breeding' of enslaved women with as much force as can a formerly enslaved woman, though. Mary Prince's mother lamented being forced to part with her children, including Prince herself, who would be sent away from her native Bermuda to work on another plantation on Turks Island: '"See, I am *shrouding* my poor children; what a task for a mother! ... I am going to carry my little chickens to market"' (15; emphasis in original). Prince's mother's comparison is fitting: she has been treated like breeding livestock, while her children will be sold and are doomed to a life of legal and existential death, or, likely, an early actual death. For enslaved women to bear children into slavery was to give them an existence permeated by death – to bring their babies into the inverted world of slavery.

Food as a Biopolitical Instrument of Enforced Life and Starvation as Insurrection

Another powerful instance of slavery as a system of enforced life revolved around the issue of eating, and the common rejection of food – usually such a great source of pleasure – by the enslaved. Significantly, the refusal to eat was the prime mode of rebellion for those kidnapped from Africa. Rediker comments:

> The Atlantic slave trade was, in many senses, a four-hundred-year hunger strike ... Because the captain's main charge from the merchant was to deliver as many live, healthy African bodies as possible to a New World port, anyone who refused sustenance ... endangered profits and subverted authority. Refusing to eat was therefore first and foremost an act of resistance. (285)

Moreover, on the slave ship, individual hunger strikes often led to mass starvation, as though the inclination to starve oneself were contagious. Of one African who starved himself, Rediker notes, 'Thus did an individual act of resistance spark a collective revolt and one form of resistance gave rise to another. The refusal to eat had led to a kind of martyrdom, to an insurrection, and, once that failed, to mass suicide' (264).

Some period writers saw starvation amongst the enslaved as a mark of what we would call 'depression' today, an interpretation that undermines its rebellious motivations, even though the effect was always subversive for the system of slavery. In his poem 'The Sailor Who Had Served in the Slave-Trade' (1798), Robert Southey tells the story of a former crew member of a 'Guinea-man' – a common term for the armed ships often enlisted for the slave trade with West Africa, then called 'Guinea' – who relates his guilty tale to a concerned minister. The sailor whipped an African woman to death when she refused to eat. However, his interpretation of the reasons for her self-starvation doesn't include rebellion:

> But some were sulky of the slaves,
> And would not touch their meat;
> So therefore we were forced by threats
> And blows to make them eat.
>
> One woman, sulkier than the rest,
> Would still refuse her food:
> O Jesus God! I hear her cries!
> I see her in her blood!
>
> The captain made me tie her up,
> And flog while he stood by;
> And then he cursed me if I stayed
> My hand to hear her cry. (69–80)

The speaker claims that he was forced into compelling the enslaved woman to eat in an intriguing account of the foundation of the slave trade upon the principles of both sovereign power and biopower: like a petty sovereign, the captain threatens the sailor with violence if he does not enforce the biopolitical imperative of ensuring the life of the enslaved woman by making her eat. The sailor's interpretation of the reason for her self-starvation, 'sulkiness', further undermines her agency. Southey, and other white abolitionist writers who depicted the self-starvation of the enslaved as an expression of their woe, sought to entice their audience with an image of victimhood: they present the enslaved as pitiful, helplessly wasting away, in need of benevolent mercy. Viewed thus, these victims were unthreatening to readers who might be so dismayed by the depiction of the enslaved as violent revolutionaries that they would be less likely to support the abolitionist movement.

Undeniably, some of the enslaved certainly starved themselves out of sheer despair. After all, even enslaved children sometimes refused to eat (Snyder, *Power* 39), and they are not likely to have been insurrectionist in their motivations. Equiano, a formerly enslaved Black person, writes of his own desolation as the cause of his suicidality as an enslaved boy in *The Interesting Narrative*: 'In this state I was constantly grieving and pining, and wishing for death rather than any thing else' (77). He suggests that the division between self-starvation from despair and obduracy is fluid and fine:

> I became so sick and low that I was not able to eat, nor had I the least desire to taste any thing. I now wished for the last friend, death, to relieve me; but soon, to my grief, two of the white men offered me eatables; and, on my refusing to eat, one of them held me fast by the hands, and laid me across I think the windlass, and tied my feet, while the other flogged me severely. (71)

Equiano attributes his self-starvation both to depression and uncooperativeness, showing that such suicidal (non-)action as avoiding food can have multiple motivations, even if the effect on slave society was always subversive.

Pro-slavery writers also often used such terms as 'sulkiness' and 'pining' to explain slave suicide. Since understanding slave suicide as resulting from depression divested it of its rebellious motive and the suicidal enslaved of agency, the slavers reasserted control through recourse to this explanation. They also implied that the enslaved had nothing to rebel against, so compassionately were they treated. In this way, proslavery writers defended a system that was increasingly under attack as the eighteenth century wore on and the abolitionist movement gained momentum. These writers commonly framed self-starvation as evidence that Africans required paternalistic treatment and the use of force was required because of it. In Planter's *West-India Trade and Islands. Commercial Reasons for the Non-abolition of the Slave Trade, in the West-India Islands, by a Planter. And Merchant* (1789), the euphemistically identified slaver writes that people of certain African nations are so lazy that they will starve to death if they are not forced to eat: 'The Eboe [or 'Igbo'] Nation ... are of the most indolent Nature ever formed, and whom the dread of the Lash alone prevents them from being poisoned with their own Sloth, as neither Interest or Reason can induce them to Work if they have the Choice of Starving' (16–17). This 'benevolent planter', to quote from the title of Thomas Bellamy's popular pro-slavery play of 1789, asserts that the slavers' paternalistic care saves the enslaved from another, more unusual means of death:

> There is also another Destruction more particularly confined to that Nation, termed the Jiggars, which arises from their natural Propensity of sitting on the Ground, which attracts that Insect, and their Indisposition to Action, suffers it to Penetrate so as to occasion the Amputation of a Limb. In such a Situation, what must be the poor Invalids [*sic*] fate? – He has no Master who considers it a Duty and his Interest to take Care of him. (17)

From this perspective, starvation is a danger not so much to the enslaved, but, rather, to the freed:

> the emancipated Negro, like those of Virginia, New York, &c. will die in the Streets, unprovided and unprotected; the Ground their wretched Bed, and the inclement sky their miserable Covering, no friendly Cott, Fuel, or Bannanah-Walk to call their own.
>
> How will they then execrate the Humane Law that so cruelly deprived them of all those Blessings, their contracted Ideas are able to enjoy; what employment is he capable of to obtain that Bread, held out to him by a careful and no Doubt an indulgent Master. (15)

The sheer audacity of such statements makes the text appear to be satirical – like Jonathan Swift's 'A Modest Proposal' (1729) for the abolition era – but it was certainly written in earnest. The gist of many pro-slavery texts like Planter's is that slavery is positive because it preserves and supports life amongst the enslaved: the very aim of biopower. Early in the tract, the anonymous writer asserts that 'barbarous as it may appear', slavery 'has been, and still is, the Preservation of Millions', since the 'Sovereign[s]' in African countries are so blood-thirsty that 'to sentence half his Subjects to an immediate Death' is often the result of a momentary whim (4). The author then concludes, 'Thus circumstanced, is not the Preservation of the Lives of Myriads a most laudable and praise-worthy Undertaking?' (4). Rediker mocks such declarations:

'The purchase of slaves was actually a humanitarian act because the unbought would routinely be slaughtered by their savage African captors. English slavers were saving lives!' (328). The pro-slavery side of the debate almost uniformly assumed that life is always good under every circumstance. Such texts provide valuable information about enforced life in the slave trade – or, at least, statements about its adherence to this principle.

When faced with undeniable facts, such as the ubiquity of slave suicide, pro-slavery writers tried to spin the topic in a way that would shift the blame. They sometimes suggested that slave suicidality occurred not as a response to the oppression of slavery, but because suicide was an inherent urge in certain African nations. Vincent Brown reports that William Beckford, slave-owner and author of the Gothic novel *Vathek* (1786), argued that 'suicide was a cultural problem, an ethnically specific practice. "The Eboe negroes," he explained, "are particularly addicted to suicide"' (183).[11] Writing on the early United States, Snyder comments on some writers' mystification over why death might be preferable to the torments of slavery: 'Early newspapers were ... at a loss to explain suicide by the enslaved', while some

> observers of slave self-destruction appealed to essentialism. They explained suicide as a predilection of newly imported slaves of a particular age or ethnicity rather than as a response to enslavement. Planters were counseled to avoid purchasing older slaves who were 'sullen and unteachable and frequently put an end to their own lives'. ('Memory' 48)

Blaming slave suicide on ethnicity and age was a way to divest the slavers of responsibility for the deaths. Brown continues:

> Henry Coor, who worked for fifteen years as a millwright in the Jamaican parish of Westmoreland, observed that unbearable workloads, physical punishment, and incessant hunger led many Africans to cut their own throats or hang themselves. 'I remember fourteen Slaves,' he told a British House of Commons committee in 1791, 'that it was generally said, and I believe it was, from bad treatment, that them [*sic*] rise in rebellion on a Sunday, who ran away into the woods, and all cut their own throats together.' (132)

Some facts were difficult to twist into a pro-slavery narrative.

Pro-slavery writers often tried to draw attention away from slave suicide altogether by painting life on the plantation as a state of ease and luxury, as does Boswell in the long poem *No Abolition of Slavery; Or the Universal Empire of Love: A Poem* (1791). Contrary to his friend Johnson, who famously toasted '"the next insurrection of the negroes in the West-Indies"' (quoted in Carey, *Rhetoric* 187 and Davis 398), Boswell was decidedly in favour of slavery. He writes,

> Lo then, in yonder fragrant isle
> Where Nature ever seems to smile,
> The cheerful *gang*! – the negroes see
> Perform the task of industry:
> Ev'n at their labour hear them sing,
> While time flies quick on downy wing;
> Finish'd the bus'ness of the day,
> No human beings are more gay:
> Of food, clothes, cleanly lodging sure,
> Each has his property secure;
> Their wives and children are protected,
> In sickness they are not neglected;
> And when old age brings a release,
> Their grateful days they end in peace. (241–54; emphasis in original)

Boswell invites the reader to view the spectacle of joy amongst the enslaved on the plantation, who live to a peaceful, apparently well-nourished old age, thanks to the beneficent slave-owners and plantation overseers. Here, then, is another pro-slavery approach to the issue of self-starvation amongst the enslaved: to pretend that it doesn't exist.

Not only did many slavers vehemently assert that they were charitable givers of life who protected and maintained the enslaved, partly through the provision of food, but they also presented themselves as providing sustenance to wider British society. These men called themselves not 'slave-masters' or 'plantation overseers', but 'planters', a euphemistic term that presents them as wholesome farmers, husbanding the land to provide life-giving products for society, making them essential contributors to the maximisation of life in Britain itself. The term also sorely misrepresents their most basic tasks, since these men had little or nothing to do with the actual planting of the land upon which their wealth depended.[12] The writer who identifies himself as 'Planter', author of the 1789 text mentioned above, echoes others of his kind who pretend that the products gained for British society by the plantation were wholesome necessities:

> Monies arising from such Sales are expended again here, or in our Sister Kingdoms, in numerous Articles, such as Beef, Pork, Butter, Cheese, Hams, Herrings, Porter, Soap, Candles, Ship Chandlery, and Dry Goods: Also Working Utensils of all Kinds, both for Agriculture and the Mechanic Arts, while our Stationary, Birmingham, Sheffield, Glass and Earthen-Ware, bear no small Part in our Exports. (10–11)

Notably absent from this list of salubrious products are sugar and rum, two of the main exports from the sugar-cane plantations in the British colonial West Indies, aptly known as the 'sugar colonies'.

We know now that the main product from the British West Indies – sugar – was unhealthy for Britons. More importantly, it was fatal to the enslaved. Radical pamphleteer William Fox takes aim at it in the title of his famous pamphlet *A Short Account of the African Slave Trade, and an Address to the People of Great Britain on the Propriety of Abstaining from West Indian Sugar and Rum* (1791). Along the same lines, in a passage that Carey calls a 'strong' 'attack' (*Rhetoric* 203), Coleridge castigates the virtue-signalling of many abolitionists in 'Lecture on the Slave-Trade' (1795):

> Had all the people who petitioned for the abolition of this execrable Commerce instead of bustling about and shewing off with all the vanity of pretended Sensibility, simply left off the use of Sugar and Rum, it is demonstrable that the Slave-merchants and Planters must either have applied to Parliament for the abolition of the Slave Trade or have suffered the West India Trade altogether to perish. (246)

Elsewhere in the 'Lecture', Coleridge states that 'nine millions of Slaves have been consumed by the Europeans' (246) – confirming metaphorically Equiano's childish fear that the slavers intended to eat the enslaved (70, 74) – and he refers to slave-grown produce as 'sweetened with the Blood of the Murdered' (248). The practice of using the enslaved to grow comestible products amounts to a kind of cannibalism, and these products are not even necessary for the consumers. As Coleridge implies, they are frivolous indulgences.

In opposition to these textual attacks on the reality of the slave trade, other literary productions continued to sugar-coat (pun intended) descriptions of the lives of the enslaved. Dumas notes that 'planters' procured poems for the 'enslaved laborers to sing while working the plantations to remind them of the benefits of their labor':

> How useful is labour, how healthful and so good!
> It keeps us from mischief, procures wholesome food;
> It saves from much sickness and loathsome disease
> That fall on the idle and pamper'd with ease. (89)

By focusing on the benefits that the enslaved gain from their labour – specifically, salubrious occupation and food – the verse obscures the real purpose of the work of the enslaved: to enrich the slavers, who only cared about the health of the former insofar as it supported such work. That the enslaved themselves were enjoined to recite these verses is tantamount to an attempt at Orwellian brainwashing – an early form of 'doublethink' – to make the victims of oppression celebrate their shackles in this system of enforced life.

Despite the slavers' best efforts to paint themselves as charitably supporting the lives of the supposedly helpless Africans they rescued from a savage land, white British abolitionists frequently attacked these claims and demonstrated the true significance of such actions as force-feeding the enslaved upon slave ships. William Roscoe addresses these enforcers of life in his bestselling abolitionist verse *The Wrongs of Africa, A Poem* (1787), using – unusually – blank verse to convey his message, thereby denying the reader the satisfaction of perfect end rhyme and leaving a sense of discomfort that echoes his theme. The following lines recognise the perversity of biopower – the tyrannical impulse not to kill, but to make live so that the enslaved may be delivered to a life of horror:

> Ye watchful guardians of the subject crew,
> That curse the lives ye cherish? 'Tis, we own,
> No common case, to shut the gates of death
> On those who wish to pass them; to retain
> Within its suffering bound, th' indignant soul
> That pants for freedom, as the hunted hart
> That seeks the coolness of the chrystal spring:
> And when the tyrant of the harmless flock,
> *That whilst he feeds them, destines them to death*,
> Is call'd humane, ye then may justly boast
> The glorious appellation: 'Tis enough
> Mean time for you, if life and health remain
> Amongst your captives, till they reach the shores
> Of those polluted Islands, that too soon
> Shall realize the evils which they dread. (26; no line numbers given, my emphasis)

Here is as apt a recognition of Foucauldian biopower as may be found in eighteenth-century literature, particularly in the statement that, through the provision of food, the ship's crew denies death to those who wish for it.

More and Eaglesfield Smith also use the image of self-starving enslaved people in their abolitionist poetry. 'The Sorrows of Yamba' repeats the sentiment of line five – 'Come, kind death! and give me rest' – as the poem's driving force, and it specifically targets the abusive response to the refusal of food as proof of the brutality that generates such a death wish in the first place:

> Nauseous horse beans they bring nigh,
>   Sick and sad we cannot eat;
> Cat must cure the Sulks they cry,
>   Down their throats we'll force the meat. (5; no lines given)

As a reference to the multiple-lashed whip called the 'cat o' nine tails', the 'Cat' resonates on several levels. As an antidote to depression that leads to the refusal of food by the enslaved, the whip symbolises the violent cruelty of the slaver, while the mention of its supposedly curative properties is an ironic recognition of the hypocritical messaging of the slave trade, which pretended both to diagnose and succor the enslaved through the use of torture. In this way, the whip is yet another of the slave trade's cruel technologies of enforced life.

Meanwhile, in a verse-protest entitled *Slavery, A Poem* (1788), More refers to another technology of enforced life on the slave ship, specifically the *speculum oris*, although this information is relegated to a footnote:

> When the sharp iron* wounds his inmost soul,
> And his strain'd eyes in burning anguish roll;
> Will the parch'd negro find, ere he expire,
> No pain in hunger, and no heat in fire? (173–6; asterisk in original as footnote marker)

More's footnote explains that she 'has seen a complete set of chains, fitted to every separate limb of these unhappy, innocent men; together with instruments for wrenching open the jaws, contrived with such ingenious cruelty as would shock the humanity of an inquisitor' (13). This tool is the *speculum oris*, described by Rediker as 'the long, thin mechanical contraption used to force open throats to receive gruel and hence sustenance' (17) (Figure 3.1). The instrument appears in other abolitionist literary works of the period, too, such as Cowper's 'Sweet Meat has Sour Sauce: or, the Slave Trader in the Dumps' (written in 1788, but not published until 1836), narrated by a slave-dealer bemoaning the potential end of his business. The verse presents an unsparing description of the *speculum oris* (along with other tortures inflicted on the enslaved) that contrasts uncomfortably with the poem's upbeat stanzaic form of three lines ending with perfect rhymes before a repeating chorus from a popular song: 'When a Negro his head from his victuals withdraws,/ And clenches his teeth and thrusts out his paws,/ Here's a notable engine to open his jaws,/ Which nobody [can deny], &c.' (22–5).[13] Meanwhile, James Stanfield's *The Guinea Voyage, A Poem in Three Books* (1789) depicts the *speculum oris* as one of the most salient manifestations of the brutality of slavery:

> Then: See the vile engines in the hateful cause
> Are plied relentless in the straining jaws
> The wrenching instruments with barbarous force
> Shew the detested food th' unwilling course. (quoted in Rediker 151)

This portrayal leaves no doubt that injury often resulted from the use of the *speculum oris*.

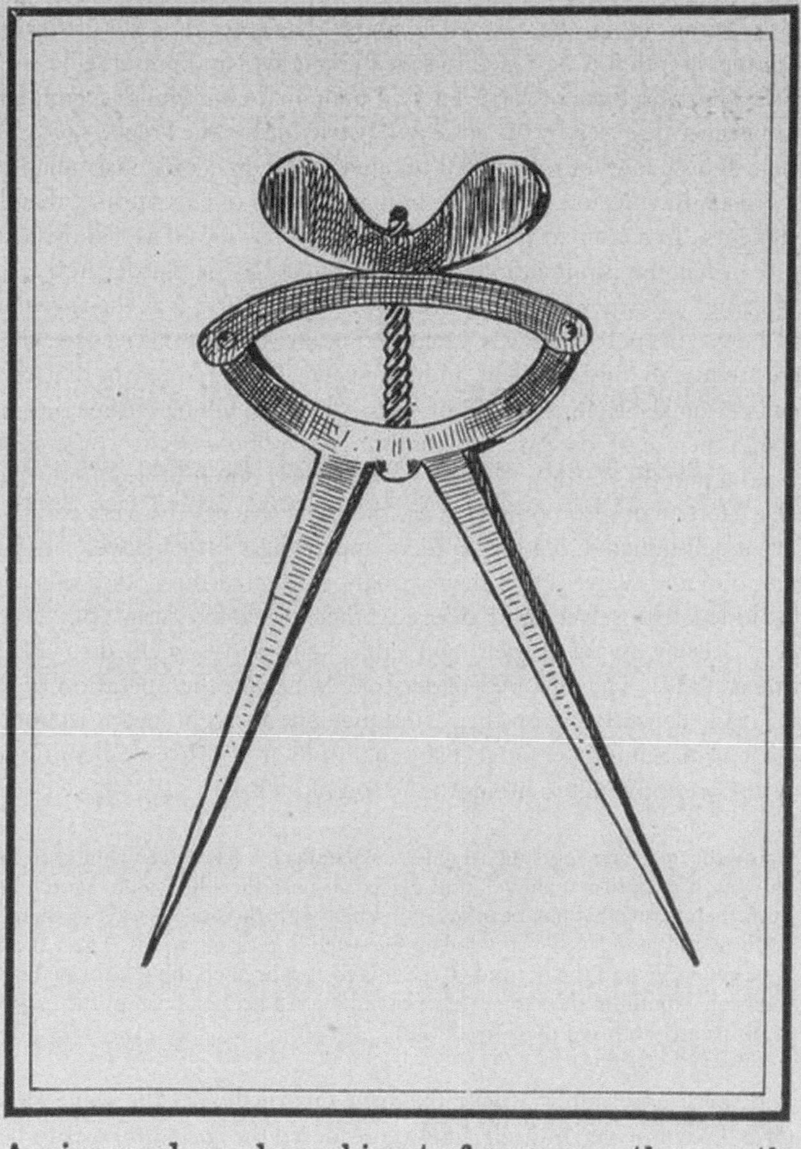

A vise used on slave ships to force open the mouths of slaves for feeding purposes.

Figure 3.1 *Speculum oris*, 1900. Available in the public domain via The New York Public Library

Particularly notable about the *speculum oris* are its medical origins, which betray yet another perversity about the inverted world of slavery: the profession that is designed to save human lives and preserve health is enlisted in the service of torturing and maiming, even while it maintains the existence despised by the enslaved. Analogously, the French physician Joseph-Ignace Guillotin invented the guillotine, the iconic instrument of the French Revolution, as a more humane means of execution. Mbembe comments, 'In a context in which decapitation is viewed as less demeaning than hanging, innovations in the technologies of murder aim ... at "civilizing" the ways of killing' (19). So, too, perhaps, was the *speculum oris* viewed as a civilised way of enforcing life, the alternatives to which were frequently more violent and agonising. Rediker reports that crew members on slave ships would often force the unwilling enslaved to eat through the use of 'the cat, the thumbscrews, a "bolus knife" or stick (to open the mouth), ... or a "horn" to force food down obstinate throats' (286). Hertzman also comments on the 'great lengths [slavers went] to prevent self-inflicted death': 'Traders and owners broke slaves' jaws to force food and water down their throats, mutilated the bodies of slaves who killed themselves, and devised other gruesome forms of "deterrence." Keenly aware of their own value, some slaves wielded suicide as a threat' (327). The enslaved understood well that the operation of the slave trade depended upon them, and they often sought means to undermine it at maximum personal cost – that of their very lives. Falconbridge describes yet other alternatives to the *speculum oris*:

> Upon the negroes refusing to take sustenance, I have seen coals of fire, glowing hot, put on a shovel, and placed so near their lips, as to scorch and burn them. And this has been accompanied with threats, or forcing them to swallow the coals, if they any longer persisted in refusing to eat. These means have generally had the desired effect. I have also been credibly informed, that a certain captain in the slave trade poured melted lead on such of the negroes as obstinately refused their food. (29)

Given these cruel alternatives, the surgeons on board the slave ships, such as Falconbridge himself, likely considered the *speculum oris* to be a preferable instrument to achieve the slave trade's goal to force as many kidnapped Africans to live as possible. To rephrase Mbembe's comment on the 'serialization of technical mechanisms for putting people to death' in the colonies (18), one might call the *speculum oris* a 'technical mechanism' for forcing people to live, a more civilised form of torture than many of the alternatives.

The *speculum oris* may be viewed as one way in which slavery perfected the technologies of enforced life that aimed at increasing subjects of colonial power, specifically by enlisting the practice of medicine in the cause. Unlike the captain, who managed the ship and its crew,[14] and the sailors, who had various jobs on board to keep the ship sailing, the slave-ship surgeon's chief task was to maintain the lives of the enslaved. He was therefore the embodiment of my point that, although many deaths occurred amongst the enslaved, the chief function of the trade in human flesh was to enforce life. While the *speculum oris* was, indeed, a veritable medical instrument and a technological advancement in comparison with hot coals, it was far from a harmless tool. It frequently caused serious damage not only to the 'soul' of the victim, as More suggests in *Slavery, A Poem* (173), but also to his or her soft tissue. Thomas Trotter, surgeon on the infamous slave ship *Brookes* – the subject of the best-known visual rendering of the stowage of the enslaved on slave-ships, published in 1788 (Figure 3.2) – details his treatment of an African who had bled profusely after cutting his own throat. Although Trotter closed the gash with stitches and wanted to force feed the enslaved man, he couldn't do so because the *speculum oris* would have reopened the throat wound (Rediker 17). In such ways these doctors, agents of biopower, became purveyors of death.

In a scene involving the torture of the enslaved who are forced to prepare food, Equiano points out the inevitability of suicide:

> I have seen a negro beaten till some of his bones were broken, for even letting a pot boil over. Is it surprising that usage like this should drive the poor creatures to despair, and make them seek a refuge in death from those evils which render their lives intolerable[?] …
>
> This they frequently do. A negro-man on board a vessel of my master, while I belonged to her, having been put in irons for some trifling misdemeanor, and kept in that state for some days, being weary of life, took an opportunity of jumping overboard into the sea; however, he was picked up without being drowned. Another, whose life was also a burden to him, resolved to starve himself to death, and refused to eat any victuals; this procured him a severe flogging: and he also, on the first occasion which offered, jumped overboard at Charles Town, but was saved. (123–4)

The irony that people tasked with preparing food to maintain the lives of the crew are tortured to the point of death, mentally and physically, is matched by Equiano's striking vocabulary in calling death an 'opportunity', thus framing it as salvation from the burden of life under slavery. Finding himself in the same situation, Equiano details his own suicidality several times in his memoir, such as in the passage describing the ship's cargo hold, where the enslaved were held. 'With the loathsomeness of the stench, and crying together', Equiano writes, he became so physically and mentally ill that he refused to eat (71). This description

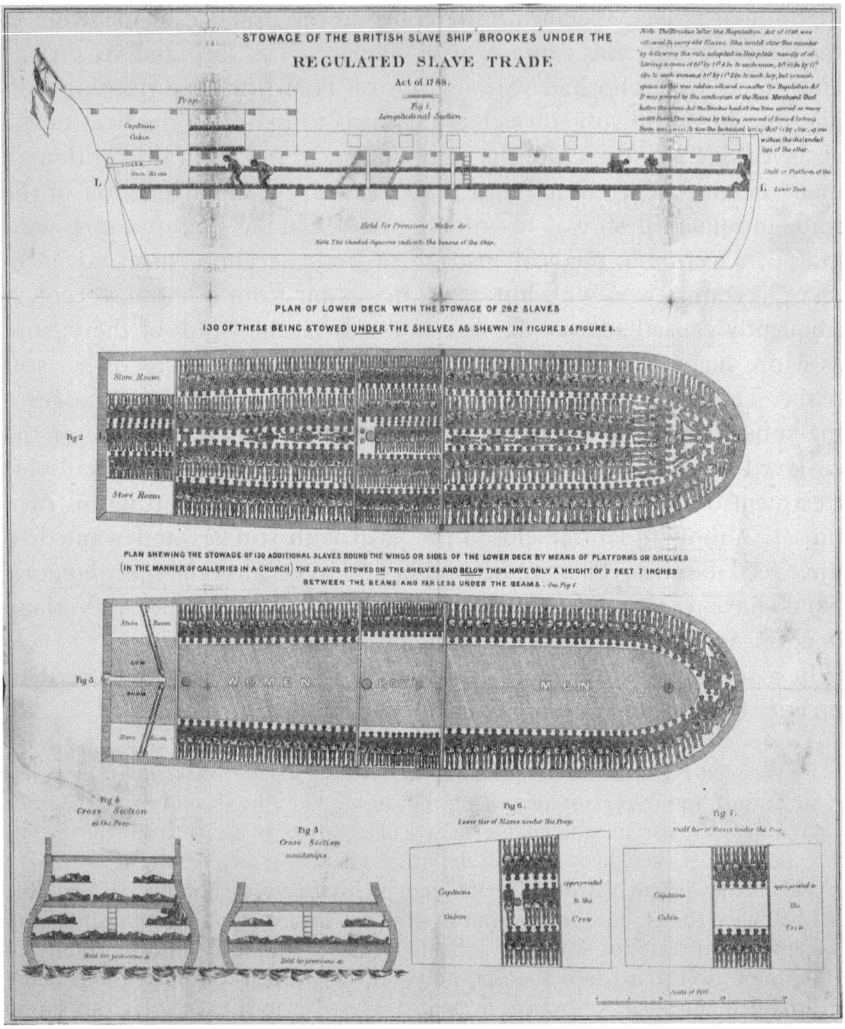

Figure 3.2 The slave ship *Brookes*, 1808. Available in the public domain via Library Company of Philadelphia

frames self-starvation as a reasonable response to an intolerable existence. Nor does Equiano's depiction of his pitiful state lessen his power as an author or the subversive resonances of his claims to the right to die: just as slave suicide always undermined the biopolitical regime of transatlantic slavery, leaving aside the individual suicide's intention, the slave memoir announces the author's place in intellectual circles of authors and presents his life as textual, ideal, a substitution for the subjugated body managed by biopower. In his memoir, Equiano 'take[s his] … flesh-and-blood reality away' (Blanchot 322) from the British public for whom it is written, and which was enriched by the same biopolitical system of slavery against which he writes, and replaces it with a text of abolitionist protest, a gesture to suicidal freedom.

Of Flying Africans and Culture Loss

Sometimes slave suicide was framed as productive of a new, positive state, rather than only a denial of the negative state of subjugation. Commenting on the common belief amongst the enslaved that they would fly home to their native land after death, Daniel Walker relates it to slave suicidality and subversion:

> Although suicide was one of the most visible manifestations of the slave's desire to hasten their spiritual and physical return to Africa, this belief also caused many African slaves to possess a noticeable contempt for death. This disposition formed the basis of many of the insurrections that occurred in the New World. With respect to the Haitian Revolution, it has continually been remarked that the African-born rebel leaders used the transmigration belief to rally their troops against the French. (13)

The belief in transmigration to Africa was far from short-lived, Snyder reports: 'As early as 1693, Captain Thomas Phillips recorded that slaves drowned or starved themselves because they believed that upon death they would transmigrate to Africa and rejoin their ancestors. As late as 1823, a Jamaican planter noted that the enslaved universally shared in this belief' (*Power* 36). Equiano also recognises this belief amongst Africans: 'I do not remember to have ever heard of it: some however believe in the transmigration of souls in a certain degree' (54). Even Zora Neale Hurston, a twentieth-century Black American writer, references it in *Their Eyes Were Watching God* (1937): one Black character says to another, 'If Ah never see you no mo' on earth, Ah'll meet you in Africa' (156). Across cultures, flying represents freedom for earthbound humans encumbered by gravity. The belief in the so-called 'flying African' is an ideal revolution, then: death is recast as freedom and suicide as the inversion of slavery. Through this belief, the enslaved who rebelled against the regime of enforced life through suicide created a new life for themselves.

The 'flying African' belief was so well known that even white people outside of the slave trade were familiar with it.[15] Upon first entering Jesus College at Cambridge University, Coleridge wrote on the theme in an anti-slavery poem, 'The Wretched Lot of the Slaves in the Islands of West India', which won the Sir William Browne gold medal in 1792

(Thomas 89). To invest the topic of slavery with the dignity and intellectualism of classical scholarship, Coleridge originally wrote the ode in classical Greek, thereafter translating a few lines of it in 1796. James Basker gives a complete translation of the text by classicist Stephen Marsh in *Amazing Grace: An Anthology of Poems about Slavery, 1660–1810* (2002). The lines are spoken from the perspective of an enslaved person wishing for death:

> O DEATH, now leave the gates of dark,
> And haste thee to a doom-bound folk.
> No nail-rent face will greet thee there,
> Nor cries of woe.
>
> But circles of the merry dance,
> And joyful leapings: feared art thou,
> But dwell'st withal with freedom fair,
> Harsh tyrant thou.
>
> I would take wing with thee to fly
> Through rugged Ocean's massy swell,
> To seats beloved of pleasures rare,
> Where I was born.
>
> There lovers tell their mistress sooth
> 'Neath fountains by the citron groves
> What mortal man to man can do,
> Such frightful things. (1–16)

The immortal place to which the speaker wishes to fly after death is clearly Africa itself, rendering Coleridge's ode an extraordinarily complete early poetic treatment of the 'flying African' myth in British literature. That the poet opens his ode with a reference to the myth moreover testifies to its importance in Coleridge's envisioning of the mental state of the enslaved, as does the fact that the only lines the poet translated into English are these ones.[16] Coleridge's interest in the slave trade was longstanding. Basker comments that, although his pursuit of the topic was 'kindled while he was still a student at Cambridge, which was a seedbed for abolitionists in the late eighteenth century (Clarkson, Wilberforce, and Wordsworth were all Cambridge graduates,) ... Coleridge never lost his antislavery fervor ... Coleridge wrote magazine articles and gave public lectures against slavery', even 'writing private letters in support of the abolitionist cause' up to 'the last year of his life' (446). He did so at some personal cost, too, according to Helen Thomas, who notes that the political climate following 1792 was one of 'suspicion and fear under the Pitt government, [meaning that] Coleridge's lecture [of 1795] took place at a time when "abolitionism" had begun to lose respectability' (89). Although Coleridge's poem might be branded as culturally appropriative today, as the white poet adopts the beliefs and perspective of an African for his speaker, he uses the trope to inspire respect and concern for Africans, whom he describes as clinging to hope and love for home even in death.

As common as the 'flying African' belief may have been, though, it should not be concluded that the native cultures of the enslaved supported suicide. Pabst Battin reveals that 'Suicide, except under certain peculiar circumstances, was formerly regarded in Ashanti as a *capital sin*. It was a sin of which the central authority took immediate cognizance' (598; emphasis in original). The change in traditional beliefs and culture under the unimaginable pressures of slavery is just one of the multitudinous ways in which the institution damaged the Africans forced into it. Slavers carefully divorced the enslaved from their native cultures, languages and identities to destroy their spirits and their will to assert themselves against their oppressors.[17] If 'society' – the stable basis out of which culture forms – signifies, at least in part, a group of people unified by the organisation of a single leadership, system and laws, then the enslaved were kept in a state of society-lessness, or social chaos, after being divorced from their native societies.

The social death that was slavery was doubly negative: not only did slavery divorce the enslaved from their culture, but it also rendered the lives affected by it lost to history. In many ways, the authentic experience of the enslaved is unrecoverable because their narratives were crafted for a largely white British audience and forced into the Procrustean bed of white genres, such as the memoir, travelogue or salvation narrative. Frantz Fanon writes in *Black Skin, White Masks* (French original 1952; English translation 1967) that simply speaking in the tongue of the colonial oppressor is an element of the Black 'man's comprehension of the dimension of *the other*' and his 'assum[ing] a culture' that is not his own puts him at odds with himself (17). As for the writing of history, Marcus Wood comments:

> The experience of the slaves is, in a very real sense, lost to the conventional resources of historical reconstruction. The evidence, and the historiography, and even the mythography, of slavery is consequently very one-sided, and comes out of a series of white records. When black authors decide to go back into the history of slavery, they still usually find themselves dependent on white sources, white propagandas, white journalisms, white theory as a starting point. (9)

British scholarly history was originally established by writers of European descent who were trained in a system that was dominated by those like them, and these circumstances have produced a rigid set of expectations, writing styles, and canons that have suppressed and often lost the voices of non-white people. Hertzman recognises 'the tension between pursuing the goal of "recovering archival traces of black life" and accepting "the archive as a site of irrevocable silence that reproduces the racial hierarchies intrinsic to its construction"', and he quotes Lisa Lowe's powerful reminder that 'any attempt to recover voices lost to slavery and the Middle Passage must be understood "within the limits of an archive that authorizes knowledge ... in terms of particular interests – those of slave owners and citizens, and not the enslaved"' (322). The pernicious effects of the slave trade on Western culture are evident even today.

Divorced from their native cultures and thrust into a world of utter mayhem – one that was devoid of a basic framework for rebuilding themselves and their culture – the enslaved were kept in a state that was ripe for suicidality. Although most Black cultures in the British transatlantic colonies would eventually thrive despite slavery, they did so against all odds. One of the first ways in which the enslaved formed a new identity was through rebellion. Rediker asserts,

> nothing was more important to the collective project of creating a group identity than resistance. This was a new language, a language of action employed every time people refused food, jumped over the side of the ship, or rose up in insurrection ... [It all] rejected enslavement and social death as it embraced creativity and a different future. (285)

Viewed thus, slave suicide was a form of identity-making – an assertion of independence from the cultural void of slavery.

The Literary Trope of Slave Suicide: A Mark of the Human or Fantasy of White Power?

Clarkson describes yet another technology for the preservation of life amongst the enslaved – the complicated and expensive system of netting around slave ships – even as he demonstrates the frequent use to which abolitionist writers like him put the concept of slave suicide, that is, to emphasise common humanity:

> The Africans, possessing equal sensibility and the like passions with the rest of the human race, are acted upon in the same manner.
>
> An effect of their situation, discoverable in some of them, is suicide, which is effected in various ways.
>
> Many of them, on the first opportunity that presents itself, leap overboard with a determination to put a period to their lives. These attempts

> are so frequent, and so much expected, that most of the vessels have netting or lattice-work of sticks from their decks up to their leading blocks. Notwithstanding this, many have accomplished their ends, and have found an asylum either in the mouths of sharks, or in the beds of their native rivers. (152)

With the mention of sharks, Clarkson raises the spectre of the terror that existed just beyond most slave ships. Several anti-slavery writers, such as Falconbridge, mention sharks as constant companions on the Middle Passage (e.g. 39), but Clarkson's reference is particularly striking for the way in which he links it to the issue of slave suicide. The implication is that the terror and pain upon the ship itself must have been great for anyone to choose death-by-shark as a sanctuary from life aboard the slave ship. With the addition of suicide netting, the vessels would be immediately recognisable and distinguished from all other ships, making it the visual declaration of the importance of suicide to the slave trade.

Clarkson's assertion that Africans are equal in sensibility to everyone else in the human race, linked with the topic of slave suicide, enunciates one of the most common uses of the topic in abolitionist writing: as proof of the humanity of the enslaved. As I have demonstrated elsewhere in this study, although suicide was regarded as sinful and selfish in many British texts throughout the long eighteenth century, the abolitionist treatment of slave suicide highlights its positive association with the characteristics that mark the human as precisely that: human.[18] Nor is this view of humankind necessarily a feature of post-Enlightenment thinking: in *Lifes Preservative Against Self-Killing* from 1637, Sym comments, 'From the consideration of self-murder we may observe: first, that man stands in more danger of destruction than any other creature. For, no creature is subject to attempts against the life of it, by itself, but only man' (297). Suicide was often associated with strong sensitivity – even sensibility – and emotion, long viewed as the marks of the feeling human being, as opposed to the so-called 'brute' animal, traditionally assumed to have no emotions. Wollstonecraft's famous opening salvo in *Rights of Woman* illustrates the common Enlightenment view that 'reason' differentiates the human from the animal ('In what does man's pre-eminence over the brute creation consist? The answer is as clear as that a half is less that the whole; in Reason' (117)); another interpretation of our difference from non-human animals may be found in the pages of abolitionist literature, where emotions so strong that they lead to suicide are frequently associated with the condition of being human. Goethe's hit sentimental novel *The Sorrows of Young Werther* and Rousseau's *Julie* popularised the perception of suicide as the mark of the sensitive person for the British public, who may have therefore been more receptive to the notion of slave suicide as a proof of African fine feeling in abolitionist texts. Alternatively, it is also possible that abolitionist texts paved the way for the British reader's reception of suicidality as a mark of sensibility in these foreign novels, Shapiro argues (*passim*). Such texts argue implicitly that Africans are equal to Europeans in feeling, manifested in suicide, to ensure the reader's sympathy for the victims of the slave trade.

By denying the humanity of the enslaved, slavers squared their treatment of the victims of the trade with their consciences and the Christian injunction to care for fellow humans. Clarkson combines the Enlightenment view of what makes a human distinctly human (reason) with the definition of the human linked to the culture of sensibility (sensitivity, feeling and emotion) in a celebrated passage that appeals to the religious awareness of his audience. He asks:

> in what volume of nature or religion is it written, that one society of men should *breed slaves* for the benefit of another? Nor is it less evident that they [Africans] would have wanted many of those qualities which they have, and which brutes have not: they would have wanted that *spirit of liberty*, that *sense of ignominy and shame*, which so frequently drives them to the horrid extremity of finishing their own existence. Nor would they have been endowed with a *contemplative power*; for such a power would have been unnecessary to people in such a situation; or rather, its only use could have been to increase their pain. We cannot suppose therefore that God has made an order of beings, with such mental qualities and powers, for the sole purpose of being used as *beasts*, or *instruments of labour*. (201–2; emphasis in original)

The motivations for suicide, such as shame, are what distinguish humans from animals. Having established the humanity of the enslaved on the basis of suicide, Clarkson contends that Africans have 'contemplative power', or what Wollstonecraft calls 'Reason'. The Christian basis for Clarkson's argument is a vital aspect of his humanising plea for readerly sympathy. Likewise, in his *Interesting Narrative*, Equiano demands, 'O, ye nominal Christians! might not an African ask you, learned you this [i.e. cruelty to the enslaved] from your God, who says unto you, Do unto all men as you would men should do unto you?' (75–6). As an African,[19] Equiano uses Christianity to underscore the humanity of his countrymen in several ways: writing about Christian teachings, he reveals his own religious fervour, closely connected to popular ideas of feeling and emotion at the time.

Ignatius Sancho discusses neither slavery nor slave suicide at length in his famous letters, even though he was born into slavery and brought from Cartagena, Colombia, to Britain as a toddler, while 'his father defeated the miseries of slavery by an act of suicide', according to Sancho's editor, Frances Crewe (49). Nevertheless, in one of Sancho's most direct references to slavery, he challenges the common association of Christianity with benevolence:

> In Africa, the poor wretched natives – blessed with the most fertile and luxuriant soil – are rendered so much the more miserable for what Providence meant as a blessing: – the Christians' abominable traffic for slaves – and the horrid cruelty and treachery of the petty Kings – encouraged by their Christian customers – who carry them strong liquors – to enflame their national madness – and powder – and bad fire-arms – to furnish them with the hellish means of killing and kidnapping. – But enough – it is a subject that sours my blood – and I am sure will not please the friendly bent of your social affections. – I mentioned these only to guard my friend against being too hasty in condemning the knavery of a people who bad as they may be – possibly – were made worse – by their Christian visitors. – Make human nature thy study – wherever thou residest – whatever the religion – or the complexion – study their hearts. – Simplicity, kindness, and charity be thy guide – with these even Savages will respect you – and God will bless you! (188)

Sancho notes that what constitutes humanity is not dependent upon a certain religion to be worthy of study, and implies that Christianity does not erase the evil of the British slavers. Consequently, the non-Christian identity of the Africans does not serve as a reliable guide to their sensibility. In this way, Sancho attempts to destabilise the common association of strong sensibility with Christianity.

One of the chief ways that literature by the formerly enslaved seeks to convey their humanity is through depictions of their suicidality as a mark of sensibility. Here is what Sidonie Smith characterises as the 'controlled distance between' the memoirist's self 'in the present as writer and himself [or herself] in the past as protagonist' (11), for slave memoirists organise their memories of utter despair in a now-fruitful way – to convince readers of the evils of slavery by enlisting their sympathy. As Laura Murphy points out, the 'slave narrative is a genre driven … [and] defined by its ambition, its desire to affect an audience' (11) in the cause of anti-slavery. Equiano's description of his suicidality fits this mould, to be sure, as does Prince's in the most heart-rending terms. Writing of her experiences as an enslaved girl, Prince prepares the reader to interpret her suicidality as an extension of her strong emotional response to her situation by describing her despair over the cruelty she endured: 'It was then … my heavy lot to weep, weep, weep, and that for years; to pass from one … misery to another, and from one cruel master to a worse', including one who flogged her continually, until, she writes, 'I was so sore with the flogging, that I scarcely cared whether I lived or died' (20, 21). At some point, she felt she was at the end of her life, one way or the other: 'I was in a dreadful state – my body all blood and bruises, and I could not help moaning piteously. The other slaves, when they saw me, shook their heads and said, "Poor child! poor child!" – I lay there till the morning, careless of what might happen, for life was very weak in me, and I wished more than ever to die', adding a few lines later, 'I was weary of my life' (22). In addition to presenting herself as full of despondent emotion to the point of suicidality, Prince also implicitly argues for the sensibility of the enslaved by describing the sympathetic reaction of her fellows in slavery.

Such depictions of Black sensibility oppose what Schuller has described as the biopolitical purpose of the aesthetic of sensibility in the nineteenth century:

> Sentimentalism, in its function as an aesthetic mode, epistemology, and ontology, was deployed to intercede in the impressibility of the civilized body by cultivating the ability to respond to sensory stimulations on the basis of emotional reflection, rather than instinctive reflex. Together, impressibility and sentimentalism distinguished civilized bodies as receptive to their milieu and able to discipline their sensory susceptibility and as such in possession of life and vitality that required protection from the threat posed by primitive bodies deemed to be impulsive and insensate, incapable of evolutionary change, whose existence was very close to running out of time. (Schuller 4)

Black bodies were cast as insensate, marked as incapable of the civilising quality of sensibility claimed by white culture. For example, MacQueen describes the practice of branding in the West Indian colonies as 'necessary to mark the initials of their master's name on some conspicuous part of the body' and claims, absurdly, that 'the operation, physicians state, occasioned scarcely any pain' (255). By recalling memories of past bodily suffering and organising them into passages meant to stimulate feelings of sympathy in the reader, these Black memoirists claim their place in the supposedly civilised realm of sensibility.

Prince's depiction of the kindness of the enslaved forms a stark contrast to heartlessness of the white people in her world. Writing of her new place of enslavement, Prince comments, 'The house was large, and built at the bottom of a very high hill; ... The stones and the timber were the best things in it; they were not so hard as the hearts of the owners' (17). More striking still is Prince's moving portrayal of her youthful feelings when she was displayed for sale alongside her siblings and accompanied by her weeping mother, in contrast with the unconcerned attitude of the white onlookers:

> My heart throbbed with grief and terror so violently, that I pressed my hands quite tightly across my breast, but I could not keep it still, and it continued

> to leap as though it would burst out of my body. But who cared for that? Did one of the many by-standers, who were looking at us so carelessly, think of the pain that wrung the hearts of the negro woman and her young ones? No, no! They were not all bad, I dare say, but slavery hardens white people's hearts towards the blacks; and many of them were not slow to make their remarks upon us aloud, without regard to our grief – though their light words fell like cayenne on the fresh wounds of our hearts. Oh those white people have small hearts who can only feel for themselves. (15–16)

Prince challenges the common British association between whiteness and sensitivity in such passages. Lee notes that she 'establishes ... an ethical relationship between self and other' (42), and she does it on her own terms: while such a bid for sympathy by white abolitionists risks subjugating the enslaved textually, as I will discuss in greater detail hereafter, memoirs by the formerly enslaved differ essentially in their affordance of control over the story to the writer, who is able to create a vastly different identity for themselves from their historical pasts. As Paquet writes in *Caribbean Autobiography* (2002), 'In the case of Mary Prince, literary agency is achieved in exile with the publication of her life story as discourse defining slave narrative' (28), rendering her memoirs an act of defiance and self-definition.

In the annals of white abolitionist literature, one of the favoured modes of enlisting readerly sympathy for the enslaved is by depicting their suicidality; but this message is often problematised by the self-serving message about white power it simultaneously conveys. While the claim to sensibility in literature can function as the Black writer's claim to humanity in their own texts, a predatory dynamic emerges in the hands of white writers, such that the author can appear to claim the coveted badge of sensibility by using the theme of the tormented Black body for their own ends. Such texts thereby confirm the status quo of white power versus Black subjugation. Some works suggest that that the enslaved are so unwaveringly faithful that they would rather choose to die than betray, be separated from or be unappreciated by their white owners, whose appearance of power increases accordingly. Maria Edgeworth's poem 'The Grateful Negro' (1802) is a case in point. In a discussion of her source for this tale about a benevolent planter, Edgeworth cites *History of Jamaica*, the author of which 'says that most of the Planters are humane' (172n). However, Edward Long, not Bryan Edwards (as Edgeworth would have it), published that text in three volumes in 1774. Edwards's most famous publication is *The History, Civil and Commercial, of the British West Indies* (1793), which Edgeworth mentions on the following page (173n). Edgeworth admits her belief in Edwards's claim regarding his own kindness to the enslaved under his power (173), a notion that supports the fiction she presents: that the enslaved are thankful for the beneficence of their white oppressors. In this so-called 'popular tale', Edgeworth portrays Edwards himself and an enslaved man named 'Caesar'. Caesar is torn between loyalty to his old 'Koromantyn[ ]' friend, Hector, who wants to lead a slave rebellion against Edwards, and Edwards himself, to whom Caesar is utterly devoted (184, 183). To resolve these competing loyalties, Caesar decides to kill himself: 'no sooner was Mr. Edwards out of sight than he knelt down, and, in a transport of gratitude, swore that, with this knife, he would stab himself to the heart, sooner than betray his master!' (197). Apparently, Edgeworth wishes to convey the sensitivity of the enslaved through Caesar's suicide, but she also satisfies the white British reader's fantasy of power by expressing the colonial dream that white ownership of the enslaved is appreciated and even savoured by the dependent Black person, who cannot live without the paternalistic 'planter's' care.[20] Such narratives often claim sympathy for the enslaved – and, indeed, Edgeworth's does so explicitly – but they also perpetuate the fiction of African inferiority and dependence upon which slavery is based.

This fantasy is most famously represented in the oft-repeated tale of the suicidal Quashi. Katherine Gaudet summarises the Quashi tale:

> In a story that was especially widely known and retold, a slave named Quashi shows his extraordinary virtue by running away to avoid the ignominy of whipping. When caught, Quashi chooses to kill himself rather than his master, thus escaping both the indignities of slavery and the taint of savagery that smeared rebelling slaves. (603)

The tale peddles the notion that Quashi sees his unblemished Black skin as representative of his relatively high status as an enslaved man. However, the fact that Quashi feels compelled to kill himself to maintain his skin in its original state demonstrates that he is, indeed, entirely in the power of his white oppressor, whose decision it is whether Quashi's skin be razed or, in effect, if Quashi die to protect it. Ramsay's original telling of the tale highlights its problematic qualities. After Quashi is condemned to be whipped by his 'master' for some minor offence, the two accidentally meet in the plantation's fields and end up struggling:

> Quashi got firmly seated on his master's breast, ... and with his weight, his thighs, and one hand, secured him motionless. He then drew out a sharp knife, and while the other lay in dreadful expectation, helpless, and shrinking into himself, he thus addressed him. 'Master, I was bred up with you from a child; I was your play-mate when a boy; I have loved you as myself; your interest has been my study; I am innocent of the cause of your suspicion; had I been guilty, my attachment to you might have pleaded for

> me. Yet you have condemned me to a punishment, of which I must ever have borne the disgraceful marks; thus only can I avoid them.' With these words, he drew the knife with all his strength across his own throat, and fell down dead without a groan, on his master, bathing him in his blood ... This is a truly mournful instance of a nobleness and grandeur of mind in a negroe. (*Essay* 252–3)

What Ramsay and so many other white British writers interpret as dignity and honourableness appear to a contemporary reader to be, rather, a kind of self-hatred and a lack of reasonable self-protectiveness in the face of utter subjugation. It is as though Quashi is himself convinced of the righteousness of the system of slavery as an expression of total white control over the Black body. Quashi refuses to murder his 'master' – whom Elizabeth Sophia Tomlins calls 'Alvaro', a 'Castilian', in her poetic retelling of the tale in 'The Slave' from 1797 (88; no line numbers given) – when he has the opportunity to enact this fully defensible response to his untenable situation. Clearly, what is more important than African dignity to the white purveyors of this story is the notion of unchallenged colonial control over the enslaved.

Many historians and critics recognise that long-eighteenth-century writers presented the Quashi tale as an abolitionist claim to African worth (Snyder, *Power* 111; Bell, 'Problem' 534; Ferguson 242), while some have noted that such tales confirm notions of Black people's inferiority (Snyder, *Power* 119). I go further to claim that the Quashi tale endorses fantasies of white power over the Black body. A more logical *dénouement* to the narrative would have included the spectacle of a dying slaver, but Tomlins avoids it in favour of showing the African's bleeding body at the end of the tale. Indeed, Tomlins's versified version of the story in 'The Slave' even teases the reader with the promise of Quashi's justifiably murderous response to his oppression and gives him words that promise warranted retribution for the wrongs against the enslaved, only to deny this conclusion. The eponymous 'Slave' himself intones,

> 'Think on the guiltless Millions, now no more,
> Whose ghosts yet hov'ring on the dreary shore,
> In sad procession strike these aching eyes,
> And bid, with all her daggers, Vengeance rise.
> Yes, injur'd Countrymen! this heart can glow,
> This hand, yet undishonour'd, deals the blow:
> This arm shall strike, this heart shall cease to groan,
> And EUROPE'S dastard Sons the great revenge shall own!'
> So spoke the Slave – and, Weep ye few who feel!
> In *his own gen'rous breast* he plung'd the steel. (100–1; no line numbers given; emphasis in original)

How this enslaved man's self-killing can be vengeance for the wrongs of slavery is entirely unclear, as Tomlins makes no other reference to the revolutionary significance of slave suicide. What is clear, from the poet's italicisation of the final line of this passage, is her recognition that this conclusion is unexpected, if not completely illogical, given what precedes it. She therefore feels compelled to emphasise the actual ending through special formatting – as though the reader might misunderstand it and believe the tale has concluded in a more plausible way (with Quashi killing Alvaro) if she does not draw attention to the absurd finale.

Notably, too, until the very last lines of the poem, Tomlins withholds Quashi's name, calling him 'the Slave' and even using the phrase as the title of the poem. With a nod to the fame of the Quashi tale for an eighteenth-century British audience, Tomlins writes from the perspective of personified Fancy,

> 'Here QUASHI lies!' – for no fictitious name
> Shall rob the injur'd Hero of his fame:
> 'Here QUASHI lies! whom Fate ordain'd a Slave,
> Whom Nature form'd just, generous and brave.
> Of Honour spotless, and of spotless Truth,
> He fell yet blooming in the days of Youth. (101; quotation marks in original)

This dramatic revelation of 'the Slave's' name as 'Quashi' at this late point in the narrative supposedly defends the glory of the 'injur'd Hero' and announces the poet's sympathy with the enslaved.[21] The belated revelation gives Tomlins the opportunity to term Quashi 'the Slave' throughout the poem, constantly reiterating his subordinate position – and suggesting that he is ontologically a slave, for, as the poem would have it, 'Fate', rather than slavers, 'ordain'd [him] a Slave'. Tomlins even attempts to forestall readerly confusion by providing an interpretation of the significance of Quashi's suicide herself: these lines announce that his character is thoroughly admirable (he is 'generous and brave'). The subsequent passage tells the eighteenth-century reader what else to conclude from this odd tale:

> No gleam of true Religion, to controul
> The wild, though noble, passions of his Soul,
> With his own hand he broke Life's galling chain,
> – Not that he fled from labour, and from pain,
> Not that he sunk beneath th' oppressive load. (102)

The message is that his suicide is excusable, although tragic, because he didn't have the benefit of Christian teachings against it. Although the lines seek to rescue the character from accusations of laziness and cowardice as motivations for choosing death, notably missing here is the implication that Quashi's suicide could be rebellious.

Perhaps the didactic last four lines of Tomlins's poem summarise the cultural significance of the Quashi narrative best. Fancy commands:

> 'Blush, EUROPE, blush! and, prostrate at his grave,
> Go learn that Conquest which adorns the brave.
> To QUASHI'S mem'ry tears of Pity shed,
> A SLAVE when living, but a Hero dead!' (102)

To move the British audience to pity the enslaved man, the poet must present him as utterly unthreatening, and what is less threatening than a corpse? Quashi bears the supposed shame of being 'a Slave' when he is alive and can only rise to the status of 'Hero' when he is 'dead', since heroes demand awe and respect, an insubordination that is intolerable in a live African for many British readers of the period. Thus, the Quashi tale implicitly demands: Does this depiction of extreme loyalty serve the function of proving the humanity of the enslaved, as the purveyors of the story often say it does? Or does it demonstrate that the enslaved are thoughtlessly devoted to their 'masters', pitiable in their helplessness, in the fashion of Josiah Wedgwood's African 'brother' in the famous 1787 medal for the Society for the Abolition of the Slave Trade, who begs to be recognised as a fellow human being with the words, 'Am I not a man and a brother?' (Figure 3.3)? I argue that, despite its apparent abolitionist purpose and use of slave suicide to engage the reader in the cause, the tale yet confirms the white colonial desire to control the Black body, a trajectory that includes, and culminates in, the system of slavery as the enforcement of life – a politics of control that makes the very existence of the enslaved a result of white power.

Insofar as abolitionist writers seek to enlist readerly sympathy through their depictions of the humanity of the enslaved, they tend to focus on pitiable qualities that lead to suicide, such as sadness, distress over a betrayal or unrequited loyalty. Clearly, though, wrath, vengefulness and insulted dignity are also decidedly human qualities, and these are evident in depictions of rebellious slave suicide, but the writers who depict these qualities risk alienating their readers, rather than drawing them in through sympathetic connection with their suicidal subject. One poem, a popular success in its day[22] and the subject of numerous critical examinations, attempts to have it both ways. *The Dying Negro: A Poetical Epistle, Supposed to be Written by a Black (Who Lately Shot Himself On Board a Vessel in the River Thames)*, as the long and descriptive title has it, was published by Day and Bicknell in 1773;

Figure 3.3 Am I not a man and a brother?', 1859. Available in the public domain via The New York Public Library Digital Collections

a second edition appeared in 1774, and 'a third edition was issued in 1775[, which] ... was further expanded, and is now the definitive edition' (Carey, 'Day' n.p.). Carey describes the difference in import between the first and third versions' depictions of suicide:

> the poem has moved sharply from a depiction of passive suffering to one of active resistance. In 1773, the poem opened:
>
> Blest with thy last sad gift – the power to dye,
> At last, thy shafts, stern fortune, I defy;
> Welcome, kind pass-port to an unknown shore! –
> The world and I are enemies no more.

> By 1775 it had become:
>
> Arm'd with thy last sad gift – the pow'r to die,
> Thy shafts, stern fortune, now I can defy;
> Thy dreadful mercy points at length the shore,
> Where all is peace and men are slaves no more.
>
> There is a crucial shift from presenting the power of suicide as a blessing to presenting it as a weapon. (*Rhetoric* 82)[23]

While the difference between 'Blest' and 'Arm'd' is certainly significant, what is surprising is that the revised version of the poem, rather than the original, presents the suicide as revolutionary, making the eponymous 'dying negro' appear potentially violent and threatening. It is not that the poets Day and Bicknell changed the poem out of a wish to ameliorate a negative public reaction to the portrayal of African violence; rather, they wished to warn the British public of the righteous revenge that may follow from colonial cruelty. Commenting on Carey's interpretation of the poem, Koretsky notes, 'in subsequent editions, Day and Bicknell shift the poem's focus from the slave's personal suffering (and therefore from his motivations to commit suicide) to the politics of slavery more generally,' moving from private despair to a vision of war between Africa and Europe ('Habeas' 22n). This bold revision of the poem speaks to the popularity of the trope of revolutionary slave suicide before the Haitian Revolution of 1791–1804, during and after which such depictions became less palatable to an alarmed British audience (Ferguson 230).

However, I would point out that both versions of the long poem deliver some satisfaction to an audience hungry for the reaffirmation of the belief in colonial supremacy. In *Death Rights*, Koretsky argues that *The Dying Negro* helps to confirm Enlightenment liberal principles by relying on the illiberal association between Blackness and death:

> Day and Bicknell present the [enslaved] speaker's capacity to reason as evidence of African-identified people's suitability for inclusion in liberal modernity's covenant of personhood [as encapsulated in the legal injunction of habeas corpus]. But, crucially, they are only able to argue this by turning the ontological relation between blackness and death into an occasion for bolstering the social structures that compel that relation in the first place. (24)

The poem's focus on the subjugated and victimised Black body reifies the structures of white society. Bell asserts that the influence of the poem was so great that it helped to create a taste for the trope of slave suicide in the literature of the early United States: 'Evidently influenced by Day and Bicknell's sorrowful masterpiece, early national writers embraced the subject of slave suicide. It proved to be a timely tactic, a means to render slaves' torments in forms that catered to novel readers' ghoulish fascination with mortality and their sweet tooth for sentimental narratives' (*No More* 206). This point about early American readers may also be applied to the British reading public, for whom the theme remained enthralling. The titular character is on the edge of death throughout and he has been thrust into this desperate state because of his treatment at the hands of British slavers. In his weakened state, he is far from menacing to the British readership, who may imagine themselves the addressees of this first-person 'poetical epistle', and he supports their self-image as liberal and sympathetic, making him an appealing, personalised figure. Sometimes British sentimental depictions of colonial enslavement support a national self-image as enlightened. A visual expression of this situation may be found in Blake's well-known etching 'Europe Supported By Africa & America', which thus appears as not only illustrative of an economic state, in which the figures of the African and American Indigenous women support that of Europe through the labour they are forced to accomplish on her behalf, but also as a representation of an ideological power dynamic (Figure 3.4).

While *The Dying Negro* is one of the most salient images of subversive suicide in abolitionist literature, its subtext nevertheless implicitly reifies the concept of white strength and superiority by appealing to the British reader's charitable sympathy for the 'dying Negro'. Throughout the poem, he is about to stab himself, Cato-like, because he will be conveyed back to the colonies, away from England and his white fiancée. More pointedly, the character is perishing, as the title confirms, throughout the poem. *The Dying Negro* gives no indication that the speaker has yet stabbed himself; the frontispiece of the 1793 edition of it (reproduced on the cover of this book) depicts him holding a dagger, rather than having plunged it into himself already – and, still, the title insists that he is presently and perpetually 'dying'. Compare this situation with the depiction of slave suicide on the last pages of John Gorton's *Tubal to Seba: The Negro Suicide. A Poem* (1797), in which the speaker kills himself in the final lines:

> The deed is done! – the poignant dagger, plung'd
> Within my bosom, rankles in my heart!
> Already I perceive triumphant death,
> In all his hostile force!
> Celestial glories open on my view. (41; no line numbers given)

Unusually, Gorton's speaker actually commits suicide in the course of the poem. As for Day and Bicknell's more famous 'dying negro', he must be understood as actively losing his life in a metaphorical or psychic sense,

Figure 3.4 William Blake, 'Europe Supported By Africa & America', 1796. Available in the public domain via Wikipedia

rather than in a literal and physical sense. Only by viewing the speaker's mental state through the lens of his enslavement may he be said to be dying throughout the span of the long poem. His death is inevitable – he is actively dying – because slavery has erased what Heidegger would call his *Dasein*, his existential reality as an autonomous human being. All that is left to him are a few words and a dagger to finish the deed. This is also why the speaker labels himself 'a thing without a name' (9; no line numbers given), a statement that Carey calls a 'self-conscious[...]' commentary on his subjugated state, and which Snyder recognises as 'an erasure of personhood' in the speaker's status as enslaved (Carey, *Rhetoric* 76; Snyder, *Power* 133). Both interpretations suggest that British colonial power has redefined the very being of the speaker, such that he has lost his existential reality, identity and even humanity.

To illustrate further that British colonial power has entirely usurped the autonomy of the African subject, Day and Bicknell make the threat of African retributive violence ideal, rather than realistic. The revenge threatened to Europe in the poem's third edition is 'the dying negro's' fantasy alone, a mere dream of bloodshed and, even then, this retributive violence is on a scale so vast that its accomplishment is unlikely. The speaker calls upon heaven to 'stain[ ] with kindred blood the impious coast' (i.e. Europe, or even Britain specifically) and

> Then the stern genius of my native land
> With delegated vengeance in his hand,
> Shall raging cross the troubled seas, and pour
> The plagues of Hell on yon devoted shore. (44; no line numbers given)

The threatened apocalyptic war of nations is of a Blakean variety: sublime, awe-inspiring and of the mental variety alone, highly unlikely to become a reality. How African nations, so internally divided and decimated by the ravages of colonialism, could unite to compose an organised army capable of attacking Europe, not to mention construct (or steal) and manage the necessary number of ships to ferry them to their righteous war on their oppressors, is entirely unclear. The British reader may have shuddered with momentary terror at the image of violent chaos, but this reaction would have been quickly subdued by the awareness of its impossibility – a comfort further confirmed via the sense of control and closure offered by the poem's rhyming couplets. *The Dying Negro* was critical in popularising the link between slavery and suicide for the British imagination, and it doubtlessly influenced Romantic writers who considered the prohibition against suicide as a form of oppression over the subject's body. However, a close reading reveals its subtext about African passivity and non-existence at the hands of colonial oppressors.

This depiction of the enslaved as non-threatening, even in suicide, confirms the racist fantasy of white power over the African body that was at the root of the institution of slavery itself. In reality, slave suicide was often insurrectionist and therefore a grievous blow to white power, as Douglas comments in 1792:

> Let us suppose ourselves in a similar predicament, and judge what would be our feelings and apprehensions; for theirs [i.e. Africans' feelings] are allowed to be, in general, no less delicate and acute. Sometimes, even before the vessels leave the coast, they make violent efforts to effectuate their escape, which prove not seldom fatal both to themselves and their tyrannizing, petty despots, who carry them away captive. (28)

Significantly, Douglas does not attribute rebellious suicide amongst enslaved Africans to some supposed national characteristic, heathen belief or wild and passionate nature; nor does he present the enslaved as helpless and pathetic, killing themselves out of despair, sorrow or misplaced loyalty. He forthrightly asks his British audience to imagine themselves in the situation of being kidnapped from their country into slavery and asks them to conclude what their feelings would be, while asserting that those of Africans are naturally the same. The answer is violent anger, which can result in the deaths of themselves and the Britons who enslave them.

The view that the literary theme of revolutionary slave suicide in the period was framed to suit colonial tastes, even when white anti-slavery writers held the pen, may seem utterly contemporary. However, some eighteenth-century commentators were just as suspicious of the motivations of a literary culture interested in scenes depicting torment for the enjoyment of the reader. Wollstonecraft draws attention to the indulgent and hypocritical representation of emotional pain in the culture of sensibility:

> Where is the dignity, the infallibility of sensibility, in the fair ladies, whom, if the voice of rumour is to be credited, the captive negroes curse in all the agony of bodily pain, for the unheard of tortures they invent? It is probable that some of them, after the sight of a flagellation, compose their ruffled spirits and exercise their tender feelings by the perusal of the last imported novel. – How true these tears are to nature, I leave you to determine. (*Rights of Men* 79)

Wollstonecraft opines that the ladies of false sensibility go so far as to orchestrate torments for the enslaved, presumably as the wives of overseers on plantations, and then seek refuge in novels of sensibility to calm the resulting disturbance to their supposedly fine feelings. It follows, then, that the pain of the enslaved, including their suicidality, would be prized by false sensibility. Stephen Ahern likewise comments on the potential for representations of slave suicide to satisfy debased tastes, rather than to encourage real-life action in the fight against slavery:

> the representation of suffering is marked by recurring problems, at times veering into a distasteful savoring of the spectacle of the body in pain, at others working to naturalize the master-slave bond, or to celebrate a quality of raw animal sensation that dehumanizes the non-European. As George Boulokos has recently observed, it is not right for us to assume that 'sentimental attention to the suffering of slaves' necessarily leads to progressive political action. (1)

Snyder asserts much the same, viewing literary representations of slave suicide as part of 'a veritable pornography of violence' (*Power* 112). Regardless of the uses to which period writers and readers put such depictions, slave suicide was undeniably a common literary theme, and is thus an important object of scholarly examination for the ways in which it influenced the broad understanding of suicide for the British public.

But what of representations of slave suicide by the formerly enslaved? Is there a danger that, as in writings about the topic by white abolitionists, 'The perverse voyeurism of audiences invested in the slave narrative' will receive what Hartman calls the '"sadistic pleasure to be derived from the spectacle of sufferance"' (quoted in Laura Murphy 59)? I suggest that this is not the case. The reader is encouraged to sympathise with these authors when they report their suicidal despair while in the state of enslavement; such 'fellow-feeling', as Adam Smith designates sympathy in *The Theory of Moral Sentiments* (1759, 5), was supposed to connect the authors emotionally with their British reading audience, a feature of the literary mode of sensibility. However, slave memoirists avoided the voyeuristic bent of sensibility through the unique features of the genre, partly through its autobiographical – rather than fictional – nature. The suffering Black body these memoirs present is not a distant spectacle for the reader's objective enjoyment. It is the embodiment of a fellow in the community of sensibility who demands recognition. These authors also maintain their dignity by choosing how and when to tell their stories, as well as by organising their memories artistically, establishing a new identity as a writer in control of his or her craft and using their past pain for productive reasons – to protest slavery – rather than for the reader's self-indulgence. Some slave memoirists' bids for readerly sympathy may also be viewed as a radical assertion of their agency. Laura Murphy affirms, 'Self-effacing narratives that concentrated on facts instead of sentiments were more highly sought after among abolitionists because they conformed to the image of the pacified slave that they wanted to project to audiences' (60). By contrast, Prince and Equiano boldly present themselves as strong, lively narrators and courageously share emotional – and not only factual – accounts of their moments of deepest despair and bodily suffering to enlist the reader's sympathy. They refuse passivity, demanding to be recognised as writers making a claim on their readers' feelings in the community of sensibility.

Racism, the colonial mindset and political circumstances constrained the depiction of slave suicide in British literature of the period, such that even the writers who were the most devoted to the abolitionist cause struggled to represent the topic in an even-handed way. This circumstance was produced, in part, by a fear of revolutionary violence stimulated by the Haitian Revolution and other uprisings before it, such as Tacky's Rebellion and the Maroons' multiple revolutions (1655, 1730s, 1795) in Jamaica (Nordius 165n; xxiii). Such anxiety was also stoked a few years earlier by the French Revolution, which Britons correctly surmised could inspire revolutionary activity in the colonies – exactly as happened in the Haitian Revolution. Carey notes that the French Revolution also discouraged British sympathy for the anti-slavery cause:

> the French Revolution was the most significant, [and] rapidly became the defining event of the 1790s, over-shadowing the abolition movement, and bringing out the conservative instincts of many who had previously supported change. After the outbreak of war with France in 1793, few of the middle or upper ranks of society had any inclination to rock the boat. While the slavery debate continued into the 1790s and beyond, by the middle of the decade, abolition of slavery had become associated in the public mind with radicals and English Jacobins. Opponents of abolition vigorously promoted this association. (*Rhetoric* 186)

What amounted to a smear campaign against abolitionists made anti-slavery a dangerous political position, when British radicals were frequently imprisoned or worse by a nervous government. Clarkson and his friends worried that his life was in danger while he collected information on the horrors of the slave trade at the docks of Liverpool (Rediker 320). It is not difficult to imagine that less courageous people would have been too frightened to support abolition in such a climate. Here, then, is another reason why abolitionist writers were sometimes loath to present slave suicide in its true aspect as a revolutionary act: they may have feared the imputation of celebrating the threat to British concerns it conveyed.

God's Suicides: Samson and Slave Suicide as Insurrection

Despite such censorship, even Britons who knew little about slavery and abolition understood slave suicide as a violent threat to the oppressors.

Two of the most influential literary sources on British Romantic-era culture, the Christian Bible and John Milton's poetry, establish the connection. Since most Britons in the period were Christians, and Milton was lauded as one of the nation's great bards, the biblical story of Samson and Milton's poetic drama based on it, *Samson Agonistes* (1671), were powerful and influential purveyors of the fear of revolutionary slave suicide. The biblical story of Samson not only presents insurrectionist slave suicide as rational and comprehensible, but also as heroic – not to mention blessed, and even inspired, by God. Beyond Britain, and in the work of other famous British writers, evidence of the influence of Samson's story is evident. As the Enlightenment *Encyclopedia*'s definition of 'suicide' details, in *Biathanatos* Donne cites Samson as proof that some suicides are divinely ordained:

> In his book he claims to prove that suicide is not against the law of nature, reason, or the revealed law of God. He shows that in the Old Testament, men acceptable to God caused their own deaths themselves, which he proves by the example of Samson, who died crushed under the ruins of a temple that he made fall on the Philistines and himself. (n.p.)

Importantly, too, the Israelite warrior was enslaved by the Philistines, the enemies of the Nazarites, Samson's tribe. The story strongly implies that God approves of slave suicide that ensures the mass murder of unjust enslavers.

To better demonstrate the power of Samson's story for British culture in this period, a short recapitulation of the plot is necessary. Samson had been tempted into marriage to the beautiful and deceitful Delilah, who promptly cut his hair, the source of his legendary strength. To further subjugate him, as the story goes in the Book of Judges, 'the Philistines took him, and put out his eyes, and brought him down to Gaza, and bound him with fetters of brass; and he did grind in the prison house./ Howbeit the hair of his head began to grow again after he was shaven' (Judges 16: 21–2). Samson slowly regains his strength along with his hair, and that is when the enslaved hero's righteous revenge begins.

One fine feast day, while the Philistines are offering sacrifices to their god Dagon and glorying in the capture of their once-powerful enemy, they force Samson to perform for them, bringing him out of the prison house and into an arena where the ruling members of Philistine society are gathered (Judges 16: 23, 27). Because the Philistines have blinded Samson, he must be led to his destination inside the arena, and, feigning fatigue,[24] he begs of his guide,

> Suffer me that I may feel the pillars whereupon the house standeth, that I may lean upon them.

> Now the house was full of men and women; and all the lords of the Philistines were there; and there were upon the roof about three thousand men and women, that beheld while Samson made sport.
>
> And Samson called unto the LORD, and said, O Lord God, remember me, I pray thee, and strengthen me, I pray thee, only this once, O God, that I may be at once avenged of the Philistines for my two eyes.
>
> And Samson took hold of the two middle pillars upon which the house stood, and on which it was borne up, of the one with his right hand, and of the other with his left.
>
> And Samson said, Let me die with the Philistines. And he bowed himself with all his might; and the house fell upon the lords, and upon all the people that were therein. So the dead which he slew at his death were more than they which he slew in his life. (Judges 16: 26–30)

This well-known biblical story clearly depicts revolutionary slave suicide as glorious, righteous and divinely ordained.

The story of Samson is justly famous, and it was the source of inspiration for such great writers as Milton because it demonstrates the workings of divine and poetic justice: the Philistines are killed through their own means, hoist with their own petard. The episode is akin to what Jacques Derrida would call 'suicidal autoimmunity' with reference to the events of 9/11 in the United States:

> here is the first symptom of suicidal autoimmunity: not only is the ground, that is, the literal figure of the founding or foundation of this 'force of law,' *seen* to be *exposed* to aggression, but the aggression of which it is the *object* … comes, *as from the inside*, from forces that are apparently without any force of their own but that are able to find the means … to get hold of an American weapon in an American city on the ground of an American airport. (Borradori 95; emphasis in original)

Similarly, the Philistines mean to demonstrate their power and authority in the space of the arena, intending to use the enslaved Samson as a foil to highlight their superiority and control: but they soon find that the aggression recoils on them. The scene is what Derrida would call 'Doubly suicidal', for it encompasses Samson's suicide as well as the unwitting self-destruction of the Philistines (95).

In Milton's *Samson Agonistes*, the Chorus helpfully proclaims the import of the action:

> O dearly-bought revenge, yet glorious!
> Living or dying thou hast fulfill'd
> The work for which thou wast foretold
> To Israel, and now ly'st victorious
> Among thy slain self-kill'd,
> Not willingly, but tangl'd in the fold
> Of dire necessity, whose law in death conjoin'd

> Thee with thy slaughter'd foes in number more
> Than all thy life had slain before. (1660–8)

Here, insurrectionary slave suicide is presented unambiguously as divinely planned martyrdom. It is not only the case that suicide and mass murder are ordained by God in this biblical story, Milton suggests. More to the point, they are consequences of Samson's enslavement.[25]

Significantly, Samson's suicidal revenge appears to have been actuated by God's will: the Israelite prays for the strength to accomplish it and he is immediately invested with this power. It is no wonder that the Samson episode was cut entirely from the so-called 'slave Bible', a severely abridged edition of the Christian Bible that was provided to enslaved people in the British Caribbean colonies. Entitled *Select Parts of the Holy Bible, For the Use of the Negro Slaves, in the British West-India Islands* (1807), it excises the Book of Judges in which the Samson story appears, and for good reason: Samson's narrative suggests that revolutionary slave suicide is nothing less than an expression of divine justice.[26] The 'slave Bible' also cuts the reference to Samson in the New Testament in Hebrews:

> And what shall I more say? for the time would fail me to tell of Gedeon, and of Barak, and of Samson, and of Jephthae; of David also, and Samuel, and of the prophets:
> Who through faith subdued kingdoms, wrought righteousness, obtained promises, stopped the mouths of lions.
> Quenched the violence of fire, escaped the edge of the sword, out of weakness were made strong, waxed valiant in fight, turned to flight the armies of the aliens. (Hebrews 11: 32–4)

Even in this passage from the New Testament – the part of the Bible devoted to God's new covenant with humankind, characterised by salvation, rather than destruction – Samson is celebrated for his suicidal mass-murder as an illustration of his faith, justice and strength. The compilers of the slave Bible must have reasoned that, had the enslaved in the colonies become familiar with the Samson story, then they would surely go the way of the Haitians and revolt. Given the outsized influence of both the Bible and Milton's writing on the formation of British culture, the importance of the Samson story cannot be underestimated. The British public's perception of slave suicide as revolutionary was centuries old, and the plethora of British abolitionist literary works on the subject only confirmed this concept and demonstrated its relevance for the period.

Conclusion: Personal Versus Outsider Depictions of Slave Suicide

The effect of slave suicide always undermined the system of colonial slavery as based on enforcing life, but that does not mean that all representations of the theme in British literature of the long eighteenth century were equally radical. Often, slave suicide in these texts aims to generate sympathy for and admiration of the enslaved by making them appear pitiful or heroic: but these depictions are complicated, in that their subtext can also demonstrate the white British public's intolerance for strong and aggressive figures of slave suicide. They are made into objects of mercy to ameliorate the insurrectionary overtones of the act. Alternatively, the threat of revolution by such suicidal figures, as in *The Dying Negro*, are made the stuff of impossible fantasy, rather than enacted in the literary work. Scenes of actualised slave rebellion are few and far between in the period. Two of the most notable appear in Southey's *Poems on the Slave Trade* (1797) and Charlotte Smith's *The Story of Henrietta* (1800),[27] while Wordsworth's sonnet 'To Toussaint L'Ouverture' (1803) celebrates the hero of the Haitian Revolution without depicting the bloody massacre of the French colonists over which L'Ouverture presided. Although neither of the latter texts identifies slave revolution as a form of slave suicide, Marcus Wood comments that 'Southey is unique among early nineteenth-century European historians, in celebrating the moral superiority of Maroons over colonial Europeans. [His character] Zumbi emerges as a charismatic man, who chooses heroic and tragic suicide rather than capture, and who is followed by a devoted group of committed revolutionaries' in the *History of Brazil* (1810 and 1819; Marcus Wood 217; see Southey 28–9). This chapter has shown the pervasive nature of literary rebellious slave suicides in acknowledgement of the influence of the trope on the Romantic-era texts I explore hereafter, but the subtext of these depictions by white authors is often that it was pitiful, which confirms the idea of Black subjugation.

However, in autobiographical works depicting the suicidality of the enslaved, such as the memoirs of Prince and Equiano, the subversive overtones of slave suicide are better maintained. Although the reader is encouraged to sympathise with the authors' depictions of themselves in a state of enslavement, the authors avoid reproducing the perception of themselves as weak and subject to the (largely white) reader's objectifying pity, suggestive of the latter's greater power, through means I have outlined in this chapter. Slave-memoirists present themselves as fellow humans, bonded to the reader in the culture of sensibility through their agonising tales. They illustrate their own control and self-mastery, so unlike life under enslavement, by organising their life events into a narrative – choosing what to include and what to omit as part of that story. Moreover, the very existence of a work by a formerly enslaved Black author subverts the biopolitical system of slavery by presenting the author's self and life as a story communicated from mind to mind, replacing the solely physical ontological existence imposed upon the enslaved Black person. A kind of suicide itself, the memoir removes the body of the (now formerly) enslaved from the field of biopower's influence.

The depiction of suicidality in slave memoirs provides another means of asserting the authors' power: they announce their independence to the British reading audience, even while the paratextual elements of the memoir may demonstrate the memoirists' embeddedness in British society. Laura Murphy states, summarising James Olney's work on the traditional elements of the slave memoir, 'the paratextual elements of the narrative provide a virtual stamp of validity and legitimacy through the testimonies of experts, abolitionists, and companions' (34). Banner claims that they 'were, at their most basic level, appended to a slave narrative to vouch for the ability of the black author to articulate and/or inscribe her own story' (298). Thus, abolitionist Pringle provides a preface to Prince's *History* and his wife Margaret Pringle follows it up with a letter to the Birmingham Ladies' Society for Relief of Negro Slaves, while the ninth edition of Equiano's *Interesting Narrative* follows several introductory paratexts written by commentators, probably all white.[28] In his foundational book on the topic, *Paratexts* (1997), Gérard Genette characterises the paratext as a

> fringe, always the conveyor of a commentary that is authorial or more or less legitimated by the author, [and] constitutes ... an influence on the public ... that ... is at the service of a better reception for the text and a more pertinent reading of it (more pertinent, of course, in the eyes of the author and his allies). (2)

Whether or not the paratextual elements of Prince's and Equiano's memoirs are 'legitimated by the author' (2) is perhaps in question, but it certainly seems to be the case that they seek to justify and establish the texts' and their authors' places in white British society. They visually enfold the authors, represented by their first-person narratives, in broader British society. However, such gestures are undermined by multiple references to the authors' own suicidality in their narratives, insofar as suicide is socially subversive. What drove the memoirists to suicidal despair in the past is the institution of slavery that has bolstered the society with which these memoirs claim kinship through their paratextual elements, putting the two impulses of the text at odds. The theme of suicidality undermines the unity conveyed by the text, destabilising it, and reveals the authors' protesting position amidst their efforts to communicate with a white British public.

My focus in this chapter has been to examine the subversive resonances of slave suicide in literature of the period, even though, importantly, the personal motivations of the enslaved in real life who chose to die may have been far from revolutionary. These people could well have chosen death for a range of reasons, including a desperate lack of choices, sheer terror over what their lives had become under slavery, or suicidal depression. The fact is that we can never fully know these motives because their voices have largely been silenced, their cultural roots having been destroyed, their native languages and modes of expression lost, and their very identities and stories co-opted by a colonial state and its readership. Just as the enslaved were renamed in the state of slavery – such that Equiano was called 'Gustavus Vassa', a name that he shed upon his emancipation – the stories of the enslaved were recast, told through the genres and conventions of their oppressors, frameworks that perforce affect the import of the works. What images of subversive slave suicide can tell us today, though, is how the later concept of suicide in the West was partially formed by it: how it associated suicide with those who are alternately deserving of sympathy or deeply suspect as rebels.

Notes

1. I avoid the term 'slave/s' as an objection to the identification of enslaved people as somehow intrinsically and ontologically enslaved, rather than people upon whom slavery has been foisted by others. However, in the interests of clarity and conciseness, I exempt some phrases referring not to people, but things, such as 'slave memoirs', 'slave suicide' and 'slave ship'.
2. In Chapter 4, I develop a similar argument about the protagonist's relationship to her life-narrative in Shelley's *Mathilda*.
3. Lee finds the most potent expression of Romantics' thinking about slavery in works about the imagination, such as Wordsworth and Coleridge's *Lyrical Ballads* and Keats's 'Lamia' (1820). For other book-length critical examinations of Romanticism and slavery, see, for example, Tim Fulford and Peter J. Kitson's edited volume of essays *Romanticism and Colonialism: Writing and Empire, 1780–1830* (1998), Bewell's *Romanticism and Colonial Disease* (1999) and Deirdre Coleman's *Romantic Colonization and British Anti-Slavery* (2005).
4. Rediker details another instance of an explicitly insurrectionist mass suicide: 'A sailor named Thompson noted that he "has known all the slaves [locked belowdecks] unanimously [to] rush to leeward in a gale of wind, on

purpose to upset the ship, choosing to drown themselves, than to continue in their situation, or go into foreign slavery"' (290; see also 18, 264, 285).

5. At times and for convenience, I use the word 'slavers' to refer to all the officials in the system of slavery, from plantation overseers through to slave-ship captains and slave-ship owners.
6. Intriguingly, though, Hertzman points out that 'for nineteenth-century Cuba it is far easier to track suicides of slaves and indentured laborers than those of whites or free people of color, due in part to wealthy families' ability to hide suicide and avoid the stigmas attached to it' (322). For contradictory reasons, then, the number and proportion (in comparison with wider colonial society) of slave suicides is difficult to establish.
7. To register the perversity and wrongness of the very concept of 'breeding' enslaved people as though they were livestock, I use scare quotation marks for the word 'breed' and its derivatives throughout this chapter.
8. The *Encyclopedia* definition for 'Negroes' is rife with othering commentary about race, including that 'they differ from other men in all the traits of their faces, with large flat noses, fat lips and wool instead of hair, and seem to constitute a new kind of men' (n.p.). At another points, the definition seems to correct its prejudicial and disparaging bent by musing, 'Did all these peoples that we have just run through, so many diverse men, come from a single mother? We are not permitted to doubt it' (n.p.).
9. Commenting on sales of the enslaved in Africa, Falconbridge notes that women seldom exceeded 'a third of the whole number. From forty to two hundred negroes are generally purchased at a time by the black traders ... and consist of those of all ages, from a month to sixty years and upwards' including pregnant women who give birth on board the ship (16). Rediker reports similar numbers, stating that 'two males for every female' were kidnapped from Africa (193).
10. For more on the issue of motherhood and the transatlantic slave trade, see the following journal issue dedicated to the topic: 'Mothering Slaves: Motherhood, Childlessness and the Care of Children in Atlantic Slave Societies', edited by Camillia Cowling et al., in *Slavery & Abolition: A Journal of Slave and Post-Slave Studies*.
11. Anita McConnell reports that Beckford's legendary wealth derived from the family's plantations: 'Beckford's grandfather Peter Beckford (bap. 1643, d. 1710) founded the greatest sugar fortune in the West Indies; the family owned twenty estates' (n.p.). Other literary slave-owners visited or even lived on their plantations in the West Indies. Matthew 'Monk' Lewis recorded his years on his plantation in Jamaica in his journals, published posthumously as *Journal of a West India Proprietor, Kept During a Residence in the Island of Jamaica* (1834) (Leask n.p.). Probably the most famous literary example of a British subject living in the colonies is that of the character Rochester in Charlotte Brontë's *Jane Eyre* (1847), an experience that takes place beyond the main plot. This structure reiterates the common British view that the colonies were foreign and unfamiliar places, beyond the ken of the average Briton. Unbeknownst to the reader and Jane Eyre herself until relatively late in the novel, Rochester married Bertha Mason, a so-called 'Creole' woman and the infamous 'madwoman in the attic', in the West Indies and brought her back with him when he returned to Britain.

12. The term 'planter' is a misleading and offensive euphemism. Therefore, I use it with scare-quotation marks throughout this text, except for when it appears in another's writing or as a capitalised pseudonym.
13. Cowper also expresses his anti-slavery views in the first forty-seven lines of Book II of *The Task*.
14. John Newton – an Anglican clergyman, composer of the beloved hymn 'Amazing Grace', and slave-ship captain on several transatlantic voyages – describes 'The eighteenth-century sea captain ... [as] a figure of almost unlimited power' in a letter to his wife Mary (Rediker 157). He also 'accounted' the job as 'a genteel employment, and ... usually very profitable' in his memoir *An Authentic Narrative* (1765) (192), suggesting that Newton was not entirely critical of the slave-ship captain's vast power, at least at the point of writing his memoir.
15. Koretsky recognises that belief in the transmigration of souls was native to some African cultures, but she contends that Europeans seized upon it to an inordinate degree to explain suicide amongst the enslaved as a response to cultural differences, rather than to the torments of slavery (*Rights* 41, 80).
16. Coleridge's own 'literal translation' from 1796 of the first lines of the poem – identified in this publication as 'Introduction to a Greek Prize Ode on the Slave-Trade' – is as follows (transcribed from a source without line breaks):

    > Leaving the gates of Darkness, O Death! hasten thou to a Race yoked to Misery! Thou wilt not be received with lacerations of Cheeks, nor with the funeral ululation, but with circling Dances and the joy of Songs. Thou art terrible indeed, yet thou dwellest with Liberty, stern Genius! Borne on thy dark pinions over the swelling of Ocean, they return to their native country. There by the side of fountains beneath Citron groves, the Lovers tell to their Beloved what horrors, being Men, they had endured from Men. (27)

17. This circumstance was no accident. Rather, it is an age-old colonial tactic used all over the world, including in early colonial Canadian society: the Catholic Church (and, to a lesser extent, other Christian churches) stole Indigenous children from their families and forced them into the 'residential school' system, where the young ones were beaten for using their native languages to 'to kill the Indian in the child'. See Bryanne Young's '"Killing the Indian in the Child": Death, Cruelty, and Subject-formation in the Canadian Indian Residential School System' (2015) for more on the Canadian colonial system's attempts to destroy Indigenous people's identity by erasing their culture.
18. This view continues to this day, as the very title of *A Very Human Ending: How Suicide Haunts Our Species* (2018) by Jesse Bering suggests.
19. In contrast with Equiano's claims in *Interesting Narrative*, historian Vincent Carretta argues that Equiano was not born in Africa, but South Carolina, in *Equiano, the African: Biography of a Self-Made Man* (1999). Because my focus is on the rhetorical techniques Equiano employs as an African writing for an eighteenth-century British audience, I take his claim regarding his native origin at face value here.
20. This problematic continues to this day in various forms, making the horror film *Get Out*, directed by Jordan Peele (2017), a powerful testament to the perseverance of the white fantasy of total power over the Black body.

21. So demeaning is the characterisation of the Quashi figure in British literature that the word 'Quashie' has come to denote 'A generic name for: a black person, esp. one considered as credulous or insignificant' ('Quashie, n.'), according to the *Oxford English Dictionary*. Also of note, Thomas Morris chooses a variant of the name for the eponymous female protagonist of his poem, *Quashy, or, The Coal-Black Maid. A Tale* (1796), which also ends with Quashy's suicide. I am indebted to Kent Lithicum for drawing my attention to this work, on which he presented at the BARS/NASSR conference *New Romanticisms* in 2022. Editor Lyndon J. Dominique lists several other period works that include the Quashi figure in a footnote to the Broadview edition of the anonymous novel *The Woman of Colour* (1808) (100).
22. Ferguson comments, 'Within two years the poem had gone into a corrected third printing' (237).
23. Snyder makes the same point in *The Power to Die* (122); see also Gaudet (604).
24. Although the biblical passage does not provide the reason Samson gives for asking to lean against the pillars, Milton reasonably ventures that he 'As over-tir'd [asks] to let him lean a while' in *Samson Agonistes* (1632).
25. For more on Christianity and slavery, see Michael Taylor's 'British Proslavery Arguments and the Bible, 1823–1833' (2016).
26. For more information on the slave Bible, see Brigit Katz's article 'Heavily Abridged "Slave Bible" Removed Passages That Might Encourage Uprisings' (2019).
27. Charlotte Smith also writes on slavery at length in her educative work, 'The Little West Indian' (1796), and she mentions the British greed that drives the nation to 'violate/ The sacred freedom of his fellow man' (58–9) early in her famous poem, *Beachy Head* (1807). For more on Romantic-era literary depictions of rebellion by the enslaved, see Kitson's 'Fictions of Slave Resistance and Revolt: Robert Southey's *Poems on the Slave Trade* (1797) and Charlotte Smith's "The Story of Henrietta" (1800)'.
28. All other references to Equiano's *Interesting Narrative* in this study are to the Broadview edition.

Chapter 4

Refusing the Burden of the Body: Mary Wollstonecraft, Mary Shelley and the Suicide Note as Literary Form

'THE END.

> 'She swallowed the laudanum; her soul was calm – the tempest had subsided – and nothing remained but an eager longing to forget herself – to fly from the anguish she endured to escape from thought – from this hell of disappointment.' (Wollstonecraft, *Wrongs* 286)

In Wollstonecraft's *The Wrongs of Woman, or Maria*, the 'mother of feminism' creates a protagonist, Maria, who attempts suicide in several of the proposed endings for the fragmentary novella – including in the most fully developed one, from which I quote above as an epigraph – to escape her husband George Venables's control over her body. Female suicide is thus presented as an escape from what the author describes as sexual slavery, which she protests is the common lot of women at the time. Wollstonecraft demonstrates that eighteenth-century British society shackles women through marriage: to explain why she continues to have sex with Venables despite hating him, Maria laments, 'women [are] the property of their husbands' (235) – a sure reference to the law of coverture in the period, which enshrined that husbands alone were the only legal personage in a marriage; wives could not own property, sue for their rights or expect custody of their children if separated from their husbands. When Venables tries to prostitute Maria to pay off his debts, it becomes apparent that, regardless of class, the women in the novella are treated chiefly as sexual objects and bound to misery by their bodies, which are utterly controlled by the patriarchy (251). The author uses the language of abolition to make this point: 'Men', Maria states in no uncertain terms, seek 'effectually to enslave us' (242). Helen Thomas similarly recognises that Wollstonecraft's protest against women's subjugation is built on the tropes of abolitionism: 'A woman's value, she [i.e. Wollstonecraft] argued, was judged not in terms of her spiritual or intellectual capacities, but upon her external and reproductive potential – a process not dissimilar to the way in which a slave's value was assessed' (87–8). Both enslaved people and women were treated as mere bodies in the period under discussion, when biopower – the form of power that concerned itself with managing and increasing the numbers of subjects in society as its assets – was gaining a foothold on a society-wide scale and when suicide gained significance as subversive of this power, as will be clear in Wollstonecraft and Shelley's framing of suicide in their fiction as rebellion against female enslavement.

In this feminist context, patriarchy is an expression and subset of biopower. The claim is consistent with Foucault's argument in both the *History of Sexuality* and *Power/Knowledge*, which maintains that power is not located only in top-down state apparatuses – such as through official legal or religious prohibitions – but throughout society, with minor deputies of power working throughout it to enforce its ideology. As Allaine Cerwonka and Anna Loutfi assert, 'the female reproductive subject has become the paradigmatic legal subject within the biopolitical state', which witnesses 'The reduction of all living beings to biological organisms under biopolitical regimes (which, for Foucault and Agamben, refers to all the populations of modern states – with the late eighteenth century as the key moment of historical transformation)' (5, 2). The patriarchy, Wollstonecraft protests through her novella, defines and controls women as bodies, which makes Maria's attempt to end her life subversive of this system of biopower. Because women are treated as bodies whose teleology is sexual attractiveness and fecundity, to deny their masculine tyrants their bodies through suicide is a radical act of protest. Suicide defies the authority of the master, who must have a subject to establish his power; a suicidal wife steals the husband's property from him and confirms her autonomy – her full control over her own body.

Defining women through their sexuality is to circumscribe them as assets to power. What is really at stake, buried under euphemisms about love and beauty, is women's fertility, their generative ability to create more assets to power by giving birth. Foucault contends in *The History of Sexuality* that biopower is ultimately interested in 'generating power', controlling life and protecting and maximising it (*Sexuality* 136).[1] Maria's baby – seized by Venables as his possession – is a reminder of why patriarchal power is always so interested in women's bodies: the patriarchy is just one element in the web of biopower that seeks to regulate and increase its influence and control through births. Foucault argues:

> The new procedures of power that were devised during the classical age and employed in the nineteenth century were what caused our societies to go from a symbolics of blood [under sovereign power] to an analytics of sexuality ... [S]exuality was on the side of the norm, knowledge, life, meaning, the disciplines, and regulations ... [And] the first dreams of the perfecting of the species inclined the whole problem toward an extremely exacting administration of sex (the art of determining good marriages, of inducing the desired fertilities, of ensuring the health and longevity of children). (*Sexuality* 148)

This predilection of modern power explains why the patriarchy attempts to own and manage women's bodies: a woman's body is the site of the generation of children, who maximise power as its assets. What Cerwonka and Loutfi claim about Agamben's theorisation of biopower also applies to Foucault's thesis: 'Agamben's biopolitical conceptual framework, which works with a particular biological conception of legal citizenship, inevitably and logically proceeds to the reproductive body of woman as a key political referent' (4). In the biopolitical state, female suicide is an immediate insult to patriarchal power and threatens the proliferation of that power that is promised in the woman's future ability to bear children. Confoundingly, though, the patriarchy's claim to women's bodies also finds expression in fantasies about women's passivity-unto-death in period texts, complicating the view of female suicide as a bid for autonomy. In recognition of the complexity of the figure of the female suicide, Wollstonecraft and Shelley represent her ambiguously: as desiring for death to escape the patriarchal demands on her body, but also as failing to accomplish the act.

This chapter explores the popularity of the theme of female suicide in Romantic literature and beyond, such as in newspapers, as well as the evolution of the theme as one that confirms the common notion of female existence and even death as defined by heterosexual love. Over and again, these texts present the woman as a parasite, so dependent on her husband or male lover that she practically ceases to exist without him, suggesting that women choose death, essentially, because they lack independence – a far cry from the notion of revolutionary suicide as a means of declaring autonomous identity. Women are thus framed as bodies alone: they are entirely defined by their bodily ties to men, and their suicidality becomes a limit expression of that identity. This cultural fantasy about women is close to what contemporary feminists call the 'docile body' theory of feminine subjecthood, which postulates that women merely submit to power's subordinating view of them, consistent with Foucault's theories of both disciplinary power and biopower. Monique Deveaux puts the thorny issue best when she claims that the 'use of the docile bodies thesis has the effect of diminishing and delimiting women's subjectivity, at times treating women as robotic receptacles of culture rather than as active agents who are both constituted by, and reflective of, their social and cultural contexts' (227). To claim that women uniformly subscribe to this oppressive view of themselves is to see them as submitting meekly to the ideological construction of themselves as docile bodies, which is misleading because – as Foucault would point out in his later work – where there is power, there is resistance. And, certainly, some female authors resisted this view of female suicidality. I choose two of the best-known period female authors and their radical novels of protest to make the point here.

The literary case studies on which I focus in this chapter challenge the view of female suicide as a capitulation to patriarchal demands of feminine dependence and bodily subordination. With reference to Wollstonecraft's novellas *Mary, A Fiction* and *The Wrongs of Woman*, I will outline the key early feminist response to this issue: the figure of the female suicide who chooses death because she refuses the role as a dependent in a patriarchal society. Shelley also tackles the joint topics of female suicidality and lack of autonomy in her suppressed novella, *Mathilda*,[2] and in a way that interrogates the significance of suicidal female protest in a culture that views women as extensions of men. Shelley's protagonist forges an autonomous identity for herself that shuns her father's strictures through the novelistic form of the long suicide note. In the mother's life and the daughter's literary work, the suicide note appears prominently as a kind of shorthand for the significance of female suicide: it functions as a replacement woman, a final chance for the suicidal woman to carve a new identity for herself and present the last word on her life and death. In this way, Mathilda dies into her text – replaces her oppressed body with a suicide note that defies her father's injunctions to secrecy – and Shelley simultaneously uses a fringe literary form separate from the male-centred literary canon. Together, these key texts outline some of the main expressions of female suicidality as rebellion against patriarchal control over the female body.

Beginning with an overview of texts on female suicide that consider why and how women killed themselves, and examining historical ideas for the prevention of female suicide – partly through punishments and treatments of female suicides' corpses – I will additionally consider discussions of female suicides in popular media. There are a number of excellent critical accounts of female suicide in the field of Romantic studies. Inaugurated with the groundbreaking work of Higonnet, this critical focus has expanded in recent years and now enjoys critical attention that suggests its enduring popularity and the perception of its significance to the study of Romanticism. An examination of female suicide as a literary theme will follow, with particular attention to the literature of sensibility, and then I will explore the literature of protest in, especially, the work of Wollstonecraft and Shelley. While Elisabeth Bronfen, Bram Dijkstra and others have shown that female suicidality may be regarded as the fulfilment of a patriarchal view of women as most attractive when dead – or well on the way there – other literary and critical treatments of the theme understand it as a woman's final claim to autonomy, her refusal to participate in the subjugating forces of patriarchal society, positioning some expressions of literary female suicide as rebellious.

The History of Female Suicide

The wider public has known very little about how, why and how often women chose death in reality. Evidence indicates that female suicides may have been more commonly misrepresented or hidden from public view than male suicides (Anderson 44). And while female suicide was a popular literary trope, the public's view of the issue was that women generally lacked the courage, strength or determination to kill themselves. Given the apparent dearth of (facts about) female suicide, then, the wide attraction to the theme in texts of the period takes on an outsized importance, suggesting that the idea was important to the culture's notion of who women were or ought to be.

The classical view of female suicide was profoundly contradictory, with some sources commenting on it as a virtual impossibility, some on its absurdity and others on its heroic and even manly qualities. Anton van Hooff acknowledges the deeply misogynistic response to the topic in the classical period, during which 'self-hanging by common women is merely ridiculous'; he goes on to cite the words of 'Diogenes the philosopher' upon 'Seeing some women hanged from an olive-tree[:] ... "Would that every tree bore similar fruit"' (20). In some classical dramas, the notion of female suicide is treated as humorous, van Hooff reports (20). Women of the period were sometimes viewed as having a 'noble motive' for choosing death, at which point their suicides were regarded as courageous and even masculine (van Hooff 20, 21) – a notion about classical-era attitudes towards women's suicide that persisted into the Romantic era, according to McGuire ('Hemans' 121). However, more typically, such suicides were not viewed in this light, rendering inaccurate the common critical perception today that suicide – male or female – was regarded almost unilaterally as an act of courage in the classical era.

The identification of suicide as courageous is doubtlessly a reflection of Seneca's famous pronouncements on the topic, such as his commentary on the gladiator who found a way to kill himself, despite the close watch of his guards:

> What a brave fellow! ... If you do not lack the courage, you will not lack the cleverness, to die. See how even the lowest of slaves, when suffering goads him on, is aroused and discovers a way to deceive even the most watchful guards! He is truly great who not only has given himself the order to die, but has also found the means. (Seneca, 'Cable' 111)

Such striking pronouncements have, perhaps, overshadowed the complex attitudes towards suicide and gender in the classical era, when suicide itself was sometimes viewed as feminine, which mostly signified weakness and timidity. Nicole Loraux recognises that the period sometimes saw suicide as 'tragic', but she maintains that it met with great disapprobation in everyday culture as 'a woman's solution and not, as has sometimes been claimed, a heroic act'; in other words, it is not true that 'in the Greek imagination all suicide was inspired by *andreia* (the Greek word for courage as a male characteristic)' (8). McGuire comments on the late-eighteenth-century afterlife of these notions about suicide and courage: 'suicide is paradoxically a feminine act, yet an act that is at the same time denied to women, since it requires both an assertion of will and a display of courage, both of which are typically seen as residing outside the purview of a female mentality' (*Dying* 143). What links the classical and Romantic periods is the view that a woman exists for her husband and family alone: patriarchal culture values women for their ability to bear children, maintain the family home, and behave as extensions of the male authorities to whom they are connected, such that they lack an autonomous identity apart from their fathers and husbands.[3] With respect to the classical period, Loraux claims that 'The death of a man inevitably calls for the suicide of a woman, his wife' (7) – a recognition that she has no life outside of her husband's – while van Hooff confirms that 'the female code of behaviour ... requires before all loyalty to one's own family' (25). If in classical times it was recognised that women did occasionally kill themselves nobly, then the act was usually viewed as inspired by bare duty, a minimum of civility and honour with respect to the men in the suicide's life, rather than a universal or more broadly political act of heroism. More to the point, for a woman's suicide to be considered noble, it must have been because her ties to the patriarchy were somehow compromised or threatened, rendering her life worthless.

This diminution of the significance of female suicide in the period did not preclude considerations of its aesthetic appeal, though, which are evident even in the Renaissance era, as a commentary by Michel de Montaigne on the suicide of a Roman general's wife illustrates:

> Nothing can be added to the beauty of the death of the wife of Fulvius, a familiar favourite of Augustus: Augustus having discovered that he had vented an important secret he had entrusted him withal, one morning that he came to make his court, received him very coldly and looked frowningly upon him. He returned home, full of, [*sic*] despair, where he sorrowfully told his wife that, having fallen into this misfortune, he was resolved to kill himself: to which she roundly replied, ''Tis but reason you should, seeing that having so often experienced the incontinence of my tongue, you could not take warning: but let me kill myself first', and without any more saying ran herself through the body with a sword. (283)

Women's suicide in the classical era could be treated as admirable and even beautiful – a troubling interpretation that I will explore in greater detail hereafter – but it was seldom admired as a heroic expression of courage or self-possession. A woman's suicide was beautiful only if it confirmed the utter entanglement of her existence with that of the man to whom she belonged.

Perhaps because female suicide was traditionally viewed as an expression of women's ties to men, rather than an assertion of personal will and autonomy, there has long existed a perceived paucity of female suicides in Western culture. Sara M. Butler comments that a propensity to view female suicidality as impossible or too distasteful for contemplation made 'gender ... an important consideration for juries in medieval England. Juries more frequently excused women of the crime' for this reason, and 'many jurors chose instead a generous reinterpretation of female self-killing, reporting deaths of this nature as accidental deaths or acts committed while *non compos mentis*' (144; italics added). When female suicides were agreed upon, the reasons given for them were equally gendered: women's physical and supposed mental weakness – the latter with respect to both their emotions and unruly imaginations – rendered them prime targets for the Devil, to whose temptations they were thought to fall easily (Butler, 'Women' 142). Notably, such women were victims, their minds and bodies acted upon rather than assertively acting. As an expression of violence and aggression, suicide was perceived as incompatible with the ideological notion of women as naturally passive, gentle and loving, the last of which supposed characteristics framed the possibilities for the motivations behind female suicide when it was recognised as having occurred. Love – be it sexual, familial or unrequited – has long been understood as the only medium in which women exist and die.

Until the late eighteenth century – when Goethe's hugely popular sentimental novel *The Sorrows of Young Werther* established the belief that unrequited love could be a reason for suicide in both sexes – one of the main explanations provided for women's suicidality was an insult to her chastity. Importantly, this interpretation has a precedent in the traditional tale of the rape of Lucretia. In Livy's telling of the story, Sextus Tarquinius (Tarquin, the last king of Rome), sneaks into the married Lucretia's room at night and puts a knife to her throat, begging and threatening her to have sex with him. However, when he sees that not even the threat of death frightens her into relenting, then he warns that he will kill her and put the corpse of a murdered slave next to her to make it look like she died in adultery with the enslaved man. She thus agrees to the sexual encounter to save her reputation from what is presented as a worse fate. Afterwards, Lucretia's shame is so great that she stabs herself in the heart in front of her father and husband (Livy 107). The Roman audience of this story was so outraged at the brutality of Tarquin – and so approving of Lucretia's response to his actions – that they overthrew his rule and instituted a republic in Rome.

While the political upheaval that followed this suicide positioned it, for many, as a deed of national significance, far beyond the realm of the family, it is undeniable that Lucretia's family ties to men drive her actions. The tale's misogynistic message that a woman's sexualised body is owned by her husband and her father, since both witness her suicide, and that her death is the only answer to the undermining of this principle – one that has never been celebrated as a noble reason for male suicide, according to my research – met with broad cultural acceptance. McGuire argues in her book on representations of female suicide in long-eighteenth-century literature that this myth was repeated ad nauseum in discussions of female suicide. Commentators used it as a touchstone to judge the ethics of the deed, and Lucretia became a patriotic heroine even to the British. One of the most famous novels of the eighteenth century, Samuel Richardson's *Clarissa*, is heavily influenced by the Lucretia tale, argues McGuire; the figure was also a favourite on the eighteenth-century stage (*Dying* 68). Nicole Reynolds also discusses the considerable number of authors who wrote on the Lucretia figure throughout the ages in addition to Livy, such as Ovid, Plutarch, St Jerome, Geoffrey Chaucer and Shakespeare. In the period under discussion, Rousseau 'refashioned an unfinished play, *La Mort de Lucrèce* (c. 1754)', into his celebrated novel *Julie*, and Gottfried Lessing's play *Emilia Galotti* (1772) 'presented a heroine who is not raped, but threatened with rape; when she begs her father to kill her so that she can retain her dignity, he stabs her to death' (Reynolds 677–8).[4] Seaver points out that Lucretia's suicide speaks to a woman's responsibility for male honour, as well as her own, since she protects her husband's reputation by choosing death after her rape ('Vicar' 42). The influence of the Lucretia tale was considerable in the formation of ideas about female suicide. Yet, not every commentator agreed that Lucretia made the right ethical decision in committing suicide, notably Kant in his *Lectures on Ethics* (145–6) and Augustine in *The City of God* (Dickenson and Boyden 107).[5] What the enduring popularity of the Lucretia tale demonstrates about female suicide is that a woman's choice to die is legitimised when viewed as a defence of sexual honour, both her own and her husband's. If she ceases to be a devoted asset to the patriarchy, an arm of biopower, then the woman must die.

Despite their religion's almost total condemnation of self-murder, even some Christian commentators celebrated female suicide committed in defence of a woman's sexual modesty – a view that is duly condemned in the Enlightenment *philosophes' Encyclopedia*. Under the entry for 'Church Father', the *Encyclopedia* comments:

> Saint Ambrose believes that virgins who cannot otherwise protect their honor do well to kill themselves. He cites Saint Pelagia and has her say that faith effaces the crime.
>
> Saint John Chrysostom reserves the highest praise for some virgins who found themselves in this predicament. He regards this type of death as an extraordinary baptism comparable to the sufferings of Our Lord Jesus Christ. Finally, all parties seem to have envisaged this action as divinely inspired. But the Holy Spirit inspires nothing of the kind. The chief reason the Supreme Being forbids suicide is that He alone is the sovereign judge of life, which he grants us out of generosity. Save its preservation, he did not intend us to have any other rights over it. (n.p.)

These saints' laudatory treatment of female self-killing demonstrates that their concerns about suicide are secondary to the view that a woman's life is worthless without her so-called 'sexual modesty'. Moreover, since the increasingly lenient attitude towards suicide throughout the eighteenth century is often attributed to the rise of Enlightenment secularism, it is also notable that this condemnation of the impiety of female suicide occurs in the *Encyclopedia*, often cited as the publication in which the most influential Enlightenment philosophers, such as Diderot, Voltaire, Jean-Baptiste le Rond d'Alembert and Rousseau, outlined the movement's principles. This entry from the *Encyclopedia* does not question the Church's celebration of female suicide out of concern for women's safety, or because they are considered valuable only if chaste. It casts women as passive responders to the pressures – especially amorous and familial – that cause suicide, rather than as agents who might choose to end their lives freely, in a way that suits them and for myriad other reasons besides love and sex, such as a desire to defy tyranny.

The long-standing interpretation of love as the main or only reason for female suicide undermines its potential significance as courageous or rebellious, since these qualities demand free will and a degree of independence that are obviated by dying for love.

One of the most influential representations of the idea of female suicide as a response to amorous pressures in British culture is Shakespeare's Ophelia in *Hamlet*. Ophelia kills herself by drowning – or, according to Gertrude, who relates Ophelia's death to her brother Laertes, she allows herself to sink into a watery grave when she falls into the river while picking flowers (4. 7. 149–66) – because, it is implied, she goes insane when her beloved Hamlet rejects her. The circumstances of her death qualify Ophelia as an idealised female suicide: she does not die violently or aggressively, but weakly and passively.[6] Nineteenth-century fascination with Ophelia's suicide is represented in countless dreamy, beautiful paintings of the scene, the most famous of which is by John Everett Millais (1852), while those by Alexandre Cabanel (1883) and John William Waterhouse (1894) (Figures 4.1, 4.2, 4.3) similarly present her death as richly sensual and attractive, revealing the cultural consensus summed up in Edgar Allen Poe's famous quip, '"the death of a beautiful woman is, unquestionably, the most poetical topic in the world"' (quoted in Bronfen 59). So much more so is the woman who chooses death because of a broken heart.

The notion that love is the prime motivator for female suicide underscores the belief that women generally do not choose to die to assert their autonomy, positioning them as being without independence and personal agency. In long-eighteenth-century literature, though, the theme of female suicide was so popular – doubtlessly influenced by the Lucretia tale and Shakespeare's Ophelia – that suicide became strongly associated with women. The act became feminised in popular perception (McGuire, *Dying* 12, 123; Franklin 213), even though individual women were still viewed as almost always unable to kill themselves. Sarah Chapone's *The Hardships of the English Laws in Relation to Wives* (1735) enshrines 'The view that a woman possesses insufficient autonomy to take her own life ... at the level of law' (McGuire, *Dying* 12). Accordingly, a medical text that appears, by its title, to be a reliable source of information on the eighteenth-century understanding of why women killed themselves – Rowley's *A Treatise on Female, Nervous, Hysterical, Hypochondriacal, Bilious, Convulsive Diseases. Apoplexy and Palsy; with Thoughts on Madness, Suicide, &c.* – contains virtually nothing on the topic of female suicide, as though it could never happen. Rowley discusses notions of female madness at length by arguing for a distinctly feminine physiological root of all female mental distempers. Under the heading 'General

Figure 4.1 John Everett Millais, 'Ophelia', 1852. Available in the public domain via Wikipedia

Figure 4.2 Alexandre Cabanel, 'Ophelia', 1883. Available in the public domain via Wikipedia

Figure 4.3 John William Waterhouse, 'Ophelia', 1894. Available in the public domain via Wikipedia

Method of preventing Female Diseases, &c.', the doctor links women's illnesses to feminine weakness and menstruation:

> THE delicate structure of the female body; the peculiar sensibility of the nervous system; the absence, presence, diminution, increase, or obstruction of the catamenia [i.e. menstrual blood]; the state of the uterus, and the singularities of each individual constitution, all require the most serious attention of the physician, who would treat the disorders of females, with integrity and success. The due regulation of the catamenia is of the utmost importance. (1–2)

However, by the time Rowley arrives at the last topic listed in his work's extensive title, suicide, he has ceased to consider women specifically and supposes a more universal – read male – patient for his considerations:

> *Jealousy* is a sensation of suspicion, where the greatest confidence is expected. In both love and marriage it has produced suicide: its remedy is indifference to the object adored, or a philosophical resignation to infidelity. In France, and other warm countries, infidelity in a mistress or wife is treated with levity or laughter; in England, with sober sadness, detestation, or self-murder. (287; emphasis in original)

That Rowley considers the topic of frustrated love leading to suicide from the perspective of the male lover alone – one whose 'mistress or wife' cheats on him – shows that he does not seriously consider women in this light. This point is surely linked to his meditation on the 'violence' of jealousy a few lines earlier (287), as women were thought incapable of real violence to themselves or others.

Despite the long-standing affinity for the literary theme of female suicide, the view that real women rarely killed themselves lasted well into the Victorian period. George Henry Lewes, the partner of George Eliot (Mary Ann Evans), wrote in 1857 that women killed themselves less often than men did because of their '"greater timidity"' and '"greater power of passive endurance, both of bodily and mental pain"', while others attributed the supposed scarcity of female suicides to women's superior obedience – presumably to society's rules that people should not take their own lives. In a similar vein, S. A. K. Strahan attributed the dearth of female suicides to women's '"lack of courage and [their] natural repugnance to personal violence and disfigurement"' (quoted in Gates 126), suggesting that women would rather live in misery than spoil their looks. Anderson reports that the only credible reasons why a woman could choose to die in the Victorian period was that her sexual relationships – forced, fulfilled or unrequited – failed her; in general, though, real female suicides were rarely discussed (57). The difference in reported suicides of males versus females in the Victorian era may reflect a reticence to report female suicides at both the official and unofficial, or familial, levels (Gates 146; see also Bailey 44, 273n; and Anderson 43–4). Arguably, the very lack of information about female suicides and, when they were acknowledged, the beliefs about the motivations for them, reveal the cultural ideal that women are weak and dependent, unable to choose suicide for their own reasons.

Another feature of the reportage of female suicide that remains remarkably constant throughout the centuries – even into our own – concerns the means through which women kill themselves. In reports from the Victorian period, drowning is the method most often chosen by women (Bailey 44, 64).[7] The most infamous would-be female suicide of the Romantic period, Wollstonecraft, would seem to underscore this claim, since she tried to drown herself in her second suicide attempt (Godwin, *Memoirs* 101), while P. B. Shelley's first wife, Harriet Shelley, succeeded in the act. Many commentators suggest that women were thought to prefer less bloody means of suicide like drowning (MacDonald, 'Secularization' 66) or poison – such as through an overdose of laudanum, the method chosen for Wollstonecraft's first suicide attempt and Fanny Godwin's death. Importantly, though, the historical record on female suicides may not reflect the true number of deaths accurately. Since, as Bailey comments, drowning is easier to conceal as an act of suicide than are some other methods, such as hanging (the preferred method of men in the Victorian period) (44), the reportage of women's accidental deaths by drowning may ignore the likelihood that many of them were, in fact, suicides.

The reasons given for why and how women choose to die may also tell us something about the constructed nature of reports about female suicides: by mixing objective fact with assumptions, they often reveal mostly cultural expectations of women, such as that they are passive bodies designed to fulfil the desires of the patriarchy. Aurelia Armstrong comments on Foucault's definition of 'docile bodies' under disciplinary power, which aimed to 'optimize the body's ... productivity and to foster its usefulness and docility' (n.p.) as a subject of biopower. The idea that women could not embrace violent death and the wish to view them as sexually attractive even in death sustain the fantasy of patriarchal power over the female body. Vera Lind argues:

> the aggressiveness and supposed coldness of the act [of suicide] appeared as a dangerous violation of early modern gender norms – women who behaved more like men threatened the order of society. With cultural interpretative models, this threat could be tracked and reintegrated into societal order. When women violated boundaries of acceptable behavior, people around them often responded by trying to put such women back into their proper

> female realm, or by making others responsible for their behavior ... [, or by tying the motivation to the] female realm of emotions. (69)

In a similar manner, commentators reveal their beliefs about female vanity or weakness in their speculations about women's motives for choosing death. Writing in 1882, James O'Dea comments:

> The mode of suicide is also governed by sex. Women occasionally end their lives ... [by] drowning or poison, because they instinctively shrink from mutilation of their bodies. Their preference for drowning over all other modes is due to a sentiment arising in them on contrasting their impressions of water – its mystery, repose, and grateful coolness, especially – with the turmoil and fever of their passions. (154)

As so many others do, O'Dea implies that women are too concerned about their attractiveness to mar their appearance intentionally through suicide, while his comment on the 'mystery, repose, and grateful coolness' of water reveals his attempt to see the world from a suicidal woman's viewpoint, which he assumes must seek beauty and sensual pleasure even in the moment of death. This aspect of his description reveals its subjective nature, which he presents otherwise as objective and quasi-scientific, or at least sociological, as the title of his treatise suggests: *Suicide: Studies on its Philosophy, Causes, and Prevention.* Here is the denial that women could kill themselves in a fit of anger, jealousy or rebellion – the denial that, perhaps, women might choose drowning because they do not have access to firearms or never learned how to tie a hangman's knot.

Such prejudices regarding the possibilities for female violence coloured not only the ideal and written but also the enacted response to female suicides. Working on the assumption that female vanity extends beyond the bounds of death, writers from the classical period to the Romantic era suggested that the threat of insult to the modesty of the female suicide's corpse could be an effective method of discouraging the act. Plutarch's *Moralia* (100 ce) recounts 'an epidemic of suicide ... among the young women of Miletus, presumably girls around the age of puberty when they were about to be married', a story that 'is well known for its account of an effective deterrent to suicide: public shame' (Pabst Battin, Introductions 128). As the story goes, a 'man of sense' suggested that the corpses should be brought naked through the town to their burial, which quickly put a stop to the suicides (Plutarch 129). What is particularly striking about this tale is its contradictory nature. Plutarch explains that an infection in the air or the gods made the girls go insane and hang themselves (Plutarch 129), which suggests that the suicides were involuntary, having been committed while the girls were *non compos mentis*. Yet, if these suicides were committed in a fit of madness, then how could a threat – to their modesty or otherwise – have effectively countered the girls' involuntary impulses? What appears to be more vital to the story than consistency is the joint affirmation of women as vain and weak, both emotionally and mentally, characteristics essential to the notion of female passivity and receptivity.

John Wesley, the founder of Methodism, tells a similar tale: 'We read in ancient history, that at a certain period, many of the women in Sparta murdered themselves. This fury increasing, a law was made, that the body of every woman that killed herself, should be exposed naked in the streets. The fury ceased at once' (164). Wesley implies that a woman's existence is so thoroughly defined by her sexual being, her body, that an offence to her modesty even in death will be enough to make her reconsider committing suicide. A text on suicide from 1819 confirms that this view of women did not change much over the years; the anonymous commentator advocates for a more 'frequent dissection of' the corpses of suicides, not only to prevent the 'resurrection men' from digging them up from graveyards to sell them to medical students, but also to deter women from killing themselves: '"the number of suicides, particularly female suicides, would be reduced; the act would therefore be humane"' (quoted in Anon., *Thoughts* 29). Although the commentator does not explain his logic, presumably he believes that the threat of a woman's naked body being exposed to (necessarily male) medical students and dissected after death would be so insulting to her modesty that she would overcome her suicidal impulses to avoid it. Such treatments of the female suicide's corpse demonstrate the belief that a woman's entire being, even unto death, is defined by sex – the only way that the arm of biopower that is the patriarchy views her.

Female Suicide in the Media

This conceptualisation of womanhood echoes throughout newspaper reports of female suicides in the long eighteenth century, too. The writers consider the victims with respect to their attractiveness, first and foremost, as though a woman's vanity must continue to be flattered even after death, and they thereby demonstrate the belief that women's bodies are their only ontological reality, even at the point of decomposition. A search of *The Times Digital Archive* from the dates 1770 to 1830 for coroner's inquests and other reports of female suicide, usually accomplished by drowning or poisoning, provides a wealth of material. Many of these anonymous reports have one thing in common: commentary on the attractive appearance of the female corpse.[8] Some of these dead women are merely 'youthful and interesting [in] appearance, respectably dressed' (24 April 1821), while others are 'extremely pretty and interesting ... even in death' (7 August 1830). So many female suicides receive such gallant treatment that one might well exclaim that death does, indeed, 'become her' (to cite the title of the 1992 film directed by Robert Zemeckis). The descriptions of the dead women range from 'fine-looking' (14 September 1819) to 'remarkably fine ... [and yo]ung' (24 March 1828); from 'possessed of uncommon personal beauty' (8 January 1827) to 'remarkably fine ... [and] possessed of features of no common attractions' (3 April 1828); and from a 'young and beautiful girl' (3 December 1825) to a 'beautiful young girl, only 17 years of age' (28 September 1789). On occasion the reporters indulge in purple prose to describe their lovely, lifeless subjects. Writing of a woman who, unusually, committed suicide by hanging – in a 'temporary fit of delirium', the coroner decided – one writer opines, 'It is not very often the Coroner has to perform his melancholy duty upon an object of so much beauty as the present deceased' (7 January 1823). Another woman, 'Found drowned', receives the royal descriptive treatment: 'A slight flush upon the face bespoke her to have once been the "rosy cheeked village beauty"; and her long light hair, which hung loosely over her neck and shoulders, presented a picture of melancholy interest' (1 September 1830), as though the dead woman were a sentimental work of art created to appeal to onlookers. Yet another woman's corpse was too decomposed, it seems, to describe it truthfully as attractive, but that does not stop the commentator from imagining the beauty that might well have graced the body once: 'it still preserved sufficient [flesh?] to indicate that she had once been beautiful. Her hair, which was raven-black, had partially fallen off, and its contrast to the skin, which was of a marble whiteness, drew forth several observations from the jury' (22 November 1829). Even in death, the suicidal female could not escape being viewed as a sexual being whose attractiveness is paramount.[9]

It should be recognised that the commentators in *The Times* occasionally point out the excellent morals of the female suicide; unsurprisingly, these, too, are mostly of a sexual nature. In an article titled 'Seduction and Suicide' that recounts a case from a French newspaper, the age-old link between women and sexual modesty is foremost. The drowned woman, young and of 'great personal beauty', is praised for her concern that her corpse should maintain a decorous appearance: 'her clothes were so pinned and fastened as to ... guard against indelicate exposure' (10 December 1822). Just as threats to submit the female suicide's corpse to sexual humiliation demonstrate that a woman could be punished or rewarded with respect to her modesty even in death, this woman's progeny stands to benefit from her chastity: the writer comments that her youth, extreme beauty, courage and misfortunes 'have excited an interest for her which will be useful to her child', who was thereafter adopted (ibid.). When other reports praise female suicides on points other than sexual modesty and beauty, they almost always do so in addition to these topics. One begins by transcribing the encomiums upon the attractiveness of the dead woman provided by her travelling companion, after which the writer moves to a more substantial assessment of her praiseworthy qualities: 'He described her as a fine figure, said she had a very graceful manner, had read a great deal, spoke very well, and entertained him with many songs as they travelled' (4 November 1786). Others echo this pattern: one reports that the suicide's 'appearance was very pleasing, and, as it yet appears, [she] was of irreproachable character' (11 September 1827), and another comments on a drowned woman, 'She was a handsome girl, 20 years of age, and was remarked for her modest, careful, and industrious conduct' (6 November 1829). These reports are distinguished from the more typical ones in their humane aspect – they recognise that a woman should not be summed up entirely with reference to her attractiveness in death – but they also share an apparent wish to elicit the sympathy of the reader, which aligns them with the popular literature of sensibility.

'The most poetical object in the world': Sensibility and the Lovely Dead

In many of these newspaper reports, the influence of the period's hugely popular literature of sensibility is evident. This literature aimed to arouse the reader's sympathy and provoke a tearful response to the pathetic subjects it describes – commonly lovely and virtuous young women beset by trials and tribulations, often of an amorous nature, and not infrequently ending with the heroine's death. Sympathy-inducing female protagonists are at the quickly beating heart of most novels of sensibility, the chief example of which is Samuel Richardson's *Clarissa*, with his *Pamela* (1740) a close second. Other immensely popular novels of sensibility feature male protagonists, foremost among them Goethe's *The Sorrows of Young Werther*, while some famous British examples also include male (less often suicidal) protagonists, such as Henry Mackenzie's *The Man of Feeling* (1771) and Laurence Sterne's *A Sentimental Journey* (1768). In novels of sensibility or sentiment readers are encouraged to be emotionally moved by the trials of the pathetic (mostly) female protagonists, for whom, in turn, extreme, trembling, emotional responses to beauty, kindness, love and the misfortunes of others provide the sure answer to the trials they witness.

The figure of the woman of sensibility who is so affected by trials in love that she sinks into death is common in such literature, although her fragility is seldom presented overtly as suicidality. On this count, female writers of sensibility – such as Burney, Charlotte Smith and even Wollstonecraft (since *Mary* may be classified as a novella of sensibility) – faced an important hurdle to inducing the desired affective response of sympathetic tears in their audience, as Eric Parisot cogently notes: 'Expressions of suicidal desire, in the real or imaginary sphere, could severely hinder any claim to sympathy and/or remembrance founded on the pathos of virtue in distress' ('Labour' 661). The virulent reaction of readers to Godwin's revelation in *Memoirs of the Author of* A Vindication of the Rights of Woman (1798) that his newly dead wife had attempted suicide twice supports this claim. For over a century after its publication, Wollstonecraft was reviled, not least – although perhaps first – by Richard Polwhele, who wrote in a footnote to *The Unsex'd Females*, a poem decrying Wollstonecraftian feminism published shortly after her death in 1798:

> I cannot but think, that the Hand of Providence is visible, in her life, her death and in [Godwin's] Memoirs ... that the fallacy of [her doctrines] and the effects of an irreligious conduct, might be manifested to the world; and as she died a death that strongly marked the distinction of the sexes [i.e. from childbirth], by pointing out the destiny of women, and the diseases to which they are liable. (327)

Polwhele's suggestion that her peculiarly feminine death was divine punishment for her immodest conduct doubtlessly refers to her feminist philosophy and extramarital pregnancies, as well as to her suicide attempts.

In the Romantic-period culture of sensibility, such sinking into death may be interpreted as the opposite of subversive, with suicide representing the culmination of the female character's role in a patriarchal culture as utterly passive – a docile body. The period's celebration of thin, quiet, reserved and selfless women reveals a preference for women who are one fainting spell away from dying. Byron links women's femininity and attractiveness to their lack of bodily desires in a letter to Lady Melbourne, dated 25 September 1812: 'I only wish she did not swallow so much supper ... a woman should never be seen eating or drinking, unless it be *lobster sallad* [*sic*] *&* *Champagne*, the only truly feminine & becoming viands' (*Letters*, ed. Lansdowne 109). Such bodilessness can easily slide into depictions of lovely female suicide. Some female writers traded in these terms. Suicide appears often in Burney's novels, where it is treated as a capitulation to patriarchal culture, rather than a protest against it, Margaret Anne Doody argues with respect to the character Elinor from *The Wanderer* (1814): 'the female suicidal gesture, though it seems defiant, original, and liberating, is an obedience to social commands ... The customary command for woman is that she be unobstrusive, slender, and quiet' (342). Bronfen makes a similar claim in *Over her Dead Body* (1992), the main argument of which is that, since women and death are 'othered' in Western culture, the constant identification of the two in art throughout the ages confirms women's alterity, their lack of agency and their marginal position in society. The critic also recognises that the theme of suicide can have protesting power:

> The choice of death emerges as a feminine strategy within which writing with the body is a way of getting rid of the oppression connected with the feminine body. Staging disembodiment as a form of escaping personal and social constraints serves to criticize those cultural attitudes that reduce the feminine body to the position of dependency and passivity, to the vulnerable object of sexual incursions. (142)

Similarly, Koretsky recognises that suicide in Romantic literature can sometimes express 'an individual's right to their own body to interrogate liberal notions of gendered subjectivity' ('Interracial' 1), and she also demonstrates that it is sometimes used to confirm conservative values in certain texts, including the link between oppressed people and death. The literary trope of female suicide is, again, like that of slave suicide: even the figures who are most evidently protesting can be interpreted as undermining a subversive purpose.

The most famous novel of sensibility with a suicidal female protagonist, Richardson's *Clarissa*, is a good example of how a female suicidal character can undermine feminine agency, rather than assert it, as the heroine is presented as attaining the height of feminine attractiveness in her weakness-unto-death.[10] In *Rights of Woman*, Wollstonecraft asks:

> Nature has given woman a weaker frame than man; but, to ensure her husband's affections, must a wife, who, by the exercise of her mind and body whilst she was discharging the duties of a daughter, wife, and mother, has allowed her constitution to retain its natural strength, and her nerves a healthy tone, is she, I say, to condescend, to use art, and feign a sickly delicacy, in order to secure her husband's affection? (138)

This 'mere nothing' with a 'sickly, die-away languor' – as Wollstonecraft describes Mary's mother in *Mary* (79) – was presented as an ideal of femininity in the period. The figure also appears in Jane Austen's *Sense and Sensibility* as Marianne, a character who almost dies, so completely does she indulge her desire to be the ultimate weak and heartbroken woman of sensibility. Marianne herself eventually recognises the suicidality in her illness:

> my own feelings had prepared my sufferings, and ... my want of fortitude under them had almost led me to the grave. My illness, I well knew, had been entirely brought on by myself, by such negligence of my own health, as I had felt even at the time to be wrong. Had I died, – it would have been self-destruction. (350)

Somewhat less gently, Burney also satirises the 'die-away' woman of sensibility in *Evelina* through the character of Lady Louisa Larpent, Lord Orville's sister. Writing to her guardian, Arthur Villars, Evelina introduces her as 'a pretty, but affected young lady', a description that she repeats later in the novel (216, 412). Lady Louisa is, it seems, always fatigued nearly to death and totally absorbed in the performance of her weakness:

> In a few minutes Lady Louisa Larpent made her appearance ... [and] passed straight forward to her seat on the sofa; where, leaning her head on her hand, she cast her languishing eyes round the room, with a vacant stare, as if determined, though she looked, not to see who was in it. (417)

Burney criticises the sickly lady of sensibility as a fraud, not to mention completely self-absorbed by her desire to appear debilitated, rather than selfless and beneficent, as she is supposed to be. (Wollstonecraft also criticises the woman of sensibility for her insincerity and lack of true benevolence in *Rights of Woman* and *Rights of Men* (e.g. 112, 79, respectively)). These female writers' distaste for the figure reflects the real damage that can ensue when living women mimic her sickly antics, so attractive is she made to appear in the sympathy-inducing literature of sensibility. This literary trend was, thus, an effective tool of biopower in encouraging women to embrace their docile bodies willingly. Armstrong notes that disciplinary power's 'perpetual surveillance is internalized by individuals to produce the kind of self-awareness that defines the modern subject' (n.p.). The woman of sensibility internalises, even prizes, her passivity as a subject of biopower – sometimes to the point of death, which, ironically, undoes biopower's aims.

We may read Wordsworth's poems about suicidal women in terms of the popular literature that depicts them as passive beings, constructed to draw out the reader's pleasurable tears, undermining the figure's potential for protest. 'The Mad Mother' and 'The Complaint of a Forsaken

Indian Woman' both feature mothers whose very existence is defined by their relationship to their children – in short, their sexual productivity. In 'The Mad Mother', the poet paints a heart-rending picture of a woman driven insane when she is abandoned by her baby's father, in yet another iteration of the woman whose suicidality is born of unrequited love. The 'mad mother' declares to her baby:

Thy father cares not for my breast,
'Tis thine, sweet baby, there to rest:
'Tis all thine own! and if its hue
Be changed, that was so fair to view,
'Tis fair enough for thee, my dove! (61–5)

She is so upset by her lover's abandonment that she has become not only suicidal, but also infanticidal:

Oh! love me, love me, little boy!
Thou art thy mother's only joy;
And do not dread the waves below,
When o'er the sea-rock's edge we go. (41–4)

Directly after this threat of violence against her infant, though, the mad mother duly promises to care for her baby:

The high crag cannot work me harm,
Nor leaping torrents when they howl;
. . . .
Without me my sweet babe would die.
Then do not fear, my boy! for thee
Bold as a lion I will be. (45–6; 51–2)

Her violent intentions are far outweighed by her devotion to the life of her child. Wordsworth thus carefully constructs a figure of female suicide that supports the sentimental view of the suicidal woman as pitiable, rather than rebellious, and, even in a state of insanity, a productive contributor to society.

Wordsworth writes of another marginalised suicidal mother in 'The Complaint of a Forsaken Indian Woman' (hereafter 'Indian Woman'), which he introduces in a prefatory note as an account of what happens when 'Northern Indian' (or Indigenous North American) people leave their sick members behind while the rest of the band migrates (151). Written from the perspective of a woman so abandoned, the poem makes her suicidality clear in the opening lines and the refrain ('Before I see another day,/ Oh let my body die away!' (1–2)). She confirms her wish to die in the second stanza:

My fire is dead: it knew no pain;
Yet is it dead, and I remain.
All stiff with ice the ashes lie;
And they are dead, and I will die.
When I was well, I wished to live,
For clothes, for warmth, for food, and fire;
But they to me no joy can give,
No pleasure now, and no desire.
Then here contented will I lie;
Alone I cannot fear to die. (11–20)

Because she is ill, she resigns herself to death and even wishes for it. This attitude becomes complicated in the subsequent stanzas, in which the speaker confesses to feeling forsaken by her community, which seems to have abandoned her because she ceased to be a productive contributor to it on account of her despondent state: 'Alas! you might have dragged me on/ Another day, a single one!/ Too soon despair o'er me prevailed;/ Too soon my heartless spirit failed' (21–4). This aspect of the poem may constitute Wordsworth's protest against society's demands upon the individual to be productive, a position he advances in 'Argument for Suicide', as discussed at the outset of this book. The Indian Woman laments:

My child! they gave thee to another,
A woman who was not thy mother.
When from my arms my babe they took,
On me how strangely did he look!
Through his whole body something ran,
A most strange something did I see;
– As if he strove to be a man,
That he might pull the sledge for me.
And then he stretched his arms, how wild
Oh mercy! like a little child. (31–40)

This character's reproductive capacity is prized by her society more than her life, it seems. Like the 'Mad Mother', her existence is defined, and perhaps decided, by her relationship to her child.

Features of the literature of sensibility are also found in the non-literary realm of the long eighteenth century, since these texts reflect their culture's values as surely as their culture reflects the sentimental author's values. The principle even applies to the medical realm. G. S. Rousseau traces the 'origins of sensibility' to the medical focus on 'nerves, spirits, and fibres', as his title goes: a major focus of the study of 'nerves, and their subsidiaries, fibres and animal spirits' was their link to the brain, which was newly posited as the seat of love and the soul, the main concerns of the novel of sensibility (145). So ingrained was sensibility in

British life that Barker-Benfield writes of the period's 'culture of sensibility' in a book bearing that title, which outlines how letter-writing became identifiable with the novel of sensibility in the form of the epistolary novel (206, 314). Arguably, then, newspaper reports of lovely, dying, virtuous women both echo and contribute to the culture of sensibility. Their selective focus on certain features of female suicides and the reasons given for these women's final choice seems to be formed by the writers' wish to satisfy their readers' expectations of them, as well as their own narrow view of the possibilities for imagining female suicide.

Literary Female Suicide as Subversive

Wollstonecraft and her daughter Shelley use the topic of female suicide to protest the limitations placed upon women in their patriarchal societies. Although their protagonists' lives are circumscribed by love, these writers do not celebrate the circumstance, as so many of their fellow period authors do. Instead, love – both amorous and familial, and it is disturbingly so at the same time in *Mathilda* – functions a lot like hate in this fiction: it chokes and punishes the female protagonists until they wish for death as a release, their suicidality a condemnation of their culture's limiting and destructive definition of women. Amorous love may be understood as a euphemism for sex, and therefore the perception that women's lives and deaths are entirely defined by it is a recognition and enforcement of their sexual objectification – of biopower's control over women and obsession with their fecundity as generators of additional assets to power through reproduction. Defined thus, these characters attempt to forge new identities for themselves beyond the demands of power through their suicidality.

In contrast with works that sentimentalise female suicide, Wollstonecraft's *Mary* and *The Wrongs of Woman*, as well as Shelley's *Mathilda*, use the theme of female suicidality as a powerful means of protest. To develop the complexities of the protagonists' relationships with patriarchy, these works take advantage of the space offered by the relatively long novella form, as well as its possibilities for the psychological development of the main characters, to explore the many ways in which women are cast as objects, as bodies alone, lacking personal agency, which renders their female suicidality as a subversive refusal of the burden of the body that weighs women down and steals their autonomy. These are not the only Romantic novels by women that feature female suicidality as a rebellion against patriarchal control; the theme may also be found in Mary Hays's *The Victim of Prejudice* (1799),

Mary Robinson's *The Natural Daughter* (1799) and Charlotte Smith's *Desmond* (1792). I focus on Wollstonecraft's and Shelley's novellas because they explore female suicidality as the consequence of patriarchal oppression throughout their long prose texts, rather than only as a single narrative episode. With respect to the theme of female suicidality in general, they contribute to a tradition established in the shorter poetic forms written by contemporary women authors, although some of that may be considered sentimental, rather than in the spirit of biopolitical protest.

Some of the best-known women writers of the Romantic period penned verses on suicide. Charlotte Smith – 'one of the most popular writers of her time' (Hunt, Jr 85) – explores the topic in *Elegaic Sonnets*, an instant hit when it was published in 1784 and one that earned the author (who was then in debtors' prison with her spendthrift husband) much-needed money, as well as literary fame; the volume went into multiple editions and, according to Loraine Fletcher, it was 'never out of print in her lifetime' (30). *Elegaic Sonnets*, Parisot argues, 'subtly gestures towards the spectre of suicide by way of quotation and allusion', with the 'most sustained consideration of the theme ... found in Smith's five-sonnet sequence supposedly written by Goethe's Werther, dramatizing the sentimental hero's decline from his complaint to his desire for solitude in nature to imaginings of an afterlife in the hearts and minds of others' (Parisot, 'Labour' 661). Mary Robinson, another well-known woman writer, also versified on suicide: her poem 'The Negro Girl' (1800) – one of many abolitionist poems by women in the period – features a young enslaved woman, Zelma, who escapes slavery and chooses death by drowning when she sees her beloved, Draco, perish after leaping into the waves from a sinking slave ship offshore. Although it may at first appear to be a sentimental treatment of female suicide that treats women as existentially dependent upon their connection to men, much like Wordsworth's 'The Mad Mother' or 'Indian Woman', Robinson's poem is subversive: referencing Jean-Luc Nancy's commentary on Kant, Higonnet comments, 'Robinson's actors refuse servitude. The Kantian sublime implies a recognition that sacrifice must lead to freedom, and it is the importance of that theme of liberty in the politically inflected representations of suicide that has perhaps been overlooked in previous studies of Romantic suicide' ('winged nature' 685). Meanwhile, Robinson's celebrated *Sappho and Phaon* sonnet sequence ends with a female suicide, that of Sappho, who rejects precarious romantic love in favour of lasting literary fame in her final moments. In Sonnet XLII, the third-last sonnet of the 44-sonnet sequence, Sappho predicts,

Soon o'er this heart, now warm with passion's flame,
The howling winds and foamy waves shall sweep;
Those eyes be ever clos'd in death's cold sleep,
And all of Sappho perish, but her name! (5–8)

The poem rejects patriarchal control by removing the woman's body from the sphere of amorous concerns and replacing her physical existence with an ideal one, represented through her literary output.

One of the most famous of all Romantic-era women poets also wrote about female suicide – and did so quite extensively. 'Hemans's poetry was admired by Lord Byron, Percy Bysshe Shelley, Marian Evans (George Eliot), Matthew Arnold, ... and countless other writers and literary critics of discerning taste', writes Paula Feldman, who adds, 'Of Hemans's contemporaries who are well-known today, only Lord Byron and Walter Scott sold more books than she in their lifetimes' (xi). Higonnet observes that Hemans presents figures of defiant female suicidality in several of her poems, including 'The Wife of Asdrubal' (1819) and 'The Last Song of Sappho' (1831) ('winged nature' 685–7). Many other poems on female suicide appear in a single volume, *Records of Woman, with Other Poems*, published in 1828 at the height of Hemans's poetic fame. Every one of the nineteen poems in it 'protests death's inevitable wrenching of the bonds of human love', comments Feldman (xxi), with no fewer than four of them featuring suicidal women: 'Imelda', 'Pauline', 'The Bride of the Greek Isle' and 'Indian Woman's Death-Song'. 'Imelda' is a tale reminiscent of Shakespeare's *Romeo and Juliet* (1597), as Hemans's Imelda kills herself after her brother kills her beloved, Azzo, and 'Pauline' features a heroic mother who joins her fate to that of her daughter, Bertha, in a conflagration. The last two poems speak most closely to the focus of this study, though, as they present female suicide as subversive. 'The Bride of the Greek Isle' features the young Eudora who sets fire to her kidnapper's ship to protest the killing of her groom, Ianthis, on their wedding day. As Higonnet points out, '"The Bride of the Greek Isle" ... assigns to the female figure the themes of slavery and republican freedom, a Byronic legacy' marked by Hemans's epigraph from *Sardanapalus*: '"Fear! – I'm a Greek, and how should I fear death?/ A slave, and wherefore should I dread my freedom?"' ('winged nature' 686). Subversive suicide also appears in 'Indian Woman's Death-Song', which is, in title and theme (an Indigenous North American woman who wishes to die after having been abandoned by her partner), strongly reminiscent of Wordsworth's 'Indian Woman'. However, Hemans depicts her 'Indian' woman with a degree of awe that is unmatched in Wordsworth's more sentimental poem. Her protagonist rushes towards a 'thunder[ing]' 'cataract[ ]' in a 'frail bark' (6, 4),

> . . . . Yet within,
> Proudly, and dauntlessly, and all alone,
> Save that a babe lay sleeping at her breast,
> A woman stood: upon her Indian brow
> Sat a strange gladness, and her dark hair wav'd
> As if triumphantly. She press'd her child,
> In its bright slumber, to her beating heart,
> And lifted her sweet voice, that rose awhile
> Above the sound of waters, high and clear,
> Wafting a wild proud strain, her song of death. (6–15)

The Indian woman's pride is mentioned twice (7, 15), while she stands 'dauntlessly' in the fearful scene, even her hair a banner to her suicidal 'triumph[ ]' (7, 11). Here, again, is a scene of suicide as heroic protest.[11] Through some of the major themes around which I organise this book – those of slave and female suicide – renowned women poets made the trope of subversive suicide familiar, and perhaps even acceptable, to a wide reading public in the Romantic period. To be sure, Wollstonecraft and Shelley contributed to an established tradition of female writers presenting women's suicide as subversive when they wrote their extensive prose treatments of the subject.

Admittedly, Wollstonecraft's and Shelley's texts are not models of humanistic protest: they indulge in a kind of predatory relationship with the subaltern[12] by invoking the figure of the enslaved person in an age of transatlantic slavery, a comparison that rings hollow, given the tortures inflicted upon enslaved Africans. At several points in Wollstonecraft's and Shelley's works, the figure of the enslaved person functions as an exemplar of one who is defined by the body, since those who perpetuate slavery treat enslaved people only as bodies that work, as mere machines. Wollstonecraft and Shelley demonstrate that women are ideologically positioned similarly, as mere bodies under biopower, specifically sexual bodies. For these authors, a woman's wish for death – the cessation of her body – is a bid for freedom from the patriarchal hegemony that traps her in this one-dimensional role.

Wollstonecraft invests women's struggle to free themselves from the shackles of patriarchy with broad political resonance by borrowing the language and tropes of abolition, especially the figure of the suicidal freedom fighter. Early women's rights activists were far from the first to use the example of slave suicide beyond the anti-slavery movement, however. Snyder reports:

> When John Locke asserted that freedom from arbitrary power was a natural right [in 1689], he used the example of a slave's choice to die to illustrate his point. Locke argued that whenever a slave found that the hardship of slavery

> outweighed the value of his life, 'it is in his power, by resisting the will of his master, to draw on himself the death he desires'. ('Memory' 51)

Catherine Macaulay Graham, Wollstonecraft's forebearer in the annals of early feminist writing, introduces the language of slavery to the 'woman question' in her influential *Letters on Education* (1790) by arguing that, although women were reduced 'to a state of abject slavery' in the past, 'Providence [did not] intend to make the condition of slavery an unalterable law of female nature' (315). Accordingly, Wollstonecraft adopts the language of slavery and abolition to protest women's lack of freedom in eighteenth-century society, and she utilises the powerful resonance of and social interest in the issue of transatlantic slavery for her purposes. Ferguson notes that Wollstonecraft makes more than eighty references to slavery in *Rights of Woman*, while Thomas, Carol Howard and Kari Winter confirm the powerful influence of abolitionist texts on her writings, both polemical and literary (Ferguson 155, 186; Thomas 86–8; Howard 71; Winter 1). By co-opting the language of abolition and slavery for feminist purposes, Wollstonecraft shows considerable insensitivity regarding the struggles of the African victims of transatlantic slavery, whose suffering far outstripped anything experienced by most British women under patriarchal rule. Nevertheless, her strategy also demonstrates that the earliest feminist struggles were waged under the banner of the human right to bodily freedom and autonomy, as were the earliest abolitionist struggles.[13] Some critics have even interpreted Wollstonecraft's own suicide attempts as tied to the Enlightenment culture of human rights. Writing at length about Wollstonecraft's attitude towards 'rational suicide' in *Gender, Art, and Death* (1993), Janet Todd muses that Wollstonecraft's attempts to drown herself may be understood as conveying that 'the rights of woman might, for a disappointed Wollstonecraft in 1795, include the revolutionary right of rational death' (115). This attitude towards suicide certainly appears in Wollstonecraft's literary works. I focus on Wollstonecraft's novellas to delineate how she advances her polemical stance against biopower by establishing the figure of the subversive suicide in the feminist literary canon, and to reveal how this figure resonates in Shelley's *Mathilda*.

In Wollstonecraft's work, slavery represents control over the body, a management of the subject's physical being that can also have a deleterious effect on her psychic existence. In *Rights of Woman*, Wollstonecraft argues that 'the weakness of women' that is commonly attributed to a kind of natural femininity is, rather, the result of 'slavish bondage to parents': 'girls, from various causes, are more kept down by their parents ... than boys ... [A]nd thus taught slavishly to submit to their parents, they are prepared for the slavery of marriage' (294–5). These 'various causes' all stem from girls' sexual reality as females, making their slavishness entirely of the biopolitical kind: parents wish to ensure their marriageability by teaching them how to behave as docile slaves. Wollstonecraft's reliance on the figure of the enslaved echoes arguments advanced by writers such as Equiano, who asserts in *The Interesting Narrative* that Africans are not innately inferior to Europeans intellectually, but their enslavement has made them appear so (31). Both writers emphasise the cultural production of subordination amongst certain groups, showing that no one is born to be oppressed. Wollstonecraft's familiarity with Equiano's text is evident in her review of it for Joseph Johnson's journal *The Analytical Review* in 1789.[14] Her intellectual debt to Equiano is thus deeper than a superficial adoption of the terms of abolitionism in her own writing. These extra-fictional examples of Wollstonecraft's familiarity with the topics of female dependence and slavery suggest the development of her thinking about themes that feature so prominently in her novellas, as well as show her understanding of them as creations of culture. The oppressed, entirely mediated by their bodies (for that is how they are made to function in society), may gain freedom and equality through a new conceptualisation of themselves – the very point of her polemical writing.

Wollstonecraft inaugurates this consideration of British womanhood in her novels by introducing female protagonists who long for the freedom from marriage promised by self-chosen death. Literary form is important here, in that Wollstonecraft chooses two novelistic genres that were particularly popular with female reading audiences – the novel of sentiment in *Mary* and the Gothic novel in *The Wrongs of Woman* – to frame her message of female subversion via suicide. By writing in these genres, Wollstonecraft addresses her rebellious stories especially to women readers, appealing to them via tropes and other literary devices with which they were familiar. This is not to say, however, that Wollstonecraft wishes to make her female audience comfortable. Her discomfiting conclusion in both novels – that women can escape their roles as mere bodies via death alone – might even undermine the efficacy of what we might assume to be her goal, feminist agitation for change.[15] One might counter: if fighting the patriarchy means choosing death, then perhaps women should accept the status quo, especially since most women's domestic situations are not nearly as dire as the lot of the enslaved. This point only serves to underscore the importance of literary genre for Wollstonecraft's feminist message, though. She conveys it via the form of the novella – as opposed to polemical prose, as in her *Vindications* – to encourage her reader to use her imagination and adopt the perspective of her protagonists, whose personal situations feel so desperate to them that they contemplate death as an escape. Objectively considered, these protagonists' lives may not seem intolerable, but by following their dawning awareness of their debased conditions as mere bodies without intellect or agency, the reader gains an appreciation of the significance of their suicidal wishes.

Shelley continues in this vein in *Mathilda*, a story about a father whose sense of ownership over his daughter extends to his desire for her body. The innovative novelistic form in which Shelley conveys this narrative – the long suicide note – becomes the character's means of forging a new, autonomous identity for herself. Indeed, the narrative protests her father's formation of her very existence into a dirty secret and becomes an attempt to redefine herself at the point of death. Together, these fictional narratives demonstrate a recognition of women's subjugation through their bodies and, through the literary trope of suicide, they agitate against it.

The Suicides of the Marys

In both *Mary* and *The Wrongs of Woman*, the autobiographically named protagonists, Mary and Maria, are both suicidal, as was Wollstonecraft herself during the interval between the writing of the novellas. Perhaps in recognition that the literary theme of female suicidality could sometimes convey female passivity, rather than autonomy, Wollstonecraft represents suicide in her fiction as a death wish rather than an accomplished act, aware that her writing could affect female readers' perceptions of themselves and ways of living as women. Thus, in the 'Advertisement' to *Mary*, Wollstonecraft declares that her protagonist redefines the possibilities for female characters in eighteenth-century novels of sensibility while recognising their link to living women in Romantic-era British society (75–6). The forematter also includes the epigraph, '*L'exercice des plus sublimes vertus éleve et nourrit le génie*', 'The exercise of the most sublime virtues raises and nourishes genius' (73). This quotation, from Rousseau's *Julie*, gestures to three of the main themes of *Mary*: female natural genius, education, and sensibility, to which the phrase 'sublime virtues' refers. Wollstonecraft reiterates the development of the female mind as the theme of her novella by describing it, in the 'Advertisement', as 'an artless tale' that is meant to 'display' 'the mind of a woman, Mary, who has thinking powers' (76). Certainly, Mary's unusual interest in 'authors whose works were addressed to the understanding' (93) surprises her friend Ann, showing that Mary is no ordinary lady of sensibility, even though she suffers for her benevolent care for others throughout the novel, as typical ladies of sensibility must. Mary cares for a dying mother who never loved her; she travels with Ann to Portugal and even studies 'physic' (97) to relieve the latter's illness, but Ann dies tragically, anyway; Mary cares for her friend (and beloved) Henry in his final illness, too, only to be devastated after his death; and, in the last pages of the novella, she devotes her life to caring for the poor, although their 'ingratitude hurt[s] her' (133). Thus, when Wollstonecraft describes Mary as 'the slave of compassion' (86), she appears to criticise this standard figure from the novel of sensibility, which was held up as an ideal for living women. Even while Wollstonecraft crafts her tale in this novelistic form, she challenges it.

Wollstonecraft's tale falls far short of showing the glorious consummation of an intelligent woman's ambition since it concludes with the eponymous protagonist's wish for death. 'Her delicate state of health did not promise long life', the last lines of the novella proclaim, adding: 'In moments of solitary sadness, a gleam of joy would dart across her mind – She thought she was hastening to that world *where there is neither marrying*, nor giving in marriage' (148; emphasis in original). The final words of *Mary* present a suggestive reworking of Jesus's teaching regarding the condition of people in heaven: 'For when they shall rise from the dead, they neither marry, nor are given in marriage; but are as the angels which are in heaven' (St Mark 12: 25).[16] Wollstonecraft suggests that a thinking woman – treated in her society as a mere body, as chattel to be traded in the marriage market – will conclude that her goal to improve her mind may only be fulfilled in the afterlife, where she will be bodiless.

Although the literary form of *Mary* might seem to confirm patriarchal power over women – since it can be classified as a novel of sensibility, with its benevolent, sensitive, too-loving protagonist – Mary's death wish opposes the patriarchal construction of woman as, above all, a body, a sexual being alone, while men are allowed to be autonomous, multidimensional figures. That Wollstonecraft uses Rousseau's words to make this point is unfortunate, though, given that she would later hold him up as a misogynist par excellence in *Rights of Woman*:

> Rousseau declares that a woman should never, for a moment, feel herself independent, that she should be governed by fear to exercise her *natural* cunning, and made a coquetish [*sic*] slave in order to render her a more alluring object of desire, a *sweeter* companion to man, whenever he chooses to relax himself. (134; emphasis in original)

Wollstonecraft clearly takes aim at Rousseau's construction of women as sexual beings, while her point that he thinks a woman exists to be a 'companion to man' expresses her complaint that women are not independent beings – they are the 'second sex', reliant upon the primary, male sex, as Simone de Beauvoir will argue. By contrast, Wollstonecraft goes on to assert that the realisation of one's selfhood – a Romantic aim for human existence if there ever was one – is also the ultimate goal of female life: 'the grand end of their [i.e. women's] exertions should be to unfold their own faculties' (*Woman* 134). In this statement, Wollstonecraft recalls the spirit of her modulated Rousseauvian epigraph to *Mary*: women are autonomous individuals (not just companions) whose minds (and not their bodies) must be fostered and educated to achieve their unique destinies. Thus, Wollstonecraft's first published novella appears more in the light of protest than it has often been received by those who focus on the author's indulgence in literary sensibility in moments that undermine the feminist message, given the misogynistic resonances of sensibility's celebration of weak and dying women.

Mary's final death wish therefore expresses a desire to be free of the burden of the female body through which she is enslaved, rather than, as with other female protagonists in novels of sensibility, a capitulation to feminine fragility. This reading of the novella explains why the protagonist feels the need to 'escape[ ]' a husband she almost never sees and about whom she demonstrates a seemingly excessive level of 'disgust' (120); why Mary considers marriage to him akin to becoming 'a slave', even though he gives her total freedom to travel and choose her companions (131); why she falls in love with a woman (Ann) and a fatherly old man (Henry), persons who are not viable sexual partners in the patriarchal scheme that devotes women to the generation of children. The answer to these queries is summarised in the novella's final statement: she wishes to be like an angel, bodiless, and therefore free from marriage (148). Notably, however, Mary does not accomplish her wish to die – to escape embodiment and thus the control of biopower. She only desires to be dead, an ending that is consistent with Wollstonecraft's condemnation of the 'sickly, die-away languor' (*Mary* 79) of the idealised woman of sensibility, since a dead Mary would align her with the Clarissas of eighteenth-century British literature. This component of the story's ending, coupled with the narrator's comment that Mary continues her energetic care for the poor and needy for the rest of her days – she 'established manufactories, threw the estate into small farms; and continually employed herself this way to dissipate care, and banish unavailing regret. She visited the sick, supported the old, and educated the young' (148) – shows that Wollstonecraft recognises the multivalent significance of female suicide in her day. 'Slave of compassion' (86) though she may be, Mary is an active, energetic protagonist, rather than a weak lady of sensibility who sinks into a femininely fragile death.

Wollstonecraft's second, fragmentary novella, *The Wrongs of Woman*, conveys the condition of a woman's body as the medium of her biopolitical enslavement in a starker and more fully developed way, partially through the Gothic setting of the madhouse. While the largely female readership of Gothic novels would recognise the commonplace trope of the imprisonment of an innocent female protagonist, Wollstonecraft politicises it in an unusually direct way. That we should understand the madhouse setting as a trap set for women by the patriarchy is clear when the protagonist, Maria, refers to 'her tyrant – her husband' (163) and muses, 'Was not the world a vast prison, and women born slaves?' (167). So begins the many references to women as enslaved throughout the narrative – at least half a dozen in this fragmentary work – although none are as striking as Maria's commentary on her pitiable landlady's battles with her abusive husband: 'These scenes awoke me at night; and, in the morning, I heard her, as usual, talk to her dear Johnny – he, forsooth, was her master; no slave in the West Indies had one more despotic' (259).[17] The insensitivity of this comparison aside, it constitutes Wollstonecraft's framing of the subjugated position of women in her culture in terms of biopower, represented by the transatlantic slave trade, and both of these realities are essential to understanding the significance of Maria's suicidality later in the text.

Such references confirm Wollstonecraft's assertion that eighteenth-century British society traps women through marriage as an institution of biopolitical control. Maria complains, 'Marriage had bastilled me for life' (243), a daring reference that heralds the political nature of her entrapment: the freeing of prisoners from the Bastille prison in Paris was the inaugurating event of the French Revolution in 1789. More pointedly, Jemima, Maria's unmarried, low-class madhouse keeper, attests, 'I was, in fact, born a slave, and chained by infamy to slavery during the whole of existence, without having any companions to alleviate it by sympathy, or teach me how to rise above it by their example' (193). Jemima goes on to tell a tale of sexual abuse and mistreatment by several men in her life. Maria's situation as a gentlewoman is less degrading, but she is also a victim of sexualised mistreatment: her dastardly husband, Venables, preys on maids and other lower-class women around him (239) while continuing to request sex from Maria, who obliges out of a sense of marital duty: 'What a task!', she complains (241). She feels forced to accede to his wishes for sex, knowing it is part of her role as a wife.

At first, Maria attempts to escape her oppression by simply leaving her husband. However, to complicate matters, she has a newborn child, and she therefore deprives her husband of two supposed possessions, for, as Maria points out, 'a wife being as much a man's property as his horse, or his ass, she has nothing she can call her own' (248). Here is the husband, then, as an agent of biopower, a possessor of life, a manager of bodies. A wife, she comments, is so powerless that 'She cannot drive an unfaithful husband from his house, nor separate, or tear, his children from him, however culpable he may be' (245). Husbands could sue for divorce on the grounds of adultery, and always maintained control over their children, but a wife would have to provide evidence of extreme cruelty ('extreme' being the operative word here, since a husband could rape and, to an extent, otherwise physically assault his wife with near impunity), incest or some other serious crime to obtain a divorce. Upon Maria's escape from the family home, Venables responds to her assertion of autonomy by imprisoning her in a madhouse. The symbolic nature of her prison further advances Wollstonecraft's point: Maria is not in a gaol, nor in a Bastille, despite her comparison of it to the French prison for victims of a tyrannical aristocracy (243). Rather, the madhouse is a place for people who have lost their minds: Venables's imprisonment of his wife there confirms that women are only sex machines, lacking intellect and the agency that attends it.

The author devotes most of the narrative to demonstrating the humiliations of the madhouse – in which Maria is denied the most basic claims to bodily autonomy, such as the right to choose or reject food freely (much like the enslaved) (164–5) – and to outlining Maria's and Jemima's complaints about the sexual enslavement of women, which arise in their accounts of themselves. At the end of the fragment, Maria composes an impassioned and well-reasoned plea to a judge, who presides over her and Venables's divorce proceedings, arguing why she should be legally free of Venables. Her speech falls on deaf ears:

> The judge ... [condemned] 'the fallacy of letting women plead their feelings, as an excuse for the violation of the marriage-vow ... It was her duty to love and obey the man chosen by her parents and relations, who were qualified by their experience to judge better for her, than she could for herself.' (284)

Women, as mere bodies, have minds so weak that they need someone else to think for them. According to two of the fragmentary endings for the novella – which was left unfinished upon Wollstonecraft's death eleven days after giving birth to her daughter Mary – this final blow plunges Maria into a state of suicidal despair. We may read Maria's suicidality as her protest against patriarchal tyranny over the female body. One potential ending is a mere sketch: 'Divorced by her husband – Her lover unfaithful – Pregnancy – Miscarriage – Suicide' (*Wrongs* 286). Here,

Maria is still defined entirely as a sexual being – a body that makes love, gets pregnant and miscarries – and this identity is linked to her suicidality. That this suicidal response can be read as Wollstonecraft's challenge to the objectification of women is confirmed by the most fully developed ending to the novella, in which Maria mistakenly believes her child is dead. Having taken a dangerous dose of laudanum, she finds that

> Still her eyes closed not – one remembrance with frightful velocity followed another – All the incidents of her life were in arms, embodied to assail her, and prevent her sinking into the sleep of death. – Her murdered child again appeared to her, mourning for the babe of which she was the tomb. (286)

Maria loses her human aspect in this passage, becoming merely a grave for her unborn baby: a fitting end for a novella in which her body has been the site of her husband's imprisonment and control.

Nor does this conclusion to the novella necessarily provide the cheerful *dénouement* that some critics believe it does, especially read in light of female suicidality as a protest against patriarchal biopower. Jemima carries Maria's baby to her while she lies swooning from a laudanum overdose, and Maria resolves to survive. Her decision to live for her baby may be interpreted as Wollstonecraft's commentary on the inescapability of women's enslavement under patriarchal rule, which traps her by means of her body, here the generator of a baby that ties her to a hated life. Richard Sanderson understands this passage as conveying that offspring can be an antidote to suicidality (51), and Thomas E. Joiner summarises a sociological study that confirms the validity of this view: 'A key finding of the study was that women with children had lower suicide rates than those with no children. The more children, the more dramatic the effect: Women with six or more children had one-fifth the risk of suicide as compared to other women' (8). Yet, viewed in the context of Wollstonecraft's extensive commentary on the enslavement of the female body under patriarchy and suicide as an escape from it, even this apparently positive ending may be interpreted as confirmation of the author's broader challenge to the status quo. Maria's baby signifies her entrapment in the web of biopower that controls her body as the site of its maximisation of power through births. Beyond the fictional realm, Wollstonecraft encourages the interpretation of Maria's continued life after her suicide attempt as a cruel disappointment. Writing to Gilbert Imlay (her daughter Fanny's father), she reflects on being saved from her own drowning attempt: 'I was inhumanly brought back to life and misery. But a fixed determination is not to be baffled by disappointment ... If I am condemned to live longer, it is a living death' (*Letters* 327). As reasoning beings trapped in and defined by their bodies, Wollstonecraft and her fictional double, Maria, live incomplete existences.

Woman as Suicide Note: Shelley's *Mathilda*

By the time Mary Shelley penned *Mathilda* in 1819, the legacy of female suicide passed down to the young author was a long one. It was not only literary. Shelley would have been aware of her mother's two suicide attempts from her father Godwin's *Memoirs*: 'she was twice', he reports, 'with an interval of four months, from the end of May to the beginning of October [of 1795], prompted ... to purposes of suicide' out of despair over her failed relationship with the unfaithful Imlay (101). It would be difficult and perhaps presumptuous to call Wollstonecraft's desire to die politically motivated in the way that her use of the trope of female suicide in her novellas is, even though she seems to have insisted on its significance thus. Prevented from dying after her second attempt at suicide, she comments in a letter, 'nor will I allow that to be a frantic attempt, which was one of the calmest acts of reason' (*Letters* 327). Knowing that female suicide was often attributed to a manic impulse associated with women's mental fragility, Wollstonecraft attempts to control the meaning of her own act by claiming that her decision to take her life was a rational one. This claim may not have been applicable to her first attempt, after which she was so irrational that she wanted to take baby Fanny's life along with her own: writing to Imlay from Scandinavia, where she was representing his business interests, she confesses, 'I have looked at the sea, and at my child, hardly daring to own to myself the secret wish, that it might become our tomb' (*Letters* 297). Troublingly, Wollstonecraft's infanticidal wish positions her as tyrannical in the way that she accuses men of being in her literary and polemical works, since it suggests a belief that her daughter Fanny Godwin is her possession to do with as she pleases, rather than an autonomous being. This parental tendency reappears in Shelley's *Mathilda*, in which the protagonist's father views Mathilda as owned by him. Arguably, Shelley obtained more than the literary trope of subversive female suicide from reading her mother's words.

Another important literary trope that Shelley reproduces from Wollstonecraft's writing is that of the woman-as-text, which Shelley conveys through the experimental form of the novelistic suicide note in *Mathilda*. In a sense, Wollstonecraft was a text to her daughter Shelley, whose only experience of her mother would have been through Wollstonecraft's writings – the most personal of which would have been her letters. Amongst those letters is the suicide note Wollstonecraft sent to Imlay, which could only have fascinated a daughter eager to understand her dead mother, and who, she would find, wished to absent herself from this earth years before Shelley was born. Passages of Wollstonecraft's suicide note, provided here in part, refer to her own faults, but the gist of it lays the blame at Imlay's feet:

> Nothing but my extreme stupidity could have rendered me blind so long. Yet, whilst you assured me that you had no attachment, I thought we might still have lived together.
>
> I shall make no comments on your conduct; or any appeal to the world. Let my wrongs sleep with me! Soon, very soon I shall be at peace. When you receive this, my burning head will be cold.
>
> I would encounter a thousand deaths, rather than a night like the last. Your treatment has thrown my mind into a state of chaos; yet I am serene. I go to find comfort, and my only fear is, that my poor body will be insulted by an endeavour to recal [*sic*] my hated existence. But I shall plunge into the Thames where there is the least chance of my being snatched from the death I seek.
>
> God bless you! May you never know by experience what you have made me endure. Should your sensibility ever awake, remorse will find its way to your heart; and, in the midst of business and sensual pleasure, I shall appear before you, the victim of your deviation from rectitude. (*Letters* 326–7)

Through these (intended) last words, Wollstonecraft conveys that she has lived for love and Imlay's cruelty has taken her life from her. Typically, then, the note provides the meaning of the would-be suicide's life and death. Wollstonecraft – like all would-be suicides who leave notes – attempts to have the last word about herself and define who she was and how those whom she leaves behind should understand her.

As the last words Wollstonecraft believed she would ever write, her suicide note may be considered as a summary of her life. A kind of snapshot of who she was at that time, the note is offered as a replacement for the writer's self, which can no longer communicate. This function is reiterated in Wollstonecraft's promise to haunt Imlay. Michael MacDonald and Terence Murphy agree that suicide notes can function as replacement existences for the suicide when they call these texts 'a means of perpetuating their [suicides'] identities beyond death, ... a last act of self-fashioning' that is closely tied to the rise of modernity: 'Suicide notes were expressions of a new emphasis on individualism, and a new psychologized conception of the self' in the eighteenth century (334, 336). Parisot offers, 'The notes are certainly devices of literary self-fashioning, but', he also recognises, these 'constructions of the self appear entirely dependent upon the reconstruction of communal ties and social context' ('Notes' 281). Accordingly, Wollstonecraft blames her suicide on Imlay and seeks to punish him for his unfaithfulness to her, casting herself in the traditional mode of the female suicide who dies for love.

In a Romantic-period context, suicide notes may be viewed as a minor literary form, thanks to their public nature. Parisot comments: 'although suicide notes only featured in a small minority of coronial inquests and even fewer still were printed in papers and magazines' in the early modern period, the published suicide note was 'well established as a literary subgenre' by the 1770s ('Notes' 278) – one that, I argue, Shelley uses to advance her feminist protest in *Mathilda*. Presumably Shelley would have been aware of the publication of suicide notes, as they appeared in a variety of venues in the period: 'From mid-century, examples can be found in all major press formats – the morning daily, the evening tri-weekly, the weekly journal, and the monthly magazine', such that 'what was once traditionally viewed as an intensely private epistolary transaction between loved ones soon became subject to public view' (Parisot, 'Notes' 278). In other words, what Betty Samraj and Jean Mark Gawron claim about suicide notes today is not true for the long eighteenth century: they comment that efforts to identify suicide notes in terms of genre are complicated by 'the absence of an identifiable discourse community ... [I]t is not the case that the writers of these suicide notes have read other notes or produced multiple iterations of these texts over time' (91). In the late eighteenth century suicide notes were indeed distinctly public, a point that Critchley underscores in *Notes on Suicide* (2015), in which he asserts that the form rose to

> prominence in its recognizable, modern form in the eighteenth century in England as a consequence of literacy and the rapid rise and spread of newspapers. The peculiar thing about eighteenth-century suicide notes is the fact that they were routinely sent to the press by those intending to take their lives ... The modern suicide note is in origin, then, a publication, and intensely public act. (46)

Some suicide notes were so well known that they might be considered famous – even classics – such as that of Budgell, as I point out in Chapter 2. Framing his death in popular terms, Budgell invokes both classical history in his reference to Cato and *Belles Lettres* in his nod to the play by Addison. By doing so, Budgell casts himself in a particular cultural mould and fashions his life and death anew.[18] No doubt influenced by reading such texts in popular media and by Wollstonecraft's suicide note – a revenant of her missing mother – Shelley structures *Mathilda* as one long suicide note. The novella is also shot through with the presence of Shelley's mother due to its engagement with Wollstonecraft's signature literary theme of female suicide. Whereas the brunt of Wollstonecraft's feminist ire is patriarchal tyranny in the form of husbands, that of her daughter Shelley is more literal: the protagonist's oppressor is her father.

Shelley's own life provided plenty of experience with suicide, too, which may have influenced her fictional portrayal of the subject. Close to the time when Shelley wrote *Mathilda*, she experienced personal feelings of suicidality over the deaths of her and P. B. Shelley's children William in 1819 and Clara in 1818, not to mention their first baby, who died shortly after birth in 1815. Shelley had also endured the suicides of her half-sister, Fanny Godwin, and Harriet Shelley, Shelley's first wife; both successful suicides were accompanied by notes, which is a relatively uncommon circumstance, since most suicides do not leave notes (Paraschakis et al. 344). Fanny's lonely death, accomplished at an inn in Wales in 1816, was preceded by a long period of melancholy, borne partly of her feelings of being unwelcome in Godwin's home at Skinner Street in London, and partly of Godwin's second marriage to Mary Jane Clairmont (Sunstein 114).[19] Shelley was well aware of Fanny Godwin's despondent mental state, but she was also likely buoyed by the latter's professions of love for her, P. B. Shelley and baby William: '"perhaps ... because I found the world deserted you, I loved you the more"', Fanny told her half sister (quoted in Sunstein 114). Shelley did not seem to know what Fanny planned in her final travels, since she and P. B. Shelley met her 'briefly at the coach stop' in Wales, apparently for a friendly visit. Emily Sunstein writes:

> On the ninth Mary had a note from her half sister indicating that Fanny Godwin intended to kill herself. Shelley rushed after her, Godwin had followed her. Both turned back after seeing a Swansea newspaper report that a young woman had committed suicide by taking laudanum. She was identified only by a gold watch (which the lovers had brought Fanny from Geneva), by corset stays marked M W (which had been her mother's), and by an unsigned suicide note referring obliquely to her bastardy. (127)

Fanny Godwin seems to have cast herself in her mother's mould in her final act – literally so, since she wore her mother's corset. But her suicide note is the most telling evidence of how she wanted to be viewed in death:

> written on 9 October 1816 at the Mackworth Arms inn, Swansea, [the note] explains clearly that she intended to take an overdose of laudanum not for her own sake, but for the good of others: '"I have long determined that the best thing I could do was to put an end to the existence of a being whose birth was unfortunate, and whose life has only been a series of pain to those persons who have hurt their health in endeavouring to promote her welfare. Perhaps to hear of my death will give you pain, but you will soon have the blessing of forgetting that such a creature ever existed as." ... Her signature was missing,

> having been torn from the note possibly by staff at the inn aware of 'the indignities which the law commanded for suicides'. (Faubert, 'Fanny' n.p.; quoting St Clair 411)

Fanny Godwin does not frame her death and life in the popular sentimental terms of the woman who dies for love. However, she reveals something about herself and, in the process, about women in her day, regarding existential concerns that are not often expressed. She believes herself unworthy to live because she is a burden on others, because she has a body that requires shelter and food, necessities that she could not finance herself as a middle-class woman in a period that offered so few avenues for work to people like her – essentially because her body is not an asset to power through work or marriage.[20]

Some months after Fanny Godwin's suicide, probably on 7 December 1816, Harriet Shelley would also take her own life by drowning herself in the Serpentine while pregnant (not with P. B. Shelley's baby) – a circumstance that might have contributed to her decision to die (Sanderson 52; see also Marshall 174). Her body was recovered on 10 December 1816. P. B. Shelley learned of her death on 15 December from a letter by his friend and publisher Thomas Hookham, according to Florence Marshall. Writing in 1889, Marshall opines, 'Life and its complications had proved too much for the poor silly woman, and she took the only means of escape she saw open to her' (174), adding that Harriet Shelley

> had, all her life, an avowed proclivity to suicide. She had been fond, in young and happy days, of talking jocosely about it, as silly girls often do; discoursing of 'some scheme of self-destruction as coolly as another lady would arrange a visit to an exhibition or a theatre.' [quoting Thomas Jefferson Hogg] But it is a wide dreary waste that lies between such an idea and the grim reality, – and poor Harriet had traversed it. (Marshall 175)

This harsh judgement of Harriet Shelley's suicide suggests another reason why people chose to write suicide notes in the period: as a means of self-defence, to influence the reaction to and perception of their choice to die. Harriet Shelley duly provided a suicide note, mainly addressed to her sister, Eliza:

> When you read this letr. I shall be [no] more an inhabitant of this miserable world. do not regret the loss of one who could never be anything but a source of vexation & misery to you all belonging to me. Too wretched to exert myself lowered in the opinion of everyone why should I drag on a miserable existence embittered by past recollections & not one ray of hope to rest on for the future. The remembrance of all your kindness which I have so unworthily repaid has often made my hert ache. (n.p.; spelling and other technical oddities in original)

In the passage she directs to P. B. Shelley, her aim is to protect their children in the way she thinks best:

> My dear Bysshe let me conjure you by the remembrance of our days of happiness to grant my last wish – do not take your innocent child from Eliza who has been more than I have, who has watched over her with such unceasing care. – Do not refuse my last request – I never could refuse you & if you had never left me I might have lived but as it is, I freely forgive you & may you enjoy that happiness which you have deprived me of. There is your beautiful boy. oh! be careful of him & his live [life? love?] may prove one day a rich reward. (n.p.)

Harriet Shelley slips into Wollstonecraftian mode when she blames her former husband for her depression, much as the mother of feminism held Imlay responsible for her would-be death in her suicide note, although most of Harriet's note is given to heaping blame upon herself. Nor does she adopt the popular literary role of the love-struck female suicide. Rather, Harriet Shelley, like Fanny Godwin, frames her suicide as an almost natural outcome of her self-hatred, a self-abnegation that fulfils what she claims is a worthless life. Also like Fanny Godwin, Harriet Shelley believes that she is a burden and those she leaves behind will be happier without her: 'My children ... are too young to regret me ... My parents do not regret me. I was unworthy your love & care. Be happy all of you. so shall my spirit find rest & forgiveness' (n.p.). Harriet Shelley's plea for sympathy did not fall on deaf ears. Some critics judge Mary Shelley's response to her death as harsh and unfeeling: Sanderson comments that she married P. B. Shelley a mere three weeks after the body was recovered (53), as though she was eagerly waiting for the first wife to die; he calls her reportage of Harriet's death in her journals 'extremely terse' (62). However, Shelley remarks on Harriet Shelley's death in her journal in 1839: 'Poor Harriet to whose sad fate I attribute so many of my own heavy sorrows as the atonement claimed by fate for her death' (quoted in Sanderson 62n). The depth of Shelley's response to Harriet Shelley's death may be discerned by the fact that she blames herself for it and continues to regret it more than twenty years later.

What of Shelley's own suicidal tendencies? She may have believed herself 'born to die' (to borrow from the title of Lana Del Rey's 2012 album) after reading of her mother's suicide attempts. She may also have been aware that Godwin and Wollstonecraft were reading together the period's most famous novel on suicide, Goethe's *Werther*, on the evening before her birth (Sanderson 61n). Some commentators attribute her suicidality in 1819, when she wrote *Mathilda*, to the deaths of her three children (see, e.g., Nitchie 455; Betty Bennett 54). Others claim, however, that Shelley threatened suicide long before this period; for instance, Harriet Shelley claimed that the author of *Frankenstein* told P. B. Shelley that she would kill herself if he did not love her (Sanderson 61n). Also significantly, P. B. Shelley flirted with death throughout his short life and urged her to do so, as well. Early in their relationship, when Godwin banned the married poet from seeing his daughter, P. B. Shelley 'burst into the house and ran up to Mary offering a bottle of laudanum, and declared, "By this you can escape from tyranny." He then brandished a small pistol saying, "they wish to separate us, my beloved, but Death shall unite us"' (Ivey White 343).[21] That P. B. Shelley associated suicide with an 'escape from tyranny' confirms the couple's familiarity with the Romantic-era notion of subversive suicide. Shelley continued to wish for death, particularly after P. B. Shelley's death, although she firmly refused to take matters into her own hands. She expresses her death wish about a dozen times in her journals and letters. However, a letter from 15 October 1822, in which she mentions her only remaining child, Percy Florence Shelley, reveals that she rejected suicide for herself: '"Percy w^{d} go too, only then I sh^{d} no longer be chained to time but sh^{d} depart – without self violence (which I wd never use) I know that I sh^{d} then die"' (Shelley, *Letters* 283; also quoted in Sanderson 64n). Undeniably, Shelley's personal familiarity with suicide – and with suicide notes – was considerable. That she should choose the form of the suicide note to structure her second completed fictional work after *Frankenstein* – which, incidentally, ends with the monster's promise to kill himself on his own funeral pyre (220–1) – is thus predictable and crucial, although this point has not received critical attention until now.

Understood in this context, *Mathilda* appears not merely as an epistolary novel – a common form for the novel of sensibility, elements of which pervade the work – but, more specifically, as a letter composed as the last statement of the suicidal protagonist.[22] Higonnet summarises the interpretive challenge of texts about suicide: 'Suicide provokes narrative, both a narrative inscribed by the actor as subject, and those stories devised around the suicide as enigmatic object of interpretation' ('Frames' 230). This point is particularly true if the narrative includes the accomplished act of suicide. It may also be so even if the narrator is only suicidal and does not actually accomplish the sad, last task by the work's end, which is the circumstance in Shelley's novella.

By seeing Mathilda's feminist protest as encapsulated in her subjective expression of herself via her narrative, rather than through her actions, we can allow for the kind of feminist reading of responses to power that have been ignored by others who employ a Foucauldian paradigm to understand such relations. Deveaux summarises this point well:

> Feminists need to look at the *inner* processes that condition women's sense of freedom or choice in addition to external manifestations of power and dominance – and Foucault's understanding of power is decidedly inadequate to this task. Women's 'freedom' does not simply refer to objective possibilities for maneuvering or resisting within a power dynamic but concerns whether a woman *feels* empowered in her specific context. Because Foucault's account of the freedom of the subject determines the presence of power or 'conduct' – as well as its opposite pole, violence or domination – based on the existence of objective points of resistance, it obscures the subjective aspects of power. (234; emphasis in original)

Mathilda's ambiguous suicide may not match the assertive power of Maria's enacted (though unsuccessful) suicidality, but it encompasses a means of women's resistance – subjective and perceptual protest – that is too often ignored. Shelley gestures to what Higonnet terms the 'enigmatic' nature of suicide ('Frames' 230) by presenting her reader with an unreliable narrator, one who promises to commit suicide for the bulk of her narrative, only to renege on her plans in the final pages.

Mathilda's repeated wish to die throughout her narrative, as well as other forms of her expression of suicidality, establish the novella as one long suicide note. At the opening of the work she claims, 'I know that I am about to die and I feel happy – joyous' (41), and later she confirms, 'Never for one moment when most placid did I cease to pray for death' (88). This orientation towards her final moments – repeatedly reminding the reader that she anticipates her death with relish – puts the novella in the company of suicide notes, the main focus of which is the anticipation of and explanation for the speaker's wished-for death. Nor does Shelley neglect to answer the chief question that suicide notes raise: Who is the note written for and why? Since Shelley wrote *Mathilda* at a time when the line between the presumed privacy of the suicide note and its increasingly public nature was blurred, it seems appropriate that the fictional addressee of the novella is unstable, too. Even though the narrator, Mathilda, claims that she writes to her friend, Woodville, she also mentions the name in the third person several times throughout the text, creating odd and confusing narrative moments. When she first introduces the character as an active participant in the past events she narrates, Mathilda writes, 'The name of my friend was Woodville' (90), even though she begins the account many pages earlier as written to Woodville himself: 'I do not know that any will peruse these pages except you, my friend [Woodville], who will receive them at my death' (41). Immediately thereafter – in an early recognition of, and perhaps awkward excuse for, these passages – Mathilda writes, 'I do not address them to you alone because it will give me pleasure to dwell upon our friendship in a way that would be needless if you alone read what I shall write. I shall relate my tale therefore as if I wrote for strangers' (41). Aside from the weak explanation that she wants to consider their friendship in an objective way through this method of narration – flimsy, indeed, since she spends most of the narrative talking about herself and her father, rather than her friendship with Woodville – it appears that writing her intimate confession pleases Mathilda, even though one might assume she would wish to hide what she characterises as her shameful story from as many people as possible. This fissure in the internal logic of the tale reveals Shelley's extra-textual intention: to contribute to the category of the public suicide note ('for strangers') and employ it as a literary form.

Mathilda is, as all suicide notes are, a document of self-fashioning. The protagonist certainly desires to exonerate herself, a common goal of the published suicide note (Parisot, 'Notes' 280). Mathilda launches into her narrative:

> I will begin my tale: it is my last task, and I hope I have strength sufficient to fulfill it. I record no crimes; my faults may easily be pardoned; for they proceeded not from evil motive but from want of judgement; and I believe few would say that they could, by a different conduct and superior wisdom, have avoided the misfortunes to which I am the victim. (42)

Mathilda offers her story as a substitute for her existence, the only evidence she wishes to leave to signify her life. Shelley encourages the reader to understand the narrative in this way – as a protagonist-manqué – by conveying Mathilda's repeated claims that she is herself a text, a drama, especially a tragedy (102, 110, 113). In a moment of petulance against the poet Woodville, Mathilda complains, 'perhaps he is already planning a poem in which I am to figure. I am a farce and play to him' (101). In refashioning herself as a suicide note – in seeking to replace her bodily existence with text – Shelley's Mathilda fulfils the view of herself as textual. But is this textual replacement reliable? Higonnet suggests that suicide notes can be misleading: 'One might argue ... that to give interpretative priority to a suicide note within a fiction is a form of surrender to the "intentional fallacy," or a privileging of the character who has authored this paradoxically autobiographical act' – paradoxical because the character speaks for herself at the moment that she removes herself ('Frames' 231). In examining the novella as a suicide note, however, the reader need not adopt Mathilda's statements about herself as entirely reliable. This reading also prompts the reader to ask what Shelley reveals about her character through this narrative form. I argue that Mathilda protests her oppression through the literary form of the public suicide note, for, in this way, she refuses to keep – and to exist as – the secret into which her father has transformed her through his incestuous desire.

Importantly, the novella's incest-plot aligns it with Wollstonecraft's fictionalised protests that women are treated as sexualised bodies alone in British culture. Through it, Shelley shows that the patriarchy views women as objects of desire even under circumstances that forbid it, and, relatedly, that women are treated as chattels possessed, controlled and managed by men. That Mathilda's father believes he owns his daughter is clear even before he returns to her after abandoning her as a baby to his stepsister and travelling abroad for sixteen years following the death of his wife, Diana. In his farewell note to Mathilda's aunt, he writes, 'I leave her under your protection. Take care of her and cherish her: one day I may claim her at your hands' (47), as though Mathilda is a hat in a coat check. The suicide note that Mathilda's father leaves her after confessing his criminal love for her is even more telling. Fulfilling the reader's expectation that the suicide note will explain his reason for choosing death, Mathilda's father describes the origin of his guilty love:

> when I saw you become the object of another's love; when I imagined that you might be loved otherwise than as a sacred type and image of loveliness and excellence, or that you might love another with a more ardent affection than that which you bore to me, then the fiend awoke within me; I dismissed your lover; and from that moment I have known no peace. (76)

Mathilda's father confesses that he cannot bear to share her love with another; he believes she should love only him, as though she does not have a life outside of his own.

Thus, the incestuous theme of the narrative signifies as more than the novella's debt to the Gothic genre. By portraying a father who desires his own daughter, Shelley decries men who believe they own women completely, whether those women are their daughters, wives or otherwise. Again, Foucault's influential commentary on modernity and biopower provides valuable insight into this situation. Since biopower seeks to increase itself through the regulation and maximisation of life – the source of its opposition to suicidality, Foucault notes (*Sexuality* 138–9) – it has reinforced the long-standing social taboo against incest, since children born of incestuous unions are prone to be fragile and therefore may not function as valuable, healthy members of the body politic.[23] Ironically, the excessive attention paid to women's sexuality in the interest of strengthening biopower creates such situations as incest, Shelley's story suggests. Men, minor deputies in the patriarchal system of biopower, are unduly interested in controlling women's bodies by regulating their choice of sexual partners, such as when fathers choose their daughters' husbands (a situation that also plagues Rousseau's *Julie* and countless other tales). To protest such disproportionate attention to women's bodies, Shelley renders it as the father's incestuous love for his daughter. Mathilda's father ought to have no interest in his daughter's sexuality; that he does is a kind of perversity, presented here as incestuous love. Mathilda's father claims that he cannot bear to think that another man looks at her as a sexual being, but his hypocrisy is obvious since he clearly desires her himself (76).

Shelley laments that even fathers may view their daughters as objects that they possess, bodies that they may claim for themselves. Tilottama Rajan notes that 'the text seems to narrate the treatment of the feminine within an incestuously patriarchal society' (45). As the letter continues, Mathilda's father confesses his desire 'to know that ... [he] was all the world to' her:

> I was lapped in a fool's paradise of enjoyment and security. Was my love blamable? If it was I was ignorant of it; I desired only *that which I possessed*, and if I enjoyed from your looks, and words, and most innocent caresses a rapture usually excluded from the feelings of a parent towards his child, yet no uneasiness, no wish, no casual idea awoke me to a sense of guilt. (75; my emphasis)

As writers of suicide notes often do, Mathilda's father seeks to exculpate himself, as though his lack of guilty feeling were the same as a lack of guilt. He also shows that he revels in his feeling of 'possess[ing]' Mathilda and becomes like a jealous lover. The idea of sharing her with another man drives his criminal love for her. Elsewhere he denies that he plans to kill himself (77) – an odd attestation for a suicide note – but Mathilda, not fooled by his attempts to deceive her, comments that he tells the lie to forego her efforts to stop his suicide (78). What confirms the text's character as a suicide note is the implied assertion underlying his words. He must die, he believes, because he cannot conquer his amorous desires: 'And now, Mathilda I must make you my last confession. I have been miserably mistaken in imagining that I could conquer my love for you; I never can' (76). He adds, 'the grave dreaded yet desired, [will] receive me free from pain: for while I feel it will be pain that must make up the whole sum of my sensations. Is not this a fearful curse that I labour under? Do I not look forward to a miserable futurity?' (77). Mathilda's father wishes for an end to his tortured state of suffering on account of a passion that can never be satisfied.

So thoroughly does Mathilda's father believe he owns his daughter that he does not distinguish her from himself. Shelley would have been primed to notice and despise the patriarchal folly of possessiveness over women from reading her mother's fiction, in which, for example, the protagonist of *Mary* is treated as just another possession in the family coffers: Mary 'feel[s] an emotion of contempt at having been thrown away – given in with an estate' (110) by her father to her husband. Shelley takes fatherly possessiveness a step further by showing how existential boundaries can become blurred for such tyrants. In Mathilda's father's suicide note, he calls her 'soul of my soul; thou in whom I breathe!' (77). Having lost his wife – Mathilda's mother – Diana, he seeks to fill the void with his daughter: 'in my madness I dared say to myself – Diana died to give her birth; her mother's spirit was transferred into her frame, and she ought to be as Diana to me' (76). Again, he shows his belief that Mathilda does not have an autonomous existence, and that she lives to serve his needs.

Believing her very being devalued and destroyed by her father's incestuous love, Mathilda becomes suicidal herself. In this way, her suicidality is a direct response to her father's claims to own her completely, even her body. The secret that began as her father's incestuous love has become her own essential being, she asserts: 'infamy and guilt was mingled with my portion; unlawful and detestable passion had poured its poison into my ears and changed all my blood, so that it was no longer the kindly stream that supports life but a cold fountain of bitterness corrupted in its very source' (97). The language of contagion, in which Mathilda focuses on physical changes, expresses aptly her perception that her very body has been altered by her father's incestuous possessiveness. Mathilda's meditation on her contaminated nature recalls Wollstonecraft's comment in *Rights of Woman*: 'A woman who has lost her honour, imagines that she cannot fall lower, and as for recovering her former station, it is impossible; no exertion can wash this stain away' (190). The stain is, indeed, deep for Mathilda, whose very spirit has been changed by her father's incestuous love: her

> soul [is] corrupted to its core by a deadly cancer. If day after day I had dwelt on these dreadful sentiments I should have become mad, and should have fancied myself a living pestilence: so horrible to my own solitary thoughts did this form, this voice, and all this wretched self appear; for had it not been the source of guilt that wants a name? (107)

Mathilda discusses her soul in terms of physical disease, demonstrating that the afflictions of physical existence – being sexually desired by her father – have corrupted her spiritual life. Her visceral description of her father's desire to possess her expresses more than intense disgust: it reveals her suicidality as a direct response to the patriarchal tyranny over her body.

However, in her wish to die, Mathilda also rebels against him, as he commands her to live after his death:

> 'You will never hear from me again: receive these then as the last words of mine that will ever reach you; and ... regard them I conjure you as a father's command. Resolutely shake of[f] the wretchedness that this first misfortune in early life must occasion you ... The sun of youth is not set for you; it will restore vigour and life to you; do not resist with obstinate grief its beneficent influence.' (78)

Mathilda rejects her father's directive to live. From the first page of the novella, she expresses her happiness at the imminent prospect of her own death (41), and at one point she actively seeks death for herself, beseeching Woodville, '"My friend, I wish to die. I am quite weary of enduring the misery which hourly I do endure, and I will throw it off"' (102). Significantly, too, Shelley frames Mathilda's urge to die as a slave suicide, as does Wollstonecraft in her novels, drawing upon the cultural associations of the many texts of abolitionist literature that frame slave suicide as a challenge to the oppression of the body in a biopolitical regime. Mathilda's invitation to Woodville to commit suicide with her leaves no doubt as to the broader meaning of her suicidality: '"What slave will not, if he may, escape from his chains? Look, I weep: for more than two years I have never enjoyed one moment free from anguish"' (102–3). She reiterates this rhetorical strategy a few lines later, pleading with Woodville, '"look, there is the key of our prison; we hold it in our own hands, and are we more debased than slaves to cast it away and give ourselves up to voluntary bondage?"' (103). Mathilda's words here closely echo those of Seneca: 'Freedom is so near; and does anyone remain a slave? ... Poor fellow, you are a slave to men, a slave to things, a slave to life; for if you lack the virtue of dying, life is slavery' (*Selected* 131).[24] Mathilda's reference to slave suicide demonstrates her awareness of its protesting power for the oppressed in body, but the long history of misogynistic fantasising about lovely female corpses in Western literature also threatens to undermine this subversive message. Is Mathilda's suicidality a capitulation to the patriarchal tyranny that enslaves her or an agitation against it?

Shelley's narrative conflict reveals her own complicated view of the issue of female suicide at a time when women were figured as ideal when closest to death in the culture of sensibility, as well as confined by husbands and fathers, against whose control of their bodies they might rebel by ending their existence. The conflict may partially explain the tale's surprising ending: Mathilda does not die by the close of the narrative, and her impending death is, at best, ambiguously suicidal.

(Notably, however, Mathilda wishes for death so intensely and often that some critics believe she does die: Diane Long Hoeveler writes, 'Mathilda wills her own early death, [and] ... that event occurs in the final pages of the novella' (369)). Mathilda is saved from overt self-violence to achieve her goal of death by contracting tuberculosis, a disease that was associated with moral purity and spirituality in the Romantic period, as Clark Lawlor recognises in *Consumption and Literature: The Making of the Romantic Disease* (2006). Thus, Mathilda's statement, 'I believed that by suicide I should violate a divine law of nature', and her assertion that in her 'calm moments' she 'considered [suicide] a crime' (89), are satisfied through her death by consumption, making her appear innocent by religious and social standards. An alternative interpretation of Mathilda's fatal illness further complicates this picture: her infection with tuberculosis may also be viewed as an illustration of her agency, in that it may be read as her chosen method of killing herself, rather than an entirely passive – or an 'innocent' – accident (111). (Durkheim himself defines suicide quite broadly and would admit of such an instance: '"Suicide" is the name given to any death that results indirectly or directly from a positive or negative act by the victim him or herself' (17)). Mathilda claims that she wanders alone in the forest until, as she puts it, 'I had lost myself' (110). The transitive verb implies that becoming lost was something that she actively did to herself, perhaps intentionally. Spending the night insufficiently dressed in the cold, damp woods brings on her consumption, and her reaction to her diagnosis further suggests a degree of suicidality in her contraction of the disease:

> every symptom of a rapid consumption declared itself ... [M]y strength became less and less; as winter came on I had a cough; and my sunken cheek, before pale, burned with a hectic fever. One by one these symptoms struck me; & I became convinced that the moment I had so much desired was about to arrive and that I was dying. (111)

Mathilda is so pleased to be dying that it is difficult to believe the fatal disease was accidentally contracted. She seems to have taken Wordsworth's speaker's advice in 'Argument for Suicide' that those who would 'die/ By licence' (9–10) should call upon illness to 'end' their lives (11). Still, though, Mathilda's impending death from disease cannot be classed as a certain suicide. Shelley's deftly ambiguous account of Mathilda's end underscores the character's contradictions throughout the novella and suggests that, for women at the time, suicide is not an unequivocal means of feminist protest.

Mathilda's textual self-fashioning by means of her long suicide note provides her with another means of escaping the prison of her female body – that which traps her in incestuous love and the command to silence that attends it. Critchley comments on the essentially communicative nature of suicide notes: 'One always speaks to someone in a suicide note. Suicide notes are attempts at communication ... The suicidal person does not want to die alone, but wants to die with another or others, to whom the note is addressed' (45). Through her narrative, Mathilda expresses her truth fully and freely, choosing Woodville and imagined strangers as her audience, and breaks free of her father's control over her expressions, which he had silenced by covering her with shame. She sees her father's passion as making her very life disgraceful in her eyes: 'my very existence was a secret known only to myself' (87); elsewhere she confesses, 'I must shrink before the eye of man lest he should read my father's guilt in my glazed eyes: I must be silent lest my faltering voice should betray unimagined horrors' (83). She professes this injunction to silence in the long suicide note that she has declared from the start as being written for others to read. Fully fashioned by herself, it also replaces her gendered body, the source of all her grief. The narrative is the last word on her existence, which is thus no longer controlled by her father – a 'revolutionary self-construction', Diana Edelman-Young calls it (124).

It may be that the purported addressee of the tale, Woodville, helps Mathilda to master her interpellation of patriarchal injunctions to secrecy by speaking of her silence, thereby bringing it into the light. 'Woodville had told me that there was in my countenance an expression as if I belonged to another world', Mathilda admits, 'so he had seen that sign: and there it lay a gloomy mark to tell the world that there was that within my soul that no silence could render sufficiently obscure', adding, 'when I saw Woodville & day after day he tried to win my confidence and *I never dared give words* to my dark tale, I was impressed more strongly with the withering fear that I was in truth a marked creature, a pariah, only fit for death' (107; my emphasis). Notice the implicit causal relationship Mathilda creates in this statement: her enforced silence increases her suicidality borne of her feeling of being soiled by, and one with, her father's incestuous desire. Thus, telling her 'dark tale' through the suicide note is a way of escaping her biopolitical imprisonment. The very narrative in which we read these words of an apparently defeated daughter is a testament to her refusal to keep her father's secret any longer. By writing this note to replace herself, Mathilda redefines her being, which she has described as corrupted by her father, through a narrative that excludes and defies his command. Betty Bennett agrees that Mathilda achieves 'a kind of redemption through her last act, the confessional writing of her story, in the end rejecting the "silence" in which she was schooled by ... her father' (*Introduction* 54). That the text is so unusual, assuming the fringe form of a public suicide note – 'written as if ... for strangers' (41) – highlights the centrality of the theme of communication. Moreover, Mathilda takes her refusal to be censored a step further: she censors her father by refusing to name him in the narrative and identifying him only in terms of his relation to her – as her father, much as he sees her only in relation to himself. He therefore loses his individual identity. Mathilda subsumes him into her tale, a recreation of herself through narrative.

Considered extra-textually, too, the novelistic suicide note as a literary form escapes the bounds of tradition and thus the confines of the canon formed by men. In a psychoanalytic reading of the text, Rajan discusses the narrative as a textual 'abject' and cites its '*unusable* negativity' in a recognition of the strangeness of the literary form (46; emphasis in original), its rejection of the usual aims of both literature and reader. I suggest we approach this odd narrative form as feminist protest. In *The Madwoman in the Attic*, Sandra Gilbert and Susan Gubar comment on the trials of female writers in the period: 'Enclosed in the architecture of an overwhelmingly male-dominated society, these literary women were also, inevitably, trapped in the specifically literary constructs of what Gertrude Stein was to call "patriarchal poetry" ... [N]ineteenth-century woman writer[s]' were 'constricted and restricted by the Palaces of Art and Houses of Fiction male writers authored' (xi). Through the form of the public suicide note, which focuses on an issue associated with feminist protest, Shelley creates a unique space for feminist dissent. This point is particularly poignant with regard to Shelley's lived situation, since she was the daughter of one famous male writer, Godwin, and the spouse of another, P. B. Shelley, her mother Wollstonecraft having died when she was an infant. Day to day, Shelley was surrounded by ambitious male writers – including Byron and Polidori at Villa Diodati, where she conceived of *Mathilda* – and she may have wished to escape being eclipsed by them by using an unusual and relatively undefined literary form.

Conclusion: Female Suicide as Self-Fashioning

Higonnet remarks that suicide is always a vehicle for meaning, a text in need of interpretation: 'To take one's life is to force others to read one's death. For when we categorize a death we do not record pure fact ... Rather, we produce a reading that depends upon the physical and subjective context' ('Feminine' 103). For the suppressed, such as women in the period, suicide can be understood as a defiant act of communication, an aggressive means of self-fashioning in a culture that would enjoin the subject to silence. Women were judged as immodest and aggressive simply for writing, giving rise to noms de plume and other forms of authorial dissimilation. Wollstonecraft did not provide her name for *Mary*; nor did Shelley do so for the first edition of *Frankenstein*. The situation did not improve much as the century wore on, as is evident from the Brontë sisters' attributions of their great novels to male-sounding authors (Currer, Ellis and Acton Bell), and from Mary Ann Evans's identification of herself as 'George Eliot'. But, in the world of fiction, women's suicides could speak volumes, sometimes much more than they could do in real life, which were too often interpreted by newspapers and other popular media to have a narrow range of significance, seemingly always about love, a euphemism for sex, and female attractiveness, the concerns of patriarchal biopower.

If it is true that all suicides are vehicles for meaning, then we may also approach the suicide of Victorian-period writer Charlotte Perkins Gilman in 1935 in this light. Her decision to end her life may be regarded as communicating her feminist rebellion – an announcement of her demand to be heard – no less poignantly than does her famous short story of feminist protest 'The Yellow Wallpaper' (1892) or the manuscript she left upon her death, 'The Right to Die', a defence of suicide and euthanasia (Pabst Battin, Introductions 634). Perkins Gilman left a suicide note, a text demanding interpretation, although the straightforward final sentence scarcely requires elucidation: 'I have preferred chloroform to cancer' (Pabst Battin, Introductions 634). In seeming defiance of the repetitious associations of women's suicide with love and family in both the popular press and literature of the foregoing centuries, Perkins Gilman describes her choice to die in the most practical terms and with the least sentimental language. As any man might, she refuses to suffer. Here is suicide as female autonomy.

Notes

1. For book-length treatments of Foucauldian theory – especially biopower – and feminism, see, for example, Jemima Repo's *The Biopolitics of Gender* (2015), Lois McNay's *Foucault and Feminism: Power, Gender and the Self* (1992), and Irene Diamond and Lee Quinby's *Feminism & Foucault: Reflections on Resistance* (1988).
2. As I detail in the Introduction to the Broadview edition of *Mathilda*, Shelley sent the manuscript of the novella to her father, Godwin, but he refused to return it after her repeated requests for it (10–11).

3. Even today in the West, women are 'given away' by their fathers at their weddings and take their husband's last names to replace that of their fathers. See Carol Blum's 'Of Women and the Land: Legitimizing Husbandry' (1996) on the establishment of patriarchal culture in early modern Britain.
4. Significantly, a volume of *Emilia Galotti* is found open on Werther's desk after he shoots himself in Goethe's *The Sorrows of Young Werther*.
5. Augustine is surprisingly modern on this point: 'in case of violent rape and of an unshaken intention not to yield unchaste consent, the crime is attributable only to the ravisher and not at all to the ravished', thereby obviating Lucretia's need to kill herself (50).
6. Although Shakespeare envisioned other types of female suicide, such as those of Lady Macbeth and Cleopatra, none were so popular in the nineteenth century as that of Ophelia.
7. This claim also appears in Gates (135), Anderson (43), and O'Dea (154).
8. Because these reports are anonymous and all from *The Times*, I distinguish them in the citation with reference to the dates on which they were published.
9. For more on media reportage about suicide in the period, see Houston's 'Fact, Truth, and the Limits of Sympathy: Newspaper Reporting of Suicide in the North of England, circa 1750–1830' (2011).
10. Importantly, most critics today agree that Clarissa is, indeed, suicidal, even though early criticism tended to skirt the subject; this point is especially striking when one considers that *Clarissa* is 'commonly viewed as the first English novel to employ the term ['suicide']', McGuire reports (*Dying* 1).
11. For more on Hemans's depictions of suicidal women in her poetry, see: McGuire's '"I leave thee not": Felicia Hemans and Maternal Suicide' (2018); Sharifah Aishah Osman's '"Mightier than death, untamable by fate": Felicia Hemans's Byronic Heroines and the Sorority of the Domestic Affections' (2006); and Jeffrey C. Robinson's 'The Poetics of Expiration: Felicia Hemans' (2003).
12. The same may be true of Hemans's and Wordsworth's treatments of 'Indian' women's suicides.
13. For more on period feminism and the rhetoric of slavery, see also: Eamon Wright's *British Women Writers and Race, 1788–1818: Narrations of Modernity* (2005) and, for the American perspective, Karen Sánchez-Eppler's *Touching Liberty: Abolition, Feminism and the Politics of the Body* (1993).
14. See my article 'The Wollstonecraftian Plot: Female Suicide as Slave Protest' for an in-depth examination of Wollstonecraft's use of abolitionist concepts and language to advance her feminist programme. Several elements in the following discussion are drawn from this publication.
15. Although Wollstonecraft published *Mary* before *Rights of Woman* – the author's feminist tour de force – and *The Wrongs of Woman* has long been considered to be her fictionalisation of her arguments in her polemical work, as I have argued in the introduction to the Broadview Press edition of the works, *Mary* contains feminist elements, too, as I will show.
16. St Luke 20: 35 and St Matthew 22: 30 feature almost identical words, but none of these biblical passages use the word 'giving' instead of 'given', as Wollstonecraft does – a change that suggests myriad interpretations about a

character who appears to live only for others, as literary ladies of sensibility often do.

17. Apparently, Shelley found this passage striking, too, as she nearly replicates it in 'The Mourner' (1830), a short story very like *Mathilda*, wherein Horace Neville complains of an older boy at Eton who bullies him: 'Speak of West Indian slavery! ... [T]he tender years of aristocratic childhood were yielded up to a capricious, unrelenting, cruel bondage, far beyond the measured despotism of Jamaica' (76).
18. See also Marc Etkind *Or Not to Be* (1997), a collection of famous suicide notes accompanied by short biographies for context.
19. I refer to Fanny Godwin and Harriet Shelley by their full names to avoid confusing them with the other Godwins and Shelleys in this examination.
20. Fanny Godwin does seem to have been viewed as an encumbrance. Godwin was terrified that the newspapers would learn of her shameful mode of death and wrote on 13 October 1816 to P. B. Shelley, begging

    > the poet to 'avoid anything that leads to publicity. Go not to Swansea; disturb not the silent dead.' ... Shelley complied, and neither he, nor any member of Fanny's family, claimed her body. Indeed, the suicide was so successfully hushed up that Fanny's stepbrother, Charles Clairmont, had not learned of her death a year later. (Faubert, 'Fanny' n.p.; quoting St Clair 412)

    Fanny Godwin was buried in an unmarked grave in Wales, finally achieving her stated goal that others should forget 'that such a creature ever existed as' herself. As if following her half-sister's lead, Shelley seems almost afraid to acknowledge the event in her journal, writing in small handwriting for the entry on the relevant date, '"Fanny died this night"' (Sunstein 127).
21. Sanderson details that Shelley remained 'preoccupied with self-destruction' until his final years:

    > Two days after Mary nearly died of a miscarriage (June 1822), Percy wrote to Trelawny in the hope of producing some prussic acid (cyanide): 'I need not tell you I have no intention of suicide at present, – but I confess it would be a comfort to me to hold in my possession that golden key to the chamber of perpetual rest.' ... A mere three weeks later, Percy was dead indeed. (61n)

    P. B. Shelley continued to indulge his fantasies about choosing death, but the ocean beat him to it.
22. As a relatively long suicide note, *Mathilda* may more properly be termed a 'suicide diary', if we take A. A. Leenaars commentary on the topic as our guide. In *Suicide Notes: Predictive Clues and Patterns* (1988), he discusses the suicide diary as 'a suicide note with a history' that 'is a lengthy, literate document kept over a fairly long period of time', in which 'the diarist writes explicitly about suicide, including his suicidal thoughts, impulses, reflections, and resistances; and, the diarist commits suicide' (cited in Samraj and Gawron 90). However, because of the cultural currency of the phrase 'suicide note' – and because most of the examples of suicides notes to which Shelley would have been privy were relatively short – I will continue to use the term 'suicide note' to interpret *Mathilda* in terms of the form.
23. This thinking may be regarded as an early iteration of Hitlerite eugenics: Foucault comments on the links of early forms of biopower to the eugenic dreams of the late nineteenth century and beyond (*Sexuality* 149–50).

24. In ‘A Family Affair: Ennobling Suicide in Mary Shelley’s *Matilda*’, I discuss this passage as part of Shelley’s contribution to the suicide debate of the period – particularly as it is articulated in Hume’s *Essays on Suicide*, Goethe’s *Werther*, and Rousseau’s *Julie*. More directly, though, Shelley’s novella is an answer, in part, to her father Godwin’s discussion of the relative merits of suicide in the appendix ‘Of Suicide’ in *Political Justice* (86). Elements of the article appear in this section and elsewhere in the present discussion.

Chapter 5

'Earth! take these atoms!': The Religious Tract War and Suicidal Rebellion in Byron's *Manfred*

Christianity was the most prevalent manifestation of biopower in Romantic-era Britain, with most anti-suicide texts approaching the topic from a religious perspective and seeking to enforce life under every circumstance. Religion may not seem to be a functionary of biopower, as it proposes to guide the spiritual life of subjects. Its undue attention to enforcing life demonstrates its role as an arm of biopower, however. This goal developed over the centuries: once, Christianity recognised self-sacrifice as the greatest act of piety for martyred saints; in the Renaissance period, the devotional poet Donne wrote an entire treatise questioning whether suicide is impermissible in Christianity; but, by the eighteenth century and Romantic period, the Christian opposition to suicide was so intense and total that nearly all of the many texts written against the individual's right to choose death invoked a Christian perspective, making it a powerful tool of the newly established, society-wide iteration of biopower. As Andrey Makarychev puts it,

> biopolitics is a utilitarian way of utilizing human bodies as an economic resource which needs to be properly administered and duly managed and taken care of, which explains the conceptual nexus between biopower and governmentality ... [, while] religion (the Foucauldian 'pastoral power') can also be analysed as a part of [the] biopower toolkit. (106)[1]

So seamless was the ideology of enforced life in British Christian society that the radical theme of religious subversive suicide rarely appears in texts, even in literary works. Although the trope of slave suicide in abolitionist literature and increased attention to other forces of biopower that took hold at this time in British life inspired a few examples on this topic, Christianity's opposition to suicide should not be understood as secondary to these other forces that shaped the heated suicide debate. Christianity's absolute enforcement of life has always afforded authority and legitimacy to biopower in other realms. In short, biopower's prohibition against choosing death has been most firmly established in and expressed through Christian doctrine, rendering its representations in the apparently separate realms of slavery and misogyny mutually enforcing. Accordingly, the literary theme of Romantic subversive suicide – slave, female, and anti-religious – that characterise texts from the period are integrally linked.

In almost every tract on suicide by Christian writers, the main argument is that suicide constitutes a rebellion against God's authority and therefore one may not choose death. Almost none of them consider the baselessness of this argument for atheists, even though the concern over what was viewed as the rise in atheism increased throughout the eighteenth century. Chief among the few Romantic-era literary works that express suicidal rebellion against religious authority is Byron's *Manfred*, my focus in this chapter, wherein the titular hero, about to launch himself off the Jungfrau, cries, 'Earth! take these atoms!' (1. 2. 109), a distinctly materialist view of the human body that both understands it in biopolitical terms and opposes the religious notion of human life as sacred. Byron's play is significant for this study because it was penned by the most famous British poet of the time and is concerned with the topic of suicide from beginning to end. Moreover, Byron sets the protagonist's quest for death alongside the play's exploration of Manfred's power struggles against religious authority, and not just Christian authority: Byron shows that all spiritual regimes seek to deny the subject autonomy. He also frames the main topic of the play, suicide, in biopolitical terms through multiple references to slavery and the sub-theme of incest, both of which suggest limitations on bodily freedom. Finally, Byron links the theme of suicide as expressive of existential independence with his protest against the Licensing Act of 1737. Through the literary form of mental drama and constant references to silence in the dialogue of the play, Byron provides a tour de force of protest against all tyrannical injunctions against autonomous self-expression.

The religious prohibition against choosing death appears not only in the Christianity of eighteenth-century Britain, but also in the classical world, such as in pronouncements by Socrates – although there were some notable exceptions, including Seneca and the other Stoics, whose cavalier attitudes towards self-killing sometimes overshadow the more familiar condemnation of suicide. Even with respect to the Christian treatment of suicide, though, there was greater debate and nuance than has generally been recognised. Although Christianity strictly condemns suicide on an official level, several commentators point out that the very basis of the Christian myth – Jesus Christ's sacrifice of himself for his followers – is a kind of suicide. This point is soundly established by Donne in *Biathanatos*, as I will show. Others would add that the revered early Christian martyrs, who offered up their lives as a testament of faith in an 'imitation of Christ', as the fifteenth-century devotional writer Thomas à Kempis would say, followed in Christ's self-destructive footsteps. In addition, writers such as Burton point out that Christianity sometimes induces suicidality (even if indirectly, through religious insanity) (52). Still others opine that condemning suicide – and especially punishing it with laws that draw upon Christian principles – is anti-Christian, as it rejects the charity, humility, and kindness that Christ commands his followers to enact, and of which suicidal people are in demonstrable need. Although the common view that religion is antithetical to suicidality is not inaccurate, it is overly simplistic and ignores the subtle realities of the issue.

The religious debate about suicide takes many forms between the contrasting positions of suicide's absolute sinfulness and its permissibility. From one extreme to another, I elucidate six basic approaches to the linked issues of suicide and religion in the period: (1) suicide is not allowable because God forbids it; (2) suicide is not allowable because God created and owns us, and therefore we have no right to destroy his property; (3) suicide is allowable because God, manifest on earth as Jesus Christ, accomplished it; (4) suicide is allowable because the Bible does not expressly condemn it (and even contains instances of heroic suicide), and it is absurd to think we can alter God's will; (5) suicide is allowable because there is no God and therefore we own ourselves; (6) suicide is allowable because, although there are gods, they have no authority over the autonomous individual. This final point – perhaps the most radical of all – is the ultimate import of Byron's *Manfred*, although its boldness can only be genuinely appreciated upon a consideration of its relation to the other arguments regarding the permissibility of suicide, religiously considered.

'This Heaven-daring crime': The Condemnation of Suicide in Religious Tracts

A common religious argument against suicide in polemical tracts is that God, figured as a divine officer, forbids it. John Herries writes in *An Address to the Public, On the Frequent and Enormous Crime of Suicide: Recommended to the Perusal of All who are Distressed in Mind, in Body, or in Worldly Circumstances* (1781):

> this Heaven-daring crime implies in it ... a disregard of that DUTY which our Maker has been pleased to assign to us ... If, therefore, we are negligent in our office, or if we relinquish it without permission, we are openly disobedient and rebellious to the Author of our being.
>
> Suppose a soldier wilfully disqualifies himself for the service of his Commander, or deserts his station without leave, is not he therefore accounted highly criminal? (13)

Like so many religious writers in the period, Herries equates Christians with soldiers in discussing their duty to God. Like a soldier, the Christian must obey the divine commander's orders immediately and without question; the trope also reveals the biopolitical view of human life as important not for its individual value, but as part of a whole, just as an army gains strength in numbers. Chloë Taylor notes of disciplinary power, part of biopower's toolkit, 'Discipline is justified by the perceived desirability of the disciplined state that its practices bring about: the well-trained soldier, the highly achieving student, the orderly ward, the productive workshop ... In disciplinary institutions, power is de-individualized' ('Familial' 203). The individual Christian is not as important as the whole of Christiandom, a view that opposes the Romantic-era focus on the value and formation of the unique self.

The view of believers as soldiers was not new to the period, although it intensified at that time. In *An Essay Concerning Self-Murther Wherein is Endeavour'd to Prove that it is Unlawful According to Natural Principles* (1700), John Adams – taking the long-standing position that 'natural' equates with 'divine' – proclaims about the classical (pre-Christian) period:

> *Pythagoras*, to shew the Unlawfulness of destroying God's Propriety, and forsaking the End for which Life was given, lays it down for one of his Rules, *That no Man ought to quit his Station, without the express Command of his Superiour Officer*; *that is, of God*, as *Cicero* explains it. (22; emphasis in original)

Meanwhile, John Calvin exhorts:

> 'Let us wait for the highest commander, who sent us into this world, to call us out of it ... God, having sent us in this world, wishes us to stay in it, and he has placed us in a post which we must not abandon until God orders us to do so.' (quoted in Watt, *Calvinism* 68)

These words render the many Calvinists in Scotland and throughout Britain as soldiers for God and their lives as their assigned duty. Even Locke echoes this view: despite his claim that each person is his own 'master' (225) and possesses his own body, he also states, 'Every one ... is *bound to preserve himself*, and not to quit his station wilfully', because people are 'all the servants of one sovereign master' (191; emphasis in original). In short, Locke at once defines the individualised Western liberal subject and, at the same time, affirms that he has a 'station' to fill in service to God. While Locke may mean to say that people have no other human master besides themselves, he does not explicitly state as much here. Locke's position aligns with that of many religious commentators who blamed the perceived rise in British suicides on the intellectual movements that he influenced, specifically empiricism and the Enlightenment. By the Romantic period, other philosophers championed Locke's point: Kant resorts to similar language in his *Lectures on Ethics*, saying that the suicide 'arrives in the next world as one who has deserted his post, and must therefore be seen as a rebel against God' (148).[2] The political language that casts believers as soldiers or rebels demonstrates religion's function as an arm of state power.

The first Christian text devoted to outlining the impermissibility of suicide published in English was Sym's *Lifes* [*sic*] *Preservative Against Self-Killing*, penned in 1637, when laws against suicide were particularly harsh, even against those who might have been insane when they ended their lives. Pabst Battin reports that, in contrast with the Romantic period, coroners returned judgements of *non compos mentis* in fewer than two per cent of cases in the Tudor and Stuart periods. Sym shared this stern attitude towards self-killing, which he perceived as an English epidemic in his time (Pabst Battin 296), a view that became shared more widely over the decades. Sym also considers a wide range of behaviours to be suicide, rather than only fatal violence against the self, and he judges the act as more sinful than murder (297). This perspective is echoed by many later religious writers, who reason that the murderer can plead for God's mercy, but that the suicide denies himself this opportunity. Sym anticipates the objections of writers like Hume and others, who point out that suicide is not specifically condemned in the Bible, when he argues, essentially, that the reason there is no written biblical law against the act is that it is too horrendous to mention:

> Here is now the specific difference of this sort of murder, whereby it transcends and is distinguished from all other murders, and consists in restraint of the act of killing, in regard of its individual object, to a man's own life and self, which is the greatest and cruellest act of hostility in the world. When a man, who by nature is most bound to preserve himself, reflects upon himself to destroy himself, the horribleness whereof is so monstrous that we read no Law made against it, as if it were a thing not to be supposed possible. (297)

Part of Sym's reasoning for the act's utter sinfulness is that, as Seaver summarises it, suicide denies 'God's sovereignty, for God gives us life as a gift, which we cannot reject or destroy without committing an act of gross disobedience' (29). However, the concepts of obedience and gift-acceptance are incompatible: those who obey accept duties, while gifts are traditionally understood as freely given, unasked for, and without the expectation of a return. It is worth considering what the nature of a gift is at this point. Montesquieu declares:

> 'Life has been given to me as a gift ... I can therefore return it when this is no longer the case ... When I am overwhelmed by pain, poverty and scorn, why does one want to prevent me from putting an end to my troubles, and to deprive me cruelly of a remedy which is in my hands?' (quoted in Szasz, *Fatal* 13–14)

More succinctly, Critchley confirms: 'a gift that we cannot reject is not a gift' (29). Other modern philosophers consider this issue: Mark Kingwell comments, 'Of course life is an amazing gift, but it is also hard, a bestowal none of us actively wished for. Martin Heidegger called this thrownness: We simply find ourselves here, without debate or decision' (O6). Thus, what some religious writers of the period identify as a gift, others have considered to be a kind of trap – not a gift at all.

For many, spirituality and faith in the divine were inconsistent with and undermined by the empiricist focus on the centrality of the material world for human knowledge and the Enlightenment's championship of reason as the all-important human faculty. Christian denouncers of the supposed rage for suicide in Britain often took aim at movements connected to empiricism, such as deism or natural religion, which favoured the notion that God is evident to everyone through nature and rejected the concept of revealed religion shared mystically (as opposed to rationally) by God with his representatives on earth, such as priests interpreting the Bible. Christian writers also decried Enlightenment thinking, often equated with 'French philosophy'. The very title of a tract by John Prince, *Self-Murder Asserted to be a Very Heinous Crime*; *In Opposition to all Arguments Brought by the Deists, To the Contrary* (1709), states the vicar's philosophical position clearly, as does John Harriott's *The Religion of Philosophy, As Contra-distinguished from Modern French Philosophy: And as an Antidote to its Pernicious Effects Lately So Evident in the Prevalence of Assassination & Suicide* (1812). Harriott, Magistrate of the Thames Police, opines, 'French atheistical philosophy, which, sapping the foundation of virtuous principles, threatens destruction to *all* religion and morality' (iv; emphasis in original), such that many people believe suicide to be an easy way out of temporary pain and into an eternity of peace (v). Enlightenment thought was deemed responsible by many authors for the decline of traditional Christian principles and resultant increase in suicide – a direct threat to pastoral power.

Another tract that wears its argument on its binding is the anonymously authored *A Dissertation or, Discourse on Suicide; Grounded on the Immovable Foundation of Scriptural, Rather than of Philosophical Principles* (1785), which similarly claims that the 'Principles of modern Atheism, Naturalism, or Deism' propose that 'an occasional SUICIDE might ... be deemed as lawful, as it would be then *personally* expedient' (5; emphasis in original). Such texts lay the blame for the perceived increase in suicides at the feet of Enlightenment thinkers. In so doing, however, they neglect the actual words of the founders of the movement, such as Locke, who also condemns suicide for religious reasons. So, too, does Diderot, the presumed writer of the entry on suicide in the *Encyclopedia* (Watt, 'Gender' 149), often viewed as the manifesto of the Enlightenment. The entry states in no uncertain terms,

> Man is not the master of his life. Since he did not give it to himself, he cannot regard it as a possession that he may dispose of as he pleases. He owes his life to his creator; it is a kind of deposit that he has entrusted to him. It is for him alone to withdraw his deposit when he finds it appropriate. Thus man does not have the right to do what he wants with it or, even less, to destroy it altogether. (n.p.)

No more traditionally Christian view on suicide may be found. The religious tract writers who oppose Enlightenment philosophy on the grounds of its supposed promotion of suicide had more support from within the movement than they appear to have realised. Still, the fear that Christian piety was declining in Britain was rampant, and it supported the generation of new religious movements that promised a return to fundamental Christian principles. Wesley laments:

> It is a melancholy consideration, that there is no country in Europe, or perhaps the habitable world, where the horrid crime of self-murder is so common as it is in *England!* One reason of this may be, that the English, in general, are more ungodly and more impatient than other nations. (164; emphasis in original)

Such complaints suggest that suicide is so tempting that only the fear of God can prevent it.

Some tracts communicate the impermissibility of suicide in God's eyes through the very forms in which they are written, such as Croft's *A Sermon, Preached ... on the 18th of September, 1791. Soon After the Riots at Birmingham, and the Self-murder of Mr Sutherland* (1791). For most of his short sermon, Croft harangues his audience about the evils of complaining:

> How can we have the presumption to set up ourselves as judges, as supreme judges, of the goodness of these days ... or of any days? How dare we dictate to the God who made us, and who placed us here? From God our maker and our heavenly father, the former and the latter days proceed: God suiteth his days to his creatures and his creatures to his days. (6)

In the last pages of the sermon, Croft addresses suicide in relation to his larger theme:

> Behold, while with the greatest folly, as well as wickedness, he grasps the instrument of self-murder in his frantick hand – behold, while he prepares to throw back his life in the face of his creator, because he is convinced that his miseries never can, by any possibility, end – his miseries are at an end, his prison doors fly open his fetters are unlocked ... Even so is it possible that some sudden and unexpected comfort may shine forth on every one. (17)

Croft's dramatic depiction of suicide underscores his authorial past as the writer of a potboiler novel on suicide titled *Love and Madness*; *or*, *A Story Too True*, which was a 'redaction of James Hackman's notorious murder of Martha Ray [the mistress of the Earl of Sandwich] and subsequent suicide attempt' (McGuire, *Dying* xvi). In his sermon, Croft insists that life is a gift from God that keeps on giving – or else.

Many Christian writers invoke the threat of hell and the eternal punishment to be visited upon the suicide's everlasting soul as a deterrent for the act. In the prefatory pages of Dawes Blackett's *Suicide*; *A Poem* (1789), the (unusually female) writer begins,

> let me ask these desperadoes how will those who shrink from the horrors of mortal and terminable disappointment be able to endure a certain and perpetual scene of sorrow and punishment, from which there is no hope of relief, no probability of pardon, and into which their own impatience has precipitated them ... He should not therefore, rush presumptuously to that tribunal, from whose sentence there is no appeal. (v)

God's eternal judgement is presented as the horrible alternative to the temporary pain of life on earth. Other writers attempt to ameliorate the traditionally harsh Christian position on suicide by offering God's love as a balm for the suffering that causes suicidality. Piggott does so in *Suicide and Its Antidotes*: *A Series of Anecdotes and Actual Narratives*, *with Suggestions on Mental Distress*, in which the Curate of Clerkenwell states his hope that, through his tract, the suicidal 'may be deterred from the perpetration of the atrocious deed; and that, by [Piggott's] displaying the happy, the blessed consequences of a providential preservation from the crime, the agitated may look to Heaven for support, and seek their refuge there' (xii). Yet others, such as John Garnons in *Sermons on Various Subjects* (1792), represent the idea of heroic resistance to the temptations of suicide, such as displayed by Job in the Old Testament. Beginning with a quotation from the Book of Job – 'all the days of my appointed time will I wait, till my change come' (Job 14:13) – Garnons lists Job's many satanic afflictions, despite which, enduring with courage and piety, he refused to end his earthly pains voluntarily (339–40). Fordyce also uses the example of Job in *A Letter on Suicide* (24). Perhaps the most famous Christian writer on this subject, however, is Calvin, the French reformer (Introductions, Pabst Battin 249). In *Sermons of Maister John Calvin, upon the Booke of Job* (1580), he writes,

> For it is not lawful for the faithful to mislike their own life, and to wish so for death. True it is that we may wish for death in one respect: which is, in consideration that we be held here in such bondage of sin, as we can not [*sic*] serve God so freely as were to be wished, because we are overfraught with vices. In respect hereof it is certain that we may sigh, and desire God to take us quickly out of the world. But (as is said afore) it may not be for that we hate our life, or for that we be weary to be held here because we be handled over rigorously: but we must bear our lot patiently, in waiting Gods [*sic*] leisure to deliver us. (251)

In Calvin's interpretation, Job demonstrates patience and humility, rather than heroism, as an exemplar of Christian piety. Romantic period writer John Coates echoes Calvin in 'An Answer to the Justification of Suicide' (1792): 'Dare you affirm, that a passionate or wicked man hath a sufficient warrant from God to dispatch himself, when he judges his station in life intolerable?' Coates adds the familiar reference to life as a gift that cannot be refused: 'That life, and every thing we here enjoy, is the gift of God, no true philosopher ever doubted; but that we should wantonly, or peevishly throw back the gift upon the donor, and destroy ourselves, I can by no means grant' (110). The decision to end a human life is God's alone, since God has given us life and is therefore the ultimate authority over it. However, Christian writers were not the first to argue that the individual's life is in the power of the divine.

Religious Anti-suicide Commentary Beyond Christianity

The first religious directives against suicide in the Western tradition are from Ancient Greece, notably in the *Phaedo* (written 360 bce), in which Plato distinguishes the suicide of Socrates from unlawful self-killing. The view that people are divine possessions is not solely Christian, as even the ancient so-called 'pagan' commentators assert it. The *Phaedo* records a conversation between Plato's teacher Socrates and Cebes. Socrates, who has been ordered to kill himself by the Athenian courts, answers Cebes' question, 'Why is suicide held to be unlawful?' under extralegal circumstances, with the answer that even

> when a man is better dead, he is not permitted to be his own benefactor, but must wait for the hand of another ... There is a doctrine whispered in secret that man is a prisoner who has no right to open the door and run away; this is a great mystery which I do not quite understand. Yet I too believe that the gods are our guardians, and that we are a possession of theirs. (76)

Socrates' declaration that he does not comprehend the prohibition against self-killing, as well as his gesture to its secretive nature (as though the prohibition – and not suicide itself – is shameful), highlights the contradiction between these statements and those made earlier in the dialogue. Nor is Socrates' subsequent confirmation of this illogical principle more conclusive, for he identifies humans as existing on the same plane as animals and other possessions when he asks Cebes:

> And if one of your own possessions, an ox or an ass, for example, took the liberty of putting himself out of the way when you had given no intimation of your wish that he should die, would you not be angry with him, and would you not punish him if you could?
>
> Certainly, replied Cebes.
>
> Then, if we look at the matter thus, there may be reason in saying that a man should wait, and not take his own life until God summons him, as he is now summoning me. (76)

The comparison between humans and domestic animals is inconsistent with Socrates' philosophy regarding the hierarchy of living creatures (*ta zoa*) that situates humans above animals. Nevertheless, Socrates reaffirms his conviction that humans are owned by the divine and, thus, our lives are not ours to dispense with.

Despite what many in the period called Socrates' 'heathen' identity, a few eighteenth-century writers, such as Adams, recognised the usefulness of his condemnation of suicide. Adams attempts to appeal to the proponents of natural law and others who look beyond Christianity for moral guidance:

> *Plato* makes *Socrates* to say, *That the Gods have a peculiar Care of us*: *That Man is one of those Things of which they have reserv'd to themselves a particular Propriety*. From which he infers, That *as a Man wou'd be angry with his Slave if he shou'd kill himself without his leave, and wou'd punish him if he cou'd for so doing, so perhaps*, says he, *God wou'd deal with Man if he should kill himself*. (21; emphasis in original)

In Adams's summary, Socrates considers humans as the slaves of God, which is another way of saying that they are divine possessions. In attempting to appeal to the Enlightenment readers whom he thought unlikely to be convinced by Christian arguments, Adams seeks to expand the sphere of influence of the anti-suicide tract writers.

Again, though, it is notable that some of the most notable Enlightenment and supposedly 'atheistical' writers, such as Rousseau, provide plenty of ammunition to support the Christian side of the period's suicide debate. In *Julie*, Rousseau's character Saint-Preux answers his friend Lord Bomston's denunciation of his suicidality with a contradictory letter that nevertheless begins with a recognition of the conventionally Christian view of self-killing:

> Yes, my lord, it is true. My soul is oppressed by the weight of life. For a long time it has been a burden to me; I have lost all that could make it dear and nothing is left but weariness. But I am told that it is not permissible for me to dispose of my life without the order from Him who gave it to me … [and] I adore the Eternal Being. (263)

Within a few lines, however, Saint-Preux launches into a much longer defence of his right to choose death – and, what's more, why Lord Bomston should agree to die with him. Most Christian writers focus on the rebellious import of Saint-Preux's letter, rather than his pious introductory statements.

Donne's *Biathanatos* and the Christian Tradition of Self-Destruction

A great many additional commentaries against the supposed eighteenth-century rage for suicide exist. Even so, Dawes Blackett expresses the fear that her society neglects discussion of the topic. She laments that even though 'The frequent and alarming acts of Suicide, which have for a series of years struck terror into the heart of every thinking being, call for the most serious consideration', British 'moralists and preachers are in a great degree silent on this awful and important head' (iii). The British desire to discuss the topic of the religious permissibility of suicide in the period was immense – and, as Dawes Blackett's statement suggests, perhaps even insatiable. Nevertheless, it was also quite new. Watt confirms, 'Only in the eighteenth century did anything resembling a debate on suicide occur' ('Gender' 149). To constitute a proper debate, an opposing position must be presented, and that demand was duly filled by the likes of Montaigne and Hume in the eighteenth century. They were preceded by

Donne, one of the few 'isolated voices', Watt points out, who spoke in defence of suicide ('Gender' 149). Donne laid the groundwork for the daring stance in favour of the right to choose death in *Biathanatos*, a word that 'literally signifies "violent death" in Greek' (McGuire, *Dying* 75). However, McGuire comments, Donne offers only 'qualified advocacy of suicide under certain circumstances and for particular ends', saying that 'self-homicide' is a sin, but that 'voluntary death in emulation of the crucifixion with a view to achieving spiritual perfection' is permissible (*Dying* 75) – or, as McGuire puts it elsewhere in *Dying to be English*, 'Donne affords a template for the erasure of the difference between suicide and self-sacrifice' (74).[3] Writing seven years before he took holy orders in the Anglican Church in 1615, after which he became Dean of St Paul's, Donne's defence of suicide is limited. Pabst Battin comments,

> in Donne's highly unconventional view, Christ himself, in not merely allowing himself to be crucified but in voluntarily emitting his last breath on the cross, was in fact a suicide ... However, Donne argues elsewhere in *Biathanatos*, because suicide is so likely to be committed for self-interested reasons rather than wholly for the glory of God, it is appropriate for both civil and canon law to prohibit it. Donne recognized that his unconventional thesis was 'misinterpretable,' and it is probably for this reason that he did not allow *Biathanatos* to be published ... Donne's work was not published until ... 1647, after his death and against his wishes, by his son. (288)

While Donne's defence of the permissibility of suicide under Christian law is qualified, it is extraordinarily powerful. The import of his position is that, under the right circumstances, suicide is the ultimate act of religious devotion – the contrary of sin. Donne not only argues that suicide can be sinless, but he also goes so far as to argue that it can be pious, an exemplary imitation of Christ.

Donne's logical argumentation in *Biathanatos* is impeccable, if dense, and he does not simply express his personal view of the matter to arrive at his shocking conclusion. Throughout the work, he refers to scripture and the most revered theological writers, such as St Augustine (289), to establish his thesis. At one point in *Biathanatos*, Donne comes to the conclusion that suicide is simply 'good' in some circumstances:

> As, ... naturally and customarily, men thought it good to die so, and that such a death, with charity, was acceptable, so it is generally said by Christ that 'the good shepherd doth give his life for his sheep,' which is a justifying and approbation of our inclination thereunto, for to say 'the good do it' is to say 'they which do it are good.' (289)

This duality out of the way, Donne cites evidence from the Bible to prove his point. Noting that St Paul approves of Christians choosing death as a testament of faith, he adds, 'one can no other way give his body for testimony of God's truth ... but by doing it himself' (289), suggesting that sometimes suicide is the only way Christians can adequately express their devotion to God. Donne is not satisfied to establish the mere acceptability of suicide in Christian terms: daringly, he goes so far as to contend that choosing death may be required as a testament of faith in some circumstances. He practically reprimands the reader for negligence in continuing to live: 'we must remember that we are commanded to do it [commit suicide] so as Christ did it' (290). Citing the example of the Christian martyrs, who were often canonised for their self-sacrifice, Donne argues,

> we are taught that all those places of giving up our bodies to death, and of laying down the soul, signify more than a yielding to death when it comes.
>
> And to my understanding there is a further degree of alacrity and propenseness to such a death, expressed in that phrase of John, 'he that hateth his life in this world shall keep it unto life eternal,' and in that of Luke, 'except he hate his own life, he cannot be my disciple'. (290–1)

Put otherwise, we should not simply accept death when it comes to us; we should actively seek it out as a means of freeing ourselves from our low and shameful earthly bodies. Only in this way, Donne suggests, can the good Christian display his disgust for this worldly life that keeps him from his beloved home in heaven. Donne adds, 'Such loatheness to live is that which is spoken of in the Hebrews: "some were racked and would not be delivered, that they might receive a better resurrection"', and then he links up the old with the comparatively new when he cites Calvin's reading of this passage from Hebrews:

> This place Calvin interprets of a readiness to die, and expresses it elegantly: to carry our life in our hands, offering it to God for a sacrifice. And this the Jesuits in their rule extend thus far, let everyone think that this was said directly to him: Hate thy life. (291)

It is notable that Donne's reference to the sacrificial piety of the Jesuits is personal – he was born into a Catholic family and had a Jesuit uncle who was executed for his faith – and would have had little influence on his largely Protestant British readers. However, he combines it with a citation of Calvinist beliefs, which are widely regarded as some of the strictest amongst the Protestant sects. In short, Donne forms his argument on the appropriateness of suicide with several Christian denominations in mind.

Donne's text inspired many Christian writers' responses, such Charles Moore's *A Full Inquiry into the Subject of Suicide* (1790), in which the author attempts to refute *Biathanatos* in a methodical manner, taking Donne's tract apart point by point (e.g. 92–6). In his essay 'On Suicide' (1823), Thomas De Quincey seeks to defend the Renaissance poet from the accusation that he champions self-killing. De Quincey further attempts to build on Donne's ideas and, Gates comments, to refine 'contemporary thinking by arguing that it was necessary to distinguish between justifiable self-homicide and culpable self-murder. The first should apply whenever interests of others were involved, the second when simple personal interest was the motivating factor' (7), thereby adding a secular conclusion to Donne's specifically religious point. However, De Quincey goes too far in his vindication of Donne when he implies that the poet piously attempts to defend the Christian martyrs from the accusation that they were suicides:

> It is a remarkable proof of the inaccuracy with which most men read – that Donne's *Biathanatos* has been supposed to countenance Suicide; and those who reverence his name have thought themselves obliged to apologize for it by urging, that it was written before he entered the church. But Donne's purpose in this treatise was a pious one: many authors had charged the martyrs of the Christian church with Suicide – on the principle that if I put myself in the way of a mad bull, knowing that he will kill me – I am as much chargeable with an act of self-destruction as if I fling myself into a river. Several casuists had extended this principle even to the case of Jesus Christ. (487)

One of these 'casuists' is Donne himself, who considers Jesus Christ's self-sacrifice in *Biathanatos*.

Many writers, indeed, attempt to excuse Donne's radical argument by pointing out that he wrote *Biathanatos* before he took holy orders in 1615. However, it is worth noting that some of his most famous religious poems further develop the theme that the Christian willingness to die is the ultimate proof of devotion to God. Donne's Holy Sonnet 5 (1635) begins,

> I am a little world made cunningly
> Of elements, and an angelic sprite;
> But black sin hath betrayed to endless night
> My world's both parts, and O, both parts must die. (1–4)

Having established the necessity of the speaker's death for religious reasons (to be cleansed of his sins), the poet develops the conceit of the human body as a 'world' that must be apocalyptically destroyed in the remainder of the sonnet. Donne also expresses a similar sentiment in Holy Sonnet 14 (1633), 'Batter my heart.' The speaker chides God for being too gentle with him – 'for you,/ As yet but knock, breathe, shine, and seek to mend' (1–2) – and therefore asks God to destroy him entirely in order to save his soul: 'That I may rise and stand, o'erthrow me, and bend/ Your force to break, blow, burn, and make me new' (3–4). Here, again, is the Christian death wish, subtly expressed, over a decade after Donne became Dean of St Paul's in 1621.

Some eighteenth-century commentators discussed Donne's text with a mix of respect and circumspection. Diderot simply provides the main points of Donne's argument in the *Encyclopedia* entry on 'suicide', denouncing suicide at the start of the entry, but not attempting to attack Donne's argument in *Biathanatos*. Describing carefully and in detail how the 'learned English theologian' establishes his thesis and 'further strengthens his argument' with a plethora of evidence, Diderot dares not refute Donne's text, even though it undermines his own condemnation of suicide on Christian principles (n.p.). By the end of the discussion, Diderot can only conclude, 'It is thus that Mr Donne establishes his system, which will certainly not be approved by orthodox theologians' (n.p.). His expectation was not incorrect.

Beyond polemics, Donne may have had personal motivations for launching a sound justification of suicide. Seaver suggests:

> In his preface Donne admitted that he often contemplated suicide, but that his conscience had assured him 'that no rebellious grudging at God's gifts nor other sinful concurrence accompanies these thoughts,' but only the conviction that 'I have the keys of my prison in my own hand, and no remedy presents itself so soon to my heart as mine own sword.' ('Vicar' 40)

While scripture and orthodox Christian theology afforded Donne the proof for his claim that self-sacrifice was religiously acceptable, personal suffering may have motivated his search for such corroboration. Regardless of the impetus for this line of argument, Donne would not be the last to develop it. Drew Daniel argues that Donne's view of suicide as an act of piety became part of the broader cultural conversation about suicide, particularly for readers of seventeenth-century philosopher Baruch Spinoza: 'a familiar gallery of self-killing worthies such as Saul, Samson, Socrates, Lucrece, St Pelagia, and many other Christian martyrs would have instantly come to mind to his [Spinoza's] early modern readers, and bold readers of Donne's *Biathanatos* would have added Christ' (101). Writing on the twentieth-century philosopher Georges Bataille, Nick Land comments that he 'reads the world historical power of Christianity through its quasi-latent content of an absolute sacrifice – that of God himself – which has created a religion of divine suicide. At the same time, he considers Christianity to have deformed and obscured this thought, burying it under a theology of redemption' (62). Christianity's formative myth affords suicide a laudatory place, from which it has struggled to distance itself.

The topic of Christian martyrdom and the mention of St Pelagia also point to the role of women in the Christian appreciation of self-sacrifice. Female martyred saints, especially virgins, have had a starring role in the Catholic faith since the early period. St Pelagia, also known as St Pelagia the Penitent, 'was a young virgin martyr of Antioch who was venerated there ... at least as early as the fourth century' (Butler and Burns 49). A number of the many martyred female saints were virgins who died heroically. Probably the most famous is Joan of Arc, the fifteenth-century patron saint of France and military ruler – sometimes called the 'Virgin Warrior' – whom representatives of the Catholic Church burned at the stake for wearing men's clothes (as did St Pelagia in some versions of her story) and following demonic orders. The Catholic Church canonised Joan of Arc in the twentieth century in an apparent admission of the mistakes of the past and a gesture in keeping with the celebration of Catholic women who sacrifice themselves for their faith, especially while chaste. As Rebecca Moore attests, 'A spiritual meritocracy, first articulated by Saint Jerome, divided women into three orders of importance: "virgins would be rewarded a hundred times their deserts; widows, sixty times; and wives, thirty times"' (77), demonstrating, again, an outsized interest in the control of female sexuality. For this reason, virginal female martyred saints have an outsized importance in the Catholic imaginary, for they sacrifice not only their sensual pleasure but also their very lives in the service of the Church. Nor have only early modern writers, such as Donne and Spinoza, considered martyrdom to be a kind of suicide. In the Romantic period, Godwin considers the issue in an appendix to *Political Justice*, titled 'Of Suicide': 'Let it be observed that all martyrs [μάρτυρες] are suicides by the very signification of the term. They die for a testimony [μαρτυρία]; that is, they have a motive for dying' (87). Godwin even considers the formative power of this concept for the establishment of Christianity: 'There is a proverb which affirms, "that the blood of the martyrs is the seed of the church"' (87). That a good deal of this blood is female confirms the importance of female suicidality to early ideas of Christianity.

Some commentators have considered that faith may be causally linked to self-destruction in other ways. Such was the case before Christianity, according to George Gregory in *Essays Historical and Moral* (1785), in which he calls suicide 'an act of religion' among 'the ancient sects of philosophers ... when it appeared necessary to preserve their persons from disgrace, or to avoid the risk of forfeiting their honour' (285). Edward Ryan concurs, claiming that pre-Christian religions encouraged suicide and championing Christianity as the bulwark against this fatal tide. In *The History of the Effects of Religion on Mankind* (1793), he lists amongst the 'advantages of Christianity' that 'it abolished those superstitions on which suicide was founded. The Indians, Gauls, Britons, Danes, and other ancient Heathen nations, imagined, that voluntary self-murder secured future happiness to suicides; and put themselves to death in compliance with their religion' (17). Closer to Donne's time – and his argument about the causal link between Christianity and self-destruction – Thomas More searched his heart to determine whether he was impiously committing suicide by refusing to renounce his Catholicism and pledge allegiance to King Henry VIII (Green 135) – which did, in fact, lead to More's execution and subsequent canonisation in the Catholic Church. Meanwhile, in *The Anatomy of Melancholy*, Burton, an Anglican clergyman, seems to justify suicide when he quotes from Ecclesiastes in the Bible ('"*Death is better than a bitter life*"') and lists many examples of noble suicide from the classical world (324; emphasis in original). However, Burton subsequently denounces these 'false and pagan positions, prophane stoical paradoxes, wicked examples: it boots not what heathen philosophers determine in this kind: they are impious, abominable, and upon a wrong ground', adding that 'God, and all good men are against it. He that stabs another, can kill his body; but he that stabs himself, kills his own soul' (325), since the suicide cannot ask for God's forgiveness. Soon thereafter Burton ameliorates his harsh comments:

> This only let me add, that, in some cases, those hard censures of such as offer violence to their own persons, ... which sometimes they do, by stabbing, slashing, &c. are to be mitigated, as in such as are mad, beside themselves for the time, or found to have been long melancholy, and that in extremity: they know not what they do, deprived of reason, judgement. (325)

When one is 'mad' with 'melancholy', one should not be held responsible for such actions. Burton concludes, 'We ought not to be so rash and rigorous in our censures, as some are: charity will judge best: God be merciful unto us all!' (326). He expresses the same point succinctly in the heading of a relevant section: 'Causes of Melancholy. God a cause' (52). Burton thus admits that God can cause suicide by driving people insane – a condition commonly called 'enthusiasm' in the long eighteenth century – and, when that happens, those people are to be held blameless.

From the Romantic period, the anonymously authored *Thoughts on Suicide, in a Letter to a Friend* echoes Burton's sentiment:

> Whether the law has any effect in the prevention of so desperate a deed I cannot tell. That can only be proved by the secret impulses of a man's own

> mind. It appears to me, that our statutes regarding this offence are founded in error, and that we arrogate to ourselves a power belonging only to God. He alone can determine the amount of the guilt incurred. He alone therefore has the right to punish. (27)

Such comments suggest that the suicide might yet be innocent, for his motivations are largely unfathomable. This writer goes so far as to suggest that it is unchristian to be harsh in the response to suicides: 'Every humane being must wish to soften the rigour of our laws respecting Suicide. They appear to be the unhallowed relics of a barbarous period, and are utterly unfit for the present state of civilized society, and the refined regulations of a Christian country' (v–vi). In other words, the responsibility of Christians is not to determine the relative sinfulness of suicide, but to respond with compassion to those who are driven to it.

Other writers argue that self-killing is allowable because the Bible does not condemn it outright. This is a main argument of Hume's essay 'Of Suicide' (1756), which was printed and withdrawn before publication as part of *Five Dissertations* in 1756, first published in 1777 (Popkin xvii) and later published in 1783 under the censorious title *Essays on Suicide, and The Immortality of the Soul, Ascribed to the late David Hume, Esq. Never Before Published. With Remarks, Intended as an Antidote to the Poison Contained in These Performances, By the Editor.*[4] In 'Of Suicide', the Scottish philosopher contends in a lengthy footnote, 'It would be easy to prove that suicide is as lawful under the Christian dispensation as it was to the Heathens. There is not a single text of scripture which prohibits it' (22n). Expectedly, this line of argument launched a great number of angry retorts by devout writers of the period, such as Fordyce, who claims that he responds to a now-dead writer of a long suicide note, but doubtlessly considers Hume his chief target: 'You have signified, that you cannot discover in the Christian system any thing *against* the practice of suicide; but you will not pretend, that you have *there* discovered any thing *for it*' (14; emphasis in original). So incensed were such writers at Hume's text that the anonymous author of *Thoughts on Suicide* laments, 'It is too much the fashion to decry Mr Hume's merits', and he notes accusations against Hume of recommending his readers to choose death – sometimes successfully (viii, vii). Such sentiments – that Hume advises people to kill themselves, rather than presents a rational argument about the permissibility of the act – were common. The anonymous author of *Thoughts on Suicide* seeks to strike a mediating note when he adds, 'Of the essay on Suicide ascribed to him [Hume] it may be said, that it is ingenious and plausible, but no more' (viii). This author may gesture to the following passage in a footnote by Hume, in which he tackles the seeming condemnation of suicide in the Sixth of the Ten Commandments brought by Moses to the Israelites:

> *Thou shalt not kill*, is evidently meant to exclude only the killing of others, over whose life we have no authority. That this precept, like most of the scripture precepts, must be modified by reason and common sense, is plain from the practice of magistrates, who punish criminals capitally, notwithstanding the letter of the law ... In all cases Christians and Heathens are precisely upon the same footing. (22; emphasis in original)

This point is apropos because British law is based on Christian principles, as Blackstone clarifies in a passage on the illegality of suicide in the *Commentaries* (e.g. 189). Hume suggests that if British law allows for the death penalty, despite the condemnation of killing in the Sixth Commandment, then British society must admit that other such loopholes may exist, and he includes suicide as one. However, no less formidable a thinker than Thomas More anticipates – and pretty soundly undermines – Hume's reasoning in a lecture on the teachings of St Augustine, in which More compares the Sixth Commandment to the Ninth, 'Thou shalt not bear false witness against thy neighbour': Paul D. Green comments, 'Augustine, on whom More as a young man had delivered a series of lectures, gave authority to the view that the Sixth Commandment must be reflexive because it does not specifically say "thy neighbor" ... as it does for the commandment against bearing false witness' (141–2). Such a retort would have been a valuable contribution to the period's suicide debate, but More was writing over two hundred years before Hume. This kind of engagement with Hume's text was uncommon, since most Christian writers simply decried it as impious, rather than attempted to refute it on rational grounds.

In addition to considering biblical silence on suicide, Hume attacks the Christian condemnation of the act in several other ways. The 'sceptical' philosopher (as Hume was often termed) argues that it is absurd to think that mere humans can ever change the course of this divinely ordered world:

> 'Tis a kind of blasphemy to imagine that any created being can disturb the order of the world, or invade the business of Providence! it supposes, that that being possesses powers and faculties, which it received not from its creator, and which are not subordinate to his government and authority. A man may disturb society no doubt, and thereby incur the displeasure of the Almighty: But the government of the world is placed far beyond his reach and violence. (17)

Despite having been accused of atheism, Hume underscores the precepts of Christianity as key to the permissibility of suicide. The philosopher shows his sound understanding of eighteenth-century British society in this line of reasoning, for most people considered Christianity to be the final authority on ethical matters; he also defers to the religion by treating it as the ultimate power to decide on the permissibility of suicide. However, in the world of Romantic literature, a few authors went beyond the Christian view of suicide in their thinking about this topic.

The Romantic Defiance of Traditional Christianity and Lord Byron's Suicidal Heresy

That literary Romanticism often rejects traditional forms of Christianity is well accepted in critical commentary. Makdisi discusses the 'bubbling variety of radicalisms' in the early decades of the period (21), while Martin Priestman outlines the outright atheism of the movement in *Romantic Atheism: Poetry and Freethought, 1780–1830* (1999). Two of the most traditionally Christian poets in the Romantic canon, Wordsworth and Coleridge, became so only in their later lives, and some of their early poetic philosophy bordered on pantheistic. Romanticism's challenge to traditional Christianity may be too commonplace to require argumentation, although the topic can scarcely be invoked without citing the best-known atheist of the era, P. B. Shelley, known as 'Shelley the Atheist' during his short term at Oxford before he was expelled for distributing a pamphlet entitled 'The Necessity of Atheism' with his friend Thomas Jefferson Hogg. It should come as no surprise that Shelley champions revolutionary suicide in two of his most powerful political poems, 'The Mask of Anarchy: Written on the Occasion of the Massacre at Manchester' (written in 1819; published 1832) and 'England in 1819' (written in 1819; published 1839), in which he suggests that oppressed people wilfully submit to the fatal violence of their persecutors as a means of overthrowing them.[5] In these poems, he frames the murder of peaceful protesters in St Peter's Field in Manchester as the victims' martyrdom – a form of suicidality, as Donne contends in *Biathanatos*. In *The Mask of Anarchy*, Shelley presents the massacred protesters as powerful 'heirs of Glory' through the sacrifice of their lives to achieve political change (147). Similarly, in 'England in 1819', 'A people starved and stabbed in th' untilled field;/ … / Are graves, from which a glorious Phantom may/ Burst, to illumine our tempestuous day' (7, 13–14): the formulation renders their deaths as socially efficacious and recasts the victims of governmental violence as martyrs to an important cause.

By comparing them to the phoenix – the mythical bird reborn from its own ashes after self-immolation every 500 years – the poet considers martyrdom in a secular light, even while gesturing subtly to its Christian analogue, Christ's sacrifice and resurrection. Shelley indicates that such stories are interchangeable, and that Britain's official religion may not be more authoritative than those of the ancient world. In both poems, he reaches beyond Hume's treatment of suicide, celebrating it – rather than simply permitting it – while undermining Christianity as the final authority on the matter.

Shelley's friend Byron conveys a similar message in *Manfred: A Dramatic Poem*. The titular protagonist yearns for death from beginning to end, and the work involves a wide variety of gods and spirits, from Christian (represented by the Abbot) to elemental (represented by the Witch of the Alps) to Zoroastrian (represented by Arimanes), and beyond. Through this diverse cast of characters, Byron establishes, like Shelley, that Christianity is no more authoritative than other religions. Byron builds a largely religious framework for his dramatic meditation on suicide, only to deny religious authority through a character who actively revolts against its attempts to subjugate him.

Byron composed *Manfred* on the shores of Lake Geneva while he was a neighbour of the Shelleys, who rented the Villa Diodati (Cochran 156). Peter Cochran comments, 'Byron began *Manfred* (we think, for he didn't date the rough *Manfred* manuscripts) at about the same time [as Shelley wrote *Frankenstein*, in June 1816]; he began fair-copying it on March 18th 1817, and revised its third act early in May. It was published on June 16th 1817' (156). Cochran also notes the similarities between *Frankenstein* and *Manfred* – such as their 'alienated' 'protagonists' who are 'scientific-philosophical overreachers' (157, 158) and rebel against 'paternal authority figures' (2) – but he does not suggest that what he calls Manfred's 'Death-Wish' is related to the character's rebellious stance, since, Cochran insists, Byron's 'play cannot be made political' (2). However, I contend that – understood in the political and religious context of Romantic-period Britain – the suicidality that permeates *Manfred* is, indeed, political insofar as it portrays a character who is utterly free from any kind of religious authority over his existence. Manfred is a rebel against pastoral power, the religious arm of biopower.

To fully appreciate the resonances of Byron's treatment of religiously considered suicide in *Manfred*, it is important to examine the poet's other comments on religion and self-destruction. Priestman's discussion of Byron's 'infidelism' helps to situate the poet in terms of the challenge to Christianity that was common in the literature of the period (219): but how do such claims relate to remarks by Byron in his letters that he was not at all against religion and, despite being raised a Calvinist, that he championed Catholicism, to the extent that he educated his daughter, Allegra, as a 'strict Catholic' in an Italian convent (*Letters*, ed. Lansdowne 406)? Such boasts from 1822 must be taken in hand with earlier pronouncements on religion from 1808, in which Byron expands:

> In Morality I prefer Confucius to the ten Commandments, and Socrates to St Paul … in Religion, I favour the Catholic Emancipation but do not acknowledge the Pope, and I have refused to take the Sacrament because I do not think eating Bread or drinking wine from the hand of an earthly vicar, will make me an Inheritor of Heaven. – I hold virtue in general … to be only in the Disposition, each a *feeling* not a principle. – I believe Truth the prime attribute of the Deity, and Death an eternal Sleep, at least of the Body. – You have here a brief compendium of the Sentiments of the *wicked* George Ld. B. (*Letters*, ed. Lansdowne 29; emphasis in original)

Byron's Catholicism seems to have been of the same sort as that of Oscar Wilde and the other dandy literati of the nineteenth-century *fin de siècle*, Byron's stylistic and philosophical inheritors. During their uninhibited lives, these figures often had little use for any kind of religion until their deathbeds, when they began to fear eternal damnation. It is also possible that a large part of their attraction to Catholicism was due to an aesthetic appreciation of the rich pageantry of its ceremony (Hanson 12, 343). Byron's rejection of the Pope as the head of the Catholic Church, the authority of priests, and the Sacrament of the Eucharist demonstrates that he was far from being a devoted adherent to Catholic principles, at least at this point in his adulthood. As with so many of his other pronouncements about what others would consider to be serious matters (again, like the Decadents), the sincerity of Byron's statements about religion may be suspect, itself symptomatic of the poet's subversive attitude towards the authority of Christianity. Byron is similarly unreliable with respect to his comments on suicide, which were alternately serious, humorous, mocking, and downright cruel.

The poet was doubtlessly aware that his maternal grandfather was a suicide (Prothero n.p.), and he might have concluded that his family history afforded him familiarity with the topic – and, perhaps, a propensity to commit suicide himself. Byron sometimes seems earnest about his own suicidality. Richard Lansdowne reports Byron's threat to kill himself if his lover, Teresa Gamba Guiccioli, should die: 'Teresa's miscarriage threatened to bring on consumption, and Byron was seriously concerned. "I do not know what I should do," he wrote …, "if She died – but I ought to blow my brains out – and I hope that I should"' (300). More often in his personal writings, Byron employs the topic of suicide in the service of black humour. In a journal entry from 10 December 1813, he jests laconically:

> I am *ennuyé* beyond my usual tense of that yawning verb, which I am always conjugating; and I don't find that society much mends the matter. I am too lazy to shoot myself – and it would annoy Augusta, and perhaps **; but it would be a good thing for George, on the other side, and no bad one for me; but I won't be tempted. (Moore, *Life* 266)

Judging by his letters, Byron's personal feelings about suicide are difficult to establish, as he often uses the topic as a vehicle for shock and humour.

In the frequent discussions of suicide in his personal writing, Byron often demonstrates a lack of horror and gravity about the topic that is unusual for the period, although utterly typical of him. Writing to Thomas Moore from Venice, 28 January 1817, the poet quips, 'I should, many a good day, have blown my brains out, but for the recollection that it would have given pleasure to my mother-in-law; and, even *then*, if I could have been certain to haunt her' (*Letters*, ed. Lansdowne 263; emphasis in original). Years earlier, writing to his half-sister Augusta Leigh on 9 April 1804, Byron muses:

> My mother Gives a *party* to night at which the principal *Southwell Belles* will be present, with one of which although I don't as yet know whom I shall so far *honour having never seen* them, I intend to *fall violently* in love, it will serve as an amusement pour passer le temps and it will at least have the charm of novelty to recommend it, then you know in the course of a few weeks I shall be quite au desespoir, shoot myself and Go out of the world with eclat, and my History will furnish materials for a pretty little Romance which shall be entitled and denominated the loves of Lord B. and the cruel and Inconstant Sigismunda Cunegunda Bridgetina &c&c princess of Terra Incognita. – Don't you think that I have a very Good Knack for *novel writing*? (*Letters*, ed. Lansdowne 14; emphasis in original)

Byron demonstrates his familiarity with popular fiction that featured desperate lovers dying on account of their devotion to each other, and he imagines himself as a hero in a tear-jerking story for the masses. Byron thus acknowledges the popularity of the theme of suicide in literature of the time, which may explain in part why he included it so often in his own verse.

Byron shows his awareness of suicide as a source of earnest cultural debate in his letters, although not always seriously. In 1813, he wrote to Thomas Moore:

> Madame de Staël ... hath published an Essay against Suicide [i.e. *Reflections on Suicide*], which, I presume, will make somebody shoot himself; – as a

sermon by Blinkensop, in *proof* of Christianity, sent a hitherto most orthodox acquaintance of mine out of a chapel of ease a perfect atheist. (Moore, *Life* 320; emphasis in original)

Byron reveals his familiarity with the suicide debate of the time, particularly as it appeared in non-fictional prose on the topic, such de Staël's, who also wrote *On the Influence of the Passions* in favour of committing suicide for love in 1798: she practically goads her readers into killing themselves lest they reveal their insufficient wisdom or courage (464, 466). Many commentators accused her of writing a suicidally contagious text. Thus, in this passage, Byron gestures not only to de Staël's recent *Reflections on Suicide*, but also to her early work and its reception when he jests that her most recent book will cause readers to commit suicide. The joke is that de Staël's 1812 essay is firmly opposed to suicide, which should have obviated its suicidal contagiousness.

Given his awareness of the Romantic-era suicide debate, we may consider Byron's use of the theme of suicide in his literary output as contributing to it. Passing references to suicide or a death wish appear throughout Byron's poetic *oeuvre*. One of the most memorable involves 'the Scorpion girt by fire' (434) in *The Giaour* (1813), which

... maddening in her ire,
One sad and sole relief she knows,
The sting she nourish'd for her foes,
Whose venom never yet was vain,
Gives but one pang, and cures all pain,
And darts into her desperate brain. – (427–32)

It is as though the scorpion has been brushing up on her Seneca, who wrote, 'If you would pierce your heart, a gaping wound is not necessary; a lancet will open the way to that great freedom, and tranquility can be purchased at the cost of a pin-prick' ('Cable' 110). Likewise, slipping into the ironic mode that characterises so many of his comments on suicide in his personal writing, Byron includes several stanzas on the topic in Canto XIV of *Don Juan* (1819, 1823–4):

The very Suicide that pays his debt
At once without instalments (an old way
Of paying debts, which Creditors regret)
Lets out impatiently his rushing breath,
Less from disgust of life than dread of death. (28–32)

In setting up his witticism about 'Creditors', Byron references what was believed to be a common reason for committing suicide in the period: debt. It was so for Polidori, author of *The Vampyre* and *Ernestus*

Berchtold (both 1819), and Byron's physician when the latter wrote *Manfred*.[6] Stanzas 5 and 6 of Canto XIV complete Byron's rumination on suicide in *Don Juan*, but he neither debates nor jokes about the matter in them. Rather, he uses the topic to contemplate the terrifying otherness of non-being, suggesting that the main reason we do not kill ourselves is that we don't know what death is and fear the '*unknown*' (46; emphasis in original): 'You look down o'er the precipice, and drear/ The gulph of rock yawns, – you can't gaze a minute/ Without an awful wish to plunge within it' (38–40). The unidentified 'you' is a general addressee, the Everyreader, as though everyone feels compelled to kill themselves at some point. Here, in the speaker's assumption that suicidality is universal, we may read, perhaps, Byron's confession to his own propensity for what he termed Polidori's 'rash act' (Medwin 119).

Byron develops the theme of suicide in other literary works besides *Manfred*. The poem 'Euthanasia' begins with a wish for oblivion that recalls Manfred's:

> When Time, or soon or late, shall bring
> The dreamless sleep that lulls the dead,
> Oblivion! may thy languid wing
> Wave gently o'er my dying bed! (1–4)

The final lines also echo the cynicism of Byron's dramatic hero: 'know, whatever thou hast been,/ 'Tis something better not to be' (35–6). Nor is *Manfred* Byron's only drama that explores the topic. In the opening scene of *Cain* (1821), Byron represents the character from the Book of Genesis in the Bible as possessing a death wish. Conversing with Lucifer, Cain complains that he

> But live[s] to die; and, living, see[s] no thing
> To make death hateful, save an innate clinging,
> A loathsome and yet all-invincible
> Instinct of life, which I abhor, as I
> Despise myself, yet cannot overcome –
> And so I live. Would I had never lived! (1. 1. 110–15)

Byron presents Cain in the same light as he does Manfred: a hero of independence in the face of tyranny. Frederick Burwick comments: 'Similar to Manfred's refusal to bow before Arimanes, or to accept the prayers of the Abbot, Cain defies both Lucifer and God. "That which I am, I am," Cain declares, "I did not seek/ For life, nor did I make myself" (3. 1. 509–10)' (56). Although the character may sound more like a spoiled child in this lament, rather than a hero of rebellious suicide, his similarities with Manfred are undeniable. Also notably, Cain's suicidality becomes more intense after he kills his brother, Abel, suggesting that one form of defiance begets another.

Byron explores the theme of rebellious suicide in another drama of the same year. *Sardanapalus* (1821) ends with the effeminate Assyrian king committing suicide with his enslaved Greek mistress, Myrrha, on a pyre of his riches, in defiance of enemies who are invading his kingdom. It is Myrrha who speaks the lines quoted in the previous chapter ('Fear! – I'm a Greek, and how should I fear death?/ A slave, and wherefore should I dread my freedom?' (1. 2. 179–80)), and there are at least forty other uses of the word 'slave' in the play. This combination of sexual nonconformity and suicide-as-resistance recalls the basic plot of *Manfred*, which features a guilt-ridden hero who wishes for death because of some unspoken crime, likely sexual and involving Astarte, who seems to be his sister. Burwick observes, 'brother-sister incest in Manfred's confession was understood by contemporary readers to be Byron's own confession of his illicit relationship with his half-sister, Augusta' (51). Far from being a mere vehicle for gossip, however, *Manfred* is one of Byron's most philosophically profound works, as it joins the question of the religious permissibility of suicide fermenting in the Romantic period with that of pastoral power's management of individuals' bodies. The topics of sexual nonconformity and choosing death are linked in Byron's protest against biopower.

Another Byronic drama that echoes themes in *Manfred* is *The Deformed Transformed* (1824). Along with *Cain* and *Manfred*, Burwick includes *The Deformed Transformed* in a grouping he calls Byron's 'Faustian plays' – a nod to the literary forebear of the plays' defiant protagonists. The last of these is also notable for exploring the suicidal despair of this character in its opening lines. In a scene that recalls Byron's own troubled relationship with his mother and physical affliction (his club foot), *The Deformed Transformed* begins with the protagonist expressing regret over having been born: when his mother Bertha commands him out of her presence, shouting, 'Thou Incubus! Thou Nightmare! Of seven sons/ The sole abortion!' (1. 1. 4–5), Arnold, a 'hunchback' (1. 1. 1), replies, 'Would that I had been so,/ And never seen the light!' (1. 1. 6–7). Soon thereafter, the beleaguered son seeks to resolve his 'trouble with being born', as Emil Cioran puts it in his book of the same title. Arnold laments his deformity and wishes he were no more in distinctly materialist, non-religious terms:

> And shall I live on,
> A burthen to the earth, myself, and shame
> Unto what brought me into life? Thou blood,
> Which flowest so freely from a scratch, let me

Try if thou wilt not in a fuller stream
Pour forth my woes for ever with thyself
On earth, to which I will restore at once
This hateful compound of her atoms, and,
Resolve back to her elements, and take
The shape of any reptile save myself,
And make a world for myriads of new worms! (1. 1. 60–70)

Arnold sets a knife in the ground so that he may fall on it and kill himself, but he is prevented from doing so by the appearance of a mysterious stranger. Despite this hindrance, the theme of suicide is already well established: almost every line so far is devoted to Arnold's suicidality, and another suicidal character will soon appear (Olimpia). Unfinished though the drama is, Byron's message is clear. Jie-Ae Yu argues: 'Byron's closet drama aims at creating subtleties that open the reader's own response to the end of the play. Byron ... wants to show a deliberately indefinite approach to the problem of the limits and powers of the human will' (20). The fragmentary character of *The Deformed Transformed* affords the reader the liberty, here of interpretation, that the play promotes through the theme of freely chosen death. Such is also the case in another 'Faustian play' about human will, *Manfred*, wherein Byron uses ambiguity to encourage readerly involvement in the making of meaning, a democratic and anti-authoritarian gesture. Through consistent references to silence and lacunae in the dramatic dialogue, Byron imbues *Manfred* with a kind of suicide of meaning that echoes the single-minded desire of its protagonist for death, thereby inviting the reader into a nihilistic world that denies the structures of belief that organise our realities, such as religion and language.

Manfred, Slavery and Suicide

Like Wollstonecraft and Shelley, Byron makes multiple references to slavery in his play on suicide and autonomy in the face of religious authority. Byron thereby develops ideas linked to biopower, rather than sovereign power, in that he does not present a character who is threatened with death by the authorities, as would be the case under sovereign power. Although the Spirits threaten to make him suffer for his refusal to bow to divine authority (e.g. 2. 4. 49–50), they repeatedly refuse or are unable to satisfy his persistent request for death, denying his will to suicide as surely as does any Christian authority. When the Christian Abbot tries to convince Manfred to live, his paternalistic care also assumes the biopolitical mode, since he aims to help him continue living, rather than threatening him with punishment for any infractions. Manfred's confirmation of his suicidality announces his refusal of a managed life, and the many references to slavery gesture at what his acceptance of such religious authority would mean for him.

By peppering the drama with references to slavery, Byron defines his hero's familiar claim to fierce independence as a rebellion against biopower. Manfred is so intent on defying authority that he announces his own supremacy over those who would subjugate him. After hearing the spirits' refusal of his request for death, he cries,

> ... Slaves, scoff not at my will!
> The mind, the spirit, the Promethean spark,
> The lightning of my being, is as bright,
> Pervading, and far-darting as your own,
> And shall not yield to yours, though coop'd in clay! (1. 1. 153–7)

If the master-slave relationship is defined by one's wielding power over another who lacks it, then Manfred attempts to deny his enslavement by making himself the master of the Spirits. A similar scene occurs in the next act, this time in relation to Manfred's request that the Witch help him die. He acknowledges,

> To do this thy power
> Must wake the dead, or lay me low with them.
> Do so—in any shape—in any hour—
> With any torture—so it be the last. (2. 2. 152–5)

Like the spirits, the Witch admits, 'That is not in my province', meaning that she cannot help him achieve death. She still wants him to 'swear obedience to ... [her] will', though (2. 2. 156, 157). True to form, Manfred retorts, 'I will not swear—Obey! and whom? the spirits/ Whose presence I command, and be the slave/ Of those who served me—Never! (2. 2. 157–9). Again, Manfred refuses to be the slave of any supernatural power with the claim that they, to the contrary, are his slaves. Lest the reader accuse Manfred of overreacting to apparently generous spirits who only want to help him (continue living, as the forces of biopower always do), Byron confirms elsewhere that the relationship they offer is, indeed, enslaving – a matter of control over the autonomous hero. Yet another group of supernatural powers, this time the Destinies, declare outright,

> Our hands contain the hearts of men,
> Our footsteps are their graves;
> We only give to take again
> The spirits of our slaves! (2. 3. 54–60)

Later in the same act, the Third Spirit acknowledges that humans like Manfred are, to the Spirits, slaves. It commands Manfred, who refuses to supplicate before the great Arimanes, 'Bow down and worship, slave! What, know'st thou not/ Thine and our Sovereign?—Tremble, and obey!' (2. 4. 32–3). When all the Spirits join in the order to Manfred – 'Prostrate thyself, and thy condemned clay,/ Child of the Earth! or dread the worst' (2. 4. 34–5) – then Byron makes his point about biopower still clearer. His body, the 'condemned clay' that makes us all 'Child[ren] of the Earth', is the source of Manfred's enslavement, and only by escaping it in death can he be free.

Byron's final reference to slavery in *Manfred* confirms suicide as a gesture of defiance against those who would control the independent agent, although the historical scene he evokes is one of sovereign power, not biopower. Canuel characterises the scene as Byron's 'criticism of the bloody culture and political executions of ancient Rome', conveyed through an 'anecdote about Nero (Byron calls him 'Rome's sixth emperor', Otho, rather than the fifth), who commits suicide rather than endure execution ... at the hands of the senators' (*Dissent* 54) who were 'once his slaves' (*Manfred* 3. 1. 91). Manfred compares himself to Nero, who escaped the punishment of sovereign power by choosing death for himself. As in other references to slavery in the drama, there is no protest against a system that involves enslavement, only Manfred's insistence that he will not be enslaved, preferring to wield power himself. Byron anchors the scene in the play's wider condemnation of the biopolitical, especially religious, control of the subject through the prohibition of suicide, as Manfred speaks the words to the Abbot to stop him from trying to dissuade Manfred from enacting his own death. He implicitly compares the Abbot to the soldier who attempted to save Nero by staunching 'The gushing throat with his officious robe' and whom Nero 'thrust ... back', rejecting the attempt to save him (3. 1. 93, 94). Analogously, Christianity's prevention of suicide amounts to an unwelcome meddling in the autonomous hero's existential choices, an enforcement of life upon the unwilling subject.

The Dramatic Form of *Manfred*, Pregnant Silence and Suicide as Autonomy

In a case of form echoing subject matter, Byron also seeks to free his play from the confines imposed upon all staged dramas in the period by choosing a relatively unconstrained literary form: the closet drama. One might assume that the genre of *Manfred* – variously called a 'closet drama', 'drama of the mind', or, as Byron would have it, 'mental theatre' or 'Dramatic Poem' – was forced on the poet by the strict governmental restrictions placed upon staged plays through the Licensing Act of 1737–1843. This assumption fails to recognise Byron's bold choice of the form as an act of dissent: he subverts traditional theatrical form along with his thematic protest against control over the individual. As Shou-Ren Wang summarises it in *The Theatre of the Mind* (1990), the legislation prevented the representation of political and religious subject matter on the stage, thereby limiting the content of acted plays to amorous and domestic topics. When the 'illegitimate' theatres that avoided censorship through melodrama began to outstrip the 'patent' or legitimate theatres (Drury Lane and Covent Garden) in revenue, they also began to offer melodramas, which were heavy in music and light on dialogue – not to mention serious content. Byron was intimately familiar with these restrictions as a member of the Drury Lane Committee of Management in 1815 (Wolfson, *Manfred* 659). He was also very critical of them and responded by writing mental dramas, which were not subject to such censorship, as they were not meant to be staged. Michael Simpson comments in *Closet Performances* (1998),

> Since the dramas of Byron and Shelley signed themselves as closet dramas and were not submitted to the London theaters, they automatically avoided the most direct form of censorship, which required, under the provisions of the Licensing Act, that all legitimate drama destined for performance be perused first by the Examiner of Plays. (233)

In typically Byronic style, then, and like Manfred himself, the poet refuses to be controlled by authorities who seek to limit his freedom, and he does so by writing in a genre, mental drama, that circumvented the censorship of topics such as suicide and incest.

In a letter upon *Manfred*'s completion, Byron himself suggests that he chose the form out of spite against the restrictions of the Licensing Act: '"*I have rendered it* quite impossible *for the stage – for which my intercourse with D[rury] L[ane] had given me the greatest contempt*"' (quoted in Lansdowne 249; italics in original), an attitude that may be linked to his apparent disdain for the play itself: 'I have really & truly no notion what it is good for' (*Letters*, ed. Lansdowne 268). The critical response to mental drama seems to have followed suit, often treating these works as underdeveloped or as generic failures. Alan Richardson points out that Romanticists 'have often had little to say about the plays as plays', and that they 'have tended to be dismissed as misguided attempts at "closet drama": plays meant to be read but never performed' (133). The genre has been overlooked as essential to and illustrative of *Manfred*'s broad message. I argue here that Byron makes silence a central element of his play through various means, the most significant of which is his choice of a form that presents the play's lines as unperformable.[7] Byron uses mental drama to emphasise the pervasive theme of silence in *Manfred* (since the play is designed not to be spoken aloud by actors), to protest the circumstance that helped to create it (control over the creative individual), and to represent suicide as a removal of the body from power's sphere of influence (since the form denies the need for actors' bodies).

Crucially, mental drama acquired the potential to relay notions about silencing and institutional control because the form gained popularity during the Romantic period in response to the censorship imposed by the Licensing Act. Simpson notes that 'More than any other form, dramatic productions ... have been subject to legislative control by the state' (44), and mental drama challenges that control. Rather than attempting to escape the confines of institutional regulation by refusing to write dramas altogether, which would only confirm the state's power to silence him, Byron actively protests such censorship by combining mental drama with a subject matter, suicide, that contests official restriction. Similarly, Byron does not attempt to escape the oppressive world of religion by ignoring it in *Manfred*; instead, he creates in Manfred 'an asocial, isolated, heroic selfhood of titanic proportions' (139), as Alan Richardson describes the protagonist, who revolts against religion throughout the text, refusing to be restricted in any way – even to the point of death.

The numerous religious tracts on suicide might seem to belie the claim that discussion of the topic was silenced or censored in the Romantic period; nevertheless, the content of what could be said about it was strictly controlled. In the 'Advertisement' to *The Dreadful Sin of Suicide*, Clayton records his confidence that his text will not result in suicidal contagion, even while he asks 'celestial influences' to ensure his success and calls upon the 'friendly candor' of the audience to receive the work in the helpful spirit in which he wrote it (n.p.); and Dawes Blackett begs her readers to 'pardon' her 'attempt to trace the evil [of suicide] to its source', arguing that she has been compelled to do so by the lack of public engagement with 'this horrid *Mania*' (iii; emphasis in original). As Watt expounds, only Donne, Montaigne, Voltaire, Montesquieu, Hume, and a few other writers (such as de Staël) dare to argue for the permissibility of the act ('Gender' 149). Even the reputedly anarchist Godwin is more condemnatory than tolerant in his appendix 'Of Suicide' in *Political Justice*, in which he asks,

'"Have I a right under any circumstances to destroy myself in order to escape from pain or disgrace?"', only to reply perfunctorily, 'Probably not' (86). Godwin closes the debate before it begins by predisposing his audience to arrive at a negative conclusion before he provides any argumentation about it. Arguing for the refusal of state power over the individual in *Political Justice*, Godwin yet denies that the subject has a right to remove his body from the purview of power's control in this appendix, demonstrating the powerful and pervasive reach of biopower over British subjects in the Romantic period – and highlighting Byron's political aim in this daring drama. Byron outdoes Godwin in radicalism, for *Manfred* frames the removal of the body from power's sphere of control as an act of heroic defiance. He champions the protagonist's insistence on choosing death over and against the religious entities' denial of his suicidal desires; the form of mental drama refuses the function of actors to physically communicate the play, in order to emphasise the removal of the body from biopolitical control; and he further underlines the silence formally intrinsic to mental drama by referring to silence throughout the play.

To highlight the experience of reading a mental drama, as opposed to viewing an actor's body and hearing his voice, Byron insists upon silence. He inserts multiple references to and demonstrations of silence, through, for instance, prominent gaps in the dialogue. The most notable instance of a linguistic lacuna occurs when the servant Manuel seems ready to announce Manfred's (probably brotherly) relation to his lover, Astarte, only to be interrupted by the entrance of the Abbot:

> Count Manfred was, as now, within his tower, –
> How occupied, we knew not, but with him
> The sole companion of his wanderings
> And watchings – her, whom of all earthly things
> That lived, the only thing he seem'd to love, –
> As he, indeed, by blood was bound to do,
> The lady Astarte, his —
> Hush! Who comes here? (3. 3. 41–8)

Upon the Abbot's arrival, Manuel breaks off, but not before he has informed the audience that Manfred was 'bound' 'by blood' to love Astarte. Byron's refusal to complete the declaration – since the lines could be interpreted as a confession of his own relationship with his half-sister Augusta Leigh – teases the audience and draws attention to itself as a pointed moment of silence. The scene's implication of incest, moreover, confirms the theme's importance in a drama about suicide as rebellion: both undermine the system of biopower.

A similar instance of emphatic silence occurs in the final scene, in which the Abbot is forced to swallow the word 'God', thanks to a Spirit's interruption. When the Spirits come to collect Manfred in his final hour, he defies them, as does the Abbot, who claims that his Christian 'piety' is enough to quell their advance:

ABBOT. What art thou, unknown being? answer! – speak!
SPIRIT. The genius of this mortal. – Come! 'tis time.
MAN[fred]. I am prepared for all things, but deny
The power which summons me. Who sent thee here?
SPIRIT. Thou'lt know anon – Come! come!
MAN. I have commanded
Things of an essence greater far than thine,
And striven with thy masters. Get thee hence!
SPIRIT. Mortal! thine hour is come – Away! I say.
MAN. I knew, and know my hour is come, but not
To render up my soul to such as thee:
Away! I'll die as I have lived – alone.
SPIRIT. Then I must summon up my brethren. – Rise!
[Other Spirits rise up
ABBOT. Avaunt! ye evil ones! – Avaunt! I say, –
Ye have no power where piety hath power,
And I do charge ye in the name —
SPIRIT. Old man!
. . . .
Waste not thy holy words on idle uses. (3. 4. 80–95; 97)

As if it weren't enough that the Abbot cannot speak the name of 'God' at line 94, his authority is also undermined when the Spirit calls him a generic 'Old man' (as does Manfred several times in the play) and announces that his supposedly efficacious sacred words are useless. Similarly, the Spirit refuses to answer Manfred's questions about its mission and master (3. 4. 84), and its response to the Abbot's question about its identity (3. 4. 80) is so mysterious (it claims to be Manfred's own 'genius' (3. 4. 81)) that it barely functions as informative at all. (Indeed, if it is Manfred's own spirit, one wonders, how can Manfred defy it, an aspect of himself?) The reader, like the Abbot, is left with more questions through these palpable silences. This effect is Byron's point in this play about the power of denial, lacunae and refusal.

Along these lines, the Phantom of Astarte steadfastly disobeys both Manfred's and Nemesis's commands for her to speak for almost fifty lines (2. 4. 104–48). Initially, Manfred quits before he starts: 'I cannot speak to her – but bid her speak' (2. 4. 104), he begs his supernatural companions. But then, neither Nemesis nor the awe-inspiring Arimanes can force the spirit of Astarte to communicate:

NEMESIS.
By the power which hath broken
The grave which enthrall'd thee,
Speak to him who hath spoken,
Or those who have call'd thee!
MAN. She is silent.
And in that silence I am more than answered.
NEM. My power extends no further. Prince of air!
It rests with thee alone – command her voice,
ARI[manes]. Spirit – obey this sceptre!
NEM. Silent still! (2. 4. 106–15)

Manfred tries his luck with the recalcitrant ghost ('Astarte! My beloved! speak to me' (2. 4. 118)), but after repeated pleas for her to utter an iota of information about herself, all she will express is his own name and that he will likely die on the morrow (2. 4. 149–52). On a smaller scale, mentions of silence recur throughout the work: Manfred makes statements such as, 'men are – what they name not to themselves' (1. 2. 46), and, 'Why should I repeat it? 'twere in vain' (2. 2. 47). Here, then, we read a suicide of meaning: a refusal to communicate, as the mental drama refuses to do in the traditional way, echoing the play's major theme.

Byron also uses silence to gesture towards taboo topics in *Manfred*. Loren Glass calls one of these topics 'the unnameable [or, at least, unnamed] incestuous sin of which Manfred is guilty' (212). The hints about incest may be viewed as secondary to and in the service of the main thrust of the plot, which revolves around Manfred's relentless wish to die, a topic even more daring than incest. Lansdowne confirms that '*incest only contravened ecclesiastical law in Britain, and was punishable by six months' imprisonment*' (125; italics in original), while suicide was a felony in law and an unpardonable mortal sin, as I detail in the Introduction to this study. However, viewed as a protest against biopower's management of the subject's body, the themes complement each other, for they both powerfully destabilise biopower's aim to increase and maintain life. This is true in obvious ways with respect to suicide, and, given that incest carries the threat of sickly progeny, it also applies to incest. The prohibition against it is a prime example of power's control over the subject's body, especially its reproductive capacities. Byron links these topics: Manfred desires death because of the disastrous outcome of what seems to have been his incestuous love for Astarte. He implies this point in his conversation with the Chamois Hunter:

MAN. Away, away! there's blood upon the brim!
Will it then never – never sink in the earth?

C. HUN. What dost thou mean? thy senses wander from thee.
MAN. I say 'tis blood – my blood! the pure warm stream
Which ran in the veins of my fathers, and in ours
When we were in our youth, and had one heart,
And loved each other as we should not love,
And this was shed: but still it rises up,
Colouring the clouds, that shut me out from heaven. (2. 1. 21–9)

Manfred's near insanity suggests that he is wracked with guilt over Astarte's death – she who, as a sister, shared familial blood with him (2. 1. 24–5). In the subsequent act, Manfred hints that they were siblings by noting their physical likeness, and implies that Astarte's death was a suicide:

MAN. She was like me in lineaments – her eyes,
Her hair, her features, all, to the very tone
Even of her voice, they said were like to mine;
But soften'd all, and temper'd into beauty;
She had the same lone thoughts and wanderings,
The quest of hidden knowledge, and a mind
To comprehend the universe: nor these
Alone, but with them gentler powers than mine,
Pity, and smiles, and tears – which I had not;
And tenderness – but that I had for her;
Humility – and that I never had.
Her faults were mine – her virtues were her own –
I loved her, and destroy'd her!
WITCH. With thy hand?
MAN. Not with my hand, but heart – which broke her heart –
It gazed on mine, and withered. I have shed
Blood, but not hers – and yet her blood was shed –
I saw – and could not staunch it. (2. 2. 106–21)

Intriguingly, in contrast to his earlier speech, in which he confesses that he and Astarte 'loved *each other* as we should not love' (2. 1. 27; my emphasis) – Manfred implies here that Astarte did not return his romantic desire; rather, she was so shocked by it that she could not continue to live after becoming aware of it (like Shelley's Mathilda after she learns of her father's passion for her) (2. 2. 18–19). What is unambiguous is that Astarte's blood was spilled, and not by Manfred, and that this fatal bloodshed followed her insight into Manfred's heart, which suggests that she killed herself as a result of discovering his incestuous passion. Franklin agrees that Astarte's death was a suicide: she 'apparently *has* committed suicide over their incestuous love' (215; emphasis in original). As a result, she is, in death, 'One without a tomb' (2. 4. 85), presumably because, as a suicide, she was buried without a Christian ceremony or in sacred ground. Both Manfred's and Astarte's suicidal desires result from incestuous love, but, significantly, these motivating circumstances are shrouded in silence, occurring offstage (even if that is an imaginative stage in this mental drama) and before the reader meets Manfred. Our only experience of Astarte consists in dialogue about her in a drama that centres on what Manfred calls his 'fierce thirst of death' (2. 1. 48), rendering the incest theme secondary to that of suicide.

Manfred boldly declares his death wish several times throughout the play. Sometimes he stops himself from enacting what he claims to desire most: again in the Jungfrau scene, Manfred wonders, 'wherefore do I pause?/ I feel the impulse [to die] – yet I do not plunge' (1. 2. 19–20). More often, others prevent him from dying: when Manfred finally does attempt to fling himself off the mountain, the Chamois Hunter detains him 'with a sudden grasp' (1. 2. stage directions between lines 109 and 110), commanding, 'Hold, madman! – though aweary of thy life,/ Stain not our pure vales with thy guilty blood' (1. 2. 110–11). Later, the Abbot attempts to talk Manfred out of choosing death, even though the latter has clearly stated his disbelief in the Abbot's holy authority (3. 1. 66). Regardless, the Abbot believes that his religious responsibilities prevent him from abandoning his attempts to stop Manfred from taking the final leap into oblivion:

> ABBOT. ... he will perish,
> And yet he must not; I will try once more,
> For such are worth redemption; and my duty
> Is to dare all things for a righteous end. (3. 1. 167–70)

Although Byron does not present the Abbot himself as tyrannical, he nevertheless declares his duty to an oppressive institution, Christianity, which judges only continued life as blameless.

For Manfred, then, suicide is a means of enacting autonomy. From the opening scene with the great Spirits, Manfred announces his refusal to yield to any other power, even that of Arimanes (1. 1. 152–7). Manfred's autonomy is his prevailing characteristic, and it is recognised at many points in the play – even by the Abbot, who tells him,

> ... I know that with mankind,
> Thy fellows in creation, thou dost rarely
> Exchange thy thoughts, and that thy solitude
> Is as an anchorite's, were it but holy. (3. 1. 39–42)

The Abbot notes Manfred's social isolation, as well as his estrangement from any community of faith, which should imply his exemption from religious strictures such as those against suicide. However, the knowledge that Manfred does not subscribe to Christian precepts does not stop the Abbot from attempting to prevent him from marching firmly towards death in the final scene: he tells him, 'I simply tell thee peril is at hand,/ And would preserve thee' (3. 4. 59–60). From the Abbot's perspective, no one can opt out of his spiritual care – his pastoral authority.

The entire plot of *Manfred* traces the protagonist's wish to die and the various means – especially religious – employed to prevent him from satisfying this wish. In the opening scene, Manfred is asked by a powerful Spirit what he requests from the great powers of the universe, whom he has gathered to serve him. He eventually names his desire for 'Oblivion, self-oblivion' (1. 1. 145), but at first he declines to answer: 'I cannot utter it' (138). Thus, Byron firmly links the topic of suicide with silence in the crucial first moments of the play. (The strangeness of the exchange highlights it, too: it is a little like calling a waiter to your table, then coyly refusing to tell him what you would like to order.) Although Manfred initially expresses uncertainty as to whether death will give him the 'oblivion' that he so desires ('Will death bestow it on me?' (1. 1. 148)), he is soon upon the Jungfrau, attempting to hurl himself off: 'Ye toppling crags of ice!/ Ye avalanches, whom a breath draws down/ In mountainous o'erwhelming, come and crush me!' (1. 2. 74–6). Despite Manfred's many requests for death, it eludes him until the last moments of the play, when he 'expires', as the stage directions inform us, upon his realisation that death is not hard to achieve, after all (3. 4. 151).

Manfred's final moments are highly equivocal, so much so that some commentators doubt that they constitute a suicide. Canuel comments:

> His death appears to be a refusal to concede to the violent imposition of authority, while reinforcing his own internal sense of 'requital' and 'desert' (3. 4. 130, 136). At the same time, though, Manfred's death is not unambiguously the suicide that the abbot supposes it to be when he urges him to 'die not thus' (3. 4. 145). Manfred interprets his death, even while he is his own destroyer, only as a form of subjection, perhaps to the law of the sceptered sovereigns who rule his spirit from their urns. It is not that he kills himself but that 'the hand of death is on me' (3. 4. 141). (*Dissent* 54)

Franklin concurs: although Byron puts the question of suicide 'right at the centre of his drama', he denies his character this finale and instead posits 'moral self-destruction ... rather than physical suicide' (214, 216). Byron certainly frames this all-important scene as ambiguously suicidal, just as Shelley frames Mathilda's end and Wollstonecraft represents her characters Mary and Maria as only wishing for death, rather than conclusively accomplishing it. In *Manfred* (and, perhaps, in *Mathilda*), ambiguously represented suicide underscores the main theme of subverting authority. The denial of suicide to a protagonist whose principal motivation is to die thwarts the text's neat closure, making it multiply interpretable and undermining the reader's expectation of a concrete message. This refusal mirrors the protagonist's refusal to live as a productive, well-managed subject of biopower. What Roland Barthes has called a 'readerly' text, featuring a neatly teleological resolution of the protagonist's struggle, casts the reader as a disciplined subject of the narrative regime – and the text itself as the formal equivalent of the disciplined subject of biopower. When Byron withholds the expected terminus of Manfred's heroically accomplished suicide, he performs a resistance to the traditional demands of plot.

Byron also emphasises his pervasive theme of silence in this ending. Instead of resolving the motivation – Manfred's wish for death – that drives the main action of the play, he leaves the reader with yet another absence. Following Blanchot, as summarised by translator Ann Smock, one might say that Byron captures the truth of death most effectively through this obliqueness:

> The suicide manqué, indeed, even the baseness apparent in his inability to face death honestly – head-on – expresses more truly, perhaps, than anything else the essence of death, which is always to elude an authentic confrontation. It never presents itself for a duel, but represents itself; it comes disguising its coming. In fact, its [death's] essence is not to come at all – ever. (8)

We cannot grasp or express our own death because it falls necessarily beyond our realm of experience; we can observe death in others and imagine its application to ourselves, but our own death can never be a reality to us. Blanchot remarks, 'One cannot "plan" to kill oneself. This apparent project sets out after something never attained, toward a goal impossible to aim for. I cannot conceive of the end as an end in itself' (*Space* 103). By refusing to represent Manfred's death wish as accomplished, Byron conveys the subjective experience of his character to the reader: we remain virtually as ignorant about his end as he is. Considered in the light of Blanchot's commentary on death and suicide, Manfred's final words, ''tis not so difficult to die' (3. 4. 151), also come into clearer focus as conveying the cessation of his will and acceptance of negation, obviating what Blanchot describes as the irony of suicide:

> He who kills himself says, 'I withdraw from the world, I will act no longer.' And yet this same person wants to make death an act; he wants to act supremely and absolutely. This illogical optimism which shines through voluntary death – this confidence that one will always be able to triumph in the end by disposing sovereignly of nothingness, by being the creator of one's

> own nothingness and by remaining able, in the very midst of the fall, to lift oneself to one's full height – this certitude affirms in the act of suicide the very thing suicide claims to deny. (*Space* 102–3)

Manfred succumbs to death's advent, rather than seizing it, and thus shows his readiness for death.

Conclusion: Byron's Romantic Independence

While Byron presents a powerful meditation on the autonomous individual's right to choose death in *Manfred*, we should not assume that the poet was therefore a champion of suicide and always sensitive to the suicidal in real life. His responses to the suicides of the politicians Romilly and Castlereagh demonstrate this point well. For reasons peripheral to his philosophical approach to suicide, Byron mocked their deaths. Besides calling Castlereagh the 'Werther of politics', as I discuss in Chapter 1, Byron's more shocking response to the death appears in an epitaph from around 1820, where he implicitly invites readers to desecrate Castlereagh's very grave by urinating on it:

> Posterity will ne'er survey
> A nobler grave than this;
> Here lie the bones of Castlereagh:
> Stop, traveller, [and] ... (1–4)

Byron followed up this poetical mockery of Castlereagh's death with a series of epigrams from 1822, such as the following:

> OH, Castlereagh! Thou art a patriot now;
> Cato died for his country, so didst thou:
> He perish'd rather than see Rome enslaved,
> Thou cutt'st thy throat that Britain may be saved!

He also wrote this one:

> So Castlereagh has cut his throat! – The worst
> Of this is, – that his own was not the first.

Byron's final epigrammatic dig at the dead politician follows:

> So He has cut his throat at last! – He! Who?
> The man who cut his country's long ago. ('Epigrams' 238)

It is as though Byron could not get enough enjoyment out of Castlereagh's suicide. Because Castlereagh was widely hated amongst the liberal literati of the period for his oppressive views and policies, it is not surprising that Byron jeers at the man. Still, these wince-inducing lines, in which Byron seems to relish repeating that Castlereagh cut his throat, reveal the depth of his hatred – that he was willing to kick Castlereagh when he was down for good – as well as that Byron's sympathy for suicides was far from seamless.

What is more surprising is Byron's mockery of Romilly's suicide, which was widely considered to be a 'national disaster' (Andrew 178), as I also discuss in Chapter 1. Byron was having none of it, even though Romilly was popular for many of the reasons that should have won him great favour with the poet; indeed, the two championed many of the same humane causes. In 1812, 'Romilly in the House of Commons spoke against capital punishment for frame-breakers ten days before Byron did so in the Lords' (Cameron 251). Nevertheless, Byron expresses his outrage over the charitable response to Romilly's suicide in a very public forum: his bestselling long poem, *Don Juan*. In Canto I, Byron describes Don Juan's mother, Donna Inez, as

> An all-in-all sufficient self-director,
> Like the lamented late Sir Samuel Romilly,
> The Law's expounder, and the State's corrector,
> Whose suicide was almost an anomaly –
> One sad example more, that 'All is vanity,' –
> (The jury brought their verdict in 'Insanity.') (115–20)

In this lighthearted treatment of Romilly's suicide, Byron suggests that his criticism is satirical – a cutting comment on the foibles of society and not just Romilly – by drawing attention to the jury's charitable finding of 'insanity' or non-criminal suicide for the politician's death. Byron's harsh response to the suicide was certainly also personal: the lawyer had agreed to represent Byron in his divorce and then switched to the side of Lady Byron (Wolfson 736n), the prototype for Donna Inez.

Even more severe is Byron's commentary on the politician in a letter to Lady Byron from 18 November 1818:

> Sir Samuel Romilly has cut his throat for the loss of his wife. It is now nearly three years since he became in the face of his compact (by a retainer – previous and I believe general) the advocate of the measures and the Approver of the proceedings which deprived me of mine ... This Man little thought when he was lacerating my heart according to law – while he was poisoning my life at it's [*sic*] sources – aiding and abetting in the blighting – branding – and Exile that was to be the result of his Counsels in their *indirect effects* – that in less than thirty six Moons – ... in the fullness of his professional Career – in the Greenness of a healthy old age [of 61] – in the radiance of Fame – and the Complacency of self-earned Riches – that a domestic Affliction would lay

> him in the Earth – with the meanest of Malefactors – in a Cross road with the Stake in his body – if the Verdict of Insanity did not redeem his ashes from the sentence of the Laws he had lived by interpreting or misinterpreting, and died in violating — The Man had eight Children – lately deprived of their Mother – could he not live? — Perhaps previous to his Annihilation he felt a portion of what he contributed his legal mite to make me feel, – but I have lived – lived to see him a Sexagenary Suicide. — It was not in vain that I invoked Nemesis in the Midnight of Rome from the awfullest of her Ruins. (*Flesh* 80–1; emphasis in original)

Evidently, Byron hated Romilly not for political reasons but because he sided with Lady Byron in their ugly separation (Cameron 249). Writing from exile in Venice, Byron relishes the news of Romilly's suicide and enjoys rubbing it in the face of the one whom Romilly championed in their separation settlement. Lest we believe that Byron approached the topic of suicide on political or philosophical grounds alone, we must put down *Manfred* and take up his other writings for a more complete view of the matter.

These personal statements about the suicides of others do not undermine Byron's message about the significance of suicide in *Manfred*. By engaging with the censored topic in a provocative way – through a hero with a death wish whom the audience may admire – Byron refuses the tyrannical control over what can be expressed about it, a move that parallels his objection to the Licensing Act. Doing so in a drama that bespeaks censorship in its very form, mental drama, and through multiple textual references to silence, further elucidates Byron's topic. Finally, by presenting a protagonist who, as Burwick puts it, 'challenges the authority of the clerisy to arbitrate or mediate over questions of individual conscience' (53), Byron challenges any form of restriction over the individual's independence. Taken all together, *Manfred* thoroughly defies the notion, so familiar in Romantic-era society, that religion is the ultimate authority on the question of one's right to choose death, instead representing suicide as a matter of personal autonomy.

Although Byron's statements about both suicide and religion were, by turns, contradictory, hectoring, cruel and humorous, he treats the matter with *gravitas* in *Manfred*. Nor does Byron's wide variety of approaches to the topic deny him a place as one of the great commentators on suicide. Treating Byron as the poster boy for Romantic suicidality, Alvarez writes in *The Savage God*, 'the Romantic stance ... was suicidal. Byron, the most selfconsciously [*sic*] doomed and dramatic of them all, remarked that "no man ever took a razor into his hand who did not at the same time think how easily he might sever the silver cord of life"'

(230). Alvarez sees Byron as the suicidal Romantic figure par excellence and suicidality as characterising the movement. Insofar as Romanticism is certainly defiant when it comes to traditional Christianity, one may safely argue that the literature was largely ranged against the punitive and controlling religious attitude to suicide of the time.

Notes

1. Viewed thus, it becomes clear why Christianity traditionally condemns homosexuality, abortion and suicide since all these practices threaten to undermine the biopolitical regime by removing (sometimes potential) assets to power: human bodies.
2. The notion that the suicide is a rebel, or traitor, in God's army may also reflect the biblical story, in the Book of Matthew, of Judas Iscariot, one of the twelve apostles: he betrayed Jesus to the Romans, leading to Jesus's crucifixion, and then 'hanged himself' (St Matthew 27: 3–5).
3. McGuire also adds that Adams was one of the first and most voluble opponents of Donne's text after it was 'published for a second time in 1700' (*Dying* 75), an indication that Adams's inspiration for penning his essay about how '*Unlawful* ... [suicide is] *According to Natural Principles*', to borrow the terms of Adams's title was, oddly, a text by an English clergyman.
4. Hume's 'Of Suicide' was suppressed and, according to Richard Popkin, Hume 'succeeded in retrieving almost all of the few copies distributed before the essays were to have been made generally available in 1755. Nonetheless, he worried about pirated editions coming out. On his deathbed he tried to persuade his publisher to offer an edition, which the publisher refused to do. The two essays finally appeared in 1777, the year after Hume's death' (xvii). For a detailed description of the complicated publication history of Hume's essay on suicide, see E. C. Mossner's 'Hume's Four Dissertations: An Essay in Biography and Bibliography' (1950).
5. A version of the following argument appears in full in my article 'Political Suicide: Castlereagh, Rebellion, and Self-Directed Violence'.
6. Polidori killed himself over gambling debts in 1821, after Byron had saved him from committing suicide in 1816 (D. L. Macdonald 130). Byron seems not to have been surprised that Polidori finally went through with the act: upon learning about Polidori's suicide, he responded,

   > Poor Polidori is gone! When he was my physician, he was always talking of Prussic acid, oil of amber, blowing into veins, suffocating by charcoal, and compounding poisons; ... he has prescribed a dose for himself that would have killed fifty Mithridates' [*sic* (apostrophe)], – a dose whose effect, Murray says, was so instantaneous that he went off without a spasm or struggle. (Medwin 119)

   Byron adds, 'It seems that disappointment [over literary failure] was the cause of this rash act' (Medwin 119), rather than insolvency. As a side note, many period quotations of this passage substitute 'Mithridates' with 'Milteades', an error that misses the point of Byron's quip, for Mithridates, the ancient king of Pontus, was well known to have taken regular sub-fatal doses of poisons to build a resistance to them, a practice now called 'Mithridatism'.

7. *Manfred* would 'enjoy theatrical success' when it was eventually performed in the nineteenth century (Wolfson 659), even though Byron created his 'Dramatic Poem' with the express intention of rendering it unperformable (Lansdowne 268).

Conclusion: The Afterlife of Romantic Subversive Suicide

Throughout this study, I have demonstrated that the society-wide establishment of biopower, which coincided with the Romantic period, was expressed in part through an explosion of the number of texts concerned with suicide – both those that inveighed against it and those that advocated its permissibility on the grounds of human rights and existential freedom. As Foucault remarks in *The History of Sexuality*, a fresh approach to suicide was concurrent with the establishment of the biopolitical regime that replaced the episteme of sovereign power, which involved a shift from the view of suicide as a crime, religious and legal, to a matter of sociological concern in texts that sought to understand and mitigate the problem (*Sexuality* 138). The establishment of biopower was not marked by an increase in punishments for suicide, a response more characteristic of sovereign power. Biopower was established ideologically, through written texts; its 'main role was to ensure, sustain, and multiply life, to put this life in order' (*Sexuality* 138) through examination and classification, the aim of newly established scientific disciplines such as early forms of psychology and sociology. Although the biopolitical regimes opposing suicide discussed in this study – slavery, patriarchy and religion – were not new to the period, biopower worked through these existing structures and intensified their efficacy in controlling bodies. Its workings also came into greater cultural focus, resulting in expressions of opposition to it. Period texts that develop the theme of subversive suicide are exemplary of this protest.

The forms of revolutionary suicide I describe in this study are subversive of enforced life, one of the most salient expressions of biopower since it always seeks to augment itself through the maintenance of its subjects' lives. In this way, I demonstrate that a familiar element in traditional ideas of what Romanticism is – its rebellious character – is bound up with the birth of biopower where suicide is concerned. However, some influential philosophers have questioned whether suicide can ever be a form of rebellion. Throughout *The Myth of Sisyphus*, Camus denies that the existential rebel can choose suicide: 'It may be thought that suicide follows revolt – but wrongly. For it does not represent the logical outcome of revolt. It is just the contrary by the consent it presupposes. Suicide ... is acceptance at its extreme. Everything is over and man returns to his essential history' (54). Camus's reasoning is unsound, as James Wood points out: he 'so widens the terms of what constitutes revolt that his leap may involve nothing more than simply remaining alive, simply refraining from killing oneself', such that,

> in the end, it [Camus's argument] is an assertion, a determination, a faith. Camus proves nothing. Perhaps Camus is right that to kill oneself would be to allow death to have dominion, and that to live rebelliously is both to be aware of and to reject death ... The difficulty of Camus's proposal for rebellion is that, at times, he seems merely to be describing life itself, which is tautological. (xvi–xvii)

Despite these limitations in Camus's argument, it seems logical to ask whether suicide can ever be revolutionary. How can suicide ever be a form of 'triumph', as Gray's Bard calls it (142), if the victor loses his life and no one therefore remains to embody the newfound freedom?

Subversive Suicide as Victory? Philosophical Views

Romantic rebellious suicide begs the question: How can choosing death establish the successful revolt of the suicide if the victorious subject is no longer? Kant summarises the quandary well in 'Of Duties to the Body, in Regard to Life' in his *Lectures on Ethics*. He explains that existential freedom depends on our having a body and, because we can have no disembodied life, the body is, in effect, our life – rendering nonsensical the concept of suicide as a bid for liberty:

> if we could slip out of one body and enter another, like a country, then we could dispose over the body, it would then be subject to our free choice, albeit that in that case we would not be disposing over our life, but only over our state, over the movable goods, the chattels, that pertained to life. But now the body is the total condition of life, so that we have no other concept of our existence save that mediated by our body, and since the use of our freedom is possible only through the body, we see that the body constitutes a part of our self. So far, then, as *anyone destroys his body, and thereby takes his own life, he has employed his choice to destroy the power of choosing itself*; *but in that case, free choice is in conflict with itself*. If freedom is the condition of life, it cannot be employed to abolish life, since then it destroys and abolishes itself; for the agent is using his life to put an end to it. Life is supposedly being

> used to bring about lifelessness, but that is a self-contradiction. So we already see in advance that man cannot dispose over himself and his life, though he certainly can over his circumstances. (144; my emphasis)

Here is a reasonable objection to suicide as a logical conundrum that carries far more weight than Kant's argument in the subsequent lecture, 'Of Suicide', in which he objects to suicide as 'contrary to the supreme self-regarding duty' by which 'all other duties ... [are] thereby abolished' (145). After all, one can simply disregard Kant's claim to be an authority on what such supposed 'supreme' duties are – or deny any exist at all – and thereby absolve oneself of responsibility to fulfil them, just as one can claim atheism to shirk the duty of living because God apparently wishes us to do so, the most common argument against suicide in the Romantic period. Contemporary philosopher Michael Cholbi agrees with this sceptical assessment of Kant's condemnation of suicide, two features of which are based on heteronomous (externally based) principles – that is, what duties we owe to God, and what is required of us as creatures of nature and subject to the rules thereof. Cholbi comments:

> Kant held that we rational agents are subject to a categorical duty of self-preservation, not to take our own lives willfully. Not to commit suicide, according to Kant, is 'the first, though not the principal, duty of a human being to himself as an animal being.'
>
> Regrettably, Kant's characteristic rigor and systematicity are absent in his discussions of suicide. (159)

By contrast, in the long passage quoted above, Kant argues essentially that the subject cannot establish his claim to existential liberty through suicide because that subject ceases to exist upon the enactment of this claim. Here is an autonomous, rather than heteronomous, argument that is far more convincing and pertinent to the present discussion, for it points to the logical absurdity of committing suicide to establish one's existential freedom. How can freedom characterise what no longer is? The short answer to the question of whether suicide can ever be subversive is that the rebel suicide's freedom lies in the act of suicide, but not necessarily the suicide's being. Subversive suicides refuse to submit to tyranny; they disallow any another person or any system to have control over their existence, including the way in which they end. Subversive suicide is established in the moment of the decision to die and the memory amongst the living of suicidal rebellion, especially as conveyed in texts.

Other philosophers claim that suicide is intricately tied to what makes us subjects, even though the subject ceases to exist beyond the final act. Mbembe cites Friedrich Hegel in his assertion that the kind of wrangling with the limits of existence that characterises suicide – here framed as the acceptance of death – is central to human subjecthood:

> the human being truly *becomes a subject* – that is, separated from the animal – in the struggle and the work through which he or she confronts death (understood as the violence of negativity [in Hegel's terms]) ... To uphold the work of death is precisely how Hegel defines the life of the Spirit. The life of the Spirit, he says, is not that life which is frightened of death, and spares itself destruction, but that life which assumes death and lives with it. (14; emphasis in original)

According to Hegel via Mbembe, the human 'Spirit' becomes itself by approaching the limit of life – by making peace with death and accepting it. And what greater acceptance of death can there be but through the act of suicide? In this light, suicide begets human subjectivity.

Other writers have emphasised suicide as the ultimate expression of human freedom. In *The Space of Literature* (1955), Blanchot comments on Fyodor Dostoevsky's character Kirilov in *The Possessed*: 'Why suicide? If he dies freely, if he experiences and proves to himself his liberty in death and the liberty of his death, he will have attained the absolute. He will be that absolute. He will be absolutely man, and there will be no absolute outside of him.' Blanchot adds: 'God is gambling his own existence in this freely chosen death which a resolute man takes upon himself. If someone becomes his own master even in death, master of himself through death, he will be master also of that omnipotence which makes itself felt by us through death' (97). Here is the motivation behind subversive suicide in an abstract form, one in which the suicide does not battle a particular master – such as the slave-owner, patriarch or God – but the very idea that he lacks independence and thus a well-defined self if he cannot freely choose death. However, Blanchot later adds that the 'optimism' that is the assertion of self through suicide is 'illogical' and therefore self-defeating (*Space* 102–3). According to Blanchot, the suicide denies that she has hope, that she has the strength to go on living: but the very act of killing oneself is itself an expression of strength and optimism. It seeks a difficult goal that, if obtained, ironically demonstrates the suicide's ability to engage with life:

> The weakness of suicide lies in the fact that whoever commits it is still too strong. He is demonstrating a strength suitable only for a citizen of the world. Whoever kills himself could, then, go on living: whoever kills himself is linked to hope, the hope of finishing it all, and hope reveals his desire to begin, to find the beginning again in the end. (*Space* 103)

I counter that Blanchot misses the point of suicide as an assertion of personal power and self-affirmation, for he seems to consider only those who choose death out of fragility, perhaps from melancholy. The Romantic subversive suicide, by contrast, powerfully asserts his will in his final act, rather than succumbing to impotence.

Blanchot attempts a different attack on suicide as an expression of self-formation, too. Responding to Heidegger's discussion of death in *Being and Time* (1927), Blanchot states that suicide:

> is what I cannot grasp, what is not linked to *me* by any relation of any sort. It is that which never comes and toward which I do not direct myself.
>
> ... To kill oneself is to mistake one death for the other; it is a sort of bizarre play on words. I go to meet the death which is in the world, at my disposal, and I think that thereby I can reach the other death, over which I have no power – which has none over me either, for it has nothing to do with me, and if I know nothing of it, it knows no more of me; it is the empty intimacy of this ignorance. That is why suicide remains essentially a bet, something hazardous: not because I leave myself a chance to survive, as sometimes happens, but because suicide is a leap. (*Space* 103–4; emphasis in original)

Blanchot represents suicide as an unknown, something beyond human reason, much as Søren Kierkegaard represents the 'leap of faith' as the surrender of our human logic to something beyond human conception, God (e.g. 30). Put otherwise, Blanchot asks, how can we posit suicide as the authentic expression of selfhood if its language, death, is foreign to us? Again, though, a logical problem plagues this approach to suicide. Martin Crowley points out that, in elaborating the argument that death is necessarily unreal to all living persons, Blanchot nevertheless implies that he somehow does understand the reality of death:

> Blanchot continues to state categorically that death 'is' this or that, grasping death firmly and apparently unproblematically within the force of his own argument in its unproblematized, binary role as The Ungraspable, The Impossible, The Unknowable. There is a separation, then, between the substance of Blanchot's argument ... and his unperturbed, assertive, even authoritarian rhetorical position. (202)

Paradoxically, Blanchot sets himself up as an authority on the unknowable.

All the same, Blanchot's enlistment of Heidegger's commentary on suicide is useful and necessary. In *Being and Time*, Heidegger examines the question of freedom and suicide: 'With death, Dasein [being there or presence] stands before itself in its *ownmost* potentiality-of-being ... Thus *death* reveals itself as one's *ownmost, nonrelational, and insuperable ... possibility*. As such, it is *an eminent* imminence.' Heidegger later adds, 'One's own potentiality-of-being becomes authentic and transparent in the understanding being-toward-death as one's *ownmost* possibility' (241, 293; emphasis in original). Here is a consideration of death as the moment of authenticity, as the articulation of self or pure autonomy – a key Romantic interest. Michael Wheeler summarises Heidegger's thought:

> My death is mine in a radical sense; it is the moment at which all my relations to others disappear. Heidegger captures this non-relationality by using the term 'ownmost' [,] ... the idea of death 'as that possibility which is one's ownmost' ... When I take on board the possibility of my own not-Being, my own being-able-to-Be is brought into proper view. Hence my awareness of my own death as an omnipresent possibility discloses the authentic self (a self that is mine) ... and my awareness of that possibility illuminates me, *qua* Dasein, in my totality. (n.p.)

What Heidegger asserts about death has clear implications for suicide as a method of self-formation, for it involves actively embracing what is framed above as a mere conceptualisation. Yet, the philosopher suggests that the triumphant expression and dramatisation of self through suicide is logically impossible. Crowley paraphrases Heidegger's query about the possibility of establishing a true relation to death:

> [I]s death something which I can grasp as the limit and guarantee of my existential authenticity, in relation to which I can come to be defined as an ontological and existential subject – or is it the very instance of that which exceeds this relation of anticipation, which happens to me without my being able to grasp it, or even to establish any sort of relation whatsoever? (191)[1]

In other words, one cannot set out to achieve one's own death because one cannot conceive of what is always beyond one's realm of experience, the point that Blanchot adopts for his own approach to suicide. As living beings, we cannot engage with our own deaths as experienced realities, and if we are dead, then we cannot conceive of anything. Thus, the successful suicide can effectuate his own death, although it is never the death for which he aimed.

In engaging thus with Heidegger's thought, Blanchot explores the utility of suicide as self-formation, even though neither philosopher is convinced that choosing death can achieve this goal. John Gregg notes about Blanchot's theorisation of suicide:

> Perhaps he who takes his own life has the aptitude to die content – provided that one considers self-destruction as *supreme self-affirmation*. Blanchot's analysis of suicide revolves around the question of whether complete consciousness of death can be achieved ... Their [i.e. suicides'] attempt to domesticate death by taking their own life constitutes an act of power ... The perpetrator of suicide sets out with great determination to conquer and

> possess death, to make it his or her own, but, suggests Blanchot, it is just the opposite that occurs. (35–6; my emphasis)

Ironically, the would-be master of death, the suicide, becomes mastered by it because, Blanchot argues, he thereby surrenders to an unknown. In Blanchot's words, the suicide announces, '"I will kill myself to affirm my insubordination, my new and terrifying liberty"' (*Space* 97), but he ultimately succumbs to a state he could never embrace because it was always beyond his comprehension.

What does Blanchot's Heideggerian wrangling over the significance of suicide mean for the concept of subversive suicide as outlined in this book? Is it thereby negated or made nonsensical? First, I would note that the very examination of this question in some of the key existentialist texts of the modern period demonstrates the lasting cultural influence of the Romantic-era suicide debate. The existentialist examination of the significance of choosing death is, however, somewhat directionless, without a target for the most part, rendering it essentially different from Romantic subversive suicide, which opposes the forces of biopower. Blanchot (and Heidegger) consider death not as a means of dividing oneself from a would-be master, as Romantic rebellious suicide is, but in relation to the individual's existence alone. By contrast, Romantic rebellious suicides assert their self-identities as autonomous and highly individualised specifically in the face of a tyrant or representatives of an institution – the agents of biopower – who presume to control subjects' bodies. In choosing death, suicides hold themselves separate from the would-be master to announce their autonomy.

It is appropriate to conclude this section on the literary-philosophical approaches to suicide with an examination of the words of a philosopher who chose death: Améry, who survived imprisonment and torture in Auschwitz during the Holocaust. In *On Suicide* (1976), Améry presents the argument that suicide is essential to human subjecthood, and that to understand it in autobiographical terms is to change its significance in key ways:

> voluntary death – with the quantitively negligible exceptions of philosophical schools or philosophizing individuals (Epicurus, Seneca, Diderot) – is nowhere recognized for what it is: a precisely free and voluntary death and a highly individual matter that … is never carried out without social reference, with which however and *finally human beings are alone with themselves, before which society has to be silent.* (97; emphasis in original)

In this statement, Améry asserts the decisive autonomy of the suicidal individual, whose death is always personal. He confirms that suicide is always committed within a social web of rules and meanings. I have endeavoured to outline the key aspects of such social references for the subversive suicides depicted in Romantic texts. However, for the individual in real life, asserts Améry, choosing death is an utterly personal experience that is out of the reach of society's rules, pronouncements, theories or criticisms. All these discourses on suicide simply dance around an idea. Genuine suicidality, Améry claims, can only be experienced, rather than explained: 'Only those who have entered the darkness can have a say in this matter' (10). Améry killed himself in 1978, two years after *On Suicide* was published.

Nevertheless, Améry's statement elucidates the basic issue of this book. I have argued that the writers of the texts I have examined in detail treat suicide as an expression of personal choice and autonomy, just as Améry does, and as a challenge to power's efforts to manage the individual subject's body, to enforce life. Their growing awareness of the workings of biopower, particularly as it was established in its exemplary form, slavery, highlighted that, despite the pronouncements of some Enlightenment thinkers, individuals in British society were not free, they did not have full disposal of their own bodies and existences, and the prohibition against suicide was the ultimate manifestation of this truth. Accordingly, suicide epitomises the individual's refusal to be so controlled.

The Enduring Legacy of the Romantic Suicide Debate

As is evident in the above discussion of the philosophical exploration of the meaning of suicide as a form of rebellion, self-formation or assertion of human rights, the literary representation of suicide as an expression of the subject's autonomy has been influential for Western thought. Watt claims that our present concept of suicide derives from the Romantic period ('Introduction' 8), and there is growing evidence to support this claim. New laws regarding euthanasia – or medical assistance in dying (MAiD) – in Canada may be said to have been influenced by the humanistic and existential strains born of the Romantic-era suicide debate as I have described it. MAiD, which has been legal in Canada since 2016, recognises individuals' rights to end their lives, but it would be going too far to say that these laws recognise a person's complete autonomy over their existence, for MAiD is currently only available to severely ill people who are deemed mentally competent to make the decision. At the time of writing, MAiD is not available to people who suffer from intractable mental illness, such as severe clinical depression or dementia.[2] Still, this important and recent change in Canadian law demonstrates that the spirit of the suicide debate lives on in the West. According to Amia Srinivasan, 'a 2010 survey suggests that 82 per cent of the British public supports medically assisted dying for terminally ill patients, and the number only drops to 71 per cent among religious people' (24). More recently, in November 2024, British MPs backed an assisted dying bill. Society is beginning to recognise the limitations of the perspective that took hold with the birth of the discipline of psychology in the Romantic period: that suicide is always a sign of mental illness and can never be considered a rational decision (of the kind I examine here in interpreting suicide as protest). This limited view of suicide is Szasz's chief complaint in *Fatal Freedom* (e.g. 128), not to mention that of Saint-Preux in Rousseau's *Julie*, who advises, 'Let us be wary of prejudices of period and nation. When killing oneself is not in fashion, one imagines that only crazy people kill themselves' (317). It is not (yet) the case, as Szasz announces, that 'When suicide is legalized, the mental illness whose treatment justifies its therapeutic prevention will ... vanish' (*Fatal* 128). However, the very existence of such broad attitudes towards the allowability of choosing death amongst the sane demonstrates that, indeed, public attitudes have altered considerably in this century. We see that rational suicide exists, and this is the very type of suicide that I have described in the present study.[3]

Such changes in our attitudes and laws would not be possible without an increased ability to discuss suicide more openly in public life. For many years, though, the topic has been censored because it was thought to be too shameful, dangerous or horrifying to consider seriously and in a measured and informed way. Such attitudes are not entirely exorcised, and stem from a variety of positions that I have outlined in this study, such as: the religious view that suicide is a sin; the moral attitude that suicide is cowardly – the easy way out of a tough situation; or the medical idea that suicide is always caused by mental illness, which itself is unjustly treated as a source of embarrassment. Relatedly, the notion of suicidal contagion from the fields of psychology and sociology have prevented open discussion: commentators have been wary of potentially provoking suicide in impressionable individuals by broaching this important topic. Lately, however, the idea has emerged that the failure or refusal to discuss suicide may be equally, if not more, dangerous and, in fact, unethical: such silence can be damaging to both survivors and the suicidal, who may be discouraged from seeking help if they feel that the topic is taboo. For those who have lost loved ones to suicide, such silence can further traumatise them, argues Ruth Golden in a recent Opinion piece for CNN, in which she mentions her documentary *The Silent Goldens* about the lasting effects of her mother's suicide when she was nineteen years old. Peggy Wehmeyer makes a similar claim in a recent article on her husband's suicide in *The New York Times*, entitled 'What Lies in Suicide's Wake', written in recognition of National Suicide Prevention Week in the US, the penultimate week of September. Wehmeyer's article encourages the discussion of suicide simply by its very existence, and it also clearly conveys the message that we must approach the topic with great care and sensitivity.

I hope I have done so in my examination of Romantic-era attitudes towards suicide, as I think understanding the origins and development of our ideas about suicide is important: it can help us to approach questions that we are still working through today. These are difficult questions that we must explore if we are to have a truly ethical society, but sometimes we are loath to do so because they are too loaded with cultural baggage or too frightening to discuss objectively. But perhaps studying these questions in historical literature can provide the distance that we need to investigate such issues dispassionately. In other words, Romantic-era literature is not irrelevant because it is old; on the contrary, it may be useful for the discussion of our most pressing contemporary ethical concerns about suicide today precisely because it is old.

Notes

1. Brent Adkins asserts that 'Heidegger denies the experience of death': 'death for Heidegger is Dasein's ownmost, non-relational possibility that is not to be outstripped. Key to Heidegger's analysis is that while Dasein exists as being towards death, Dasein can never experience its own death' (189).
2. Changes to this aspect of MAiD's availability in Canada is a major point of debate at the time of writing. Miriam Toews's novel *All My Puny Sorrows* (2014) – now a major motion picture directed by Michael McGowan (2021) – explores the question of whether severely depressed, intractably suicidal adults should be offered assistance in dying. See also Anna Mehler Paperny's moving account of her over decade-long struggle with an overwhelming wish to die in *Hello I Want to Die Please Fix Me: Depression in the First Person* (2019).
3. By no means do I deny that suicide is sometimes linked to mental illness, however. Interestingly, Donald Antrim suggests that suicidality may be understood as a mental illness in its own right in the memoir, *One Friday in April: A Story of Suicide and Survival* (2021).

Works Cited

Adams, John. *An Essay Concerning Self-Murther Wherein is Endeavour'd to Prove that it is Unlawful According to Natural Principles*. London, 1700. *Early English Books Online*, http://name.umdl.umich.edu/a26335.0001.001. Accessed 5 May 2021.

Addison, Joseph. *Cato: A Tragedy. As it is Acted at the Theatre-Royal in Drury-Lane, by Her Majesty's Servants*. London, 1713. *Google Books*, https://www.google.ca/books/edition/Cato/RkMJAAAAQAAJ?hl=en&gbpv=0. Accessed 17 June 2022.

Adkins, Brent. *Death and Desire in Hegel, Heidegger and Deleuze*. Edinburgh UP, 2007.

Agamben, Giorgio. *Homo Sacer: Sovereign Power and Bare Life*. Translated by Daniel Heller-Roazen, Stanford UP, 1998.

Ahern, Stephen. 'Introduction: The Bonds of Sentiment'. *Affect and Abolition in the Anglo-Atlantic, 1770–1830*, edited by Stephen Ahern, Routledge, 2016, pp. 1–22. *Taylor & Francis*, https://doi.org/10.4324/9781315263243. Accessed 24 January 2024.

Alderson, Ralph. *A Chemical Analysis and Medical Treatise on the Shap Spaw, in Westmoreland, With Some Remarks on a Peculiar Affection of the Heart, the Consequence of Dyspepsia; Together with Observations on that Corporeal Derangement and Painful Mental Sympathy which Not Unfrequently Leads to The Commission of Suicide*. Kendal [1828]. *Google Books*, https://www.google.ca/books/edition/A_Chemical_Analysis_and_Medical_Treatise/8zltQVi_3MIC?hl=en&gbpv=1&dq=Alderson,+Ralph.+A+Chemical+Analysis+and+Medical+Treatise+on+the+Shap+Spaw&printsec=frontcover. Accessed 25 January 2022.

Allen, Jessica L. 'Pringle's Pruning of Prince: The History of Mary Prince and the Question of Repetition'. *Callaloo*, vol. 35, no. 2, 2012, pp. 509–19. *JSTOR*, https://www.jstor.org/stable/23274295. Accessed 5 January 2023.

Alvarez, Al. *The Savage God: A Study of Suicide*. 1971. Norton, 1990.

Améry, Jean. *On Suicide: A Discourse on Voluntary Death*. 1976. Translated by John D. Barlow, Indiana UP, 1999.

Anderson, Olive. *Suicide in Victorian and Edwardian England*. Clarendon Press, 1987.

Andrew, Donna T. 'The Suicide of Sir Samuel Romilly: Apotheosis or Outrage?' *From Sin to Insanity: Suicide in Early Modern Europe*, edited by Jeffrey R. Watt, Cornell UP, 2004, pp. 175–88.

Anon. 'Slavery and the British Transatlantic Slave Trade'. *The National Archives* (UK), https://www.nationalarchives.gov.uk/help-with-your-research/research-guides/british-transatlantic-slave-trade-records/. Accessed 9 August 2022.

Anon. *A Remedy for Self-Murder. Suggested in a Letter to a Friend.* 1819. *The History of Suicide in England, 1650–1850*, edited by Daryl Lee, Part II, vol. 7, 1st ed., Routledge, 2016, https://doi.org/10.4324/9781003113966, pp. 51–62. Accessed 13 June 2023.

Anon. *Thoughts on Suicide, in a Letter to a Friend.* London, 1819. *Google Books*, https://www.google.ca/books/edition/Thoughts_on_Suicide_in_a_Letter_to_a_Fri/H4wUAAAAQAAJ?hl=en&gbpv=0. Accessed 27 March 2020.

Anon. 'Verses Found Inscribed on a Skull in a Church-yard'. *Essay on the Application of the Organology of the Brain to Education.* London [1816?], pp. 14–16.

Anon. 'Portrait of the engraver James Neagle'. Museum number: 1892,0714.822. *The British Museum* (website), https://www.britishmuseum.org/collection/object/P_1892-0714-822. Accessed 10 August 2023.

Anon., editor. *Tributes of the Public Press to the Memory of the Late Mr Whitbread. Being the Memorials and Characters of that Eminent Man.* London, 1815. *Google Books*, https://books.google.ca/books?id=kn9ZAAAAcAAJ&printsec=frontcover#v=onepage&q&f=false. Accessed 18 January 2024.

Anon. *A Dissertation or, Discourse on Suicide; Grounded on the Immovable Foundation of Scriptural, Rather than of Philosophical Principles.* Northampton, 1785.

Antrim, Donald. *One Friday in April: A Story of Suicide and Survival.* W. W. Norton, 2021.

Armstrong, Aurelia. 'Michel Foucault: Feminism'. *The Internet Encyclopedia of Philosophy*, https://iep.utm.edu/foucfem/. Accessed 20 June 2022.

Augustine, St (of Hippo). *Saint Augustine. The City of God, Books I–VII.* Catholic University of America Press, 2008. *EBSCOhost*, search.ebscohost.com/login.aspx?direct=true&db=e000xna&AN=498860&site=ehost-live. Accessed 30 May 2024.

Austen, Jane. *Sense and Sensibility.* 1811. Edited by Kathleen James-Cavan, Broadview Press, 2001.

Bailey, Victor. *This Rash Act: Suicide Across the Life Cycle in the Victorian City.* Stanford UP, 1998.

Bamborough, J. B. 'Burton, Robert (1577–1640), writer'. *Oxford Dictionary of National Biography*, Oxford UP, 2004, https://doi-org.uml.idm.oclc.org/10.1093/ref:odnb/4137. Accessed 28 May 2021.

Banner, Rachel. 'Surface and Stasis: Re-reading Slave Narrative via "The History of Mary Prince"'. *Callaloo*, vol. 36, no. 2, 2013, pp. 298–311. *JSTOR*, https://www.jstor.org/stable/24264910. Accessed 5 February 2023.

Barker-Benfield, G. J. *The Culture of Sensibility: Sex and Society in Eighteenth-Century Britain.* U of Chicago P, 1992.

Barry, Edward. *The Present Practice of a Justice of the Peace.* Vol. 2, London, 1790. *Eighteenth Century Collections Online*, https://go.gale.com/ps/i.do?p=GDCS&u=univmanitoba&id=GALE|CW0124343115&v=2.1&it=r&sid=bookmark-GDCS&sPage=413&asid=3b4ae912. Accessed 9 December 2021.

Barthes, Roland. *S/Z.* Hill and Wang, 1974.

Basker, James G., editor. *Amazing Grace: An Anthology of Poems about Slavery, 1660–1810*. Yale UP, 2002.

Baumgartner, Barbara. 'The Body as Evidence: Resistance, Collaboration, and Appropriation in "The History of Mary Prince"'. *Callaloo*, vol. 24, no. 1, 2001, pp. 253–75. *JSTOR*, https://www.jstor.org/stable/3300499. Accessed 1 March 2023.

Behn, Aphra. *Oroonoko: Or, The Royal Slave. The Broadview Anthology of British Literature: One Volume Compact Edition*, edited by Joseph Black et al., Broadview Press, 2015, pp. 880–914.

Bell, Richard. *We Shall be No More: Suicide and Self-Government in the Newly United States*. Harvard UP, 2012. *EBSCOhost*, https://doi.org/10.4159/harvard.9780674064799. Accessed 23 January 2024.

——. 'Slave Suicide, Abolition and the Problem of Resistance'. *Slavery & Abolition: A Journal of Slave and Post-Slave Studies*, vol. 33, no. 4, 2012, pp. 525–49. *Taylor & Francis*, https://doi.org/10.1080/0144039X.2011.644069. Accessed 10 December 2012.

Bennett, Andrew. *Suicide Century: Literature and Suicide from James Joyce to David Foster Wallace*. Cambridge UP, 2017.

Bennett, Betty T. *Mary Wollstonecraft Shelley: An Introduction*. Johns Hopkins UP, 1996.

Bergner, Gwen. 'Introduction: The Plantation, the Postplantation, and the Afterlives of Slavery'. *American Literature*, vol. 91, no. 3, 2019, pp. 447–57, https://doi.org/10.1215/00029831-7722078. Accessed 12 March 2021.

Bergner, Gwen, and Zita Cristina Nunes, editors. *The Plantation, the Postplantation, and the Afterlives of Slavery*. Issue of *American Literature*, vol. 91, no. 3, 2019.

Bering, Jesse. *A Very Human Ending: How Suicide Haunts Our Species*. Penguin Random House, 2018.

Bewell, Alan. '"The Stranger and the Exile Who Is in Our Land within Our Gates": Mary Prince as a Black British Immigrant'. *Modern Philology*, vol. 118, no. 2, 2020, pp. 234–51. *EBSCOhost*, https://doi.org/10.1086/711084. Accessed 5 January 2023.

——. *Romanticism and Colonial Disease*. Johns Hopkins UP, 1999.

Black, Joseph, et al. Introductory matter to Aphra Behn's 'Oroonoko'. *The Broadview Anthology of British Literature: One Volume Compact Edition*, edited by Joseph Black et al., Broadview Press, 2015, pp. 878–80.

Blackburn, Robin. 'Review of Peter Kitson and Debbie Lee, eds., *Slavery, Abolition and Emancipation: Writings in the British Romantic Period*'. *Bryn Mawr Review of Comparative Literature*, vol. 6, no. 2, 2007, pp. 1–5, https://repository.brynmawr.edu/bmrcl/vol6/iss2/7. Accessed 18 August 2021.

Blackstone, William. *Commentaries on the Laws of England: In Four Books*. 5th ed., 4 volumes, Clarendon Press, 1773. Volume 4. *Eighteenth-Century Collections Online*, link.gale.com/apps/doc/CW0125377502/ECCO?u=univmanitoba&sid=bookmark-ECCO&xid=b8b4395c&pg=195. Accessed 18 January 2024.

Blair, Robert. *The Grave. The Poetical Works of Beattie, Blair, and Falconer with Lives, Critical Dissertations, and Explanatory Notes*, edited by George Gilfillan, [no place], [no year], [n.p.]. *Project Gutenberg*, https://www.gutenberg.org/files/8695/8695-h/8695-h.htm. Accessed 25 January 2022.

Blanchot, Maurice. *The Space of Literature: A Translation of 'l'Espace Littéraire'*. Translated and introduced by Ann Smock, U of Nebraska Press, 2015.

——. 'Literature and the Right to Death'. 1948. *The Work of Fire*. Translated by Charlotte Mandell, Stanford UP, 1995, pp. 300–44.

Blum, Carol. 'Of Women and the Land: Legitimizing Husbandry'. *Early Modern Conceptions of Property*, edited by John Brewer and Susan Staves, Routledge, 1996, pp. 161–9.

Borradori, Giovanna. *Philosophy in a Time of Terror: Dialogues with Jurgen Habermas and Jacques Derrida*. U of Chicago P, 2003.

Boswell, James. *The Life of Samuel Johnson, L. L. D.: Including A Journal of a Tour to the Hebrides*. 1791. Edited by John Wilson Croker, vol. 2, New York, 1837. *Google Books*, https://books.google.vu/books?id=z5sEAAAAYAAJ&printsec=frontcover&source=gbs_ge_summary_r&cad=0#v=onepage&q=whelp&f=false. Accessed 13 February 2021.

——. *No Abolition of Slavery; Or the Universal Empire of Love: A Poem*. London, 1791. *Google Books*, https://www.google.ca/books/edition/No_Abolition_of_Slavery_Or_The_Universal/vZ31DiXkZegC?hl=en&gbpv=1&dq=No+Abolition+of+Slavery%3B+Or+the+Universal+Empire+of+Love&pg=PP6&printsec=frontcover. Accessed 23 May 2021.

Bronfen, Elisabeth. *Over Her Dead Body: Death, Femininity and the Aesthetic*. Manchester UP, 1992.

Brontë, Charlotte. *Jane Eyre*, edited by Margaret Smith, Oxford UP, 2000.

Brown, Vincent. *The Reaper's Garden: Death and Power in the World of Atlantic Slavery*. Harvard UP, 2007.

Burney, Frances. *Evelina, or The History of a Young Lady's Entrance into the World*. 1778. Edited by Susan Kubica Howard, Broadview Press, 2000.

Burton, Robert. *The Anatomy of Melancholy, What it is, with all the Kinds, Causes, Symptomes, Prognostics, and Several Cures of It*. 1621. Vol. 1, 13th ed., London, 1827. *HathiTrust*, https://babel.hathitrust.org/cgi/pt?id=uc1.31175011983346&view=plaintext&seq=9. Accessed 27 March 2020.

Burwick, Frederick. 'Lord Byron's Faustian Plays: *Manfred* (1817), *Cain* (1821), and *The Deformed Transformed* (1822)'. *Faust Adaptations from Marlowe to Aboudoma and Markland*, edited by Lorna Fitzsimmons, Purdue UP, 2016, pp. 46–65.

Butler, Alban, and Paul Burns. *Butler's Lives of the Saints*. Revised by Peter Doyle, vol. 10, Burns & Oates, 1997. *Google Books*, https://www.google.ca/books/edition/Butler_s_Lives_of_the_Saints/RhzAkvei_U8C?hl=en&gbpv=1. Accessed 6 February 2024.

Butler, Sara M. 'Women, Suicide, and the Jury in Later Medieval England'. *Signs*, vol. 32, no. 1, 2006, pp. 141–66, *JSTOR*, https://doi.org/10.1086/505270. Accessed 26 March 2020.

Byron, George Gordon. *The Deformed Transformed. A Drama*. 2nd ed., London, 1824. *Internet Archive*, https://archive.org/stream/deformedtransfor01byro/deformedtransfor01byro_djvu.txt. Accessed 9 December 2019.

——. Preface to *Don Juan*, Cantos VI–VIII. 1823–4. *The Major Works*, edited by Jerome McGann, Oxford UP, 2008, pp. 589–90.

——. *Don Juan*. 1819, 1823–4. *The Major Works*. 1985. Edited by Jerome McGann, Oxford UP, 2008, pp. 373–879.

——. 'Epigrams'. 1822. *The Complete Poetical Works of Lord Byron*, edited by Paul Elmer More, Houghton Mifflin, 1905, p. 235. *HathiTrust*, https://babel.hathitrust.org/cgi/pt?id=hvd.32044037088457&seq=11. Accessed 7 February 2024.

——. *Cain: A Mystery*. 1821. *The Major Works*. 1985. Edited by Jerome McGann, Oxford UP, 2008, pp. 881–938.

——. 'Euthanasia'. *Lord Byron's Works*. Vol. 3, Paris, 1821, pp. 219–20. *Google Books*, https://www.google.ca/books/edition/Lord_Byron_s_Works/5ZsgAAAAMAAJ?hl=en&gbpv=1&dq=%22Lord+Byron%E2%80%99s+Works%22+euthanasia&pg=RA1-PA219&printsec=frontcover. Accessed 1 April 2020.

——. *Sardanapalus*. 1821. *The Broadview Anthology of Romantic Drama*, edited by Jeffrey N. Cox and Michael Gamer, Broadview Press, 2003, pp. 263–309.

——. 'POSTERITY will ne'er survey'. 1820? *The Complete Poetical Works of Lord Byron*, edited by Paul Elmer More, Houghton Mifflin, 1905, p. 235. *HathiTrust*, https://babel.hathitrust.org/cgi/pt?id=hvd.32044037088457&seq=11. Accessed 7 February 2024.

——. *'The Flesh is Frail': Byron's Letters and Journals*. Vol. 6 (1818–19). Edited by Leslie Marchand, Harvard UP, 1976. *Google Books*, https://www.google.ca/books/edition/The_Flesh_is_Frail/W9LhyLadkgMC?hl=en&gbpv=1. Accessed 12 February 2024.

——. *Manfred*. 1817. *The Major Works*. 1985. Edited and introduced by Jerome McGann, Oxford UP, 2008, pp. 274–314.

——. *The Giaour. A Fragment of a Turkish Tale*. 1813. *The Major Works*. 1985. Edited and introduced by Jerome McGann, Oxford UP, 2008, pp. 207–47.

——. *Byron's Letter and Journals. August 1811–April 1814*, edited by Rowland E. Prothero, vol. 2, London, 1898. *Project Gutenberg*, http://www.gutenberg.org/files/9921/9921-h/9921-h.htm#frg82. Accessed 31 March 2020.

——. *Byron's Letters and Journals: A New Selection: From Leslie A. Marchand's Twelve-Volume Edition*, edited by Richard Lansdowne, Oxford UP, 2015. *EBSCOhost*, search-ebscohost-com.uml.idm.oclc.org/login.aspx?direct=true&db=nlebk&AN=960656&site=ehost-live. Accessed 24 June 2020.

Calvin, John. From *Sermons of Maister John Calvin, upon the Booke of Job*. 1580. *The Ethics of Suicide: Historical Sources*, edited by Margaret Pabst Battin, Oxford UP, 2015, pp. 249–52. *ProQuest*, http://ebookcentral.proquest.com/lib/umanitoba/detail.action?docID=2145420. Accessed 26 March 2020.

Cameron, Kenneth Neill, editor. *Shelley and His Circle: 1773–1822*. Harvard UP, 1970.

Camus, Albert. *The Myth of Sisyphus*. 1955. Translated by Justin O'Brian, introduced by James Wood, Penguin, 2000.

Canuel, Mark. *Justice, Dissent, and the Sublime*. Johns Hopkins UP, 2012.

——. *Religion, Toleration, and British Writing, 1790–1830*. Cambridge UP, 2002.

Carey, Brycchan. *British Abolitionism and the Rhetoric of Sensibility: Writing, Sentiment, and Slavery, 1760–1807*. Palgrave, 2005.

——. 'Thomas Day (1748–1789)'. *Brycchan Carey, Author and Academic*. https://brycchancarey.com/abolition/day.htm. Accessed 14 February 2024.

Carretta, Vincent. *Equiano, the African: Biography of a Self-Made Man*. U of Georgia P, 2005.

Cerwonka, Allaine, and Anna Loutfi. 'Biopolitics and the Female Reproductive Body as the New Subject of Law', *feminists@law*, vol. 1, no. 1, 2011, https://journals.kent.ac.uk/index.php/feministsatlaw/article/view/18/76. Accessed 29 June 2022.

Cheyne, George. *The English Malady: or, A Treatise of Nervous Diseases of All Kinds, as Spleen, Vapours, Lowness of Spirits, Hypochondriacal, and Hysterical Distempers &c*. London, 1733.

Cholbi, Michael, 'Kant and the Irrationality of Suicide'. *History of Philosophy Quarterly*, vol. 17, no. 2, 2000, pp. 159–76. *JSTOR*, https://www.jstor.org/stable/27744847. Accessed 7 February 2024.

'Church Father'. *Encyclopédie ou Dictionnaire Raisonné des Sciences, des Arts et des Métiers*. 1762–72. *The Encyclopedia of Diderot & d'Alembert Collaborative Translation Project*. Translated by Emily Jane Cohen, Michigan Publishing, 2002. http://hdl.handle.net/2027/spo.did2222.0000.336. Accessed 16 March 2020.

Cioran, E. M. *The Trouble with Being Born*. 1973. Seaver Books, 2012.

Cisney, Vernon W., and Nicolae Morar. 'Introduction: Why Biopower? Why Now?' *Biopower: Foucault and Beyond*, edited by Vernon W. Cisney and Nicolae Morar. U of Chicago P, 2016, pp. 1–25.

Clarkson, Thomas. *An Essay on the Slavery and Commerce of the Human Species, Particularly the African; Translated from a Latin Dissertation, Which Was Honoured with the First Prize in the Unviersity of Cambridge, for the Year 1785*. 2nd ed., rev., 1788. *Thomas Clarkson and Ottobah Cugoano: Essays on the Slavery and Commerce of the Human Species*. By Thomas Clarkson, Ottobah Cugoano. Edited by Marie-Antoinette Smith, Broadview Press, 2010, pp. 57–220.

Clayton, George. *The Dreadful Sin of Suicide. A Sermon Preached at The Rv. D. Winter's Meeting House*. London, 1812. *Google Books*, https://www.google.ca/books/edition/The_Dreadful_Sin_of_Suicide_A_Sermon_Etc/JGlpAAAAcAAJ?hl=en&gbpv=1&dq=The+Dreadful+Sin+of+Suicide&printsec=frontcover. Accessed 21 July 2021.

Coates, John. 'An Answer to the Justification of Suicide'. 1792. *The History of Suicide in England, 1650–1850: Volume 6. 1750–1799: Legal, Medical, Literary and Miscellaneous Texts, and Newspapers and Magazines*, edited by Jeffrey Merrick, Pickering & Chatto, 2013, pp. 107–16.

Cochran, Peter. *Manfred: An Edition of Byron's Manuscripts and a Collection of Essays*. Cambridge Scholars Publishing, 2015. *EBSCOhost*, search.ebscohost.com/login.aspx?direct=true&db=e000xna&AN=960135&site=ehost-live. Accessed 6 February 2014.

Coleman, Deirdre. *Romantic Colonization and British Anti-Slavery*. Cambridge UP, 2005.

Coleridge, Samuel Taylor. 'The Suicide's Argument. With Nature's Answer'. 1811. *The Collected Works of Samuel Taylor Coleridge: Poetical Works I Poems (Reading Text): PART 2*, edited by J. C. C. Mays, Princeton UP, 1969, p. 895.

——. 'Lecture on the Slave-Trade'. *The Collected Works of Samuel Taylor Coleridge, Volume 1: Lectures, 1795: On Politics and Religion*. Princeton UP, 1971,

2015, pp. 231–52. *EBSCOhost*, https://doi.org/10.1515/9781400867844-008. Accessed 1 June 2023.

——. 'Monody on the Death of Chatterton'. 1794. *English Poetry 1579–1830: Spenser and the Tradition*, http://spenserians.cath.vt.edu/TextRecord.php?action=GET&textsid=35143. Accessed 18 January 2019.

——. 'The Wretched Lot of the Slaves in the Islands of West India'. 1792. *Amazing Grace: An Anthology of Poems about Slavery, 1660–1810*, edited by James Basker, Yale UP, 2002, pp. 446–9.

——. 'Literal Translation' of 'Introduction to a Greek Prize Ode on the Slave-Trade'. 1791. *The Complete Poetical Works of Samuel Taylor Coleridge*, edited by Ernest Hartley Coleridge. Clarendon Press, 1912, vol. 1, pp. 146, footnote 2. *Project Gutenberg*, https://www.gutenberg.org/files/29091/29091-h/29091-h.htm. Accessed 24 January 2024.

Coroner's Inquest (Peter Cope). 1789. London Metropolitan Archives, LL ref: LMCLIC650020414. *London Lives 1690 to 1800 – Crime, Poverty and Social Policy in the Metropolis*, https://www.londonlives.org/browse.jsp?div=LMCLIC65002IC650020414. Accessed 13 July 2020.

Coroner's Inquest (Thomas Philpot). 1762. Westminster Abbey Muniment Room, Westminster Coroners' Inquests, 1760–99, LL ref: WACWIC652020368. *London Lives 1690 to 1800 – Crime, Poverty and Social Policy in the Metropolis*, https://www.londonlives.org/browse.jsp?div=WACWIC65202IC652020368. Accessed 13 July 2020.

Corry, John. *The Suicide*; *or*, *The Progress of Error. A Moral Tale*, *for the Instruction of Young Persons*. London, [1805?].

Cowling, Camillia, Maria Helena Pereira Toledo Machado, Diana Paton, and Emily West, editors. *Mothering Slaves: Motherhood*, *Childlessness and the Care of Children in Atlantic Slave Societies* issue. *Slavery & Abolition: A Journal of Slave and Post-Slave Studies*, vol. 38, no. 2, 2017, https://doi.org/10.1080/0144039X.2017.1316959. Accessed 18 March 2020.

Cowper, William. *The Works of William Cowper. His Life*, *Letters*, *and Poems*, *Now First Completed by the Introduction of Cowper's Private Correspondence*, edited by T. S. Grimshawe, London, 1849. *Project Gutenberg*, https://www.gutenberg.org/files/47790/47790-h/47790-h.htm. Accessed 25 March 2021.

——. 'Sweet Meat has Sour Sauce: Or, the Slave Trader in the Dumps'. 1836. 'Antislavery Poems by William Cowper'. *Brycchan Carey*, *Author and Academic*, https://brycchancarey.com/slavery/cowperpoems.htm#sweet. Accessed 4 March 2019.

——. 'The Castaway'. 1803. *The Norton Anthology of English Literature*, edited by M. H. Abrams, vol. 1, 5th ed., W. W. Norton & Company, 1986, pp. 2531–2.

——. *The Task and Other Poems*. 1785. Edited by Henry Morley, London, Cassell & Company, 1899. *Project Gutenberg*, https://www.gutenberg.org/files/3698/3698-h/3698-h.htm. Accessed 2 June 2023.

Crewe, Frances. 'Letter from the Editor'. *Letters of the Late Ignatius Sancho*, *an African*. 1782. By Ignatius Sancho. Edited by Vincent Carretta, Broadview Press, 2015, pp. 47–8.

Critchley, Simon. *Notes on Suicide*. Fitzcarraldo Editions, 2015.

Croft, Herbert. *A Sermon*, *Preached … on the 18th of September*, *1791. Soon After the Riots at Birmingham*, *and the Self-murder of Mr Sutherland*.

London, 1791. *Eighteenth-Century Collections Online*, link.gale.com/apps/doc/CW0122112498/GDCS?u=univmanitoba&sid=bookmark-GDCS&xid=2110a21b&pg=1. Accessed 25 March 2020.

Croker, John Wilson. Notes. *The Life of Samuel Johnson, including A Journal of a Tour to the Hebrides*. By James Boswell. Edited by John Wilson Croker, vol. 3, London, 1831. *Internet Archive*, https://archive.org/details/dli.granth.36203. Accessed 13 April 2021.

Crowley, Martin. 'Possible Suicide: Blanchot and the Ownership of Death'. *Paragraph*, vol. 23, no. 2, pp. 191–206. *EBSCOhost*, https://doi.org/10.3366/para.2000.23.2.191. Accessed 11 April 2021.

Cugoano, Ottobah. *Thoughts and Sentiments on the Evil and Wicked Traffic of the Slavery and Commerce of the Human Species, Humbly Submitted to the Inhabitants of Great Britain.* 1787. *Thomas Clarkson and Ottobah Cugoano: Essays on the Slavery and Commerce of the Human Species.* By Thomas Clarkson, Ottobah Cugoano. Edited by Marie-Antoinette Smith, Broadview Press, 2010, pp. 221–326.

Daniel, Drew. 'Self-Killing and the Matter of Affect in Bacon and Spinoza'. *Affect Theory and Early Modern Texts Politics, Ecologies, and Form*, Palgrave Macmillan, 2017, pp. 89–108. *SpringerLink*, https://doi.org/10.1057/978-1-137-56126-8. Accessed 6 February 2024.

Darcy, Jane. 'Religious Melancholy in the Romantic Period: William Cowper as Test Case'. *Romanticism: The Journal of Romantic Culture and Criticism*, vol. 15, no. 2, 2009, pp. 144–55. *EBSCOhost*, https://doi.org/10.3366/E1354991X09000622. Accessed 2 April 2013.

Davis, David Brion. *The Problem of Slavery in the Age of Revolution, 1770–1823*. 1975. Oxford UP, 1999. *EBSCOhost*, search.ebscohost.com/login.aspx?direct=true&db=e000xna&AN=151346&site=ehost-live. Accessed 23 January 2024.

Dawes Blackett, Mary. *Suicide*; *A Poem*. London, 1789.

Day, Thomas, and John Bicknell. *The Dying Negro: A Poem*. 3rd ed., London, 1775. 'Poems Against Slavery'. *Brycchan Carey, Author and Academic*, https://brycchancarey.com/slavery/dying.htm. Accessed 14 January 2022.

De Quincey, Thomas. From 'On Suicide'. *The Ethics of Suicide: Historical Sources*, edited by Margaret Pabst Battin, Oxford UP, 2015, pp. 487–9. *ProQuest*, http://ebookcentral.proquest.com/lib/umanitoba/detail.action?docID=2145420. Accessed 26 March 2020.

de Staël, Madame [Anne Louise Germaine de Staël-Holstein]. *Reflections on Suicide*. 1812. *The Ethics of Suicide: Historical Sources*, edited by Margaret Pabst Battin, Oxford UP, 2015, pp. 467–71. *ProQuest*, http://ebookcentral.proquest.com/lib/umanitoba/detail.action?docID=2145420. Accessed 26 March 2020.

——. From *On the Influence of the Passions*. 1798. *The Ethics of Suicide: Historical Sources*, edited by Margaret Pabst Battin, Oxford UP, 2015, pp. 464–6. *ProQuest*, http://ebookcentral.proquest.com/lib/umanitoba/detail.action?docID=2145420. Accessed 26 March 2020.

Del Rey, Lana. *Born to Die*, Interscope Records and Polydor Records, 2012.

Deveaux, Monique. 'Feminism and Empowerment: A Critical Reading of Foucault'. *Feminist Studies*, vol. 20, no. 2, 1994, pp. 223–47. *JSTOR*, http://www.jstor.org/stable/3178151. Accessed 19 August 2021.

Diamond, Irene, and Lee Quinby. *Feminism & Foucault: Reflections on Resistance*. Northeastern UP, 1988.

Dickenson, Elizabeth G., and James M. Boyden. 'Ambivalence toward Suicide in Golden Age Spain'. *From Sin to Insanity: Suicide in Early Modern Europe*, edited by Jeffrey R. Watt, Cornell UP, 2004, pp. 100–15.

Diderot, Denis, et al. *Encyclopédie ou Dictionnaire Raisonné des Sciences, des Arts et des Métiers*. 1762–72. *The Encyclopedia of Diderot & d'Alembert Collaborative Translation Project*. Translated by Pamela Cheek, Michigan Publishing, 2003, https://quod.lib.umich.edu/d/did/. Accessed 16 June 2021.

Dijkstra, Bram. *Idols of Perversity: Fantasies of Feminine Evil in Fin-de-Siècle Culture*. Oxford UP, 1986.

Dominique, Lyndon J. Footnotes to *The Woman of Colour*, by Anonymous. 1808. Edited by Lyndon J. Dominque, Broadview Press, 2008.

Donne, John. From *Biathanatos* [*: A Declaration of that Paradoxe, or Thesis, That Self-homicide is Not So Naturally Sin, That It May Never be Otherwise. Wherein the Nature, and the Extent of All those Lawes, Which Seeme to be Violated by this Act, are Diligently Surveyed*]. 1647. *The Ethics of Suicide: Historical Sources*, edited by Margaret Pabst Battin, Oxford UP, 2015, pp. 289–91. *ProQuest*, http://ebookcentral.proquest.com/lib/umanitoba/detail.action?docID=2145420. Accessed 26 March 2020.

——. '[Holy Sonnet] 5 ['I am a little world made cunningly.']' 1635. *The Norton Anthology of English Literature*, edited by M. H. Abrams, vol. 1, 5th ed., W. W. Norton & Company, 1986, p. 1098.

——. '[Holy Sonnet] 14 ['Batter my heart, three-personed God.']' 1633. *The Norton Anthology of English Literature*, edited by M. H. Abrams, vol. 1, 5th ed., W. W. Norton & Company, 1986, p. 1100.

Doody, Margaret Anne. *Frances Burney: The Life in the Works*. Cambridge UP, 1988.

Douglas, Niel. *The African Slave Trade: Or a Short View of the Evidence, Relative to That Subject, Produced Before the House of Commons*. Edinburgh, 1792. *Slavery and Anti-Slavery: A Transnational Archive*, link.gale.com/apps/doc/U0102445883/SAS?u=univmanitoba&sid=bookmark-SAS&xid=5ebade07&pg=1. Accessed 25 January 2022.

Drescher, Seymour. *Econocide: British Slavery in the Era of Abolition*. 1977. 2nd ed., foreword and preface by David Brion Davis, U of North Carolina P, 2010. *EBSCOhost*, https://search-ebscohost-com.uml.idm.oclc.org/login.aspx?direct=true&db=e000xna&AN=343669&site=ehost-live. Accessed 7 February 2024.

Driver, Julia. 'The History of Utilitarianism'. *The Stanford Encyclopedia of Philosophy*, edited by Edward N. Zalta, 2014, https://plato.stanford.edu/archives/win2014/entries/utilitarianism-history/. Accessed 2 August 2020.

Dumas, Paula E. *Proslavery Britain Fighting for Slavery in an Era of Abolition*. Palgrave Macmillan, 2016. *SpringerLink*, https://doi.org/10.1057/9781137558589. Accessed 24 January 2024.

Durkheim, Émile. *On Suicide*. 1897. Translated by Robin Buss, introduced by Richard Sennett, notes by Alexander Riley, Penguin, 2006.

Edelman, Lee. *No Future: Queer Theory and the Death Drive*. Duke UP, 2004. *JSTOR*, https://doi.org/10.2307/j.ctv11hpkpp. Accessed 14 June 2022.

Edelman-Young, Diana. '"Kingdom of Shadows": Intimations of Desire in Mary Shelley's "Mathilda"'. *Keats-Shelley Journal*, vol. 51, 2002, pp. 116–44. *JSTOR*, http://www.jstor.org/stable/30213309. Accessed 25 August 2023.

Edgeworth, Maria. 'The Grateful Negro'. 1802. *Popular Tales: The Contrast. The Grateful Negro. Tomorrow*. London, 1811, pp. 171–210. *Google Books*, https://www.google.ca/books/edition/Popular_Tales_The_contrast_The_grateful/h1XEqwK9w1sC?hl=en&gbpv=1&dq=Popular+Tales:+The+Contrast.+The+Grateful+Negro.+Tomorrow.+London,+1811&pg=PP13&printsec=frontcover. Accessed 23 April 2020.

Edwards, Bryan. *The History, Civil and Commercial, of the British West Indies*. 1793. 5th ed., London, 1818–19. *World Scholar: Latin America & the Caribbean*, http://worldscholar.tu.galegroup.com/tinyurl/4wmed0. Accessed 16 June 2017.

Equiano, Olaudah. *The Interesting Narrative of the life of Olaudah Equiano, or Gustavus Vassa, the African, Written by Himself*. 1789, 2001. Edited by Angelo Costanzo, Broadview Press, 2004.

——. 'The Interesting Narrative of the Life of Olaudah Equiano: Or Gustavus Vassa, the African. Written by Himself'. London: Printed and sold by the author, 1794. 9th ed. *Google Books*, https://www.google.ca/books/edition/The_Interesting_Narrative_of_the_Life_of/4GM6AAAAcAAJ?hl=en&gbpv=0. Accessed 17 June 2022.

Etkind, Marc. *Or Not to Be: A Collection of Suicide Notes*. Riverhead Books, 1997.

Falconbridge, Alexander. *An Account of the Slave Trade on the Coast of Africa*. London, 1788. *Google Books*, https://books.google.ca/books?id=_lTrja-FFXEC&printsec=frontcover&dq=alexander+falconbridge&hl=en&sa=X&ved=0ahUKEwjy6qPouoTpAhXMrZ4KHeirDf4Q6AEICDAA#v=onepage&q=alexander%20falconbridge&f=false. Accessed 1 May 2020.

Fanon, Frantz. *Black Skin, White Masks*. 1967. Translated by Charles Lam Markmann, Grove Press, 2008.

Faubert, Michelle. 'Political Suicide: Castlereagh, Rebellion, and Self-Directed Violence'. *Commemorating Peterloo: Violence, Resilience and Claim-making During the Romantic Era*, edited by Michael Demson and Regina Hewitt, Edinburgh UP, 2019, pp. 160–82.

——. 'Calvinism, Enthusiasm, and Suicide: The Regulation of Subjectivity in the Romantic Period'. *Studies in the Literary Imagination*, vol. 51, no. 1, 2018, pp. 79–102.

——. 'Introduction to Suicidal Romanticism: Origins and Influences'. *Studies in the Literary Imagination*, vol. 51, no. 1, 2018, pp. v–xv.

——. Suicidal Romanticism: Origins and Influences. Issue of *Studies in the Literary Imagination*, vol. 51, no. 1, 2018, pp. 1–162.

——. 'Introduction'. *Mathilda*. By Mary Shelley. 1819, 1959. Edited by Michelle Faubert, Broadview Press, 2017, pp. 9–33.

——. '*Werther* Goes Viral: Suicidal Contagion, Anti-Vaccination, and Infectious Sympathy'. *Literature and Medicine*, vol. 34, no. 2, 2016, pp. 389–418.

——. 'The Fictional Suicides of Mary Wollstonecraft'. *Literature Compass*, vol. 12, no. 12, 2015, pp. 652–9. https://doi.org/10.1111/lic3.12282. Accessed 25 January 2022.

——. 'Romantic Suicide, Contagion, and Rousseau's *Julie*'. *Romanticism, Rousseau, Switzerland: New Prospects*, edited by Diane Piccitto, Angela Esterhammer and Patrick Vincent, Palgrave, 2015, pp. 38–53.

——. 'The Wollstonecraftian Plot: Female Suicide as Slave Protest'. *Bodyscapes: Embodied Selves, Embodied Spaces and Legible Bodies in the Romantic Age*, edited by Gerold Sedlmayr, Wissenschaftlicher Verlag Trier, 2015, pp. 123–44.

——. 'A Family Affair: Ennobling Suicide in Mary Shelley's *Matilda*'. *Essays in Romanticism*, vol. 20, no. 7, 2013, pp. 101–28.

——. 'Fanny Imlay/Godwin (1794–1816)'. *Oxford Dictionary of National Biography*, Oxford UP, 2012, https://doi-org.uml.idm.oclc.org/10.1093/ref:odnb/103421. Accessed 13 August 2019.

——. Introduction. *Mary, A Fiction and The Wrongs of Woman, or Maria.* By Mary Wollstonecraft. Edited by Michelle Faubert. Broadview Editions, 2012, pp. 11–50.

Faubert, Michelle, and Nicole Reynolds. 'Introduction: Romanticism and Suicide'. *Literature Compass*, vol. 12, no. 12, 2015, pp. 641–51. https://doi.org/10.1111/lic3.12285. Accessed 25 January 2022.

Feldman, Paula R. Introduction. *Records of Woman, with Other Poems.* By Felicia Hemans. Edited by Paula R. Feldman, The UP of Kentucky, 1999, pp. xi–xxix. *EBSCOhost*, http://uml.idm.oclc.org/login?url=https://search.ebscohost.com/login.aspx?direct=true&db=e000xna&AN=938104&site=ehost-live&ebv=EB&ppid=pp_xi. Accessed 5 February 2024.

Ferguson, Moira. *Subject to Others: British Women Writers and Colonial Slavery, 1670–1834.* 1992. Routledge, 2014. *Taylor & Francis Evidence Based Ebook Collection*, https://doi.org/10.4324/9781315758008. Accessed 24 January 2024.

Ferriar, John. *The Prince of Angola, a Tragedy, Altered from the Play of* Oroonoko. *And Adapted to the Circumstances of the Present Times.* J. Harrop, 1788. *Eighteenth Century Collections Online*, link.gale.com/apps/doc/CW0109503288/ECCO?u=univmanitoba&sid=bookmark-ECCO&xid=2be46e39&pg=1. Accessed 16 January 2024.

Fisher, D. 'Whitbread, Samuel (1764–1815), politician'. *Oxford Dictionary of National Biography*, Oxford UP, 2008, https://doi-org.uml.idm.oclc.org/10.1093/ref:odnb/29231. Accessed 19 May 2021.

Fleming, Thomas. *The Intimate Lives of the Founding Fathers.* Harper Collins, 2009.

Fletcher, Loraine. Introduction. *Emmeline, the Orphan of the Castle.* 1788. By Charlotte Smith. Edited by Loraine Fletcher, Broadview Press, 2003, pp. 9–35.

Fordyce, James. *A Letter on Suicide, to a Friend who Meditated that Dreadful Crime.* In *Poems, by Charles James*, vol. 2, 3rd ed., London, 1797, pp. 9–29. *Google Books*, https://books.google.ca/books?id=ImIRAAAAYAAJ&printsec=frontcover&source=gbs_ge_summary_r&cad=0#v=onepage&q&f=false. Accessed 17 January 2024.

Foucault, Michel. *Power/Knowledge: Selected Interviews and Other Writings, 1972–1977*, edited by Colin Gordon, translated by Colin Gordon, et al., Pantheon Books, 1980.

——. *The History of Sexuality: An Introduction.* Translated by Robert Hurley, vol. 1, Pantheon Books, 1978.

Fox, William. *A Short Account of the African Slave Trade, and an Address to the People of Great Britain on the Propriety of Abstaining from West Indian Sugar and Rum.* 11th ed., London, 1791.

Franklin, Caroline. '"Stand not on that brink!": Byron, Gender and Romantic Suicide'. *Byron and Marginality*, edited by Norbert Lennartz, Edinburgh UP, 2018, pp. 207–32.

French, Howard W. 'Slavery, Empire, Memory'. *The New York Review*. 7 April 2022. https://www.nybooks.com/articles/2022/04/07/slavery-empire-memory-britain-howard-french/. Accessed 20 July 2022.

Fulford, Tim, and Peter J. Kitson, editors. *Romanticism and Colonialism: Writing and Empire, 1780–1830*. Cambridge UP, 1998.

Gadpaille, Michelle. 'Trans-Colonial Collaboration and Slave Narrative: Mary Prince Revisited'. *ELOPE*, vol. 8, no. 2, 2011, pp. 63–77. https://doi.org/10.4312/elope.8.2.63-77. Accessed 1 February 2023.

Garnons, John. *Sermons on Various Subjects*. 1792. *The History of Suicide in England, 1650–1850. Sermons, Discourses, Essays and Treatises*. Part 2. Edited by Mark Robson, Paul S. Seaver, Kelly McGuire, Jeffrey Merrick, Daryl Lee, vol. 5, Routledge, 2013, pp. 337–45. https://doi.org/10.4324/9781003113942-22. Accessed 14 June 2023.

Gates, Barbara T. *Victorian Suicide: Mad Crimes and Sad Histories*. Princeton UP, 1988.

Gaudet, Katherine. 'Liberty and Death: Fictions of Suicide in the New Republic'. *Early American Literature*, vol. 47, no. 3, 2012, pp. 591–622. *JSTOR*, https://www.jstor.org/stable/41705692. Accessed 20 September 2019.

Genette, Gérard. *Paratexts: Thresholds of Interpretation*. Translated by Jane E. Lewin, foreword by Richard Macksey. Cambridge UP, 1997. *EBSCOhost*, search.ebscohost.com/login.aspx?direct=true&db=e000xna&AN=675642&site=ehost-live. Accessed 6 March 2023.

Get Out. Directed by Jordan Peele, Universal Pictures, 2017.

Gibson, Robert. *Best of Enemies: Anglo-French Relations Since the Norman Conquest*. 2nd ed., Impress Books, 1995, 2004.

Gilbert, Sandra M., and Susan Gubar. *The Madwoman in the Attic: The Woman Writer and the Nineteenth-Century Literary Imagination*. 2nd ed., Yale UP, 2000.

Glass, Loren. 'Blood and Affection: The Poetics of Incest in "Manfred" and "Parisina"'. *Studies in Romanticism*, vol. 34, no. 2, 1995, pp. 211–26. *JSTOR*, https://www.jstor.org/stable/25601113. Accessed 7 February 2024.

Godineau, Dominique. 'Pratiques du Suicide à Paris Pendant la Révolution Francaise'. *French History and Civilization: Papers from the George Rudé Seminar*, edited by Ian Coller, et al., no. 1, 2005, pp. 126–40. https://h-france.net/rude/wp-content/uploads/2017/08/vol1_Godineau1.pdf. Accessed 18 January 2024.

Godwin, William. *Memoirs of the Author of* A Vindication of the Rights of Woman. 1798. Edited by Pamela Clemit and Gina Luria Walker, Broadview, 2001.

——. *An Enquiry Concerning Political Justice, and Its Influence on General Virtue and Happiness*. Vol. 1, Dublin, 1793.

Goethe, Johann Wolfgang von. *The Sorrows of Young Werther*. Translated and introduced by David Constantine, Oxford UP, 2012. *ProQuest*, https://

ebookcentral.proquest.com/lib/umanitoba/detail.action?docID=5891581. Accessed 12 July 2022.

Golden, Ruth. 'Opening up about my mother's suicide was life-changing'. *CNN Opinion*, https://www.cnn.com/2019/09/18/opinions/suicide-loss-time-to-open-up-golden/index.html. Accessed 18 September 2019.

Gorton, John. *Tubal to Seba: The Negro Suicide. A Poem*. London, 1797. *Google Books*, https://books.google.ca/books?id=v65YAAAAcAAJ&lpg=PP17&dq=Tubal%20to%20Seba%3A%20The%20Negro%20Suicide.&pg=PP13#v=onepage&q=Tubal%20to%20Seba:%20The%20Negro%20Suicide.&f=false. Accessed 16 March 2020.

Grafton, Anthony, et al. *The Classical Tradition*. Harvard UP, 2010.

Gray, Thomas. 'The Bard: A Pindaric Ode'. 1757. *Representative Poetry Online*. University of Toronto. https://rpo.library.utoronto.ca/content/bard-pindaric-ode. Accessed 24 October 2018.

——. 'Elegy Written in a Country Churchyard'. 1751. *The Norton Anthology of English Literature*, edited by M. H. Abrams, vol. 1, 5th ed., W. W. Norton & Company, 1986, pp. 2480–3.

Green, Paul D. 'Suicide, Martyrdom, and Thomas More'. *Studies in the Renaissance*, vol. 19, 1972, pp. 135–55. *JSTOR*, DOI: 10.2307/2857090. https://www.jstor.org/stable/2857090. Accessed 5 April 2021.

Gregg, John. *Maurice Blanchot and the Literature of Transgression*. Princeton UP, 1994.

Gregory, George. *Essays Historical and Moral*. London, 1785.

Griffin, James. *On Human Rights*. Oxford UP, 2008.

Groom, Nick. 'The Death of Chatterton'. *From Gothic to Romantic: Thomas Chatterton's Bristol*, edited by Alistair Heys, Redcliffe Press, 2005, pp. 116–25.

Hale, Matthew. *Historia Placitorum Coronæ: The History of the Pleas of the Crown*. Vol. 1, London, 1778. *Google Books*, https://www.google.ca/books/edition/Historia_Placitorum_Coronae/PWpKAAAAYAAJ?hl=en&gbpv=1&dq=Historia+Placitorum+Coron%C3%A6+1778&pg=PA627&printsec=frontcover. Accessed 25 January 2022.

Hanson, Ellis. *Decadence and Catholicism*. Harvard UP, 1997.

Harriott, John. *The Religion of Philosophy, As Contra-distinguished from Modern French Philosophy: And as an Antidote to its Pernicious Effects Lately So Evident in the Prevalence of Assassination & Suicide*. London, 1812.

Hartman, Saidiya V. 'Venus in Two Acts'. *Small Axe: A Journal of Criticism*, vol. 26, no. 26, 2008, pp. 1–14. *ProjectMuse*, DOI:10.2979/SAX.2008.-.26.1. Accessed 27 October 2021.

——. *Scenes of Subjection: Terror, Slavery, and Self-Making in Nineteenth-Century America*. Oxford UP, 1997.

Hays, Mary. *The Victim of Prejudice*. 1799. Edited by Eleanor Ty, 2nd ed., Broadview Press, 1998.

Hebrews (The Epistle Paul the Apostle to). *The King James Version of the Bible*. n.p. *Project Gutenberg*, http://www.gutenberg.org/files/10/10-h/10-h.htm. Accessed 18 April 2020.

Heidegger, Martin. *Being and Time*. 1927. Translated by Joan Stambaugh, revised and foreword by Dennis J. Schmidt, SUNY Press, 2010.

Hemans, Felicia. 'The Bride of the Greek Isle'. *Records of Woman, with Other Poems*, edited by Paula R. Feldman, The UP of Kentucky, 1999, pp. 17–23.

EBSCOhost, search.ebscohost.com/login.aspx?direct=true&db=e000xna&AN=938104&site=ehost-live. Accessed 24 May 2023.

——. 'Imelda'. *Records of Woman, with Other Poems*, edited by Paula R. Feldman, The UP of Kentucky, 1999, pp. 35–9. *EBSCOhost*, search.ebscohost.com/login.aspx?direct=true&db=e000xna&AN=938104&site=ehost-live. Accessed 24 May 2023.

——. 'Indian Woman's Death-Song'. *Records of Woman, with Other Poems*, edited by Paula R. Feldman, The UP of Kentucky, 1999, pp. 57–9. *EBSCOhost*, search.ebscohost.com/login.aspx?direct=true&db=e000xna&AN=938104&site=ehost-live. Accessed 24 May 2023.

——. 'Pauline'. *Records of Woman, with Other Poems*, edited by Paula R. Feldman, The UP of Kentucky, 1999, pp. 63–7. *EBSCOhost*, search.ebscohost.com/login.aspx?direct=true&db=e000xna&AN=938104&site=ehost-live. Accessed 24 May 2023.

Herries, John. *An Address to the Public, On the Frequent and Enormous Crime of Suicide: Recommended to the Perusal of All who are Distressed in Mind, in Body, or in Worldly Circumstances*. 2nd ed., London, 1781. *Eighteenth-Century Collections Online*, link.gale.com/apps/doc/CW0105994046/ECCO?u=univmanitoba&sid=bookmark-ECCO&xid=e7db730e&pg=1. Accessed 14 May 2013.

Hertzman, Marc A. 'Fatal Differences: Suicide, Race, and Forced Labor in the Americas'. *The American Historical Review*, 2017, vol. 122, no. 2, pp. 317–45. *EBSCOhost*, https://doi.org/10.1093/ahr/122.2.317. Accessed 23 January 2024.

Higonnet, Margaret R. 'Frames of Female Suicide'. *Studies in the Novel*, vol. 32, no. 2, 2000, pp. 229–42. *JSTOR*, https://www.jstor.org/stable/29533392. Accessed 6 February 2013.

——. '"this winged nature fraught": Suicide and Agency in Women's Poetry'. *Literature Compass*, vol. 12, 2015, pp. 683–9. doi: 10.1111/lic3.12283. Accessed 2 June 2023.

——. 'Suicide: Representations of the Feminine in the Nineteenth Century'. *Poetics Today*, vol. 6, no. 1/2, 1985, pp. 103–18. *JSTOR*, https://www.jstor.org/stable/1772124. Accessed 5 February 2024.

Hogg, James. *The Private Memoirs and Confessions of a Justified Sinner*. 1824. Edited by Adrian Hunter, Broadview Press, 2001.

Houston, Robert. 'Fact, Truth, and the Limits of Sympathy: Newspaper Reporting of Suicide in the North of England, circa 1750–1830'. *Studies in the Literary Imagination*, vol. 44, no. 2, 2011, pp. 93–108.

——. *Punishing the Dead?: Suicide, Lordship, and Community in Britain, 1500–1830*. Oxford UP, 2010.

——. 'The Medicalization of Suicide: Medicine and the Law in Scotland and England, circa 1750–1850'. *Histories of Suicide: International Perspectives on Self-Destruction in the Modern World*, edited by John C. Weaver and David Wright, U of Toronto P, 2009, pp. 91–118.

Howard, Carol. 'Wollstonecraft's Thoughts on Slavery and Corruption'. *Eighteenth Century: Theory and Interpretation*, vol. 45, no. 1, 2004, pp. 61–86. *EBSCOhost*, http://uml.idm.oclc.org/login?url=https://search.ebscohost.com/login.aspx?direct=true&db=a9h&AN=18077500&site=ehost-live. Accessed 5 February 2024.

Hulse, Michael. Introduction to *The Sorrows of Young Werther*. By Johann Wolfgang von Goethe. Edited by Michael Hulse, Penguin, 1989, pp. 5–19.

Hume, David. *Essays on Suicide, and The Immortality of the Soul, Ascribed to the late David Hume, Esq. Never Before Published. With Remarks, Intended as an Antidote to the Poison Contained in These Performances, By the Editor*. London, 1783.

Hunt, Bishop C., Jr. 'Wordsworth and Charlotte Smith'. *The Wordsworth Circle*, vol. 1, 1970, pp. 85–103. *JSTOR*, http://www.jstor.org/stable/24039615. Accessed 24 May 2023.

Hurston, Zora Neale. *Their Eyes Were Watching God*. 1937. Foreword by Edwidge Danticat and afterword by Henry Louis Gates Jr, Amistad, 1999.

Ingram, Allan. *Boswell's Creative Gloom: A Study of Imagery and Melancholy in the Writings of James Boswell*. Barnes & Noble Books, 1982.

Ivey White, Newman. *Shelley*. Vol. 1. A. A. Knopf, 1940.

James, C. L. R. *The Black Jacobins: Toussaint L'Ouverture and the San Domingo Revolution*. 2nd ed., Vintage, 1989.

Job, The Book of. *The King James Version of the Bible*. n.p. *Project Gutenberg*, http://www.gutenberg.org/files/10/10-h/10-h.htm. Accessed 10 October 2019.

Johnson, Samuel. *Lives of the Most Eminent English Poets with Critical Observations on Their Works*. 1779. London, [1879]. *Google Books*, https://www.google.ca/books/edition/Lives_of_the_Most_Eminent_English_Poets/-RNCAAAAcAAJ?hl=en&gbpv=0. Accessed 25 January 2022.

Joiner, Thomas E. *Myths About Suicide*. Harvard UP, 2010.

Judges, The Book of. *The King James Version of the Bible*. *Project Gutenberg*, http://www.gutenberg.org/files/10/10-h/10-h.htm. Accessed 15 June 2020.

Kant, Immanuel. *Lectures on Ethics*. Translated by Peter Heath, edited by Peter Heath and J. B. Schneewind, Cambridge UP, 2001.

Katz, Brigit. 'Heavily Abridged "Slave Bible" Removed Passages That Might Encourage Uprisings'. *Smithsonian Magazine*, 4 January 2019, https://www.smithsonianmag.com/smart-news/heavily-abridged-slave-bible-removed-passages-might-encourage-uprisings-180970989/. Accessed 4 January 2019.

Keats, John. 'Oh Chatterton! how very sad thy fate'. 1848. *John Keats. Complete Poems*, edited by Jack Stillinger. The Belknap Press of Harvard UP, 1982, pp. 5–6.

——. 'Ode to a Nightingale'. 1820. *John Keats. Complete Poems*, edited by Jack Stillinger. The Belknap Press of Harvard UP, 1982, pp. 279–81.

——. *Endymion: A Poetic Romance*. *John Keats. Complete Poems*, edited by Jack Stillinger. The Belknap Press of Harvard UP, 1982, pp. 64–162.

Ketton-Cremer, Robert. *Thomas Gray*. Cambridge UP, 1955.

Kierkegaard, Søren. *Fear and Trembling*, edited by C. Stephen Evans and Sylvia Walsh, Cambridge UP, 2006.

Kingwell, Mark. 'In coronavirus quarantine, use boredom as a window to wisdom'. *Globe and Mail*. Prairie edition. 4 April 2020. O1-O6.

Klibansky, Raymond, and Ernest C. Mossner. *New Letters of David Hume*. Oxford UP, 2011.

Knapp, Andrew, and William Baldwin. *The Newgate Calendar; Comprising Interesting Memoirs of the Most Notorious Characters Who Have Been Convicted of Outrages on the Laws of England Since the Commencement of the Eighteenth Century; With Occasional Anecdotes and Observations,*

Speeches, Confessions, and Last Exclamations of Sufferers. Vol. 3, London, 1824? *Crime, Punishment, and Popular Culture, 1790–1920*. link.gale.com/apps/doc/BEOZRP688575252/CPPC?u=univmanitoba&sid=bookmark-CPPC&xid=007a6180&pg=1. Accessed 7 February 2024.

Koretsky, Deanna. *Death Rights: Romantic Suicide, Race, and the Bounds of Liberalism*. SUNY Press, 2021. *ProQuest*, https://ebookcentral.proquest.com/lib/umanitoba/detail.action?docID=6499940. Accessed 13 July 2021.

——. 'The Interracial Marriage Plot: Suicide and the Politics of Blood in Romantic-era Women's Fiction'. *Studies in the Literary Imagination*, vol. 51, no. 1, 2018, pp. 1–18. DOI: 10.1353/sli.2018.0001. Accessed 24 October 2021.

——. 'Habeas Corpus and the Politics of Freedom: Slavery and Romantic Suicide'. *Essays in Romanticism*, vol. 22, no. 1, 2015, pp. 21–33.

Kitson, Peter J. 'Fictions of Slave Resistance and Revolt: Robert Southey's *Poems on the Slave Trade* (1797) and Charlotte Smith's "The Story of Henrietta" (1800)'. *Race, Romanticism, and the Atlantic*, edited by Paul Youngquist, Routledge, 2013, pp. 107–23. https://doi.org/10.4324/9781315603384-5. Accessed 2 June 2023.

Land, Nick. *The Thirst for Annihilation: Georges Bataille and Virulent Nihilism*. Routledge: 1992. *Taylor & Francis*, https://doi.org/10.4324/9780203411902. Accessed 6 February 2024.

Langley, Eric. *Narcissism and Suicide in Shakespeare and his Contemporaries*. Oxford UP, 2009.

Lansdowne, Richard. Commentary. *Byron's Letters and Journals: A New Selection: From Leslie A. Marchand's Twelve-Volume Edition*. By Lord Byron. Edited by Richard Lansdowne, Oxford UP, 2015. *EBSCO Host*, search-ebscohost-com.uml.idm.oclc.org/login.aspx?direct=true&db=nlebk&AN=960656&site=ehost-live. Accessed 5 August 2021.

Lawlor, Clark. *Consumption and Literature: The Making of the Romantic Disease*. Palgrave, 2006.

Leask, Nigel. 'Lewis, Matthew Gregory. (1775–1818)'. *Oxford Dictionary of National Biography*, Oxford UP, 2004, https://doi-org.uml.idm.oclc.org/10.1093/ref:odnb/16597. Accessed 21 May 2021.

Lee, Debbie. *Slavery and the Romantic Imagination*. 2002. U of Pennsylvania P, 2004.

Lind, Vera. 'The Suicidal Mind and Body: Examples from Northern Germany'. *From Sin to Insanity: Suicide in Early Modern Europe*, edited by Jeffrey R. Watt, Cornell UP, 2004, pp. 64–80.

Livy. From *The History of Rome: The Rape of Lucretia*. In *The Ethics of Suicide: Historical Sources*, edited by Margaret Pabst Battin, Oxford UP, 2015, pp. 106–7. *ProQuest*, http://ebookcentral.proquest.com/lib/umanitoba/detail.action?docID=2145420. Accessed 2 April 2020.

Locke, John. *Two Treatises of Government*. 1689. London, 1821. *Internet Archive*, https://archive.org/details/twotreatisesofg00lockuoft. Accessed 25 March 2020.

London Lives. 'Coroners' Inquests into Suspicious Deaths (IC)'. *London Lives 1690 to 1800 – Crime, Poverty and Social Policy in the Metropolis*, https://www.londonlives.org/static/IC.jsp. Accessed 15 March 2021.

Long, Edward. *The History of Jamaica. Or, General Survey of the Antient and Modern State of that Island: With Reflections on Its Situation, Settlements,*

Inhabitants, Climate, Products, Commerce, Laws, and Government. T. Lowndes, 1774. 3 vols.

Long Hoeveler, Diane. 'Screen-Memories and Fictionalized Autobiography: Mary Shelley's *Mathilda* and "The Mourner"'. *Nineteenth-Century Contexts*, vol. 27, no. 4, 2005, pp. 365–81.

Loraux, Nicole. *Tragic Ways of Killing a Woman.* Translated by Anthony Forster, Harvard UP, 1991.

Macaulay Graham, Catharine. From *Letters on Education: With Observations on Religious and Metaphysical Subjects.* 1790. In *Mary, A Fiction* and *The Wrongs of Woman, or Maria.* 1788 and 1798. By Mary Wollstonecraft. Edited by Michelle Faubert, Broadview Press, 2012, pp. 311–16.

McConnell, Anita. 'Beckford, William Thomas (1760–1844), writer and art collector'. *Oxford Dictionary of National Biography*, Oxford University Press, 2009, https://www-oxforddnb-com.uml.idm.oclc.org/view/10.1093/ref:odnb/9780198614128.001.0001/odnb-9780198614128-e-1905. Accessed 14 February 2024.

Macdonald, D. L. *Poor Polidori: A Critical Biography of the Author of* The Vampyre. U of Toronto P, 1991. *EBSCOhost*, search.ebscohost.com/login.aspx?direct=true&db=e000xna&AN=682304&site=ehost-live. 7 February 2024.

MacDonald, Michael. 'The Secularization of Suicide in England 1660–1800'. *Past and Present*, no. 111, 1986, pp. 50–100. *JSTOR*, https://www.jstor.org/stable/650502. Accessed 19 January 2024.

MacDonald, Michael, and Terence R. Murphy. *Sleepless Souls: Suicide in Early Modern England.* Clarendon Press, 1990.

McGowan, Michael, director. *All My Puny Sorrows.* 2021. Carousel Pictures, et al. Canada.

McGuire, Kelly. '"I leave thee not": Felicia Hemans and Maternal Suicide'. *Studies in the Literary Imagination*, vol. 51, no. 1, 2018, pp. 121–37. DOI: 10.1353/sli.2018.0007. Accessed 3 October 2021.

——. *Dying to be English: Suicide Narratives and National Identity, 1721–1814.* Pickering & Chatto Publishers, 2012. *Proquest*, https://ebookcentral.proquest.com/lib/umanitoba/detail.action?docID=1035034. Accessed 25 January 2022.

McNay, Lois. *Foucault and Feminism: Power, Gender and the Self.* Polity Press, 1992.

MacQueen, James. *The West India Colonies: The Calumnies and Misrepresentations Circulated Against Them by the Edinburgh Review, Mr Clarkson, Mr Cropper, &c. &c.* London, 1824. *Google Books*, https://www.google.ca/books/edition/The_West_India_Colonies/PJ2kIpRKlz0C?hl=en&gbpv=1&dq=The+West+India+Colonies:+The+Calumnies+and+Misrepresentations+Circulated+Against+Them&printsec=frontcover. Accessed 30 April 2020.

Macready, William Charles. *Macready's Reminiscences, and Selections from His Diaries and Letters*, edited by Frederick Pollock, vol. 1, London, 1875. *Google Books*, https://www.google.ca/books/edition/Macready%CA%BCs_Reminiscences_and_Selections/CUwZFfyAiE4C?hl=en&gbpv=1&dq=Macready%E2%80%99s+Reminiscences,+and+Selections+from+His+Diaries+and+Letters&printsec=frontcover. Accessed 19 January 2024.

Makarychev, Andrey. 'Introduction. Biopower at Europe's Eastern Margins: New Facets of a Research Agenda'. *Journal of Contemporary Central and Eastern Europe*, vol. 26, no. 2–3, 2018, pp. 105–7. https://doi.org/10.1080/25739638.2018.1526491. Accessed 29 January 2022.

Makdisi, Saree. *William Blake and the Impossible History of the 1790s*. U of Chicago P, 2003.

Man Burrows, George. *Commentaries on the Causes, Forms, Symptoms, and Treatment, Moral and Medical, of Insanity*. London, 1828. *Google Books*, https://www.google.ca/books/edition/Commentaries_on_the_Causes_Forms_Symptom/tfARAAAAYAAJ?hl=en&gbpv=1&dq=Commentaries+on+the+Causes,+Forms,+Symptoms,+and+Treatment,+Moral+and+Medical,+of+Insanity&printsec=frontcover. Accessed 19 January 2024.

Marley, Bob. 'Buffalo Soldier'. *Confrontation*. By Bob Marley and the Wailers, Tuff Gong/Island Records, 1983.

Marsh, Ian. *Suicide: Foucault, History and Truth*. Cambridge UP, 2010.

Marshall, Florence A., editor. *The Life & Letters of Mary Wollstonecraft Shelley*. Vol. 1, London, 1889. *Google Books*, https://www.google.ca/books/edition/The_Life_Letters_of_Mary_Wollstonecraft/Mb0_AQAAMAAJ?hl=en&gbpv=1&dq=The+Life+and+Letters+of+Mary+Wollstonecraft+Shelley&printsec=frontcover. Accessed 5 February 2024.

Mays, J. C. C. Notes to 'The Suicide's Argument. With Nature's Answer'. 1811. By S. T. Coleridge. *The Collected Works of Samuel Taylor Coleridge: Poetical Works I Poems (Reading Text): PART* 2, edited by J. C. C. Mays, Princeton UP, 1969, p. 895.

Mbembe, Achille. 'Necropolitics'. Translated by Libby Meintjes. *Public Culture*, vol. 15, no. 1, 2003, pp. 11–40.

Medwin, Thomas. *Conversations of Lord Byron. Noted During a Residence with His Lordship at Pisa, in the Years 1821 and 1822*. London, 1824. *Google Books*, https://www.google.ca/books/edition/Conversations_of_Lord_Byron/vV75pOPkDL8C?hl=en&gbpv=1&dq=Conversations+with+Lord+Byron&printsec=frontcover. Accessed 6 February 2024.

Mehler Paperny, Anna. *Hello I Want to Die Please Fix Me: Depression in the First Person*. Penguin Random House Canada, 2019.

Melikan, R. A. 'Romilly, Sir Samuel (1757–1818)'. *Oxford Dictionary of National Biography*, Oxford UP, 2008, https://doi-org.uml.idm.oclc.org/10.1093/ref:odnb/24050. Accessed 19 May 2021.

Merrick, Jeffrey. 'Suicide and Politics in Pre-Revolutionary France'. *Eighteenth-Century Life*, vol. 30, no. 2, 2006, pp. 32–47. *Project MUSE*. muse.jhu.edu/article/198565. Accessed 18 January 2024.

Milton, John. From *Samson Agonistes*. 1671. *Representative Poetry Online*. University of Toronto, https://rpo.library.utoronto.ca/content/samson-agonistes-0. Accessed 29 April 2020.

Montaigne, Michel de. From *A Custom of the Isle of Cea*. In *The Ethics of Suicide: Historical Sources*, edited by Margaret Pabst Battin, Oxford UP, 2015, pp. 280–4. *ProQuest*, https://ebookcentral.proquest.com/lib/umanitoba/detail.action?docID=2145420. Accessed 23 July 2021.

Montesquieu. From *The Spirit of the Laws*. In *The Ethics of Suicide: Historical Sources*, edited by Margaret Pabst Battin, Oxford UP, 2015, pp. 395–6.

ProQuest, http://ebookcentral.proquest.com/lib/umanitoba/detail.action?docID=2145420. Accessed 26 March 2020.

Moore, Charles. *A Full Inquiry into the Subject of Suicide*. London, 1790. *HathiTrust*, https://catalog.hathitrust.org/Record/008622664. Accessed 27 March 2020.

Moore, Dafydd. 'Heroic Incoherence in James Macpherson's "The Poems of Ossian"'. *Eighteenth-Century Studies*, vol. 34, no. 1, 2000, pp. 43–59. *JSTOR*, http://www.jstor.org/stable/30054103. Accessed 15 January 2024.

Moore, John. *Zeluco: Various Views of Human Nature Taken from Life and Manners, Foreign and Domestic*. 2nd ed., London, 1789. *Google Books*, https://books.google.ca/books?redir_esc=y&id=b8I1AAAAMAAJ&q=cuba#v=snippet&q=cuba&f=false. Accessed 4 June 2021.

Moore, Marianne. 'To a Steam Roller'. *The Complete Poems of Marianne Moore*. Macmillan, 1967, p. 102.

Moore, Rebecca. *Women in Christian Traditions*. NYU Press, 2015. *EBSCOhost*, https://doi.org/10.18574/9781479817887. Accessed 6 February 2024.

Moore, Thomas. *The Life of Lord Byron. With the Letters and Journals*. Vol. 1. Philadelphia, 1869. *Google Books*, https://books.google.ca/books?id=AMYUAAAAYAAJ&printsec=frontcover#v=onepage&q&f=false. Accessed 6 February 2024.

More, Hannah. *Slavery, A Poem*. 1788. 'Poems Against Slavery'. *Brycchan Carey, Author and Academic*, https://brycchancarey.com/slavery/morepoems.htm. Accessed 14 January 2022.

More, Hannah, and Eaglesfield Smith. 'The Sorrows of Yamba, or The Negro Woman's Lamentation'. 1797. 'Poems Against Slavery'. *Brycchan Carey, Author and Academic*, https://brycchancarey.com/slavery/yamba.htm. Accessed 14 January 2022.

More, Thomas. From *Utopia*. 1516. *The Ethics of Suicide: Historical Sources*, edited by Margaret Pabst Battin, Oxford UP, 2015, p. 239. *ProQuest*, http://ebookcentral.proquest.com/lib/umanitoba/detail.action?docID=2145420. Accessed 26 March 2020.

Morris, Thomas. *Quashy, or, The Coal-Black Maid. A Tale*. London, 1796. *Google Books*, https://www.google.ca/books/edition/Quashy/SEJDAQAAMAAJ?hl=en&gbpv=1&pg=PA3&printsec=frontcover. Accessed 8 August 2022.

Mossner, E. C. 'Hume's Four Dissertations: An Essay in Biography and Bibliography'. *Modern Philology*, vol. 48, no. 1, 1950, pp. 37–57.

Murphy, Laura. *The New Slave Narrative: The Battle Over Representations of Contemporary Slavery*. Columbia UP, 2019. *EBSCOhost*, https://doi.org/10.7312/murp18824. Accessed 16 June 2022.

'Negroes'. By Le Romain, Jean-Baptiste-Pierre. *Encyclopédie ou Dictionnaire Raisonné des Sciences, des Arts et des Métiers*. 1762–72. *The Encyclopedia of Diderot & d'Alembert Collaborative Translation Project*. Translated by Pamela Cheek, Michigan Publishing, 2003, http://hdl.handle.net/2027/spo.did2222.0000.028. Accessed 26 June 2020.

Newton, Huey P. *Revolutionary Suicide*. 1973. Penguin, 2009.

[Newton, John.] *An Authentic Narrative of Some Remarkable and Interesting Particulars in the Life of ********. 4th ed. London, 1775. *Google Books*, https://www.google.ca/books/edition/An_Authentic_Narrative_of_Some_Remarkabl/viZPAAAAYAAJ?hl=en&gbpv=1&dq=1775+An+Authentic+Nar

rative+of+Some+Remarkable+and+Interesting+Particulars+in+the+Life+of&pg=PP7&printsec=frontcover. Accessed 13 October 2021.

Nitchie, E. 'Mary Shelley's "Mathilda": An Unpublished Story and its Biographical Significance'. *Studies in Philology*, vol. 40, no. 3, 1943, pp. 447–62. *JSTOR*, https://www.jstor.org/stable/4172624. Accessed 25 January 2022.

Nordius, Janina. Introduction and notes. *The Story of Henrietta*. 1800. By Charlotte Smith. Edited by Janina Nordius. Valancourt Books, 2012, pp. vii–xliii, pp. 149–66.

O'Dea, James. *Suicide: Studies on its Philosophy, Causes, and Prevention*. New York, 1882.

Osman, Sharifah Aishah. '"Mightier than death, untamable by fate": Felicia Hemans's Byronic Heroines and the Sorority of the Domestic Affections'. *Romanticism on the Net*, no. 43, 2006, https://doi.org/10.7202/013590ar. Accessed 12 August 2020.

Pabst Battin, Margaret, editor. Introductions to entries. *The Ethics of Suicide: Historical Sources*, edited by Margaret Pabst Battin, Oxford UP, 2015. *ProQuest*, https://ebookcentral.proquest.com/lib/umanitoba/detail.action?docID=2145420. Accessed 25 January 2022.

Paquet, Sandra Pouchet. *Caribbean Autobiography: Cultural Identity and Self-Representation*. U of Wisconsin P, 2002. *EBSCOhost*, search.ebscohost.com/login.aspx?direct=true&db=e000xna&AN=336116&site=ehost-live. Accessed 23 January 2024.

Paraschakis, Antonios, et al. 'Differences Between Suicide Victims Who Leave Notes and Those Who Do Not: A 2-Year Study in Greece'. *Crisis*, vol. 33, no. 6, 2012, pp. 344–9. doi:10.1027/0227-5910/a000150. Accessed 2 February 2024.

Paris, John Ayrton, and John Samuel Martin Fonblanque. *Medical Jurisprudence*. Vol. 2, London, 1823. *HathiTrust*, https://babel.hathitrust.org/cgi/pt?id=hvd.hc37hy&view=1up&seq=9&skin=2021. Accessed 25 January 2022.

Parisot, Eric. 'Living to Labour, Labouring to Live: The Problem of Suicide in Charlotte Smith's *Elegiac Sonnets*'. *Literature Compass*, vol. 12, no. 12, 2015, pp. 660–6. *JSTOR*, https://doi.org/10.1111/lic3.12286. Accessed 25 January 2022.

——. 'Suicide Notes and Popular Sensibility in the Eighteenth-Century British Press'. *Eighteenth-Century Studies*, vol. 47, no. 3, 2014, pp. 277–91. https://doi.org/10.1353/ecs.2014.0016. Accessed 5 February 2024.

Percy, Thomas. *Reliques of English Poetry*. 1765. Edited by Nick Groom, vol. 1, Routledge, 1996.

Phillips, David P. 'The Influence of Suggestion on Suicide: Substantive and Theoretical Implications of the Werther Effect'. *American Sociological Review*, vol. 39, no. 3, 1974, pp. 340–54. *JSTOR*, https://doi.org/10.2307/2094294. Accessed 19 January 2024.

Piggott, Solomon. *Suicide and Its Antidotes: A Series of Anecdotes and Actual Narratives, with Suggestions on Mental Distress*. London, 1824. *Google Books*, https://www.google.ca/books/edition/Suicide_and_Its_Antidotes/YQ6-VWSmgTIC?hl=en&gbpv=1&dq=Suicide+and+Its+Antidotes&printsec=frontcover. Accessed 9 March 2020.

Pinckard, George. *Notes on the West Indies: Including Observations Relative to the Creoles and Slaves of the Western Colonies and the Indian of South America: Interspersed with Remarks Upon the Seasoning Or Yellow Fever of Hot Climates*. 2 vols. London, 1816. *Google Books*, https://www.google.ca/books/edition/Notes_on_the_West_Indies/Fx0TAAAAYAAJ?hl=en&gbpv=1&dq=Notes+on+the+West+Indies&printsec=frontcover. Accessed 22 March 2024.

Planter. *West-India Trade and Islands. Commercial Reasons for the Non-abolition of the Slave Trade, in the West-India Islands, by a Planter. And Merchant*. London, 1789. *Google Books*, https://www.google.ca/books/edition/West_India_Trade_and_Islands_Commercial/0iJcAAAAcAAJ?hl=en&gbpv=1&dq=West-India+Trade+and+Islands&pg=PA1&printsec=frontcover. Accessed 30 April 2020.

Plato. From 'Phaedo: The Death of Socrates'. 360 bce. *The Ethics of Suicide: Historical Sources*, edited by Margaret Pabst Battin, Oxford UP, 2015, pp. 75–81. *ProQuest*, http://ebookcentral.proquest.com/lib/umanitoba/detail.action?docID=2145420. Accessed 26 March 2020.

Plutarch. From *Moralia: The Women of Miletus*. In *The Ethics of Suicide: Historical Sources*, edited by Margaret Pabst Battin, Oxford UP, 2015, p. 129. *ProQuest*, http://ebookcentral.proquest.com/lib/umanitoba/detail.action?docID=2145420. Accessed 25 April 2020.

Polwhele, Richard. 'The Unsex'd Females'. *The Longman Anthology of British Literature: The Romantics and Their Contemporaries*, edited by Susan Wolfson and Peter Manning, vol. 2A, 3rd ed., Pearson Longman, 2010, pp. 323–7.

Popkin, Richard H. Introduction. *Dialogues Concerning Natural Religion*. 1980. By David Hume. Edited by Richard H. Popkin. 2nd ed., Hackett Publishing, 1998, pp. vii–xx.

Porter, Roy. Introduction. *George Cheyne: The English Malady*. 1733. Edited and introduced by Roy Porter, Routledge, 1991, 2013, pp. ix–li.

Powell Jones, William. *Thomas Gray, Scholar: The True Tragedy of an Eighteenth-Century Gentleman*. Harvard UP, 1937.

Priestman, Martin. *Romantic Atheism: Poetry, and Freethought: 1780–1830*. Cambridge UP, 1999. *EBSCOhost*, https://doi.org/10.1017/CBO9780511484452. Accessed 6 February 2004.

Prince, John. *Self-Murder Asserted to be a Very Heinous Crime*; *In Opposition to all Arguments Brought by the Deists*, *To the Contrary*. London, 1709. *Eighteenth-Century Collections Online*, link.gale.com/apps/doc/CW0105366324/ECCO?u=univmanitoba&sid=bookmark-ECCO&xid=7faa7a6d&pg=1. Accessed 16 May 2012.

Prince, Mary. *The History of Mary Prince, a West Indian Slave: Related by Herself*. 1831. The University of North Carolina at Chapel Hill Library, 2017. *EBSCOhost*, https://doi.org/10.5149/9781469633299_prince. Accessed 2 October 2020.

Pringle, Thomas. Preface. *The History of Mary Prince, a West Indian Slave: Related by Herself*. 1831. By Mary Prince. The University of North Carolina at Chapel Hill Library, 2017, pp. i–ii. *EBSCOhost*, https://doi.org/10.5149/9781469633299_prince. Accessed 2 October 2020.

Prothero, Rowland E. Commentary. *The Works of Lord Byron, Letters and Journals*, edited by Roland E. Prothero, [location not given], 1898.

Project Gutenberg, http://www.gutenberg.org/files/8901/8901-h/8901-h.htm. Accessed 1 April 2020.

'Quashie, n.' *OED Online*, Oxford UP, September 2021, https://doi.org/10.1093/OED/3354015943. Accessed 15 November 2021.

Quinlan, Maurice J. 'William Cowper and the Unpardonable Sin'. *The Journal of Religion*, vol. 23, no. 2, 1943, pp. 110–16. *JSTOR*, https://www.jstor.org/stable/1198480. Accessed 22 February 2013.

Rajan, Tilottama. 'Mary Shelley's *Mathilda:* Melancholy and the Political Economy of Romanticism'. *Studies in the Novel*, vol. 26, no. 2, 1994, pp. 43–68.

Ramsay, James. *Objections to the Abolition of the Slave Trade, with Answers: To which are Prefixed, Strictures on a Late Publication, Intitled, 'Considerations on the Emancipation of Negroes, and the Abolition of the Slave Trade, by a West India Planter'*. 2nd ed., London, 1788. *Google Books*, https://www.google.ca/books/edition/Objections_to_the_Abolition_of_the_Slave/axzFeRsksP0C?hl=en&gbpv=1&dq=Objections+to+the+Abolition+of+the+Slave+Trade&printsec=frontcover. Accessed 1 May 2020.

——. *An Essay on the Treatment and Conversion of African Slaves in the British Sugar Colonies*. James Phillips, 1784. *Google Books*, https://www.google.ca/books/edition/An_Essay_on_the_Treatment_and_Conversion/Zf9AAAAAcAAJ?hl=en&gbpv=1&dq=An+Essay+on+the+Treatment+and+Conversion+of+African+Slaves&printsec=frontcover. Accessed 16 August 2020.

Rediker, Marcus. *The Slave Ship: A Human History*. Penguin, 2007.

Reid, John. *Essays on Insanity, Hypochondriasis, and Other Nervous Affections*. London, 1816. *Google Books*, https://www.google.ca/books/edition/Essays_on_Insanity_Hypochondriasis_and_O/yDBAAQAAMAAJ?hl=en&gbpv=1&dq=Essays+on+Insanity,+Hypochondriasis&printsec=frontcover. Accessed 28 May 2021.

Repo, Jemima. *The Biopolitics of Gender*. Oxford UP, 2015.

Reynolds, Nicole. 'Suicide, Romance, and Imperial Rebellion: Sati and the Lucretia Story in Sydney Owenson's *The Missionary: An Indian Tale*'. *Literature Compass*, vol. 12, no. 12, 2015, pp. 675–82. https://doi.org/10.1111/lic3.12287. Accessed 25 January 2022.

Richardson, Alan. 'Byron and the Theatre'. *The Cambridge Companion to Byron*, edited by Drummond Bone, Cambridge UP, 2004, pp. 133–50. *ProQuest*, https://uml.idm.oclc.org/login?url=https://www.proquest.com/books/byron-theatre/docview/2137988915/se-2. Accessed 7 February 2024.

Richardson, Samuel. *Clarissa, or The History of a Young Lady*. 1747–8. Edited by Angus Ross, Viking, 1985.

Robinson, Jeffrey C. 'The Poetics of Expiration: Felicia Hemans'. *Romanticism on the Net*, vol. 29–30, 2003, https://doi.org/10.7202/007715ar. Accessed 15 February 2019.

Robinson, Mary. 'The Negro Girl'. 1800. *Selected Poems*, edited by Judith Pascoe, Broadview Press, 2000, pp. 234–9.

——. *A Letter to the Women of England* and *The Natural Daughter*. 1799. Edited by Sharon M. Setzer, Broadview Press, 2003.

——. 'Sonnet XLII'. *Sappho and Phaon. In a Series of Legitimate Sonnets, with Thoughts on Poetical Subjects*. London, 1796, p. 80. *Online Archive of California*, https://oac.cdlib.org/view?docId=kt929016dt&brand=oac4&doc.view=entire_text. Accessed 15 June 2023.

——. 'Monody to the Memory of Chatterton'. *A Celebration of Woman Writers*. University of Pennsylvania. https://digital.library.upenn.edu/women/robinson/1791/1791-chatterton.html. Accessed 19 January 2024.

Roscoe, William. *The Wrongs of Africa, A Poem. Part the First*. 1787. 'Poems Against Slavery'. *Brycchan Carey, Author and Academic*, https://brycchancarey.com/slavery/roscoe1.htm. Accessed 14 January 2022.

Rousseau, G. S. 'Nerves, Spirits, and Fibres: Towards Defining the Origins of Sensibility'. *Studies in the Eighteenth Century III: Papers Presented at the Third David Nichol Smith Memorial Seminar*, edited by R. F. Brissenden, U of Toronto P, 1976, pp. 137–57.

Rousseau, Jean-Jacques. *Julie, Or, The New Heloise: Letters of Two Lovers who Live in a Small Town*. 1761. Edited by Philip Stewart and Jean Vaché. UP of New England, 1997. *ProQuest*, https://ebookcentral.proquest.com/lib/umanitoba/detail.action?docID=1084937. Accessed 19 January 2024.

——. *La Nouvelle Héloïse. Julie, or The New Eloise*. 1761. Translated by Judith McDowell, Pennsylvania State UP, 1968.

Rowley, William. *A Treatise on Female, Nervous, Hysterical, Hypochondriacal, Bilious, Convulsive Diseases; Apoplexy and Palsy; with thoughts on Madness, Suicide, &c.* London, 1788. *Eighteenth Century Collections Online*, link.gale.com/apps/doc/CW0107178100/ECCO?u=univmanitoba&sid=bookmark-ECCO&xid=a490655a&pg=353. Accessed 19 January 2024.

Ryan, Edward. *The History of the Effects of Religion on Mankind*. Vol. 2. London, 1793. *Eighteenth Century Collections Online*, link.gale.com/apps/doc/CB0131912523/ECCO?u=univmanitoba&sid=bookmark-ECCO&xid=39ab789a&pg=1. Accessed 25 January 2022.

Samraj, Betty, and Jean Mark Gawron. 'The Suicide Note as a Genre: Implications for Genre Theory'. *Journal of English for Academic Purposes*, vol. 19, no. 25, 2015, pp. 88–101. *CRKN Elsevier Additional Journals*. https://doi.org/10.1016/j.jeap.2015.04.006. Accessed 5 February 2024.

Sánchez-Eppler, Karen. *Touching Liberty: Abolition, Feminism and the Politics of the Body*, U of California P, 1993.

Sancho, Ignatius. *Letters of the Late Ignatius Sancho, an African*. 1782. Edited by Vincent Carretta, Broadview Press, 2015.

Sanderson, Richard K. 'Glutting the Maw of Death: Suicide and Procreation in *Frankenstein*'. *South Central Review*, vol. 9, no. 2, 1992, pp. 49–64. *JSTOR*, https://doi.org/10.2307/3189529. Accessed 25 January 2022.

Schama, Simon. *Citizens: A Chronicle of the French Revolution*. Vintage Books, 1989.

Schlenther, Boyd Stanley. 'Whitefield, George (1714–1770), Calvinistic Methodist leader'. *Oxford Dictionary of National Biography*, Oxford UP, 2004, https://doi-org.uml.idm.oclc.org/10.1093/ref:odnb/29281. Accessed 15 November 2021.

Schopenhauer, Arthur. 'On Suicide'. *The Essays of Arthur Schopenhauer. Studies in Pessimism*. Vol. 4. Translated by T. Bailey Saunders. Pennsylvania State UP, 2005, pp. 22–7.

Schuller, Kyla. *The Biopolitics of Feeling: Race, Sex, and Science in the Nineteenth Century*. Duke UP, 2018. *ProQuest*, https://ebookcentral.proquest.com/lib/umanitoba/detail.action?docID=5208903. Accessed 24 January 2024.

Seaver, Paul S. 'Suicide and the Vicar General in London: A Mystery Solved?' *From Sin to Insanity: Suicide in Early Modern Europe*, edited by Jeffrey R. Watt, Cornell UP, 2004, pp. 25–47.

Seaver, Paul. S. et al., editors. *The History of Suicide in England, 1650–1850*. Pickering & Chatto, 2012–13.

Select Parts of the Holy Bible, For the Use of the Negro Slaves, in the British West-India Islands. Law and Gilbert, 1807.

Seneca. From 'Letter 70: On the Proper Time to Slip the Cable'. 65 bce? *The Ethics of Suicide: Historical Sources*, edited by Margaret Pabst Battin, Oxford UP, 2015, pp. 109–11. *ProQuest*, http://ebookcentral.proquest.com/lib/umanitoba/detail.action?docID=2145420. Accessed 2 April 2020.

——. *Selected Letters*. Translated and introduced by Elaine Fantham, Oxford UP, 2010.

Sennett, Richard. 'Introduction'. *On Suicide*. 1897. By Émile Durkheim. Translated by Robin Buss, introduced by Richard Sennett, notes by Alexander Riley, Penguin, 2006, pp. xi–xxiv.

Sha, Richard C. *Perverse Romanticism*, Johns Hopkins UP, 2009. *Project MUSE*, doi:10.1353/book.3494. Accessed 15 June 2022.

Shain, Barry Alan. *The Myth of American Individualism: The Protestant Origins of American Political Thought*. Princeton UP, 1996.

Shakespeare, William. *The Tragedy of Hamlet, Prince of Denmark*. In *William Shakespeare: Complete Works*, edited by Jonathan Bate and Eric Rasmussen, The Modern Library, 2007, pp. 1924–99.

Shapiro, Stephen. 'Mass African Suicide and the Rise of Euro-American Sentimentalism: Equiano's and Stevenson's Tales of the Semi-Periphery'. *Revolutions & Watersheds: Transatlantic Dialogues, 1775–1815*, edited by W. M. Verhoeven and Beth Dolan Kautz, Rodopi, 1999, pp. 123–44.

Sharp, Granville. *A Tract on the Law of Nature and Principles of Action in Man*. 2nd ed., London, 1777, 1809. *Google Books*, https://www.google.ca/books/edition/A_Tract_on_the_Law_of_Nature_and_princip/YHtjAAAAcAAJ?hl=en&gbpv=1. Accessed 19 January 2024.

Shelley, Harriet. 'Harriet Shelley's Suicide Letter'. ?7 December 1816. *Shelley's Ghost: Reshaping the Image of a Literary Family*, https://wayback.archive-it.org/org-467/20160519095811/http://shelleysghost.bodleian.ox.ac.uk/harriet-shelleys-suicide-letter. Accessed 10 March 2020.

Shelley, Mary. *The Letters of Mary Wollstonecraft Shelley*, edited by Betty T. Bennett, vol. 1, Johns Hopkins UP, 1980.

——. *Mathilda*. 1959. Edited by Michelle Faubert, Broadview Press, 2017.

——. 'The Mourner'. *The Keepsake*, edited by Frederic Mansel Reynolds, London, 1830, pp. 71–97.

——. *The Last Man*. 1826. Edited by Anne McWhir, Broadview Press, 1996.

——. *Frankenstein; or, The Modern Prometheus*. 1818. Edited by Kathleen Scherf and D. L. MacDonald, 3rd ed., Broadview Press, 2012.

Shelley, Percy Bysshe. 'England in 1819'. 1839. *Romanticism: An Anthology*, edited by Duncan Wu, Blackwell Publishers, 1996, p. 876.

——. 'The Mask of Anarchy'. 1832. *Romanticism: An Anthology*, edited by Duncan Wu, Blackwell Publishers, 1996, pp. 943–53.

——. 'Adonais'. 1821. *Romanticism: An Anthology*, edited by Duncan Wu, Blackwell Publishers, 1996, pp. 969–87.

——. 'Alastor; or, The Spirit of Solitude'. 1816. *Romanticism: An Anthology*, edited by Duncan Wu, Blackwell Publishers, 1996, pp. 834–52.

Sherwood, Marika. *After Abolition: Britain and the Slave Trade Since 1807*. I. B. Tauris & Co., 2007.

Simpson, Michael. *Closet Performances: Political Exhibition and Prohibition in the Dramas of Byron and Shelley*. Stanford UP, 1998.

'Slave trade'. *Encyclopédie ou Dictionnaire Raisonné des Sciences, des Arts et des Métiers*. 1762–72. By Louis Jaucourt. Translated by Stephanie Noble. *The Encyclopedia of Diderot & d'Alembert Collaborative Translation Project*. Michigan Publishing, 2007, http://hdl.handle.net/2027/spo.did2222.0000.114. Accessed 7 May 2021.

Smith, Adam. *The Theory of Moral Sentiments*. 2nd ed., London, 1761. *Google Books*, https://www.google.ca/books/edition/The_Theory_of_Moral_Sentiments/xVkOAAAAQAAJ?hl=en&gbpv=1&dq=The+Theory+of+Moral+Sentiments+1759&printsec=frontcover. Accessed 25 January 2022.

Smith, Charlotte. *The Poems of Charlotte Smith*, edited by Stuart Curran, Oxford UP, 1993.

——. *Beachy Head: With Other Poems*. London, 1807. *Proquest*, https://www.proquest.com/docview/2147605166/Z200488842/CD0A14B5667B4EBDPQ/1?accountid=14569. Accessed 2 June 2023.

——. *The Story of Henrietta*. 1800. Introduction and notes by Janina Nordius, Valancourt Books, 2012.

——. 'The Little West Indian'. 1796. *The Works of Charlotte Smith*. 1st ed., vol. 12, edited by Elizabeth A. Dolan, Routledge, 2007, pp. 117–24. https://doi.org/10.4324/9780429348884-16. Accessed 2 February 2024.

——. *Desmond*. 1792. Edited by Antje Blank and Janet Todd, Broadview Press, 2001.

Smith, Charlotte Turner. *Elegiac Sonnets, and Other Essays*. 2nd ed., London, 1784. *Eighteenth Century Collections Online*, link.gale.com/apps/doc/CW0111304415/ECCO?u=univmanitoba&sid=bookmark-ECCO&xid=b7241fa4&pg=1. Accessed 9 August 2024.

Smith, Sidonie. *Where I'm Bound: Patterns of Slavery and Freedom in Black American Autobiography*. Greenwood Press, 1974.

Smock, Ann. 'Translator's Introduction'. *The Space of Literature: A Translation of 'l'Espace Littéraire'*. By Maurice Blanchot. Translated and introduced by Ann Smock, U of Nebraska Press, 2015, pp. 1–15.

Snyder, Terri L. *The Power to Die: Slavery and Suicide in British North America*. The U of Chicago P, 2015. *EBSCOhost*, search-ebscohost-com.uml.idm.oclc.org/login.aspx?direct=true&db=nlebk&AN=1044859&site=ehost-live. Accessed 15 December 2017.

——. 'Suicide, Slavery, and Memory in North America'. *The Journal of American History*, vol. 97, no. 1, 2010, pp. 39–62. *EBSCO Host*, https://doi.org/10.2307/jahist/97.1.39. Accessed 5 May 2017.

Southey, Robert. *History of Brazil*. Vol. 3, London, 1819. *HathiTrust*, https://babel.hathitrust.org/cgi/pt?id=gri.ark:/13960/t6j115964&view=1up&seq=9&skin=2021. Accessed 25 January 2022.

——. 'The Sailor Who Had Served in the Slave-Trade'. 1798. *The Longman Anthology of British Literature*, edited by David Damrosch and Kevin J. H. Dettmar, et al., vol. 2A, 3rd ed., Pearson, 2012, pp. 246–9.

Sowell, Thomas. 'Malthus and the Utilitarians'. *The Canadian Journal of Economics and Political Science / Revue Canadienne d'Economique et de Science Politique*, vol. 28, no. 2, 1962, pp. 268–74.

Srinivasan, Amia. 'This won't hurt'. Review of *Notes on Suicide*, by Simon

Critchley. *TLS: Times Literary Supplement*, issue 5890, p. 24. Accessed 19 February 2016.

St Clair, William. *The Godwins and the Shelleys: The Biography of a Family*. Johns Hopkins UP, 1989.

St Luke. *The King James Version of the Bible*. n.p. *Project Gutenberg*, http://www.gutenberg.org/files/10/10-h/10-h.htm. Accessed 7 October 2019.

St Mark. *The King James Version of the Bible*. n.p. *Project Gutenberg*, http://www.gutenberg.org/files/10/10-h/10-h.htm. Accessed 10 October 2019.

St Matthew. *The King James Version of the Bible*. n.p. *Project Gutenberg*, http://www.gutenberg.org/files/10/10-h/10-h.htm. Accessed 7 October 2019.

Sterne, Laurence. *A Sentimental Journey*. 1768. William Tegg, 1868.

Stewart, William. *An A-Z of Counselling Theory and Practice*. 1992. 4th ed., Nelson Thornes, 2005.

'Suicide'. *The Encyclopedia of Diderot & d'Alembert Collaborative Translation Project*. Translated by Jeffrey Merrick. Michigan Publishing, 2003, http://hdl.handle.net/2027/spo.did2222.0000.346. Accessed 16 March 2020.

Sunstein, Emily W. *Mary Shelley: Romance and Reality*. Johns Hopkins UP, 1989.

Swift, Jonathan. *A Modest Proposal for Preventing the Children of Poor People from Being a Burden to Their Parents or the Country, and for Making Them Beneficial to the Country*. 3rd ed., Dublin, 1730.

Sym, John. From 'Lifes Preservative against Self-Killing'. 1637. *The Ethics of Suicide: Historical Sources*, edited by Margaret Pabst Battin, Oxford UP, 2015, pp. 297–8. *ProQuest*, http://ebookcentral.proquest.com/lib/umanitoba/detail.action?docID=2145420. Accessed 26 March 2020.

Szasz, Thomas. *Suicide Prohibition: The Shame of Medicine*. Syracuse UP, 2011.

——. *Fatal Freedom: The Ethics and Politics of Suicide*. Syracuse UP, 1999.

Taylor, Chloë. 'Biopower'. *Understanding Foucault, Understanding Modernism*, edited by David Scott, Laci Mattison, Paul Ardoin, and S. E. Gontarski, Bloomsbury, 2017, pp. 237–8.

——. 'Foucault and Familial Power'. *Hypatia*, vol. 27, no. 1, 2012, pp. 201–18. *JSTOR*, https://www.jstor.org/stable/41328905. Accessed 22 June 2022.

Taylor, Michael. 'British Proslavery Arguments and the Bible, 1823–1833'. *Slavery & Abolition*, vol. 37, no. 1, 2016, pp. 139–58, DOI: 10.1080/0144039X.2015.1093394. Accessed 13 July 2021. https://publicdomainreview.org/collection/the-newgate-calendar-1795. Accessed 21 May 2021.

The Public Domain Review. 'The Newgate Calendar'. https://publicdomainreview.org/collection/the-newgate-calendar-1795. Accessed 21 May 2021.

The Times Digital Archive. *Gale Primary Sources*, com.uml.idm.oclc.org/apps/doc/CS51009858/GDCS?u=univmanitoba&sid=bookmark-GDCS&xid=bea73737. Accessed 12 July 2020.

Thomas, Helen. *Romanticism and Slave Narratives: Transatlantic Testimonies*. Cambridge UP, 2000. *EBSCOhost*, search-ebscohost-com.uml.idm.oclc.org/login.aspx?direct=true&db=e000xna&AN=77514&site=ehost-live. Accessed 17 April 2020.

Thorsona, Jan, and Per-Arne Öbergb. 'Was There a Suicide Epidemic after Goethe's *Werther*?' *Archives of Suicide Research*, vol. 7, no. 1, 2003, pp. 69–72. *EBSCO-host*, https://doi.org/10.1080/13811110301568. Accessed 19 January 2024.

Thorvaldsen, Gunnar. *Censuses and Census Takers: A Global History*. Routledge, 2018. *EBSCOhost*, https://doi.org/10.4324/9781315148502. Accessed 19 July 2021.

Todd, Janet. *Gender, Art, and Death*. Polity Press, 1993.

Toews, Miriam. *All My Puny Sorrows*. Knopf Canada, 2014.

Tomlins, Elizabeth Sophia. 'The Slave'. *Tributes of Affection: with The Slave; and Other Poems. By a Lady; and her Brother*. London, 1797, pp. 87–102. *Eighteenth-Century Collections Online*, link.gale.com/apps/doc/CW0111246336/ECCO?u=univmanitoba&sid=bookmark-ECCO&xid=8a31478d&pg=1. Accessed 25 January 2022.

Tuite, Clara. *Lord Byron and Scandalous Celebrity*. Cambridge UP, 2015.

van Hooff, Anton J. L. *From Autothanasia to Suicide: Self-killing in Classical Antiquity*. Routledge, 1990. *EBSCOhost*, https://doi.org/10.4324/9780203032930. Accessed 2 February 2024.

Voltaire. 'Cato. On Suicide, and the Abbe St Cyran's Book Legitimating Suicide'. *The Works of Voltaire. A Contemporary Version. A Critique and Biography*, edited by John Morley, notes by Tobias Smollett, translated by William F. Fleming, vol. 4, E. R. DuMont, 1901. *Online Library of Liberty*, https://oll.libertyfund.org/title/fleming-the-works-of-voltaire-vol-iv-philosophical-dictionary-part-2#lf0060-04_head_011. Accessed 13 July 2021.

Walker, Daniel E. 'Suicidal Tendencies: African Transmigration in the History and Folklore of the Americas'. *The Griot*, vol. 18, no. 2, 1999, pp. 10–18.

Walling, Mary Anne. 'Suicide Contagion'. *Current Trauma Reports*, vol. 7, no. 4, 2021, pp. 103–14. https://doi.org/10.1007/s40719-021-00219-9. Accessed 25 March 2022.

Walsh, Robert, Jr. 'The Life of Dr Cotton'. *The Works of the British Poets, with Lives of the Authors*. Vol. 35, Boston, 1822, pp. 313–17. *HathiTrust*, https://babel.hathitrust.org/cgi/pt?id=nyp.33433067302442&seq=423&q1=dr+cotton. Accessed 23 January 2024.

Wang, Shou-Ren. *The Theatre of the Mind: A Study of Unacted Drama in Nineteenth-Century*. Palgrave Macmillan, 1990.

Watt, Jeffrey R. 'Introduction: Toward a History of Suicide in Early Modern Europe'. *From Sin to Insanity: Suicide in Early Modern Europe*, edited by Jeffrey R. Watt, Cornell UP, 2004, pp. 1–8.

——. 'Suicide, Gender, and Religion: The Case of Geneva'. *From Sin to Insanity: Suicide in Early Modern Europe*, edited by Jeffrey R. Watt, Cornell UP, 2004, pp. 138–57.

——. *Choosing Death: Suicide and Calvinism in Early Modern Geneva*. Truman State UP, 2001.

Wedderburn, Robert. *The Horrors of Slavery; Exemplified in the Life and History of the Rev. Robert Wedderburn*. London, 1824. *Google Books*, https://www.google.ca/books/edition/The_Horrors_of_Slavery_Exemplified_in_th/-uEvYjI0XVoC?hl=en&gbpv=1&dq=horrors+of+slavery+wedderburn&printsec=frontcover. Accessed 23 April 2020.

Wehmeyer, Peggy. 'What Lies in Suicide's Wake'. *The New York Times*. 7 September 2019, https://www.nytimes.com/2019/09/12/opinion/suicide-prevention.html. Accessed 25 January 2022.

Wehrs, Donald R. 'Desire and Duty in *La Nouvelle Héloïse*'. *Modern Language Studies*, vol. 18, no. 2, 1988, pp. 79–88. https://doi.org/10.2307/3194768. Accessed 12 August 2022.

Weinbaum, Alys Eve. *The Afterlife of Reproductive Slavery: Biocapitalism and Black Feminism's Philosophy of History*. Duke UP, 2019, https://doi.org/10.1215/9781478003281-001. Accessed 23 May 2020.

Wesley, John. *The Works of the Rev. John Wesley. Containing, Tracts and Letters on Various Subjects*. Vol. 10, New York, 1827. *Google Books*, https://www.google.ca/books/edition/The_Works_of_the_Rev_John_Wesley_Tracts/FokYAAAAYAAJ?hl=en&gbpv=1&dq=The+Works+of+the+Rev.+John+Wesley.+Containing,+Tracts+and+Letters+on+Various+Subjects&printsec=frontcover. Accessed 2 February 2024.

West-India Planter. *Considerations on the Emancipation of Negroes and on the Abolition of the Slave-trade. By a West-India Planter*. London, 1788. *Slavery and Anti-Slavery: A Transnational Archive*, link.gale.com/apps/doc/U0102138640/SAS?u=univmanitoba&sid=bookmark-SAS&xid=b09b407f&pg=1. Accessed 25 January 2022.

Wheeler, Michael. 'Martin Heidegger'. *The Stanford Encyclopedia of Philosophy*, edited by Edward N. Zalta, 2020, https://plato.stanford.edu/archives/fall2020/entries/heidegger/. Accessed 4 August 2020.

White, Daniel E. *Early Romanticism and Religious Dissent*. Cambridge UP, 2007.

Whyte, Jessica. '"The work of men is not durable": History, Haiti and the Rights of Man'. *Agamben and Colonialism*, edited by Marcelo Svirsky and Simone Bignall, Edinburgh UP, 2012, pp. 239–60. *EBSCOhost*, https://doi.org/10.3366/j.ctt1g0b67k.15. Accessed 3 July 2020.

Wiltshire, John. *Frances Burney and the Doctors: Patient Narratives Then and Now*. Cambridge UP, 2019.

Winter, Kari J. *Subjects of Slavery, Agents of Change: Women and Power in Gothic Novels and Slave Narratives, 1790–1865*. U of Georgia P, 1992.

Wolfson, Susan, and Peter Manning. Introduction to *Manfred. The Longman Anthology of British Literature: The Romantics and Their Contemporaries*, edited by Susan Wolfson and Peter Manning, vol. 2A, 3rd ed., Pearson Longman, 2010, pp. 659–60.

——. Notes. *The Longman Anthology of British Literature: The Romantics and Their Contemporaries*, edited by Susan Wolfson and Peter Manning, vol. 2A, 3rd ed., Pearson Longman, 2006, *passim*.

Wollstonecraft, Mary. *The Collected Letters of Mary Wollstonecraft*, edited by Janet Todd, Columbia UP, 2003.

——. *Mary, A Fiction* and *The Wrongs of Woman, or Maria*. 1788 and 1798. Edited by Michelle Faubert, Broadview Press, 2012.

——. *The Vindications: The Rights of Men* and *The Rights of Woman*. 1790 and 1792. Edited by D. L. Macdonald and Kathleen Scherf, Broadview Press, 1997.

——. Review of *The Interesting Narrative of the Life of Olaudah Equiano, or Gustavus Vassa, the African. Written by Himself. The Analytical Review, Or History of Literature, Domestic and Foreign, on an Enlarged Plan*. Vol. 4, London, 1789. *Google Books*, https://books.google.ca/books?id=2O4vAAAAYAAJ&pg=PA27&dq=The+Analytical+Review+equiano+J.+

Johnson,+1789&hl=en&sa=X&ved=0ahUKEwiWxIWh7qLWAhUh_4MKHe-HoDj8Q6AEINjAD#v=onepage&q=The%20Analytical%20Review%20equiano%20J.%20Johnson%2C%201789&f=false. Accessed 25 February 2013.

Wood, James. Introduction. *The Myth of Sisyphus*. By Albert Camus. 1955. Translated by Justin O'Brian, introduced by James Wood, Penguin, 2000, pp. vii–xx.

Wood, Marcus. *Slavery, Empathy, and Pornography*. Oxford UP, 2002. *EBSCOhost*, search-Ebscohost-com.uml.idm.oclc.org/login.aspx?direct=true&db=e000xna&AN=150002&site=ehost-live. Accessed 17 April 2020.

Wordsworth, William. 'Resolution and Independence'. 1807. *The Longman Anthology of British Literature: The Romantics and Their Contemporaries*, edited by Susan Wolfson and Peter Manning, vol. 2A, 3rd ed., Pearson Longman, 2006, pp. 520–4.

——. 'It is not to be Thought of'. 1803. *Representative Poetry Online*. University of Toronto. https://rpo.library.utoronto.ca/content/it-not-be-thought. Accessed 19 October 2021.

——. 'To Toussaint L'Ouverture'. 1803. *The Longman Anthology of British Literature*, edited by David Damrosch and Kevin J. H. Dettmar, et al., vol. 2A, 3rd ed., Pearson, 2012, pp. 259–60.

——. From Preface to *Lyrical Ballads*. 1800, 1802. *The Longman Anthology of British Literature: The Romantics and Their Contemporaries*, edited by Susan Wolfson and Peter Manning, vol. 2A, 3rd ed., Pearson Longman, 2006, pp. 408–20.

——. 'The Complaint of a Forsaken Indian Woman'. *Wordsworth and Coleridge: Lyrical Ballads*, edited with introduction, notes and appendices by R. L. Brett and A. R. Jones, Routledge, 2005, pp. 151–3. https://doi.org/10.4324/9780203823613. Accessed 30 May 2024.

——. 'The Mad Mother'. *Wordsworth and Coleridge: Lyrical Ballads*, edited with introduction, notes and appendices by R. L. Brett and A. R. Jones, Routledge, 2005, pp. 127–30. https://doi.org/10.4324/9780203823613. Accessed 30 May 2024.

——. 'Argument for Suicide'. 1797. *The Cornell Wordsworth: The Borderers*, edited by Robert Osborn, Cornell UP, 1982, p. 810.

Wright, Eamon. *British Women Writers and Race, 1788–1818: Narrations of Modernity*. Palgrave Macmillan, 2005.

Young, Bryanne. '"Killing the Indian in the Child": Death, Cruelty, and Subject-formation in the Canadian Indian Residential School System'. *Mosaic: An Interdisciplinary Critical Journal*, vol. 48, no. 4, 2015, pp. 63–76. *JSTOR*, https://www.jstor.org/stable/44030407. Accessed 6 July 2021.

Young, Edward. *Young's Night-Thoughts With Life, Critical Dissertation and Explanatory Notes*. 1742–5. Edited by George Gilfillin, Edinburgh, 1853, *Project Gutenberg*, https://www.gutenberg.org/files/33156/33156-h/33156-h.htm. Accessed 25 January 2022.

Youngquist, Paul. *Monstrosities: Bodies and British Romanticism*. U of Minnesota P, 2003.

Yu, Jie-Ae. 'Byron's *The Deformed Transformed*'. *The Explicator*, vol. 63, no. 1, 2004, pp. 19–21. *Taylor & Francis*, https://doi.org/10.1080/00144940409597246. Accessed 6 February 2004.

Zeuske, Michael. 'The Rise of Atlantic Slavery in the Americas'. *The Palgrave Handbook of Global Slavery Throughout History*, edited by Damian A. Pargas and Juliane Schiel, Palgrave Macmillan, 2023, pp. 379–93. *SpringerLink*, https://doi.org/10.1007/978-3-031-13260-5_21. Accessed 8 February 2024.

Index

EU Authorised Representative:
Easy Access System Europe Mustamäe tee 50, 10621 Tallinn, Estonia
gpsr.requests@easproject.com

Printed and bound by CPI Group (UK) Ltd, Croydon, CR0 4YY
29/09/2026
02224981-0018